Short Sea Shipping in the Age of Sustainable Development and Information Technology

This book provides a thorough understanding of short sea shipping (SSS) and its role in transport chains, presenting a revision of EU policies for SSS.

Infrastructure and equipment required for the success of SSS are discussed, including critical features of modern roll-on/roll-off (Ro-Ro) ships and terminals. Models are proposed for the evaluation of transportation demand in SSS, including the potential effects of external costs and its results are used within the scope of methods for Ro-Ro ship and fleet sizing. A discussion of methods used to calculate such costs is provided, and a comparison of aggregated demand with and without internalisation of external costs is carried out, pointing towards solutions for 'greening' freight transportation. Applications of multi-criteria decision-making and simulation techniques to supply chains based on SSS are presented. The role of information and communication technologies (ICT) in the promotion of SSS is also discussed. A number of case studies illustrate the different research methods and techniques.

This book is a useful resource for students and researchers studying transportation, as well as policymakers and practitioners involved in this field and anyone with an interest in the promotion of environmentally sound transport solutions.

Tiago A. Santos is Assistant Professor in Instituto Superior Técnico (IST) and the Principal Researcher at the Centre for Marine Technology and Ocean Engineering (CENTEC) in the group 'Safety and Logistics of Maritime Transportation'. He currently coordinates the national research project SHORTSEACHAIN, dealing mainly with short sea shipping integrated in intermodal supply chains.

C. Guedes Soares is a Distinguished Professor of Naval Architecture and Ocean Engineering in Instituto Superior Técnico (IST) and President of the Centre for Marine Technology and Ocean Engineering (CENTEC). He has participated or coordinated numerous international and national research projects in the field of maritime transportation and ports, including the Concerted Action on Short Sea Shipping, INTRASEAS, TOHPIC, TRAPIST, TRESHIP, FLAGSHIP and EFFORTS EU projects.

Short Sea Shipping in the Age of Sustainable Development and Information Technology

Edited by Tiago A. Santos
and C. Guedes Soares

LONDON AND NEW YORK

First published 2020
by Routledge
2 Park Square, Milton Park, Abingdon, Oxon OX14 4RN

and by Routledge
605 Third Avenue, New York, NY 10017

First issued in paperback 2021

Routledge is an imprint of the Taylor & Francis Group, an informa business

© 2020 selection and editorial matter, Tiago A. Santos and C. Guedes Soares; individual chapters, the contributors

The right of Tiago A. Santos and C. Guedes Soares to be identified as the authors of the editorial material, and of the authors for their individual chapters, has been asserted in accordance with sections 77 and 78 of the Copyright, Designs and Patents Act 1988.

All rights reserved. No part of this book may be reprinted or reproduced or utilised in any form or by any electronic, mechanical, or other means, now known or hereafter invented, including photocopying and recording, or in any information storage or retrieval system, without permission in writing from the publishers.

Trademark notice: Product or corporate names may be trademarks or registered trademarks, and are used only for identification and explanation without intent to infringe.

Publisher's Note
The publisher has gone to great lengths to ensure the quality of this reprint but points out that some imperfections in the original copies may be apparent.

British Library Cataloguing-in-Publication Data
A catalogue record for this book is available from the British Library

Library of Congress Cataloging-in-Publication Data
A catalog record for this book has been requested

ISBN 13: 978-1-03-223709-1 (pbk)
ISBN 13: 978-0-367-23242-9 (hbk)

Typeset in Times New Roman
by Apex CoVantage, LLC

Contents

List of figures	vii
List of tables	xi
List of contributors	xiv
Preface	xv

PART I
Short sea shipping policies, infrastructure and equipment   1

1   European policies for short sea shipping and intermodality   3
    HARILAOS N. PSARAFTIS AND THALIS ZIS

2   Ro-Ro ships and dedicated short sea shipping terminals   22
    MANUEL VENTURA, TIAGO A. SANTOS AND
    C. GUEDES SOARES

PART II
Quantitative methods for short sea shipping   59

3   Ro-Ro ship and fleet sizing in intermodal transportation   61
    TIAGO A. SANTOS AND C. GUEDES SOARES

4   Sustainability in short sea shipping-based intermodal
    transport chains   89
    TIAGO A. SANTOS, MÓNICA M. RAMALHO AND
    C. GUEDES SOARES

5   Simulating Ro-Ro operations in the context of supply chains   116
    TIAGO A. SANTOS, JOÃO ESCABELADO, RUI BOTTER AND
    C. GUEDES SOARES

vi *Contents*

6 Multi-criteria decision method applied to Motorways of the Sea 141
ALBA MARTÍNEZ-LÓPEZ AND LOURDES TRUJILLO

7 The economic impact of tourism on the Motorways of the Sea Nantes–Gijón 163
JOSÉ F. BAÑOS PINO, LUIS VALDÉS PELÁEZ, EDUARDO DEL VALLE TUERO AND EMMA ZAPICO FERNÁNDEZ

PART III
Regional studies on short sea shipping 181

8 Ro-Ro short sea shipping and Motorways of the Sea: evolutionary patterns of road hauliers' operating strategies 183
MIGUEL ÁNGEL LÓPEZ-NAVARRO

9 The competitiveness of Motorways of the Sea: a case study in Italy 199
MARINO LUPI, ALESSANDRO FARINA AND ANTONIO PRATELLI

10 The cost of modal shift: the case of Greece 224
EVANGELOS SAMBRACOS AND MARINA MANIATI

11 Short sea shipping in the Association of Southeast Asian Nations 242
AMINUDDIN MD AROF AND AMAYROL ZAKARIA

12 Short sea shipping in Latin America: analysis of the current logistics system 259
DELMO MOURA AND RUI BOTTER

PART IV
Information and communications technology in support of short sea shipping 275

13 Short sea shipping in the age of information and communications technology 277
TIAGO A. SANTOS AND C. GUEDES SOARES

Index 297

Figures

1.1	Core network corridors.	7
1.2	Modal performance, EU-28 (billions of tonne-km).	8
2.1	Typical examples of Ro-Ro cargo and Ro-Pax ships.	24
2.2	General arrangement of Ro-Ro cargo ship (142 m length overall, 23 m breadth, 1830 m lane length).	25
2.3	General arrangement of Ro-Pax ship (199.8 m length overall, 27.8 m breadth, 2980 m lane length, 640 passengers).	26
2.4	Number of operators and Ro-Ro ships involved in SSS.	29
2.5	Newbuilding year and ship age profile of Ro-Ro cargo ships and Ro-Pax ships.	29
2.6	Evolution of lane length of Ro-Ro ships fleet over time.	30
2.7	Relation between length overall (Loa) and length between perpendiculars (Lpp).	32
2.8	Relation between length between perpendiculars and lane length.	33
2.9	Relation between breadth, depth and draught and lane length.	34
2.10	Relation between dimensional ratios of Ro-Ro ships and lane length.	36
2.11	Estimate of the gross tonnage as function of length between perpendiculars, breadth and depth.	37
2.12	Number of Ro-Ro cargo decks of ships in the Ro-Ro fleet.	38
2.13	Relation between the deadweight and the lane length.	39
2.14	Relation between speed and lane length.	40
2.15	Relation between main engines maximum continuous rating and lane length.	41
2.16	Relation between installed auxiliary power and lane length.	42
2.17	Relation between newbuilding price and lane length.	43
2.18	Relation between crew size, passenger capacity and lane length.	45
2.19	Types of intermodal units.	46
2.20	Double stacking of containers in the weather deck of a Ro-Ro cargo ship.	47
2.21	Ro-Ro cargo terminal in Trieste, Italy, showing in-dock rail terminal adjacent to quay.	50

viii *Figures*

2.22	Typical layout of a Ro-Ro cargo terminal (Pendik, Istanbul, Turkey) and a Ro-Pax ferry terminal (Caen-Ouistreham, France).	51
3.1	Transport problem between multiple origin and destination NUTS 2 regions.	65
3.2	Cases in comparison of unimodal and intermodal costs and times.	68
3.3	Lanemeter capacity as function of length overall for ships in the database.	74
3.4	Main propulsion power installed on board ships in the database (kW).	74
3.5	Service speed of ships included in the database.	75
3.6	Auxiliary power installed on board ships in the database.	76
3.7	Map of the maritime routes to the three ports (with nautical distances in and out of ECA).	77
3.8	Geographical distribution of import cargos (expressed in TEUs) through NUTS 2 regions.	78
3.9	Cargo volume conveyed by intermodal and road transport solutions as function of ship speed and maritime freight rate (exports), port of Rotterdam.	80
3.10	NUTS 2 regions using the intermodal transport solution through Le Havre.	81
3.11	NUTS 2 regions using the intermodal transport solution through Rotterdam.	82
3.12	NUTS 2 regions using the intermodal transport solution through Hamburg.	82
3.13	Technical and financial feasibility of points of operation for Le Havre.	83
3.14	Technical and financial feasibility of points of operation for Rotterdam.	83
3.15	Technical and financial feasibility of points of operation for Hamburg.	83
3.16	Cumulative technical and financial feasibility of points of operation for Rotterdam (left) and Hamburg (right).	84
4.1	General formulation of transport problem between origin and destination NUTS 2 regions.	94
4.2	Transport networks supporting the intermodal and unimodal routes.	105
4.3	Transit time in intermodal and unimodal routes.	108
4.4	Transport cost in intermodal and unimodal routes.	108
4.5	Air pollutant and climate change emissions for the various scenarios.	109
4.6	External costs comparison of the different scenarios.	110
4.7	External costs comparison of the different scenarios.	111
4.8	Total cost per trailer comparison of the different scenarios.	111
5.1	Definition of the many-to-many transport problem.	120

Figures ix

5.2	Distribution of cargo units to be carried between origin-destination pairs.	121
5.3	Distribution of average truck speed in intermodal (pre-carriage and on-carriage) and unimodal (long-distance haulage) transport.	122
5.4	Distribution of booking times in relation to contracted delivery time.	122
5.5	Distribution of bad weather occurrences over the year.	123
5.6	Distribution of delays in departure time from port.	124
5.7	Distribution of average ship speed in summer and winter.	125
5.8	General layout of the simulation model.	127
5.9	General layout of Intermodal Sub-model 1.	128
5.10	General layout of the simulation Intermodal Sub-model 2.	129
5.11	Location of cargo origins in Portugal, loading port (Leixões) and logistics company truck park.	131
5.12	Location of cargo destinations in northern France, unloading port (Le Havre) and logistics company park.	131
5.13	Average reliability as a function of the number of iterations.	133
5.14	Annual cost of the system and number of late deliveries corresponding to different reliability levels.	133
5.15	Occupancy of the truck fleet in Portugal.	134
5.16	Occupancy of the truck fleet in France.	134
6.1	The 'many-to-many' model applied to study transport alternatives.	143
6.2	Port indexes in terms of time (PI^T_k) and cost (PI^C_k) for the intermodality through Rosyth port.	149
6.3	Probability distributions of the port indexes for the case of Scotland–continental Europe, obtained using Monte Carlo simulations in terms of time PI^T_k (top) and costs PI^C_k (bottom).	152
6.4	The 'one-to-many' model applied for eastern Africa application.	155
6.5	Port indexes (PI_k), Port indexes in terms of time (PI^T_k) and cost (PI^C_k) for the eastern African ports.	158
7.1	MoS Gijón–Nantes.	165
7.2	MoS Gijón–Nantes passenger traffic in 2013.	166
7.3	MoS Nantes–Gijón passenger traffic in 2013.	167
7.4	Users of MoS Gijón–Nantes.	168
7.5	Passenger load factor (%) MoS Gijón–Nantes.	176
9.1	The existing routes considered in the research (solid lines) and the proposed new routes (dashed lines).	207
10.1	Ports of Eleusis and Patras – road and sea transport.	225
10.2	Loaded/unloaded trucks/trailers at the port of Patras.	228
10.3	Break-even point analysis results for a new-built Ro-Ro (line Patras–Eleusis–Patras).	235
10.4	Break-even point analysis results for a second-hand Ro-Ro (line Patras–Eleusis–Patras).	236

x *Figures*

11.1	The ASEA.	244
11.2	The Philippines Nautical Highways.	246
11.3	The routes covered by JICA's feasibility study.	246
11.4	Short sea shipping in ASEAN.	248
11.5	Decision-making model for interstate Ro-Ro SSS.	253
12.1	Port activities in 2018 – Latin America and the Caribbean.	266
13.1	Scope of electronic facilities involved in the logistics chain.	278
13.2	Sea traffic management implementation and deployment strategy.	282
13.3	Scope of port single window (JUP) and logistic single window (JUL).	288
13.4	Services provided by transport data sharing platform.	290
13.5	Synchromodal options between Rotterdam and Tilburg.	292

Tables

1.1	Ports in Europe with cold ironing facilities.	14
2.1	Technical characteristics of ships of importance for economic studies.	31
2.2	Main dimensions of intermodal units.	47
3.1	Characteristics of the routes to the three ports.	77
3.2	Cargo volumes (TEU) when using different ports.	81
3.3	Characteristics of optimum ships for the different routes.	85
4.1	Emission reduction factors of IWW fuel technologies for various air pollutants and CO2.	92
4.2	External cost correction factors per alternative fuel technology in SSS.	93
4.3	Intermodal transportation network links definition.	95
4.4	Characteristics of the modes of transportation used in the intermodal and unimodal routes.	104
4.5	Characteristics of the different scenarios studied.	106
4.6	Characteristics of the operation in seaport terminals.	107
5.1	Definition of scenarios for simulations.	132
5.2	Trucks and driver's occupancy (fraction of full occupancy) form the various scenarios.	135
5.3	Characteristics and results of the transport system for different levels of reliability.	136
5.4	Detailed costs of the intermodal and unimodal operations.	137
6.1	Information about the trucking between Scotland and the European continent.	147
6.2	Information about the capillary hauls in European continent and trunk hauls.	147
6.3	Information about the capillary hauls in Scotland.	148
6.4	Port index in terms of time for the application case in Europe.	150
6.5	Contribution of the inputs to the variance of the port index distributions.	153
6.6	Statistical results from the Monte Carlo simulations.	154
6.7	Technical features for standard vessels operating under SSS conditions.	157

6.8	Disaggregation of the port index in terms of time for the eastern African ports.	159
6.9	Disaggregation of the port index in terms of cost for the eastern African ports.	159
7.1	Motorways of the Sea (MoS) timetables.	165
7.2	Final holiday destination of inbound tourism in Spain.	169
7.3	Final holiday destination of outbound Spanish tourism.	170
7.4	Definitions and sample statistics of the explanatory variables.	171
7.5	Semiparametric estimation results of the tobit model.	172
7.6	Marginal effects of the semiparametric tobit model.	172
7.7	Expected tourism expenditure by category and sector of activity (€).	176
7.8	Expected economic impacts in terms of GVA (€) of MoS Gijón–Nantes, 2021.	177
7.9	Expected economic impacts in terms of employment (FTE) of MoS Gijón–Nantes, 2021.	177
8.1	Main challenges in the process of change from all-road transport to unaccompanied Ro-Ro short sea shipping.	187
8.2	Road hauliers' characteristics ($n = 47$).	189
8.3	Agent responsible for the decision to use Ro-Ro SSS ($n = 47$).	190
8.4	Ro-Ro SSS vs all-road transport (road hauliers' assessments).	191
8.5	Road hauliers' evolution (2007–2014).	192
8.6	Variation in the number of semi-trailers loaded per week considering only the road hauliers that continue using Ro-Ro SSS ($n = 23$).	192
9.1	Synthesis of the comparison among 2008, 2010, 2012, 2015 (low and high season) and 2019 data.	203
9.2	Number of routes calling at a given number of ports in 2008, 2010, 2012, 2015 (low and high season) and 2019.	204
9.3	Characteristics of MoS routes in operation in the Ligurian area (data refer to the last week of October 2015).	206
9.4	Comparison, in terms of monetary cost, travel time, generalized cost and distance, between the all-road and the intermodal alternatives.	212
9.5	Comparison, in terms of monetary cost, travel time, generalized cost and distance, between the all-road and the intermodal accompanied and unaccompanied alternatives, for the improvement scenario M2.	215
9.6	Comparison between all-road and intermodal accompanied transport in the M3 scenario.	217
9.7	Comparison between all-road and intermodal unaccompanied transport in the M3 scenario.	219
10.1	Annual operational and voyage cost for road transport (one truck, Athens–Patras–Athens, first year).	230
10.2	Ro-Ro annual operational and voyage cost (line Patras–Eleusis, first year).	232

10.3	Cash flows analysis results for Ro-Ro (line Patras–Eleusis–Patras).	234
10.4	Sensitivity analysis for Ro-Ro (line Patras–Eleusis–Patras).	236
10.5	Marginal external costs for road and sea freight transport (line Patras–Eleusis–Patras).	237
10.6	External costs per round trip and tonne (Patras–Eleusis–Patras).	238
11.1	Outcome of JICA's feasibility study.	247
11.2	Results of AHP paired comparisons.	252
11.3	Mean score for selected routes.	254
11.4	Total ratings of selected routes.	255
12.1	Main trade flows.	265
12.2	Exports of some Mercosul (Common Market of the South) member/associate countries.	265

Contributors

Aminuddin Md Arof, Universiti Kuala Lumpur, Malaysian Institute of Marine Engineering Technology, Malaysia

Rui Botter, University of São Paulo, Brazil

João Escabelado, CENTEC, Instituto Superior Técnico, ULisboa, Portugal

Alessandro Farina, Università di Pisa, Italy

Emma Zapico Fernández, University of Oviedo, Spain

Miguel Ángel López-Navarro, Universitat Jaume I, Spain

Marino Lupi, Università di Pisa, Italy

Marina Maniati, University of Piraeus, Greece

Alba Martínez-López, Universidad de Las Palmas de Gran Canaria, Spain

Delmo Moura, Universidade Federal do ABC, Brazil

Luis Valdés Peláez, University of Oviedo, Spain

José F. Baños Pino, University of Oviedo, Spain

Antonio Pratelli, Università di Pisa, Italy

Harilaos N. Psaraftis, Technical University of Denmark (DTU)

Mónica M. Ramalho, CENTEC, Instituto Superior Técnico, ULisboa, Portugal

Evangelos Sambracos, University of Piraeus, Greece

Lourdes Trujillo, Universidad de Las Palmas de Gran Canaria, Spain

Eduardo Del Valle Tuero, University of Oviedo, Spain

Manuel Ventura, CENTEC, Instituto Superior Técnico, ULisboa, Portugal

Amayrol Zakaria, Universiti Kuala Lumpur, Malaysian Institute of Marine Engineering Technology, Malaysia

Thalis Zis, Technical University of Denmark (DTU)

Preface

The concept of short sea shipping (SSS), in general, relates to maritime transport of goods over relatively short distances, as opposed to oceanic deep sea shipping. In the European Union (EU) context, it relates to maritime transport of goods between ports in the EU, or between ports in the EU and ports of other countries situated in geographical Europe or across the Mediterranean and Black seas.

SSS has been promoted within the EU as a potential means for increasing the sustainability of freight transport and for meeting the ever-increasing needs for freight transport capacity, while promoting the emergence of a truly common EU market. Accordingly, several support programmes (directed to SSS but also to intermodality, in general) have been in place since at least 1995, but this mode of transportation has seen its market share decrease from 32.7% to 31.5% in 2017, according to Eurostat data. Nevertheless, SSS remains a potential alternative to road haulage, especially along Motorways of the Sea corridors and when resorting to roll-on/roll-off ships (Ro-Ro cargo ships, Ro-Pax ships, ferries), due to its good ability to integrate with other modes of transportation. This explains why the focus of this book is primarily directed towards SSS using Ro-Ro ships.

Notwithstanding this potential of SSS, the fact remains that road haulage has slightly expanded its market share in the EU over the period 1995–2017, from 45.3% to 50.1%, despite the increasing pressure to decarbonize transport and decongest the European road network. Several countries have meanwhile intensified efforts to prevent the increasing freight traffic on their roads, which has increased competitiveness, partially by using controversial employment schemes. Other modes of transportation, such as rail and inland waterways, have similarly failed to gain market share or, in the particular case of rail, have lost some ground. Consequently, the European Commission is now pushing the concept of rail freight corridors in an attempt to foster the competitiveness of rail freight transportation. On the other hand, SSS appears to have lost some appeal in the mind of EU decision makers.

This book presents recent developments in research illustrating diverse quantitative and qualitative analysis techniques to improve our understanding of SSS, potentially leading to significant improvements in its competitiveness. The structure of the book is organized in the following way. *Part I* includes *Chapter 1* and *Chapter 2*, which form an introduction to the theme of SSS, providing, respectively, a general background dealing with policy developments and current challenges in SSS, and information on technical characteristics of Ro-Ro ships (including a database of existing ships), which are the main focus of this book. *Chapter 2* also discusses the characteristics of port terminals engaged in SSS, thus providing reference information on the basic infrastructure and equipment required for successfully implementing transport solutions in this field.

After this broad introduction, *Part II* includes *Chapters 3 through 7*, which present different quantitative methods and techniques and their application in the study of SSS. *Chapter 3* details an approach to the quantification of demand for SSS, considering the flows of cargo between pairs of NUTS 2 regions in western Europe and the sizing of the ship/fleet necessary to meet such demand. *Chapter 4* shows how models of transport networks may be used in the assessment of the sustainability of different transport modes or combinations of such modes, providing relevant information on emissions and external costs for different transport solutions. *Chapter 5* describes a discrete event simulation model applied to the study of intermodal operations (including an SSS link) of a logistics company, aiming at quantifying reliability of this type of operations (a major concern for shippers) while considering a number of uncertainties related to the ship, port and road haulage. *Chapter 6* details a multi-criteria decision method to identify the most suitable pair of ports in a given transport corridor, with interesting applications to the western Europe Motorways of the Sea and also to the East Africa region. *Chapter 7* introduces an economic impact assessment approach to evaluating the contribution of tourism to the development of coastal regions connected through an SSS line which uses Ro-Pax ships.

Following this section dealing with quantitative methods, Part III of this book includes *Chapters 8 to 12*, primarily dedicated to regional studies across the globe, starting with the western area of the Mediterranean Sea. *Chapter 8* applies yet another research technique, the use of questionnaires, to assess the evolution of the road hauliers' operating strategies in the use of Ro-Ro based SSS in the West Mediterranean. *Chapter 9* considers the same geographical area and applies a network-based approach to explore the possibilities of improvement of Ro-Ro routes in this area. Turning now to the East Mediterranean area, *Chapter 10* presents an economic study, drawing mainly on shipping finance techniques, that assesses the feasibility of using SSS in short routes between Greek ports. *Chapter 11* takes the reader to Southeast Asia (ASEAN) and shows how important SSS is in this region, but it also points out the relevant natural and infrastructure bottlenecks hampering further development. These difficulties are studied using an analytic hierarchy process (AHP) technique to assess qualitatively the potential of different routes. Regarding the American continent, *Chapter 12* elaborates on the negative role that bureaucratic and protectionist barriers have in preventing the development of SSS in Latin America, focusing primarily on South America, where road and rail infrastructure are still frequently insufficient and where SSS could play a decisive role in improving the connection between densely populated areas, situated mostly in coastal regions.

Part IV of this book includes *Chapter 13*, which deals with a significantly different but still crucial topic: the role that information and communication technology will certainly play in the future of SSS. Three types of electronic systems are described: vessel traffic systems, maritime single windows and multimodal transport platforms. The different ways in which these systems may be used to address key issues currently hindering further development of SSS are discussed.

Finally, we would like to point out that this book draws on the significant expertise of many reputed academicians, who have provided the aforementioned chapters. The editors would like to thank all of them for their relevant contributions and availability to participate in this project. This book also results from the long experience on SSS of the research centre, Centre for Marine Technology and Ocean Engineering (CENTEC) of Instituto Superior Técnico (IST) University of Lisbon (UL).

Tiago A. Santos
Carlos Guedes Soares
Centre for Marine
Technology and Ocean Engineering
Instituto Superior Técnico
Universidade de Lisboa

Part I
Short sea shipping policies, infrastructure and equipment

1 European policies for short sea shipping and intermodality

Harilaos N. Psaraftis and Thalis Zis

1 Introduction

The objective to encourage and strengthen short sea shipping (SSS) has always been at the forefront of the transport policy of many countries. Perhaps none has been more active in that regard than the European Union. In the European Commission's 2001 White Paper on Transport (EU, 2001a), shifting freight from the road mode to the maritime mode has been adopted as a central policy goal, and specific actions have been promulgated to move towards that goal. As growth in European road transport has been acknowledged to be accompanied by important side effects, such as congestion, pollution, noise accidents and others, these problems create substantial 'external' costs. According to the 2001 White Paper, the most recent (at the time) estimate of the external costs of road congestion was 0.5% of the European Union's GDP, something that was projected to increase by 142% to 80 billion € a year in 2010 (that is, approximately 1% of GDP) if no action was taken.

In the European Commission's more recent White Paper (EU, 2011), at first glance SSS figures less prominently than before, at least explicitly, for the main reason that things like decarbonization of transport and the spectrum of technologies and other measures to achieve it have received a more explicit attention. However, the stated goal of greenhouse gas (GHG) emissions reduction from transport of at least 60% by year 2050 implicitly keeps the SSS sector at the centre stage of EU transport policy. In addition, the official establishment of the Trans-European Transport Network (TEN-T) guidelines and the Connect Europe Facility in 2013 have provided a new push to intermodality and SSS. More recent developments include developments as regards European sulphur emissions control areas (2015) The new port package in 2017, the global sulphur cap in 2020, and the so-called Initial IMO Strategy to reduce maritime GHG emissions by at least 50% by 2050. We have also seen the birth of the Belt and Road Initiative promoted by the Chinese, in their quest to better connect China to Europe, with implications that touch at least the European SSS feeder market segment and provide an increased focus on rail connections to China, which might reduce maritime transport in general. All of these developments may impact intermodality and SSS in Europe in the years ahead.

Taking in consideration the aforementioned, this chapter takes stock of these and other related developments and discusses the policy dimension of European SSS and intermodality. An earlier view of the same subject, mostly focusing on the role of ports in SSS, was presented in Psaraftis (2012). As several developments have occurred since then, an interesting question is to what extent the overall picture and the prospects have changed.

Before we proceed, two clarifications are in order. First, because the scope of this subject is immense, one would have to be very selective to conform to the space limitations of a book chapter. To that effect, we only highlight what we think are some of the main issues and provide some references for further study, without claiming an encyclopaedic treatment. For that purpose (and this is the second clarification), material in this chapter mainly draws from and expands upon earlier works of the authors and their colleagues. These include Psaraftis (2005a, 2012, 2016, 2018), Zis and Psaraftis (2017, 2018) and Zis *et al.* (2019).

The rest of this chapter is organized as follows. Section 2 provides some background, focusing mainly on basic legislative developments and traffic growth statistics. Section 3 continues with a discussion of a number of factors that are relevant as regards SSS and intermodality in Europe, including the fate of the port package, the EU enlargement, the rail freight corridors, the impact of environmental regulation, the impact of sulphur regulations, the internalization of external costs, the impact of port security and the drive for decarbonization and the 'Initial IMO Strategy'. Finally, Section 4 presents the chapter's conclusions.

2 Background

In the period that preceded the Commission's adoption of the 2011 White Paper on Transport (EU, 2011), a spectrum of initiatives have been supportive to the overall objective of shifting freight from road to sea. Among these, the 2004 EC Communication on SSS (EU, 2004a) took stock on where the SSS sector stood since 1999 and what the plans were in this area. Its 2006 update (EU, 2006a) performed a mid-term review of its program to promote SSS. Even earlier, the Commission had adopted the proposals by the High-Level Group headed by EC Commissioner Karel van Miert regarding the revision of the TEN-T (EU, 2003a). In particular, the proposed creation of a network of 'Motorways of the Sea' (MoS) was worthy of note, with four such maritime corridors identified across Europe. The aim of the MoS, to be fully implemented by 2020, is to concentrate flows of freight on a few sea routes in order to establish new viable, regular and frequent maritime links for the transport of goods between member states and thus reduce road congestion and improve access to peripheral and island countries.

Previously, the Commission had launched the first *Marco Polo* programme (EU, 2003b), the programme that succeeded the previous *PACT* programme (Pilot Actions for Combined Transport) to support intermodality. The goal of the first *Marco Polo* programme was to shift some 12 billion tonne-kilometres a year from road to non-road modes, which is approximately 1% of the traffic. *Marco Polo II*

(2007–2013) had a much more ambitious goal, to shift some 140 billion tonne-kilometres a year off the road, which is approximately 10% of the traffic (EU, 2006b).

Moreover, the Commission stated in their Freight Transport Logistics Action Plan (EU, 2007), launched in October 2007, that 'Logistics policy needs to be pursued at all levels of governance' (p. 2), which is also the reason behind this action plan as one in a series of policy initiatives to improve the efficiency and sustainability of freight transport in Europe. In the Freight Transport Logistics Action Plan, a number of short- to medium-term actions were presented that would assist Europe in addressing its current and future challenges and ensure a competitive and sustainable freight transport system. Among the actions are the 'green transport corridors for freight'. The Green Corridors were characterized by a concentration of freight traffic between major hubs and by relatively long distances of transport. Green Corridors are meant to be in all ways environmentally friendly, safe and efficient. Green technologies and smart utilization of ICT, where available, may even improve them. The EU FP7 project SuperGreen,[1] which was characterized a 'success story' by the European Commission, provided a cross-disciplinary investigation of these issues, and a book on green transportation logistics included many of its results (Psaraftis, 2016).

The 'new EU White Paper' on transport policy was released in 2011 (EU, 2011). A basic element of this policy is the so-called decarbonization of transport. In fact, the ambitious goal of reducing GHG emissions from all modes of transport by at least 60% from 1990 levels by 2050 has been set. To reach the EU 2050 decarbonization goal, the 2011 White Paper stipulated, among other things, that

> 30% of road freight over 300 km should shift to other modes such as rail or waterborne transport by 2030, and more than 50% by 2050, facilitated by efficient and green freight corridors. To meet this goal will also require appropriate infrastructure to be developed.
>
> (p. 9)

Interestingly enough, the International Maritime Organization (IMO) set a similar goal in 2018, to reduce GHG emissions from international shipping by at least 50% from 2008 levels by 2050 (IMO, 2018).

Two years later after the 2011 White Paper, the EU adopted two regulations, one on the TEN-T guidelines (EU, 2013a) and one on the so-called Connect Europe Facility (CEF), which finances EU priority infrastructure in transportation, energy and digital broadband and lists nine 'core network corridors' (EU, 2013b). The core network corridors constitute the backbone of the EU transport network. They bring together public and private resources and concentrate EU support from the CEF, particularly to:

- remove bottlenecks;
- build missing cross-border connections; and
- promote modal integration and interoperability.

They also aim at:

- integrating (as ongoing modal measure, these corridors shall be integrated into the multi-modal TEN-T) rail freight corridors;
- promoting clean fuels;
- promoting innovative transport solutions;
- advancing telematics applications for efficient infrastructure use;
- integrating urban areas into the TEN-T; and
- enhancing safety.

The nine core network corridors were identified in the annex to the CEF regulation, which included a list of projects pre-identified for possible EU funding during the period 2014–2020, based on their added value for TEN-T development and their maturity status. The core network corridors are shown in Figure 1.1.

At first glance, the developments mentioned earlier look very promising. In particular, if one compares the European scene with the situation in North America or elsewhere, where similar road congestion problems exist but the approach to solve them using SSS has still a long way to go (especially in the United States, where the Jones Act and other pieces of legislation that hamper SSS development are in force), then one may get the impression that Europe is far ahead in this area and things are looking bright for the future. The question is, however, to what extent this is indeed the case.

Figure 1.2 is from the most recent (2018) European Commission's Statistical Pocketbook ('EU Transport in Figures') and shows traffic figures in tonne-km for all freight transport modes in the EU-28. One can clearly see that the gap between road transport (which is the top EU transporter among all modes) and sea transport (the second transporter) is significant and shows no signs of narrowing. In fact, road had surpassed SSS as the top transporter in intra-EU trades as early as 1985 (when the EU had just 15 members), a position it has maintained (and further reinforced) through and beyond the enlargement. It is interesting to note that in the interval 1995–2016, the SSS share in tonne-km dropped (marginally) from 32.7% to 32.3%, whereas the share of road transport volume increased from 45.3% to 49.3%. The absolute increases of volumes in tonne-km from 1995 to 2016 were 26.9% for SSS and 40.0% for road. Thus, these statistics show that the situation, at least regarding the policy goal shift of freight from land to sea, has gotten progressively worse over the years.

In several papers and talks as early as 2004, the first author of this chapter had raised several concerns for the future of European SSS, the European port sector and related sectors. In a *Lloyds List* article (Psaraftis, 2004), it was argued that the patchwork in EU port policy should be redefined if the port sector were to meet the challenges it faced. In a journal paper (Psaraftis, 2005a), it was mentioned that

> for all the noble intentions as regards short sea shipping, ports and intermodality described in high-profile EU transport policy declarations and documents, much confusion and uncertainty exists as to how, when or if these

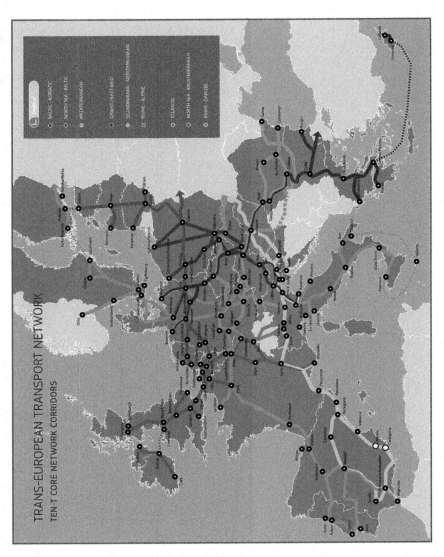

Figure 1.1 Core network corridors.

Source: European Commission, Connect Europe Facility.

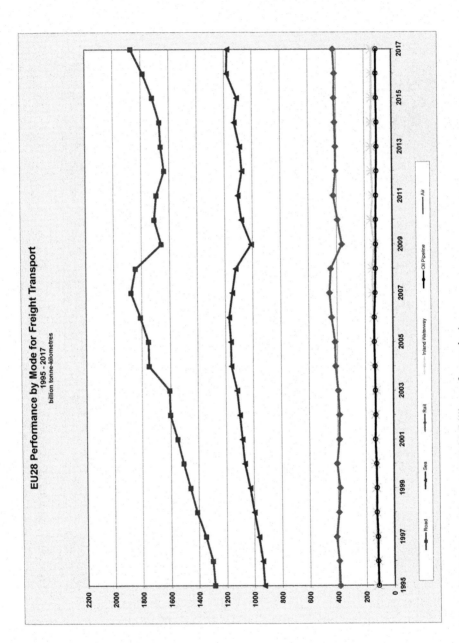

Figure 1.2 Modal performance, EU-28 (billions of tonne-km).

Source: European Commission (2018).

intentions will ever be reached, [and that] if over-regulated ports are affected adversely by a maze of additional requirements, short sea shipping effectiveness is bound to be affected, and this will help road transport increase its share in intra-community transport even further.

(p. 80)

In another talk that year (Psaraftis, 2005b), the picture of European SSS was described as not very bright, and it was suggested that politicians and legislators should abandon the patchwork *modus operandi* and adopt a more proactive policy philosophy. Finally yet importantly, in Psaraftis (2012) a discussion of the role of ports in SSS was made, with a similar less-than-optimistic outlook. The next section discusses the problem further, commenting also on some developments that took place after 2011.

3 Factors that may affect SSS and intermodality

It is difficult to single out any one issue as solely responsible for the less than desirable growth of SSS versus the road mode in Europe. In the following, we identify some factors or issues that may have contributed thus far or are likely to contribute in the future. Included also are some other relevant factors whose impact or potential impact on SSS and intermodality, positive or negative, is not yet fully understood. The next sections present some of these factors, focusing on their policy context.

3.1 Port package failure and subsequent resurrection

Regulating the port sector in Europe proved to be a major challenge. After the admittedly successful conclusion of the Green Paper on Sea Ports and Maritime Infrastructure EU (1997b), things went downhill. The laudable attempt of the Commission to take the next step and regulate market access to port services was not successful, and this certainly did not make things any better for European SSS and intermodality. After years of negotiations among regulators and port stakeholders, in January 2006 the European Parliament rejected with a majority of 532 out of 677 the second proposal of the European Commission for a directive to regulate market access to port services, the so-called port package (EU, 2004b). At face value, this was a failure bigger than the narrow parliamentary defeat of the first proposal in November 2003. Perhaps more important, it was a serious setback for the European port industry, and, by extension, for the European SSS and intermodal sector. The failure was attributed on the one hand to inadequate consultation with stakeholders and on the other on the perception that it forced a 'one-size-fits-all' model onto a widely diversified industry. This, coupled with the common opposition of forces that had little or nothing to do with one other (such as, for instance, dockers' unions and private British ports) but still were united in opposing the port package for various reasons, led to its ultimate defeat.

It took seven years after that setback to see any visible signs of recovery. In 2013 the European Parliament and Council came up with a proposal for a regulation on market access to port services and financial transparency in ports. All 329 TEN-T ports were covered by the proposed regulation, and the following services were included: bunkering, cargo handling, dredging, mooring, passenger services, port reception facilities, pilotage and towage. However, and after some hard discussions, it was finally stipulated that cargo handling and passenger services would be subject to the financial transparency rules but exempt from the market access provisions, as initially proposed by the Commission. Member states would remain free to decide on market access rules for these services, in compliance with Court of Justice case law. Many, particularly from the ship operators' side, were disappointed by the 'watering down' of the proposed regulation in such a manner; however, some others felt that the alternative would be no regulation. After this hurdle was sidestepped, the regulation was finally approved in 2017 (EU, 2017). It is still too early to ascertain what the effects of the new regulation will be on the EU ports sector, and by extension, on EU SSS and intermodality.

3.2 EU enlargement

At face value, the EU enlargement cannot be held accountable for the decline of SSS's share, as the decline had started before the enlargement. However, it is a fact that things did not improve after the enlargement. According to the European Sea Ports Organization (ESPO),

> since May 2004, when Latvia, Lithuania and Estonia became EU members, maritime transport in the Baltic Sea decreased 10 percent; while road transport increased almost 50 percent. This is due to a decrease in bureaucracy and administrative procedures for road transport, while legislation on shipping has not or has unsatisfactorily been transposed. This means that an inverse modal shift (from sea to road) is taking place as the result of the enlargement.
> (ESPO, 2005)

A similar situation may exist with Bulgaria's and Romania's entry in the EU in January 2007, as traffic from the south of the Balkan peninsula to central Europe and vice versa might find road a more attractive mode than waterborne transport (via the Adriatic, for instance), for the same reasons as in the Baltic. A shipment from Turkey to central Europe and vice versa can very well travel by truck and stop only at one EU border (Greece or Bulgaria) instead of having to stop at one or two borders plus two ports via the Adriatic. Port infrastructure, and (more important) customs procedures in ports may be found to be lagging, if SSS is to grow in these countries and in the countries and regions linked to them as trade partners (Turkey, Black Sea, Middle East, North Africa). The cause seems clear: at least for the time being, road is better than SSS procedurally. Section 3.7 on the internalization of external costs provides some additional insights on this issue.

Another factor that may have contributed to the increase of competitiveness of road versus SSS during this period is the influx of lower-wage drivers, mainly from eastern Europe (both EU such as Bulgaria, Romania and Poland and non-EU such as Belarus). Adopting labour employment conditions and wages that are not necessarily legitimate, some road companies have created a non-level playing field, both for road competitors that play by the book and for SSS companies that try to compete with road haulage. This has been recognized as a problem (IP, 2015), but a comprehensive solution is not yet in sight.

3.3 Development of rail freight corridors

An interesting parallel development, whose origins can be traced to the 2007 Freight Logistics Action Plan, was Regulation No. 913/2010 (EU, 2010a). This laid down rules for the establishment, organization and management of international rail corridors with a view to developing a European rail network for competitive freight. Nine so-called rail freight corridors (RFCs) were established across the European Union. The regulation set up rules for the governance of each RFC and measures for implementing the RFC. It also established a process of allocating capacity to freight trains with better coordination of priority rules and prioritizing, among freight trains, those that cross at least one border. This mechanism is described in the regulation for the RFCs, and more details are given in Panagakos (2016).

The emphasis that the EU has put into developing freight railway corridors is important not only in its own right and as one of the basic elements of the strategy of shifting freight away from the roads, but also in connection with SSS and intermodality. One can see that the development of RFCs may cut two ways. On the one hand, SSS can only function efficiently if adequate rail connections are established to interface the maritime mode, but on the other hand, traffic that could be shifted from road to the maritime mode may be shifted to the rail mode instead. Which of the two opposing forces has thus far prevailed or is likely to prevail in the future is not very clear; however, it can be seen from Figure 1.2 that the performance of the rail mode in Europe has yet to take off.

A related development is the Belt and Road Initiative (BRI), previously known as One Belt One Road (OBOR). This a massive infrastructure project sponsored by China to promote their trade to Europe. All modes of transport are involved; however, what is most striking is the contemplated increased use of rail across Asia instead of shipping. The rail option involves considerably shorter distances and times than does the maritime mode, and even though the current capacity of existing rail links (for instance via Russia or Kazakhstan) is limited, the future potential exists and may be exploited further. To what extent this may decrease deep sea shipping traffic from the Far East to Europe and vice versa, and hence also decrease (or seriously reconfigure) the associated SSS traffic due to feedering to and from the main lines, remains to be seen.

3.4 Port security issues

Turning now to port security, it is known that ships and ports had to comply with the IMO's International Ship and Port Security (ISPS) code by 1 July 2004 (ISPS,

2004). And whereas ships more or less found a way to comply with that goal, the situation with ports was far more difficult. Perhaps adding to the difficulty, the EU has adopted a regulation on ship and port security (EU, 2004d), which transposed the ISPS code into EU law. Parts of this regulation are more stringent than the ISPS code, by making mandatory some parts of ISPS that are not mandatory. In addition to this regulation, there is also a specific directive on port security (EU, 2005) and also a proposal for a regulation on supply chain security (EU, 2006c). Moreover, one also needs to add the various bilateral and global US-EU agreements on ship and port security, for instance under the 'Container Security Initiative' and other programmes. And it is worthy to mention that under the 'International Port Security Program' of the US Coast Guard (Angelo, 2004) all major ports, including EU ports, will be under intense US scrutiny as regards security.

It seems self-evident that the objective of adequate security should be pursued wherever possible. However, delays in ports due to security regulations may constitute another barrier against SSS and in favour of road transport. A cargo load from (for instance) Madrid to Frankfurt will not stop anywhere along its route if it travels by truck, but it will be subject to security checks if its route involves a sea leg. The stipulation of the US that all containers destined to the US will have to be screened (SAFE, 2006) will certainly add to the bottlenecks in European ports and will thus impact European SSS, even though it is not directly connected to intra-European freight.

It is also noted here that it is very difficult, or nearly impossible, to establish dedicated SSS terminals, as most ships, and even SSS feeders, carry a mix of short sea and deep sea cargos. If it were possible to separate such cargos, a dedicated SSS terminal would conceivably be able to provide faster security procedures for SSS traffic.

3.5 Environmental issues in ports

Looking at environmental matters, a number of EU environmental directives come into play. Many of these are the basis of the 'Natura 2000' initiative. These include the Bathing Water Directive (EU, 1976a), the Dangerous Substances Directive (EU, 1976b), the Wild Birds Directive (EU, 1979), the Health and Safety in the Workplace Directive (EU, 1989), the Shellfish Directive (EU, 1991a), the Urban Waste Water Treatment Directive (EU, 1991b), the Habitats Directive (EU, 1992), the Environmental Impact Assessment Directive (EU, 1997a), the Waste Reception Facilities Directive (EU, 2000a), the Water Framework Directive (EU, 2000b), the Strategic Environmental Assessment Directive (EU, 2001b) and the Environmental Liability Directive (EU, 2004c).

Port authorities are obliged to comply to the rules and other provisions stipulated in these directives, by taking measures that ensure compliance. These measures entail costs which impact any transport chain that uses these ports, and, as such, the competitive position of that chain versus a chain that avoids these ports (for instance, a road-only chain). All these directives apply to ports, and as such, impact also SSS and intermodality.

In addition, other initiatives stemming from port associations are relevant. These port associations, the most prominent of which at a global level is the International Association of Ports and Harbors (IAPH), (in Europe) the European Sea Port Organization (ESPO) and national ports associations. Such associations typically represent their members and suggest guidelines for efficient operations. In addition, they promote the exchange of lessons learned on successful green strategies developed by port authorities around the world. Unfortunately, the qualitative approach followed is not backed by quantitative procedures to verify the potential in environmental improvement.

The IAPH has launched the World Ports Climate Initiative (WPCI) targeting GHG emission reductions for its members. The WPCI supports ports to monitor and reduce their CO_2 footprint. The IAPH has additionally designed a toolbox that showcases successful implementation of port initiatives and clean air programmes for all operations taking place in a terminal. Finally, in March 2018 the IAPH launched the World Ports Sustainability Program (WPSP) to guide port members on how to achieve progress on the Sustainable Development Goals (SDGs) of the United Nations (UN). The IAPH has observer status at the IMO and has recently been increasing its visibility in IMO matters, particularly as regards the decarbonization of shipping (more on this in Section 3.8).

The European equivalent of IAPH is ESPO, which is also a strategic partner of the WPSP. ESPO has developed the self-diagnosis method (SDM) framework for port authorities within the EcoPorts network. This is meant to provide insight on problematic areas within the port that should be prioritized for environmental improvement. ESPO has also published a green guide for the systematic port environmental management and designed the Port Environmental Review System (PERS). PERS complements the SDM and assists port authorities to introduce environmental management systems (ESPO, 2012).

While tools such as PERS and the SDM are useful for providing a qualitative indication of improvement over the years, they are not sufficient. The lack of quantitative evidence in the agendas of port associations around the world raises the issue of efficiently estimating, monitoring and mitigating emissions near and at ports. In recent years, researchers have tried to address this gap. A quantitative estimate of actual reductions in energy use, emissions generated or other environmental issues is necessary to ensure that each port is able to track its progress. The review of Davarzani et al. (2015) suggests that the topic of green ports is at a very early stage, but it will continue to grow as practitioners and governments continue to face challenges that research can solve.

Emissions are estimated typically using bottom-up approaches based on fuel consumption estimations for ship emissions activity at ports. Other studies consider emissions concentrations from shipping using monitoring stations at ports and dispersion modelling. Saxe and Larsen (2004) modelled emissions of NO_x and particulate matter (PM) from three Danish ports using a meteorological air quality model. Ng et al. (2013) used automatic identification system (AIS) data to compile an emissions inventory for exhaust emissions of ocean-going vessels in Hong Kong and found that container ships were the top polluters. Zis et al.

(2014) constructed a modelling methodology that allows the estimation of emissions from ship activity near and at ports and the potential for reduction through different abatement methods. Dragović et al. (2015) focused on near-port emissions from cruise ships and their externalities, with a case study on the cruise ports of Dubrovnik and Kotor. Cullinane et al. (2016) used a bottom-up methodology to estimate emission at berth from container ships in the three largest ports in Taiwan.

As evidenced, the majority of these studies focus on container or cruise terminals due to the higher fuel consumption and associated emissions in these ship types. Emissions reduction actions that are relevant to SSS include the provision of shore power for ships at berth, commonly known as cold ironing. The European Commission has promoted the further provision of shore power to its member states via an official recommendation. Cold ironing allows vessels to switch off their auxiliary engines at berth and eliminate local emissions, but the ship and the terminal need to invest (retrofitting the vessel and acquiring the shore power unit at port respectively). Zis (2019) argues that for cold ironing to be a viable solution, it is necessary that regulatory bodies assist its further adoption from ship operators and ports. Cold ironing is mandatory in California (USA) for ocean-going vessels, while in Europe all ports will be required to have some capability to provide shore power by 31 December 2025, according to an EU directive (EU, 2014a). Table 1.1 shows a summary of existing European terminals with cold

Table 1.1 Ports in Europe with cold ironing facilities.

Port with cold ironing provision	Terminal type	Country
Antwerp	Container, barges	Belgium
Zeebrugge	Ro-Ro	
Helsinki	Ro-Ro	Finland
Kemi	Ro-Ro	
Kotka	Ro-Ro	
Oulu	Ro-Ro	
Le Havre	Ferries	France
Marseille	Ferries	
Lübeck	Ro-Ro	Germany
Hamburg	Cruise (powered by LNG Barges)	
Amsterdam	River Boats	Netherlands
Rotterdam	Barges	
Oslo	Ro-Pax	Norway
Bergen	Supply Vessels	
Gothenburg	Ro-Ro	Sweden
Helsingborg	Ferries	
Piteå	Ferries	
Stockholm	Ro-Pax	
Milford Haven	Tugs	UK

Source: Adapted from Zis (2019).

ironing facilities, where it can be seen that most of these terminals are primarily concerned with SSS.

Another grave environmental concern globally are the issues of ballast water treatment and, in the context of ports, the provision of facilities for treatment. Large vessels carry massive amounts of water in their ballast tanks to stabilize the ship. When cargo is loaded the ballast water is discharged, and when cargo is removed from the ship water is pumped in to compensate for changes in weight distribution. However, pumping in ballast water in one port and discharging it at a different geographical area can lead to the invasion of alien species, resulting in serious environmental damage to the aquatic environment. This is also a concern for short sea shipping because of the many voyages between different waters (for example, services between the North Sea and the Baltic Sea, where the waters have different salinity levels). At present there is no direct EU law on ballast water, and only one EU regulation that merely recognizes the Ballast Water Management (BWM) Convention as a possible measure for containing the spread of invasive species (EU, 2014b). The BWM Convention proposed by the IMO entered into force in September 2017, and among other issues it sets guidelines for port state control.

Other environmental issues affecting ports are related to dredging operations, waste disposal, potential oil spillage from ships and the visual intrusion of ships, cargo handling equipment and other superstructure. The latter are responsible for noise, dust and lighting pollution during nighttime operations.

3.6 The impact of sulphur regulations

Sulphur emissions entail a broader spectrum of environmental issues, which may also impact SSS. Although SO_x emissions are not GHGs, they are highly undesirable, as they cause acid rain and negative health effects in humans and animals. To mitigate these negative effects, the international shipping community has taken substantial policy measures. With the introduction of a 0.1% ceiling for the content of sulphur in marine fuels (and hence also to the percentage of SO_x emissions) in northern European and North American emission control areas (ECAs) as of 1/1/2015, SSS companies operating in these areas will face substantial additional fuel cost. In addition, the IMO has decided on a global 0.5% cap on sulphur content as of 1/1/2020. Both these developments may have important consequences in maritime logistics. In fact, one of the obvious implications of ECAs is on ship speed, as low-sulphur fuel like marine gas oil (MGO) or marine diesel oil (MDO) are almost double the price of heavy fuel oil (HFO). This would induce ships to slow down whenever they sail within ECAs, but indeed the implications are much more far-reaching.

In addition to the introduction of sulphur emissions control areas (SECAs), as of January 2010 the European Union (EU) had already set a sulphur limit of 0.1% for ships at berth in EU ports with stays longer than 2 hours, as well as when sailing on inland waterways. Significant as these might be, such developments may also have an important impact on other, seemingly unrelated policy subjects regarding other modes of transport, especially road. ECSA (the European Community Shipowners' Association) has already voiced concern that the use of fuel with lower sulphur within designated SECAs may have a reverse impact on the policy goal to shift freight from land to sea, by making SSS less favourable than road transport, something that would ultimately lead to more CO_2 pollution overall (Lloyds List, 2008). Clearly, it would not make sense to reduce air pollution at sea, only to see the savings being more than offset by an air pollution increase on land.

Even after the precipitous drop of fuel prices after mid-2014, which saw the prices of MGO and MDO in 2015 go lower than the price of HFO in early 2014, a significant price gap still exists, not to mention that fuel prices are rising again and may rise even more in the future. Unlike its deep sea counterpart, in SSS a freight rate increase due to more expensive fuel may induce shippers to use land-based alternatives (mainly road). A reverse shift of freight would go against the EU policy to shift traffic from land to sea to reduce congestion and road emissions and might ultimately (under certain circumstances) increase the overall level of CO_2 emissions along the entire supply chain.

In a recent project at the Technical University of Denmark (DTU) called RoRoSECA, the possible impacts of sulphur regulations on the Ro-Ro sector in northern Europe, as well as possible mitigation actions and policy alternatives, have been investigated by developing enhanced modal split models that attempt to calculate the possible shifts to other modes. Zis and Psaraftis (2017) were the first to examine the potential modal shifts in European short sea shipping because of the sulphur regulation. They showed that due to unexpectedly low fuel prices, the sector was unharmed by the regulation, but should fuel prices rise again it may be a concern. In follow-up works they examined the potential of Ro-Ro operator's measures (Zis and Psaraftis, 2018) and policy measures (Zis et al., 2019) in order to reverse potential modal shifts due to the regulation.

The impact of the 0.5% global sulphur cap as of 1/1/2020 on European SSS is less understood and is, at this point in time, only subject to speculation. One could conceivably envisage a scenario in which SSS traffic in areas previously not subject to sulphur regulations (e.g. the Mediterranean) might be back-shifted to land modes due to the anticipated increase of fuel prices. However, the extent of these shifts, if any, is mostly unknown.

3.7 Internalization of external costs

Transport generates significant 'external costs' that affect society as opposed to individual private users. In addition to congestion, accidents and environmental impacts in terms of climate change, air pollution and noise, transport activities contribute to the degradation of nature, landscape and sensitive areas, pollute soil and water, and aggravate energy dependency (Maibach et al., 2008). The internalization of the external costs of transport has been an important policy goal for many years in Europe and elsewhere in the world. To this day, this goal is not yet fully achieved.

From a welfare economics point of view, internalizing external costs aims at efficiency gains through conveying the right price signal to economic actors. The right prices would encourage the use of safer, more silent and environmentally friendlier vehicles, as well as the planning of trips according to expected traffic. In 2011 the European Commission set 2020 as the deadline for the full and mandatory internalization of external costs for all modes, with emphasis on road and rail transport. However, and with 2020 already here, one can say that even though some progress has been made (for instance the implementation of road toll schemes such as the Euro-vignette and others), the road to a full application of this principle is still a long one. With respect to SSS, Zis *et al.* (2019) included the internalization of external costs as one of the candidate policies for reversing possible negative modal shifts concerning the impact of sulphur regulations on Ro-Ro shipping in northern Europe.

3.8 The drive to decarbonize shipping and the initial IMO strategy

Finally but importantly, perhaps no other maritime policy has greater potential to influence the maritime industry, including SSS, than the so-called Initial IMO Strategy to reduce maritime GHG emissions, adopted in April 2018 (IMO, 2018). This includes, among others, the following elements: (a) the vision, (b) the levels of ambition, (c) the guiding principles, (d) a list of short-term, medium-term and long term candidate measures with a timeline and (e) miscellaneous other elements, such as follow-up actions and others. We next briefly highlight some of these elements.

The vision is that IMO remains committed to reducing GHG emissions from international shipping and, as a matter of urgency, aims to phase them out as soon as possible in this century. The Initial IMO Strategy identifies levels of ambition for the international shipping sector, noting that technological innovation and the global introduction of alternative fuels and/or energy sources for international shipping will be integral to achieve the overall ambition. Reviews should take into account updated emission estimates, emissions reduction options for international shipping and the reports of the Intergovernmental Panel on Climate Change (IPCC).

The levels of ambition directing the Initial Strategy are as follows:

1. Carbon intensity of the ship to decline through implementation of further phases of the energy efficiency design index (EEDI) for new ships.
2. To reduce CO_2 emissions per transport work, as an average across international shipping, by at least 40% by 2030, pursuing efforts towards 70% by 2050, compared to 2008.
3. To peak GHG emissions from international shipping as soon as possible and to reduce the total annual GHG emissions by at least 50% by 2050 compared to 2008 while pursuing efforts towards phasing them out.

The IMO decarbonization goals look very similar to the goals of the 2011 Transport White Paper. For a discussion of the main issues, see Psaraftis (2018, 2019).

At the time this chapter was being completed, no concrete prioritization scheme had been adopted among the set of short-term, medium-term and long-term candidate measures. Among those, speed limits are being advocated by various groups, and the risk here is that such a measure may induce reverse modal shifts in European SSS (and possibly also deep sea shipping) and divert traffic to land-based modes, as in general transit time is a major drawback of maritime transportation. How SSS might be affected in the long run by low-carbon fuels or other energy-saving technologies to reduce GHG emissions from ships is less clear. If anything, the Initial IMO Strategy may provide an excellent opportunity for the renewal of the European SSS fleet, which is a prerequisite for that mode to successfully compete with land-based alternatives.

4 Conclusions

In this chapter we highlighted some of the challenges faced by the intermodal and SSS sectors in Europe and presented where we stand today, in the context of recent policy initiatives. In that context, the chapter can be considered as an update of the earlier work by Psaraftis (2012). What is common with the situation in 2011, the year of the 2011 White Paper, is mainly the continuing gap between road and SSS in terms of the transport modal split in Europe. Thus, and despite much regulatory activity, including action after 2011 (for instance, TEN-Ts, CEF, port package and others), there are no visible signs that the gap is narrowing.

The Initial IMO Strategy to decarbonize shipping has added some momentum to the strong decarbonization drive of the 2011 White Paper. One hopes that both will provide a similarly strong incentive for shifts from road to SSS. However, these shifts (and therefore the much-sought reduction in GHG emissions from transport) will not happen by themselves. More concrete actions will need to take place, in terms of lifting administrative barriers in ports, particularly as regards security, fully internalizing the external costs of road transport, or implementing some other action that would make a difference.

Until and unless those shifts happen, and in spite of the whole spectrum of regulatory-legislative initiatives, declarations and other noble intents that have been presented and advanced over the years as regards SSS and intermodality, we believe that road transport will continue to be the undisputed king of intra-European transport. To reverse this situation, it would seem that, at a minimum, there should exist a strong political will to ensure that special interests, mainly those from the trucking and automotive industries, are put aside in the quest to implement a sensible policy concerning how environmental matters in transport should be treated.

Note

1 http://martrans.org/supergreen/

References

Angelo, J. (2004), *Port and Maritime Security After 1 July 2004*. European Sea Ports Conference, Rotterdam, June.

Cullinane, K., Tseng, P.H., & Wilmsmeier, G. (2016), Estimation of container ship emissions at berth in Taiwan. *International Journal of Sustainable Transportation*, 10 (5), pp. 466–474.

Davarzani, H., Fahimnia, B., Bell, M., & Sarkis, J. (2016), Greening ports and maritime logistics: A review. *Transportation Research Part D: Transport and Environment*, 48, pp. 473–487.

Dragović, B., Tzannatos, E., Tselentis, V., Meštrović, R., & Škurić, M. (2015), Ship emissions and their externalities in cruise ports. *Transportation Research Part D: Transport and Environment*, 61, pp. 289–300.

ESPO (2005), *ESPO News*, Aug. 2005.

European Sea Ports Organisation (2012) Green Guide, http://www.ecoports.com/templates/frontend/blue/images/pdf/espo_green%20guide_october%202012_final.pdf

EU (1976a), *Bathing Water Directive*, 76/160/EEC.

EU (1976b), *Dangerous Substances Directive*, 76/464/EEC.

EU (1979), *Wild Birds Directive*, 79/409/EEC.

EU (1989), *Safety and Health of Workers at Work Directive*, 89/391/EEC.

EU (1991a), *Shellfish Hygiene Directive*, 91/492/EEC.

EU (1991b), *Waste Water Treatment Directive*, 91/271/EEC.

EU (1992), *Habitats Directive*, 92/43/EEC.

EU (1997a), *Directive 97/11/EC* amending directive 85/337/EEC on the assessment of the effects of certain public and private projects on the environment.

EU (1997b), COM(1997) 678 final, green paper on seaports and maritime infrastructure.

EU (2000a), *Waste Reception Facilities Directive*, 2000/59/EC.

EU (2000b), *Water Framework Directive*, 2000/60/EC.

EU (2001a), European transport policy for 2010 – time to decide, mid-term review COM(2006) 314 final – 'Keep Europe moving -sustainable mobility for our continent'.

EU (2001b), *Strategic Environment Assessment Directive*, 2001/42/EC.

EU (2003a), *COM(2003) 564 Final*, amended proposal for a decision of the European parliament and of the council amending the amended proposal for a decision of the European parliament and of the council amending decision no. 1692/96/EC on community guidelines for the development of the trans-European network.

EU (2003b), *Regulation (EC) No. 1382/2003* of the European parliament and of the council of 22/07/2003 on the granting of community financial assistance to improve the environmental performance of the freight transport system (Marco Polo program).

EU (2004a), *COM(2004) 453 Final*, communication from the commission to the council, the European parliament, the European economic and social committee and the committee of the regions, on short sea shipping.

EU (2004b), *COM(2004) 654(01)*, proposal for a directive of the European parliament and of the council on market access to port services.

EU (2004c), *Directive 2004/35/EC* of the European parliament and of the council on environmental liability with regard to the prevention and remedying of environmental damage.

EU (2004d), *Regulation (EC) No. 725/2004* of the European parliament and of the council on the enhancing ship and port security.

EU (2005), *Directive 2005/65/EC* of the European parliament and of the council, on enhancing port security.

EU (2006a), *COM(2006) 380 Final*, communication from the commission to the council, the European parliament, the European economic and social committee and the committee of the regions, mid-term review of the programme for the promotion of short sea shipping.

EU (2006b), *Regulation (EC)* No. 1692/2006 of the European parliament and of the council of 24 October 2006 establishing the second Marco Polo programme for the granting of community financial assistance to improve the environmental performance of the freight transport system (Marco Polo II) and repealing regulation (EC) No. 1382/2003.

EU (2006c), *COM(2006), 79*, proposal for a regulation of the European parliament and of the council, for enhancing supply chain security.

EU (2007), *COM(2007) 607 Final*, communication from the commission: 'Freight transport logistics action plan.'

EU (2010a). *Regulation (EU) No. 913/2010 of 22 September 2010 Concerning a European Rail Network for Competitive Freight*. Strasbourg, 22 September 2010.

EU (2011), *COM(2011) 144 Final*, white paper, 'roadmap to a single European transport area – towards a competitive and resource efficient transport system,' 28.3.2011.

EU (2014a), Directive 2014/94/EU on the development of alternative fuels infrastructure. *Official Journal of the European Union L* 307 (1).

EU (2014b), Regulation (EU) No. 1143/2014 of the European parliament and of the council on the prevention and management of the introduction and spread of invasive alien species.

EU (2017), Regulation (EU) 2017/352 of the European parliament and of the council of 15 February 2017 establishing a framework for the provision of port services and common rules on the financial transparency of ports.

European Parliament & Council (2013a), Regulation (EU) no 1315/2013 of 11 December 2013 on union guidelines for the development of the trans-European transport network and repealing decision no 661/2010/EU. Strasbourg.

European Parliament & Council (2013b), Regulation (EU) no 1316/2013 of 11 December 2013 establishing the connecting Europe facility, amending regulation (EU) no 913/2010 and repealing regulations (EC) no 680/2007 and (EC) no 67/2010. Strasbourg.

IMO (2018), Resolution MEPC. 304(72) (adopted on 13 April 2018) initial IMO strategy on reduction OF GHG emissions from ships, IMO doc. MEPC 72/17/Add.1, Annex 11.

IP (2015), Employment conditions in the international road haulage sector, study for the European parliament, IP/A/ECON/2014-07, April.

ISPS (2004), *International Ship and Port Security Code*, an amendment to the SOLAS Convention, adopted in the IMO diplomatic conference on 12 December 2002.

Lloyds List (2008), IMO Sulphur limits deal could see more freight hit the road.00 *Lloyds List*, 10 April 2008.

Maibach, M., Schreyer, C., Sutter, D., van Essen, H.P., Boon, B.H., Smokers, R., Schroten, A., Doll, C., Pawlowska, B., & Bak, M. (2008), *Handbook on Estimation of External Costs in the Transport Sector*. Delft, CE: IMPACT Study.

Ng, S.K., Loh, C., Lin, C., Booth, V., Chan, J.W., Yip, A.C., & Lau, A.K. (2013), Policy change driven by an AIS-assisted marine emission inventory in Hong Kong and the Pearl River Delta. *Atmospheric Environment*, 76, pp. 102–112.

Panagakos, G. (2016), The policy context. In H.N. Psaraftis (ed.), *Green Transportation Logistics: The Quest for Win-Win Solutions*. Cham, Switzerland: Springer.

Psaraftis, H.N. (2004), *European Port Patchwork Needs to be Redesigned. Lloyds List*, 22 January.

Psaraftis, H.N. (2005a), EU ports policy: Where do we go from here? *Maritime Economics and Logistics*, 7 (1), pp. 73–82.

Psaraftis, H.N. (2005b), *Short Sea Shipping: Towards a Great Fiasco?* Invited lecture, Mare Forum Conference, Rome, Italy, September.

Psaraftis, H.N. (2012), The role of ports in short sea shipping. In C.G. Soares, N. Fonseca & A.P. Texeira (eds.), *Marine Technology and Engineering: CENTEC Anniversary Book*. Portugal: Technical University of Lisbon.

Psaraftis, H.N. (ed.) (2016), *Green Transportation Logistics: The Quest for Win-Win Solutions*. Cham, Switzerland: Springer.

Psaraftis, H.N. (2018), Decarbonization of maritime transport: To be or not to be? *Maritime Economics and Logistics*. doi:10.1057/s41278-018-0098-8.

Psaraftis, H.N. (2019), Speed optimization vs speed reduction: The choice between speed limits and a bunker levy. *Sustainability*, 11. doi:10.3390/su11080000.

SAFE (2006), Security and accountability for every port act (SAFE Port Act of 2006), signed into law by President George W. Bush in October 2006.

Saxe, H., & Larsen, T. (2004), Air pollution from ships in three Danish ports. *Atmospheric Environment*, 38 (24), pp. 4057–4067.

Zis, T., North, R.J., Angeloudis, P., Ochieng, W.Y., & Bell, M.G.H. (2014), Evaluation of cold ironing and speed reduction policies to reduce ship emissions near and at ports. *Maritime Economics & Logistics*, 16 (4), pp. 371–398.

Zis, T., & Psaraftis, H.N. (2017), The implications of the new Sulphur limits on the European Ro-Ro sector. *Transportation Research Part D: Transport and Environment*, 52, pp. 185–201.

Zis, T., & Psaraftis, H.N. (2018), Operational measures to mitigate and reverse the potential modal shifts due to environmental legislation. *Maritime Policy & Management*, pp. 1–16.

Zis, T.P. (2019), Prospects of cold ironing as an emissions reduction option. *Transportation Research Part A: Policy and Practice*, 119, pp. 82–95.

Zis, T.P., Psaraftis, H.N., Panagakos, G., & Kronbak, J. (2019), Policy measures to avert possible modal shifts caused by Sulphur regulation in the European Ro-Ro sector. *Transportation Research Part D: Transport and Environment*, 70, pp. 1–17.

2 Ro-Ro ships and dedicated short sea shipping terminals

Manuel Ventura, Tiago A. Santos and C. Guedes Soares

1 Introduction

Short sea shipping (SSS) has been for many years now an important component of transport policies in the European Union (EU). It is useful first to review its definition, which may be found in, for example, European Commission (1999). This communication indicates that SSS is the transport of cargo and passengers between the Union and non-Union ports of countries along the Mediterranean Sea, the Black Sea and the Baltic Sea, Norway and Iceland, including national and international traffic along the coast and up to islands, rivers and lakes in those countries. The same document indicates that feeder services (typical in the container market) are also included in the definition of SSS. The concept of SSS also includes routes, which traditionally were considered as maritime cabotage. The Council of the European Communities (1992) defines maritime cabotage as transport services within a member state, including mainland cabotage, off-shore supply services and island cabotage.

This broad definition of SSS can be seen as comprising many different shipping segments, such as dry bulk, liquid bulk, containerized cargo, general cargo and roll-on/roll-off (Ro-Ro) cargo. However, the success of SSS in shifting cargos away from congested land infrastructure (mainly road but also rail) is dependent especially on Ro-Ro ships, as most bulk and containerized cargo is already carried by sea, most notably over medium to large distances. In contrast, significant amounts of general cargo and Ro-Ro cargo are carried using trucks (heavy goods vehicles – HGVs), contributing significantly to the congestion and wear of European roads. This is the motivation to concentrate this chapter on Ro-Ro ships, as this ship type is the one that can really promote modal shifts due to its good integration in the intermodal door-to-door transport network. The study of the technical characteristics of Ro-Ro ships capable of loading large numbers of HGVs or containers on wheeled platforms is important for developing more competitive SSS services.

It is then necessary to establish which types of Ro-Ro ships will be considered in this chapter, as there are many different sub-types. Wijnolst and Wergeland (2009) discuss extensively innovation in shipping, including also the so-called ferry industry. These authors distinguish, within this industry, many sub-types of ferries: commuter ferries, car ferries, fast ferries, cruise ferries, Ro-Pax ferries

(Roll-on/Roll-off passenger ferries) and Ro-Ro liners. This chapter does not consider the first three types, as these belong to the high-speed ferry segment used in shorter voyages often across lakes, rivers or sheltered sea areas. Furthermore, these three types, because of their small size and absence of enclosed vehicle deck, often fall out of the general spirit of the definition of ferry given by the leading ferry information provider ShipPax: 'a ship larger than 1,000 GT that sails on a regular line, has passenger accommodation and is using Ro-Ro technology for the transportation of cars and commercial vehicles (if any), having sufficient free height on car deck(s) for this'.

Therefore, this chapter will focus only on cruise ferries, Ro-Pax ferries and Ro-Ro liners. The term Ro-Ro liners refers to Ro-Ro cargo ships (restricted, as such, to carrying not more than 12 passengers, generally truck drivers). Ro-Pax ferries are those with typical passenger capacities of a few hundred, and cruise ferries are those carrying many hundreds to a few thousand passengers. Likewise, the analysis excludes other types of Ro-Ro ships which exist in the world fleet and are out of the scope of the 'ferry industry', namely the deep sea Ro-Ro ships, which belong to two different sub-types: conventional Ro-Ro ships (often called Con-Ro as they also have some container capacity) and vehicle carriers (PCC – pure car carriers or PCTC – pure car and truck carriers). These ships are, as the name implies, used in deep sea routes, and this excludes them in a study dedicated to SSS.

Having efficient Ro-Ro ships is a necessity, but this by itself does not ensure the success of a modal shift from road to sea. This is because SSS services, integrated necessarily in intermodal supply chains, suffer from disruptions in the transportation chain occurring in ports, where the transfer to/from road or, in some cases, to/from rail, is carried out. The provision of suitable dedicated SSS terminals is also generally taken as of paramount importance to decrease such disruptions and smoothen the overall transportation process. It is important therefore to study the technical characteristics desirable for such terminals, and that is the reason for including a final section in this chapter dedicated to SSS port terminals.

The remainder of this chapter is organized as follows. A characterization of the European Ro-Ro ship fleet based on a database of ships is first presented. Based on this, the influence of ship technical characteristics, particularly speed and propulsion power, on the economic performance of Ro-Ro operations and the technological developments occurring in the different ship sub-types are discussed. A subsequent section deals with the technical features necessary in dedicated SSS Ro-Ro terminals and their influence on the success of intermodal operations. Organizational and procedural matters in SSS terminals are also briefly discussed, just before a short section summarizing the conclusions of this chapter.

2 Typical ship configurations and undergoing technological innovations

Examples of the two main types of Ro-Ro ships are shown in Figure 2.1, with a typical Ro-Ro cargo ship on the left and a typical Ro-Pax ship on the right. It may be seen that Ro-Ro cargo ships generally have a superstructure located at one third

Figure 2.1 Typical examples of Ro-Ro cargo and Ro-Pax ships.

of the ship's length, whereas Ro-Pax ships possess a much larger superstructure, due to the necessity of carrying passengers, located forward and extending aft as much as necessary to accommodate the passengers. Loading Ro-Ro cargo ships is generally done using one or more stern ramps, while Ro-Pax ships typically have a drive-through capability (may be loaded/unloaded through a bow ramp in addition to the stern ramp). In some cases Ro-Pax ships allow a double-level loading/unloading using special link spans.

Figure 2.2 shows the general arrangement of a typical Ro-Ro cargo ship. In this case, the ship is fitted with three Ro-Ro cargo decks (lower, main and upper decks), with the lower deck located forward of the engine room within B/10 lateral void spaces. In this case, the third Ro-Ro deck (upper deck) is the weather deck. Some larger ships now have four, five or even more cargo decks. The superstructure is located forward and is not very large, as it only needs to support the crew (limited in number). A significant number of ships have a superstructure at the extreme aft or at one third of the ship's length. The engine room is, in the case of this ship, located aft and contains two medium-speed diesel engines. Very rarely, a forward engine room may exist in correspondence with a forward superstructure, but this leads to very long shaft lines, prone to technical problems such as vibrations.

Figure 2.3 shows the general arrangement of a typical Ro-Pax ship. The ship is fitted with two full-length Ro-Ro cargo decks (main and upper decks) but no lower deck. However, some of these ships are also fitted with a lower deck, forward of the engine room, within B/5 lateral void spaces. The superstructure is located forward and extends to slightly aft of amidships, as it needs to provide accommodations for over 600 passengers, in addition to crew members. The engine room is located aft and holds four medium-speed diesel engines, coupled in pairs to two shaft lines. Very rarely, the superstructure of a Ro-Pax ship may be located aft, and this occurs for ships with limited passenger capacity. Ro-Pax ships with very high passenger capacity may have full-length superstructures and, in some cases, have only one Ro-Ro cargo deck. These ships are often called cruise ferries.

Regarding technological innovation, the focus of recent developments has been not only on increasing the efficiency of the propulsion system, but also on

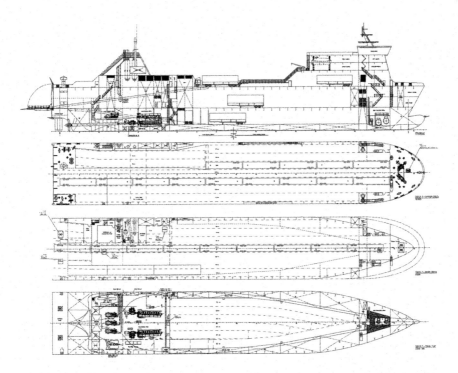

Figure 2.2 General arrangement of Ro-Ro cargo ship (142 m length overall, 23 m breadth, 1830 m lane length).

Source: Adapted from Seatruck (2013).

reducing or eliminating emissions, either by adopting electric propulsion or by using alternative fuel solutions such as liquified natural gas (LNG), methanol or even hydrogen fuel cells.

One example of efficiency improvement design measures was presented within the scope of the EU project STREAMLINE (2010–2014). Rolls Royce proposed the concept of a contra rotating pod (CRP) drive, developed for a medium-sized Ro-Ro vessel as an alternative to the conventional twin screw arrangement (European Technology Platform Waterborne, 2016). In this concept, two controllable pitch propellers rotating in opposite directions are installed, in series, in a common shaft inside a pod. After a set of model tests, the project claims that power savings of up to 15.6% are obtained, in comparison with four different twin-screw arrangements for a Ro-Ro vessel.

Alternative fuels have also made some gains in Ro-Ro ships, especially for newbuilding. The ferry *Viking Grace* was built by STX Turku yard in 2013 to operate on the Baltic, between Turku and Stockholm, and was the first large LNG-fuelled passenger ship with dual-fuel electric propulsion. It has capacity for 2,800 passengers and 1,275 m lane length on the main deck and additional 550 m on a

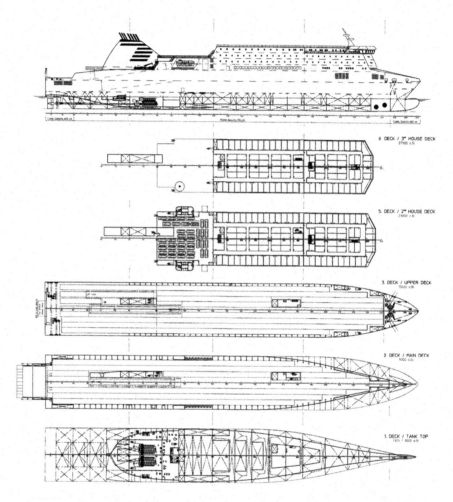

Figure 2.3 General arrangement of Ro-Pax ship (199.8 m length overall, 27.8 m breadth, 2980 m lane length, 640 passengers).

Source: Adapted from FSG (2002).

hoistable deck. More recently (2018), the ship was equipped with a rotor sail to reduce further fuel consumption and emissions. However, Viking Lines already have under construction a new larger LNG-powered ferry, with 218 m length, 63,000 GT and capacity for 2,800 passengers and 1,500 m lane length. This ship is to be delivered in 2020 and is expected to consume less 10% in fuel. Also in the Baltic Sea, the Swedish operator Destination Gotland has received in 2018 a LNG-powered Ro-Pax ferry, the *Visborg*, with 200 m length, and a sister vessel is under construction in China. These are the first LNG Ro-Pax ships built in

Chinese yards. Finally, the Estonian company Tallink also has in operation since 2017 an LNG-fuelled Ro-Pax named *Megastar*, and another ship in currently on order.

In the English Channel and the Atlantic, Brittany Ferries has ordered three LNG-powered electric propulsion Ro-Pax ships (E-Flexer class), the first of which will be named *Honfleur*. These ships feature an innovative re-fuelling system, which consists of four interchangeable 40-feet ISO containers, installed in place using a shipboard crane. Ships are being built in a German shipyard, FSG, for delivery from 2019 onwards. In the Mediterranean, Baleària in 2017 ordered two new ferries with dual-fuel LNG propulsion, the first of which (*Hypatia de Alexandria*) started operating in 2019. Finally, CLdN Ro-Ro company built two new Ro-Ro cargo ships, *Celine* and *Delphine*, with 74,000 GT, 235 metres length, and 8,000 lane-metres capacity, for operation on North Sea and Atlantic coasts. These ships were designed with the LNG-ready class notation and will be able to switch to LNG as soon as bunkering infrastructure is available and LNG prices are attractive (DNV-GL, 2018).

While waiting for new buildings, some investment is being made in converting existing ships with conventional diesel-based propulsion systems to other types of propulsion and fuel. The project HYBRIDShip, started in 2016 by Fiskerstrand Holding AS, aims at converting an existing diesel-powered ferry to hydrogen and fuel cells, complemented by batteries. The Norwegian government is supporting a project launched in 2017 that intends to build a hydrogen-electric ferry to operate on the Hjelmeland–Nesvik route.

Some effort has also been put into converting Ro-Pax ships to fully electric (battery-based) propulsion. The *Tycho Brahe* ferry and its sister ship *Aurora of Helsingborg*, with 12,000 GT and a length of 111 m, operating between Denmark and Sweden, have been converted from diesel propulsion to fully electric propulsion (2017). The ships are fitted with four thrusters of 1.5 MW each, with the power provided by 640 Li-ion batteries of 6.5 kWh each. Batteries are re-charged in ports in a matter of minutes. Another similar project has been undertaken by Stena Line, which installed a 1 MWh battery pack in the weather deck of *Stena Jutlandica*, for powering the bow thrusters while manoeuvring in port. In subsequent steps, a 20 MWh battery pack will enable operating on electricity up to 10 miles from port and, finally, a 50 MWh battery pack will enable covering the 50 miles from Gothenburg to Frederikshavn entirely on batteries.

Other shipping companies are engaged in converting diesel engines to run on LNG. One example is Balearia, which in addition to the aforementioned new-building, plans to convert a series of six Ro-Pax ships to use LNG in dual-fuel engines. The first one, the *Nápoles*, with 186 m length and capacity for 1,600 passengers and 1,430 m lane length, is already back in operation (2018), after being re-fit in Gibraltar's Gibdock shipyard.

Finally, Stena Line has promoted an innovative conversion of one of its Ro-Pax ships, *Stena Germanica*, to run on methanol. The conversion was carried out in Poland (Remontowa) in 2015. Methanol, in comparison with conventional marine bunker fuels, reduces emissions significantly: SO_x emissions by 99%, NO_x by

60%, CO_2 by 25% and particulate matter (PM) by 95%. The existing engines were modified with new dual-fuel injection nozzles but are still able to run on marine gas oil as backup. This ship had already been fitted in 2012 with a shore-to-ship power supply system, enabling the shutdown of its diesel engines while at port in Gothenburg.

3 Assessment of the Ro-Ro ship fleet

3.1 Ro-Ro ship database

A comprehensive database of Ro-Ro ships has been developed to estimate a number of ship technical characteristics necessary to necessary to assess ship's economic performance on a given route, aiming at further developing the work presented in Santos and Guedes Soares (2017a) on the evaluation of transport demand on a given SSS Ro-Ro route. This demand is finally expressed as a weekly demand in lane length (meters). Later, Santos and Guedes Soares (2017b) used a small database of Ro-Ro cargo ships to estimate the size of the ship(s) necessary to carry the estimated cargo demand per week, as derived in the previous paper. This chapter aims at improving the estimates of ship characteristics with a much-enlarged database, comprising also Ro-Pax ships. Furthermore, very few databases of this type have been presented in the open literature, an exception being that presented by Kristensen and Psaraftis (2016).

The ship database has been created based on the report from Baltic Press (2017), containing the main shipowners and ship operators in the SSS Ro-Ro market, namely those operating ferries across different routes in four areas: North Sea, Baltic Sea, Irish Sea and Mediterranean Sea. For those shipowners, their fleet was identified and the technical characteristics of the ships were registered. As a result, 25 operators were identified with a fleet of 164 Ro-Ro cargo ships and 38 operators with a fleet of 225 Ro-Pax ships. Therefore, the European fleet in 2018 comprises about 401 ships. It should be noted that some companies offer services with both ship types. Figure 2.4 shows that the percentages in number of operators and ships do not differ much for Ro-Ro cargo and Ro-Pax ships.

Figure 2.5 shows that the number of Ro-Ro cargo ships built in the last few years has been continuously increasing, unlike the number of Ro-Pax ships that has decreased in the last five years recorded. This justifies the fact that very few Ro-Ro cargo ships have more than 20 years of age, whereas a significant number of Ro-Pax ships have more than 20 years. This is, in fact, typical of passenger ships, known to have substantially longer operational lives than cargo ships have.

Data from ships built between 1980 and 2018 were compiled and analyzed to try to characterize Ro-Ro ships used in short sea shipping. To collect this data, sources such as RINA (1992–2013) and shipyards', shipping companies', classification societies' and other publicly available websites were used. Figure 2.6 shows the results for both ship types, regarding lane length, and it may be seen that most cargo ships have between 1,500 m and 4,000 m in lane length, whereas most Ro-Pax ships have between 500 m and 4,000 m in lane length. Ro-Ro cargo ships thus have a higher lower boundary for cargo capacity (1,500 m rather than

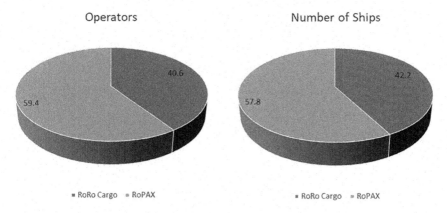

Figure 2.4 Number of operators and Ro-Ro ships involved in SSS.

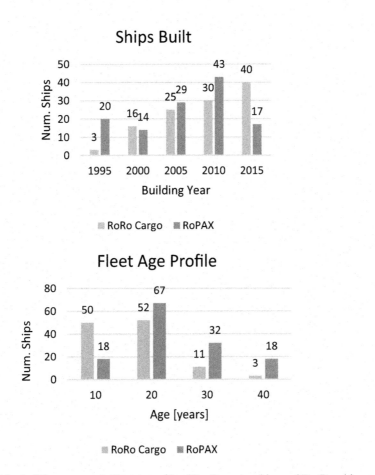

Figure 2.5 Newbuilding year and ship age profile of Ro-Ro cargo ships and Ro-Pax ships.

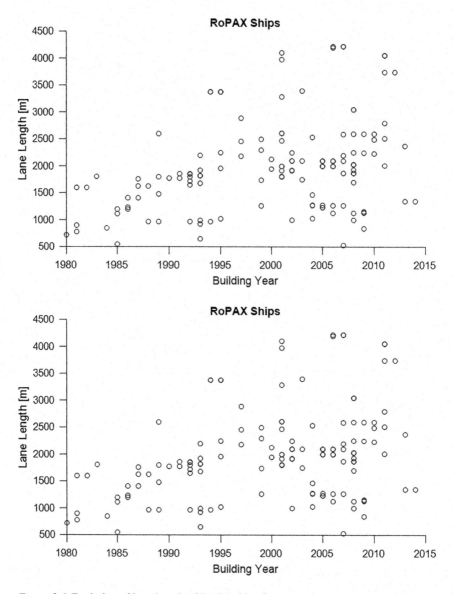

Figure 2.6 Evolution of lane length of Ro-Ro ships fleet over time.

500 m). Regarding the evolution in time of the lane length capacity, no clear trend exists, although it appears that the maximum lane length of ships has been increasing significantly.

It should be mentioned that in very recent years (or even throughout 2019, the reason why the ships are not included in the database) a few Ro-Ro cargo ships have been delivered with even larger lane lengths. That is the case of ships forming recent classes of Ro-Ro cargo ships, ordered by DFDS (lane length of 6,690 m), Grimaldi (7,800 m) and CLdN (also 7,800 m). These ships carry between 450 and 600 trailer units, certainly putting a heavy burden on the infrastructure of Ro-Ro terminals where these ships call.

3.2 Ro-Ro ship characteristics

When studying the economic performance of ships on a given route, it is necessary to evaluate the different costs involved in ship operation. These costs may be categorized in different ways, but the categorization by Stopford (2009) will be followed in this study, broadly sub-dividing into capital costs, operating costs and voyage costs. Capital cost depends on the ship's newbuilding cost, which is in turn function of the main dimensions and passenger capacity, among others. Operating costs depend on the main dimensions of the ship (length, breadth, depth), gross tonnage, deadweight, newbuilding price, crew size, type of propulsion, propulsion power, number and type of main engines, among others. Finally, voyage costs depend on propulsion power, auxiliary power, speed actually used, the characteristics of the voyage and the price and type of fuel used. Considering the dependencies of these three cost categories, Table 2.1 summarizes the technical characteristics of interest from an economic point of view, which should be recorded in the database, as a function of lane length.

The length overall (Loa) is an important dimension of the ship from the point of view of its operation. Some ports, terminals and waterways present physical limitations of this dimension, which is also relevant concerning the mooring space occupied and the determination of some port tariffs. Therefore, Figure 2.7 presents the relations between the Loa and the length between perpendiculars (Lpp), a dimension that is quite relevant from the point of view of naval architecture. As

Table 2.1 Technical characteristics of ships of importance for economic studies.

Technical characteristic	
Length overall	Loa
Breadth	B
Depth	D
Gross tonnage	GT
Deadweight	DW
Type of propulsion	TP
Type and number of main engines	NME
Propulsion power	MCR
Auxiliary power	Pe
Service speed	Vs
Newbuilding price	Nwb
Crew size	Crew

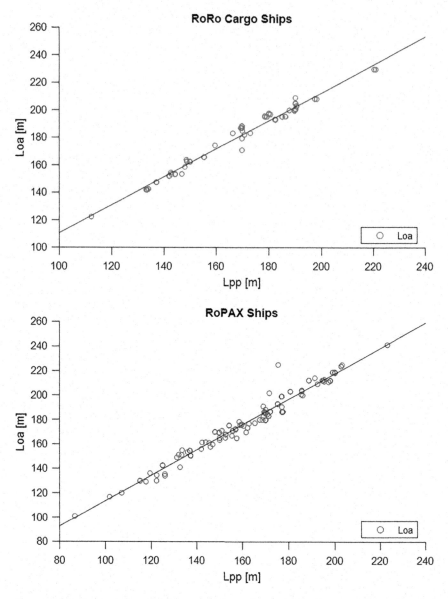

Figure 2.7 Relation between length overall (Loa) and length between perpendiculars (Lpp).

can be seen, the relation is practically linear. The figure also shows that the ships in the database range from Lpp of 100 m to 220 m, with most ships concentrated in the range between 140 m and 200 m (for Ro-Ro cargo ships) and 120 m and 220 m (for Ro-Pax ships).

As complementary information, Figure 2.8 depicts the variation of the main dimensions with the lane length (meters). There is definitely a relationship between Lpp and the ship's lane length, but still a wide variation of Lpp may exist for each lane length capacity, reflecting the fact that ships of the same size may be designed with different numbers of cargo decks leading to much different cargo capacities. It can be seen that there is a larger dispersion of the values of the ship's length versus the lane length in the Ro-Pax ships than in the Ro-Ro cargo ships.

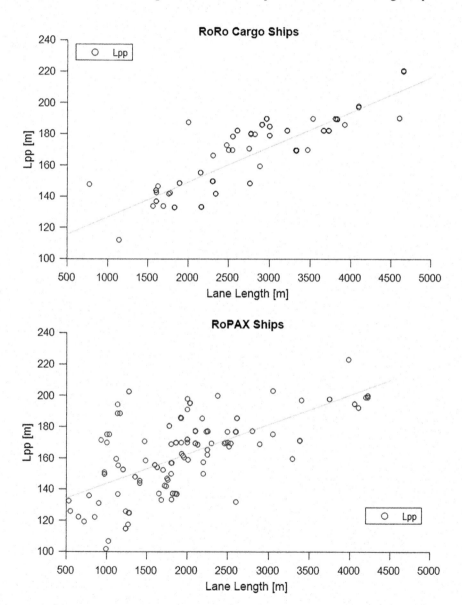

Figure 2.8 Relation between length between perpendiculars and lane length.

Figure 2.9 shows the relation between the breadth, depth and draught of the ships and their lane length. All these characteristics appear to increase with lane length. It may be seen that most Ro-Ro cargo ships have breadths between 20 m and 27 m, with a few aligned with the Panamax breadth (32.2 m). Also for cargo ships, the depth (measured to upper deck) increases from 13 m to approximately

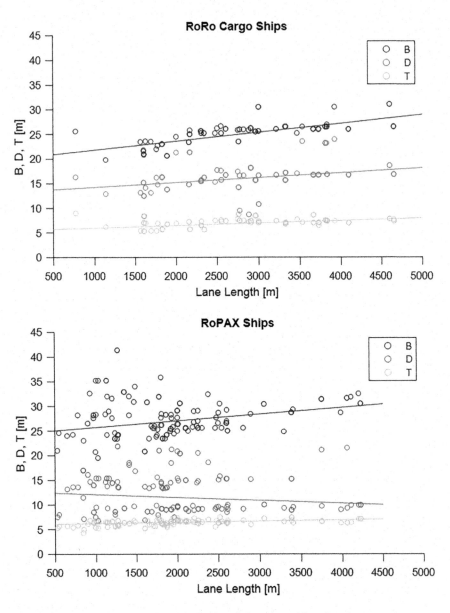

Figure 2.9 Relation between breadth, depth and draught and lane length.

17 m and the draught from 5 m to approximately 8 m. For Ro-Pax ships the dispersion is wider, namely regarding the breadth of the ship, which in many cases is much larger than for Ro-Ro cargo ships of the same size. Regarding depth, the database clearly shows ships (particularly Ro-Pax ships) in which the recorded depth is that up to the main cargo deck, while in other cases the recorded depth is that measured to an upper deck (weather deck or not). In a few cases, the depth appears to be that to the weather deck. However, also for these ships, it appears that the three characteristics increase steadily with lane length.

Figure 2.10 shows the dimensional ratios typical of both types of ships. Although the dispersion is large in all cases, it appears that the L/B ratio increases with lane length in both types of ships. The other two ratios appear more or less constant.

Most administration (flag) and port authority tariffs and fees applied to a ship are determined as a function of the size of the ship measured through its gross tonnage (GT). In Figure 2.11 are represented the gross tonnages of Ro-Ro cargo ships and Ro-Pax ships in the database, expressed as function of a length between perpendiculars, breadth and depth.

Considering the results in Figure 2.11, the values of GT can be estimated for Ro-Ro cargo ships by the expression:

$$GT = -4.124 Lpp^{1.134} B^{2.399} D^{2.227E-1} \tag{2.1}$$

For Ro-Pax ships, the values of GT can be estimated by the expression:

$$GT = -1.416 Lpp^{1.024} B^{1.935} D^{3.213E-2} \tag{2.2}$$

The number of cargo decks is an essential parameter of the configuration of the cargo space of Ro-Ro ships. From the database, as shown in Figure 2.12, the most frequent number of decks for Ro-Ro cargo ships is three, while Ro-Pax ships most frequently have two or three decks. These are only the fixed cargo decks, ignoring any movable intermediate platforms (used generally for light vehicles).

Figure 2.13 shows the deadweight of the ships as a function of the lane length. It may be seen that there is a clear increase of deadweight with the size of the ship, which might be expected. Also, the deadweight of Ro-Ro cargo ships is clearly larger than that of a similar size (lane length) Ro-Pax ship.

Figure 2.14 shows the relation between service speed and the lane length of ships of the two types. Although the dispersion is large, a trend appears to exist towards a slight growth of service speed with lane length. It is also clear that the service speed of most Ro-Pax ships is slightly larger than that of Ro-Ro cargo ships of similar size, as could be expected. Most Ro-Ro cargo ships have service speed between 16 knots and 22 knots, while Ro-Pax ships show service speeds widely scattered between 18 knots and 30 knots.

This is in line with the findings of Lloyd's Register-Fairplay (2008), which show that actual speeds of operation of Ro-Pax ships are generally higher than those of Ro-Ro cargo ships. In any case, the same study also shows that the actual speeds of

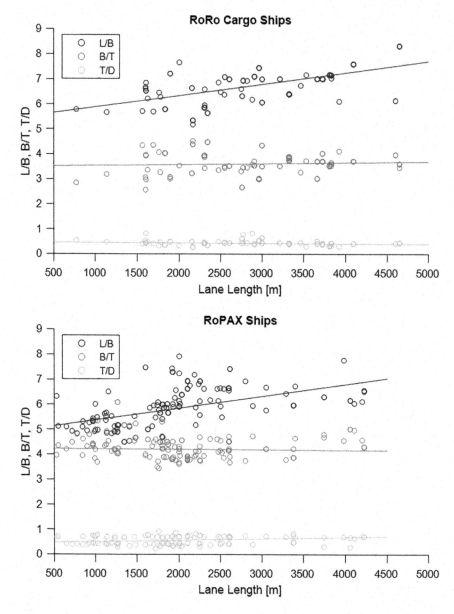

Figure 2.10 Relation between dimensional ratios of Ro-Ro ships and lane length.

operation are, in many cases, much lower than the service speeds of ships (as defined during design), as the practice of slow steaming is very common nowadays. Differences of 3 knots for Ro-Ro cargo ships and of 5 knots for Ro-Pax ships are common.

Figure 2.15 shows the variation of the installed propulsive power (total maximum continuous rating – MCR) with the total lane length. It can be seen that

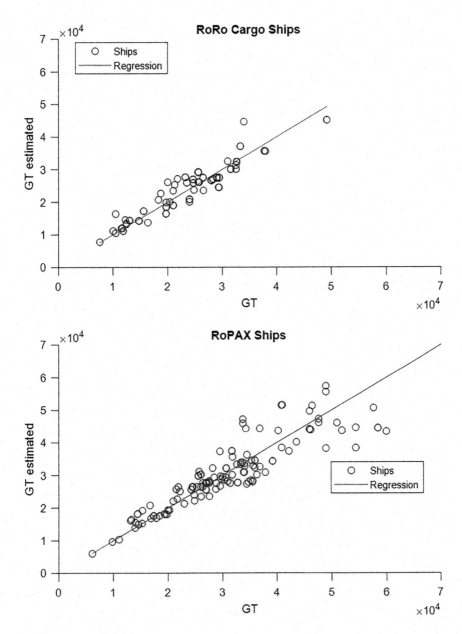

Figure 2.11 Estimate of the gross tonnage as function of length between perpendiculars, breadth and depth.

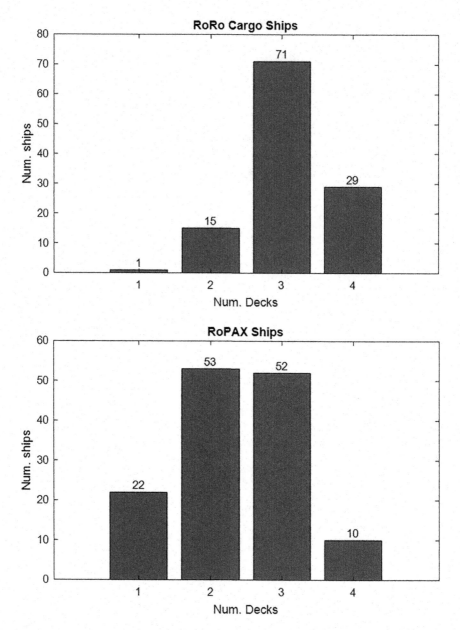

Figure 2.12 Number of Ro-Ro cargo decks of ships in the Ro-Ro fleet.

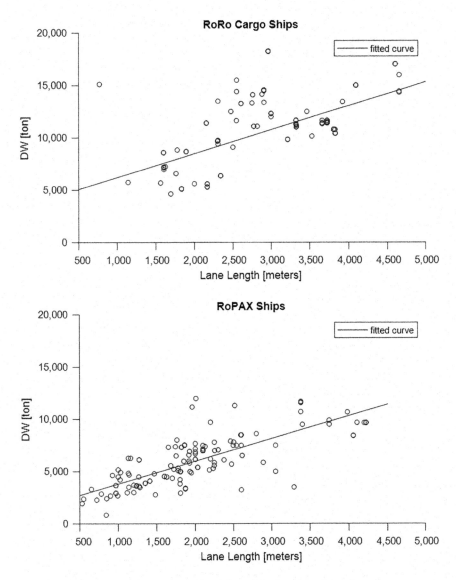

Figure 2.13 Relation between the deadweight and the lane length.

the dispersion is much higher in Ro-Pax ships and, as might be expected from the previous figure, the installed power is much higher than that of Ro-Ro cargo ships.

Another technical characteristic of importance is the total power of the auxiliary engines, used for generating electrical power on board, as this is an important component of voyage costs. Figure 2.16 shows the ship's total auxiliary power

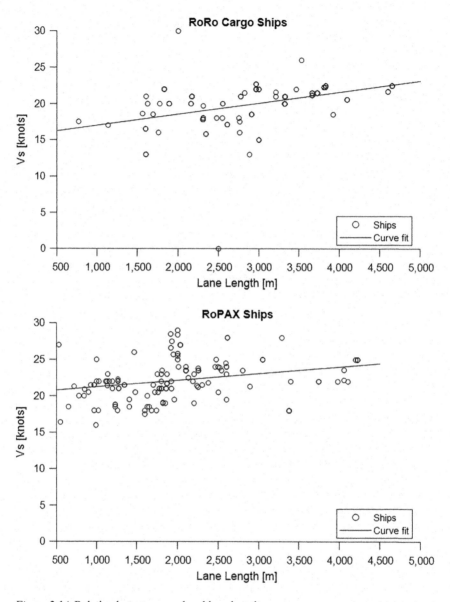

Figure 2.14 Relation between speed and lane length.

and the lane length of the ships. The dispersion is now very significant, with some tendency for an increase as the ship's size grows, motivating the representation in the figures of only a lower bound, which appears consensual. For a ship of a given size (lane length), the auxiliary engine's power may be somewhere above this lower bound, depending on such parameters as main engine power, number of Ro-Ro decks, number of passengers and power of bow/stern thrusters.

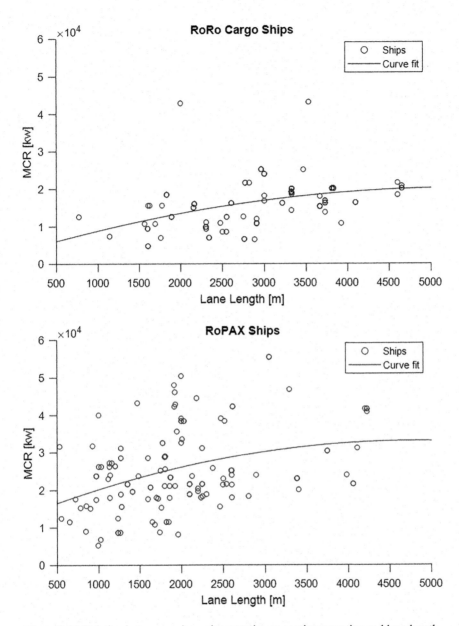

Figure 2.15 Relation between main engines maximum continuous rating and lane length.

Figure 2.17 shows the newbuilding price of Ro-Ro ships. Information on these prices is relatively rare, especially for Ro-Ro cargo ships. For Ro-Ro cargo ships there are data (Bartlett, 2012) regarding average prices for different ship sizes. For Ro-Pax ships, more information is publicly available in specialized magazines. In general, it may be seen that Ro-Ro cargo ships are much less costly

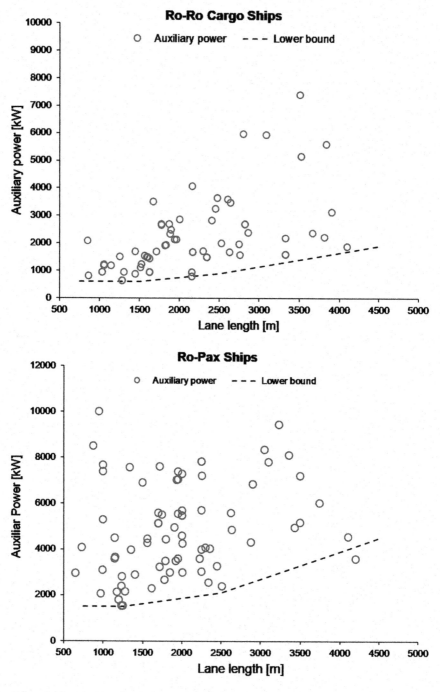

Figure 2.16 Relation between installed auxiliary power and lane length.

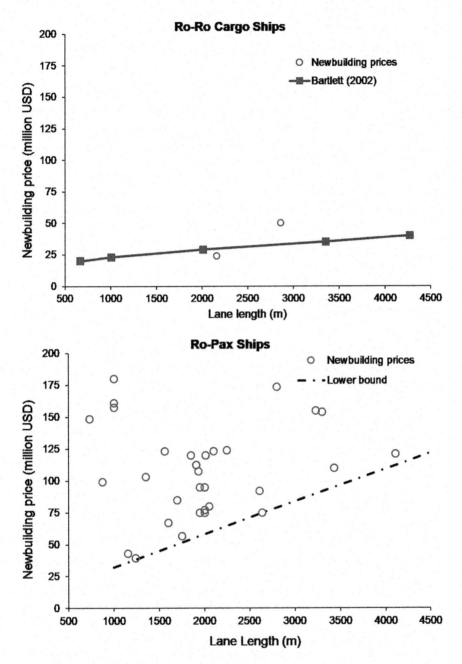

Figure 2.17 Relation between newbuilding price and lane length.

than Ro-Pax ships are. Newbuilding price for a Ro-Ro cargo ship is below 50 million USD, while for Ro-Pax it is above this threshold in most of the upper size range. For Ro-Pax ships, Figure 2.17b shows a lower boundary for ship prices, but the dispersion of newbuilding prices is very wide due to large variations in cargo and passenger capacities and in amenities (and quality of public spaces) provided on board.

Figure 2.18 shows the crew and passenger capacity of Ro-Ro ships. Most Ro-Ro cargo ships have crews with less than 25 members, with a slight tendency to increase with the lane length. Ro-Pax ships have crews which may number 100 members or more, still substantially less than the number of passengers on board, which may be as large as 3,000 and generally not less than 250. The figure also shows the upper and lower bounds for the number of crew members as a function of the lane length. Within these bounds the ships will have more or less crew depending on the number of passengers on board, which leads to the necessity of more comprehensive amenities. For cargo ships, the complexity of the ship's machinery and cargo spaces may lead to more numerous crews. Two or three ships in the database fall outside of the bounds for crew size, but these are cruise ferries with very high passenger capacities.

4 Intermodal units

Before discussing the characteristics and problems specific of Ro-Ro SSS terminals, a brief review of intermodal cargo units is provided in this section. Figure 2.19 shows the main types of intermodal cargo units currently in use in such terminals and of interest in this chapter (see dotted boxes). The most common intermodal units are full road trucks (lorries, articulated vehicles, road trains), trailers or semi-trailers, roll trailers and cassettes. Containers of different sizes are also common and are carried generally on top of roll trailers or cassettes. For convenience, it is common to use the expression 'platform' to indicate the different types of intermodal cargo units used in SSS terminals.

In general, platforms are mounted on wheels and can be towed by tractor units. If they have a height of 1.2–1.4 m above the ground, they correspond to trailers or semi-trailers prepared to circulate in roads. There are also low cargo platforms, called roll trailers, with a height above the ground of about 0.6 m and wheels at the rear end, which cannot circulate outside the terminal. These are used for over-dimensioned cargos or containers and generally can take more weight than the standard platforms. Their length is generally enough to fit a 20 ft or a 40 ft container. Roll trailers are towed by terminal tractor units using an intermediate piece of equipment called gooseneck to lift the forward end of the roll trailer. The set of the tractor unit, gooseneck and roll trailer is often called a 'mafi roll trailer system'. Shipping companies generally operate fleets of roll trailers for the use of their customers. Another type of platform, which is wheelless, is called a cassette. These are handled using special terminal tractors called lift-trailers (or translifters). They may also take containers and generally have a length of 40 ft. Both

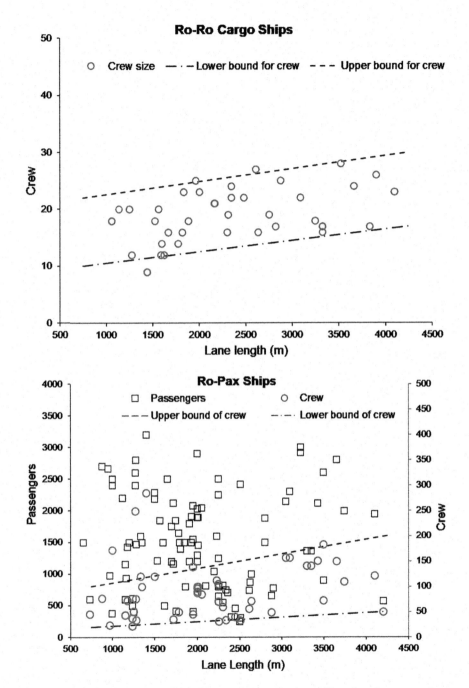

Figure 2.18 Relation between crew size, passenger capacity and lane length.

46 *Manuel Ventura et al.*

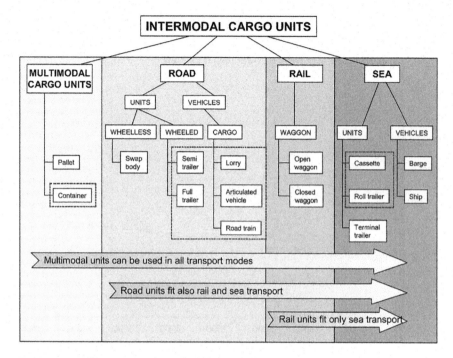

Figure 2.19 Types of intermodal units.
Source: Adapted from Wijnolst and Wergeland (2009).

these types of cargo units, roll trailers and cassettes, can be tightly stowed side by side inside the ship and, therefore, need less space on the cargo deck than do trucks or trailers. They may also carry heavier cargos than trucks, but the strength of the Ro-Ro decks must be taken in consideration, as well as the slope of the ramps and the pulling power of the terminal tractor, as these parameters may limit, in practice, the permissible load in these units. Table 2.2 shows a summary of the main characteristics of these intermodal units.

In recent years a number of Ro-Ro ships, mainly of the cargo ship sub-type, have been designed with internal decks having sufficient deck free height to make it possible to double stack containers on top of roll trailers or cassettes, as shown in Figure 2.20. The complete set will have a total height up to 7.0 m, so enough free height below the deck beams must be provided for this. The main advantage of this type of arrangement is that it allows a much better utilization of the ship's cargo spaces and will allow important transport cost savings. Another consideration in the design of the shore ramp and ship's internal deck spaces is that, in order to allow an efficient cargo handling of the full road trucks, trailers, semi-trailers, roll trailers or cassettes, it is necessary to ensure that the slope of the shore ramps and internal ramps between the different decks in the Ro-Ro ship is less than 7 degrees.

Table 2.2 Main dimensions of intermodal units.

		Length (m)	Breadth (m)	Height (m)	Weight loaded (t)
Road trucks	Lorries	10.72	2.55	4.00	18–26
	Articulated trucks	16.50	2.55	4.00	40
	Road train	18.75	2.55	4.00	40
	Road train (national traffic)	25.25	2.55	4.00	60
Semi-trailers		13.60	2.55	4.00	40
Trailers	Small	7.82	2.55	4.00	18
	Full trailer	13.60	2.55	4.00	30
Roll trailers	40 ft	12.40	2.59	0.77	100
	62 ft	18.90	2.60	0.85	100
	72 ft	22.00	2.80	0.97	90
Cassettes	40 ft	12.20	2.60	0.85	80–120
Containers	TEU	6.06	2.44	2.59	28.2
	FEU	12.19	2.44	2.59	26.6
	High cube 40 ft	12.19	2.44	2.90	30.8
	High cube 20 ft	13.72	2.44	2.90	30.4

Figure 2.20 Double stacking of containers in the weather deck of a Ro-Ro cargo ship.

5 Dedicated short sea shipping terminals

5.1 Integration of port terminals in SSS

Short sea shipping faces some difficulties in its interaction with port terminals. SSS has to use terminals more frequently than does deep sea shipping, which makes it critical to have efficient port operations. In fact, one of the prerequisites for the efficient integration of SSS in Motorways of the Sea, a concept first proposed by European Commission (2001), is the provision of dedicated port infrastructures, mainly Ro-Ro terminals fitted with ample parking space, logistics equipment and even accommodation for drivers. The terminals should allow cargo to flow rapidly to ensure that the overall transit time across the transport chain is not compromised (generally should be not higher than a fully road-based alternative). In addition to these requirements, in the literature on SSS, one may find many other requirements applicable to these terminals:

- Avoiding discrimination of SSS in relation to deep sea shipping;
- Clear and uniform rules on pilotage, cargo handling and stevedoring;
- Flexible stevedoring for 24-hour operations, 365 days per year;
- Improvement of the terminal's overall reliability;
- Simplification of rules governing the operation of ports;
- Reduction of bureaucracy and complex documentation, namely in customs;
- Integration of the logistics chain stakeholders (shipowners, carriers, forwarders) in a one-stop shop (IT systems), allowing the monitoring of cargo flows and transparency;
- Provision of high-capacity land access (road and rail);
- Year-round navigability (no restrictions due to ice, bad weather or drought);
- Available water depth with no tidal restrictions;
- Tight security measures in the terminal in accordance with ISPS;
- Provision of services to cargo and truck drivers and even some value-added logistics services;
- Establishment and monitoring of a set of service performance indicators; and
- Continuous effort for improving the image of the terminal and, in general, of SSS performance.

Shipping companies involved in SSS frequently voice their concerns over port terminals' performance, covering different aspects affecting both time and the costs incurred in ports. Shipping companies frequently suggest that the mandatory obligation in most ports to use pilotage is an area of possible improvement. Their argument is that SSS services are regular lines, and the ships' captains are therefore expected to be familiar with the natural conditions in the port, making mandatory pilotage unnecessary. It could therefore be waived in most cases, and in some ports it already occurs through pilotage exemption certificates (PEC). Also, sometimes tug utilization is mandatory, but SSS ships typically have good manoeuvrability due to the presence of bow thrusters (in some cases also stern thrusters) and do not need the assistance of tugs. Finally, the utilization of specialized mooring companies is often mandatory, but in most cases mooring could easily be done by terminal or shipping company personnel.

5.2 Types of Ro-Ro SSS terminals

According to PIANC (2014), there are mainly three types of Ro-Ro terminals, depending on the type of vessels that they service. One is the Ro-Ro cargo terminal, which handles primarily road trucks (also called heavy goods vehicles), mostly unaccompanied. Ships using these terminals usually have very limited driver accommodation as they are classified as cargo ships. Tractor units are often decoupled from the trailers and semi-trailers and carried aboard the ships. The trailers or semi-trailers are loaded and unloaded using special equipment. In some terminals the entire full road truck may also be taken aboard, with or without accompanying drivers. Routes are typically of mid to high distance (in SSS terms), and the frequency is from weekly to daily.

A second type of Ro-Ro terminal is the Ro-Pax ferry terminal, which handles a combination of road trucks, passenger cars and passengers (travelling with or without car). The term 'ferry' commonly designates the ship type, and the routes are typically short and of high frequency (several departures per day). Ships have capacity for passengers, ranging widely from dozens to a few thousands. Trucks may be carried accompanied or not. In some cases, only the semi-trailer is carried on board.

Finally, a third type of Ro-Ro terminal is the car carrier terminal, which receives car carriers (vehicle carriers) loaded with combinations of new cars, trucks and wheeled machinery. Most of these terminals receive regular deep sea Ro-Ro lines (long distance), so they will be left out of this study on short sea shipping. The frequency of deep sea lines is lower, usually monthly. However, a small number of shipping companies do operate small- to medium-size vehicle carriers in typical short sea trades in the EU, namely Flota Suardiaz and UECC.

5.3 General organization and operations

Ro-Ro terminals generally have the following functional areas:

- Reception and delivery area: includes terminal gates and their access;
- Storage area: includes the spaces allocated to storage of trucks, cars, trailers, semi-trailers, platforms with cargo on top (general cargo, containers) and containers, but also the roadways for circulation. Segregation of cargo flows (import/export) and of cargo types is generally used;
- Cargo handling area: includes the quay, apron and ramps through which loading/unloading of the ship is carried out;
- Service area: space for workshops, parking or terminal equipment, administration and management offices, customs, bar, toilets and showers; and
- Added-value area: space for facilities allowing cargo servicing.

The cargo handling area is quite important, and the layout of berths may actually follow several different designs. Because most Ro-Ro ships and ferries have bow or stern ramps (or both), the ship needs to be in a corner, but the details of the disposition of the berths vary. Some terminals have berths located along a longitudinal quay, others have finger piers along which the ships berth (cargo handling through the stern or bow ramps), others have berths at an angle to the quay and, finally, the berth may simply take a corner of the dock. The different dispositions have all their advantages and disadvantages, as discussed in UNCTAD (1985).

The reception and delivery area is common to all terminals, but it is relatively uncommon that Ro-Ro terminals possess dedicated in-dock rail facilities. There are, however, some examples of this type of facility. For example, the Samer terminal in Trieste (Italy), shown in Figure 2.21, sends over 25 trains per week to six different intermodal terminals in Germany, Austria and Luxembourg (data from late 2018). Various types of trains transport full road trucks, semi-trailers (even if non-cranable) and containers. The loading/unloading of trains is carried out using reach-stackers.

Cargo handling operations in Ro-Ro terminals dedicated to SSS is generally done by stevedores employed by the terminal operator. The terminal operator is usually the shipping company whose ships use the terminal. This is especially true when large volumes of passengers use the terminal. Terminal tractors used to tow the unaccompanied cargo (platforms) to/from the ship, for example, are operated by the terminal operator's contracted stevedores. In some ports, the stevedores may need to be provided by a port-wide labour pool. The stowage of the cargo on board the ship, namely the lashing of trucks, vehicles and intermodal units inside the ship, is generally done by the crew itself (self-handling). In countries or ports where this is not accepted by local authorities, the need to use local stevedores for this task is generally considered a major hindrance to the development of SSS in such ports.

Figure 2.21 Ro-Ro cargo terminal in Trieste, Italy, showing in-dock rail terminal adjacent to quay.

Ro-Ro ships and dedicated SSS terminals 51

Regarding loading practices, Morales-Fusco (2016) indicates that when both accompanied and unaccompanied transport is to be handled, platforms of different types are loaded first, together with new cars and other vehicles. This operation is carried out by the stevedores. Once this is completed, vehicles (light vehicles, trucks and buses) driven by their own occupants are loaded last to minimize the time passengers spend on board (drivers are regarded as passengers).

The storage of all these vehicles in the terminal yard is also done separately, with unaccompanied transport parked in oblique rows (trucks and trailers) or blocks (new cars), typically for a few days. Accompanied transport is generally parked in a separate block where typically it will wait for a few hours. Unloading generally starts with the accompanied transport, which drives directly out of the terminal, apart from some required border or customs controls. Stevedores then unload the unaccompanied cargo and park it in designated areas in the yard, again in blocks or rows. Figure 2.22 shows an example of a cargo Ro-Ro terminal, with semi-trailers parked in oblique rows, and a Ro-Pax ferry terminal, with the same type of area (in the background) and areas for accompanied transport (trucks or cars) in the foreground.

5.4 Productivity and dwell time

Productivity of loading/unloading operations in Ro-Ro terminals varies substantially. First, in cargo Ro-Ro terminals, transport is mostly unaccompanied, and therefore the terminal operator must provide tractor units to tow the trailers or semi-trailers into the ship. When the transport is accompanied, the truck drivers will load and unload their own trucks. The Ro-Ro deck must be at least 25 metres wide for the truck and semi-trailer to make a 180-degree turn and drive out through the stern gate. Otherwise, the ship should use the bow ramp in one terminal and the stern ramp in another terminal to speed up operations (drive-through cargo handling).

PIANC (2014) indicates for the productivity per Ro-Ro berth in Ro-Pax ferry terminals a value of 100 units per hour and for Ro-Ro cargo terminals 50 units

Figure 2.22 Typical layout of a Ro-Ro cargo terminal (Pendik, Istanbul, Turkey) and a Ro-Pax ferry terminal (Caen-Ouistreham, France).

per hour. Tractors are generally able to take in or out about six units per hour (may be as low as five or as high as seven), leading to the conclusion that this productivity of 50 units per hour requires simultaneous operation of about eight tractor units. For Mafi tractors, their speed is generally about 6.4 m/s, and engaging or disengaging takes about 2.5 min. In addition, Morales-Fusco (2016) reports that field observations in Barcelona's Ro-Ro terminals showed, presumably for accompanied transport, that 60–90 trucks may be loaded per hour, while 120–150 trucks may be unloaded per hour. Passenger vehicles are moved at a faster rate of 120–180 vehicles per hour.

The number of terminal tractors needs to be balanced with the size and arrangement of the ship and with the number of hours available to complete the unloading and loading of the ship. In most Ro-Ro cargo terminals, the ship will actually have to be fully unloaded and then fully loaded over a full day (preferably during daytime). As guidance, the number of equipment used to fully load/unload a ship in 6 hours is dependent on the size of the vessel, for example ships with capacity up to 75 platforms require one Mafi tractor; up to 135 platforms, two Mafis and more than 135 platforms, three Mafis. FEPORTS (2007) indicate that for a ship with capacity for 150 platforms, a fleet of four to five tractors is required.

In Ro-Pax ferry terminals, most of the transport is accompanied, and the loading or unloading operations are much faster. In some cases, double deck linkspans allow the simultaneous loading or unloading of two vehicle decks. This infrastructure is required for rapid turnaround of high-capacity Ro-Pax ships. Such an operation puts the road access infrastructure to the terminal under significant pressure, and its design needs to consider carefully these peaks of traffic.

As mentioned before, the terminal operator generally provides the personnel (stevedores) and the equipment (tractor units) for loading unaccompanied cargo in the ships. Personnel come in gangs, which often include (but vary between terminals) one chief, one cargo controller, four operators, one land controller and one auxiliary. Depending on the size of the ship and the available time for completing the operations, the number of gangs is adjusted. The typical gang working period (shift) is approximately 6 hours, implying that for large Ro-Ro ships, two consecutive shifts will be needed to operate the ship during the normal daylight hours.

Yard capacity is mainly determined by the yard area available. An important parameter to define is the proportion of unaccompanied transport that the terminal will handle. A larger proportion of unaccompanied vehicles generally requires more yard area because parking is carried out in rows and not in blocks. Larger dwell times in the terminal also lead to the need for more yard area.

Another important issue in Ro-Ro shipping is the shorter dwell times characteristic of this type of cargo. Although the dwell time will vary between terminals, PIANC (2014) indicates a typical dwell time in Ro-Ro cargo ferry terminals of 1 to 2 days, in Ro-Pax ferry terminals less than 1 day and in car carrier terminals generally 7 to 10 days (more than usual for containers in container terminals). Ligteringen (1999) indicates that in Ro-Pax ferry terminals the dwell time for trucks is as low as 1 to 3 hours. It is important to note that the dwell time is often very different for import and export. For example, outbound unaccompanied trucks will arrive any time between 7 days and 1 day (some predominance for 1 to 2 days) before departure, while inbound trucks will be picked up, in the vast majority of cases, 1 to 2 days after arrival.

Notwithstanding the dwell times mentioned, most shipping companies nowadays accept unaccompanied trucks to be delivered up to about 6 hours before departure, while complete trucks (accompanied) may be accepted up to about 2 hours before departure. Trucks with dangerous goods will be required to arrive earlier than these times. In any case, the individual conditions of each regular line need to be checked for the actual specifics, with variations on these arrangements existing even between different ports in the same line.

5.5 Cargo handling costs

The handling of unaccompanied cargo units in Ro-Ro terminals may be charged separately to the forwarder or shipper or may be included in a freight all kind rate, together with the maritime freight rate. Several European studies have gathered evidence regarding the levels of this handling cost in the EU. RECORDIT (2003) reports a broad range of values between 23 and 101 euros per unit, PLATINA(2012) shows values between 25 and 70 euros, while more recently TRT and MDS (2017) report an average of 67 euros. The higher values relate to modal transfer to rail or barges. Although these sources are not entirely clear, it is considered that these values include the operation of loading/unloading in the ship and the loading/unloading to/from a truck, train or barge. In the terminal tariffs, when these are publicly available, the two operations are generally mentioned and priced separately.

Additionally, if the cargo units spend more than 2 days in the terminal, the operator generally charges a storage or parking tariff (on a daily basis). Many European terminals, especially those handling a significant amount of unaccompanied transport, publish their annual tariffs, in many cases through their web pages. Sometimes, the tariffs include discounts applicable when large volumes (typically in excess of about 20,000 units per year) are handled by a forwarder.

5.6 Design of Ro-Ro short sea shipping terminals

The design and operation of Ro-Ro terminals dedicated to SSS, notwithstanding its specificities, follow the general procedures applicable for Ro-Ro terminals. Most of these terminals are generally very simple, as the infrastructure consists of a duly prepared surface for parking trucks, trailers, containers and cars and a quay fitted with a ramp for accessing the ship. In the case of terminals handling large volumes of passengers, infrastructure needs to be more comprehensive, as it is necessary to have buildings for receiving passengers, duly connected with the ship and, quite often, double deck linkspans to facilitate the loading and unloading of the ferries, as the typical turnaround times are much shorter.

The parameters characterizing the yard area are the following:

- Total area;
- Parking space area;
- Pavement type;
- Type of parking system (blocks, oblique);
- Type of traffic segmentation (import/export; Schengen/extra Schengen);
- Number of parking slots;
- Number of reefer slots (if any);
- Ro-Ro equipment (terminal tractors, translifters, fork-lift trucks, reach-stackers); and
- Garage and warehouse buildings (if any).

Concerning the quay of the terminal, the following are characteristic parameters:

- Quay length;
- Number of berths;
- Berth layout;
- Depth of water;
- Number of Ro-Ro ramps (fixed, floating); and
- Number and type of the linkspans.

Concerning the interface with land-based modes of transportation, the following are characteristic parameters:

- Number of gates (in/out);
- Gate management system (appointment, identification);
- In-dock rail terminal (if any) with number and length of rail tracks; and
- Barge terminal (if any).

Concerning regulatory compliance and additional services, the following are characteristic parameters:

- Cold ironing facilities;
- Fencing;
- Security system;
- Electrical lighting;
- Yard management software;
- Services provided to users (truck drivers); and
- Added-value services (if any).

For the design of Ro-Ro terminals, a number of useful references can be found in the literature, starting with monographs from the UNCTAD series. UNCTAD (1985) provides a complete handbook on port development, which includes a chapter on Ro-Ro terminal design providing some valuable insight. Some years later, Agós (1991) presented a monograph on the planning and management of multi-purpose terminals, including Ro-Ro terminals, but also container and general cargo terminals (also in a UNCTAD series). More recently, PIANC (2014) produced updated information for the master planning of ports, including a specific chapter dealing with Ro-Ro terminal planning. These references, and also Thoresen (2014), cover a number of design aspects related predominantly to the terminal's capacity for handling ships and cargo: marine capacity (ship manoeuvring), berth capacity (berth length, number of berths, vessel timetables and berth throughput), internal capacity (landside assembly, check-in, security, border controls and passenger facilities) and external capacity (hinterland connections for entry and exit).

In the case of Ro-Pax terminals, these require much more extensive built-up facilities, namely a passenger reception building. The main services provided in this building include the commercial check-in, immigration and customs checks, travel information desk, waiting space (lounges), some shops and a bar/restaurant. In some cases, these buildings have elevated walkways leading directly to the ship, making it very convenient for the prompt embarkation of foot passengers. Inbound and outbound traffic segregation within this building and, overall, in the terminal, will also be necessary for safety, security and traffic flow assurance reasons. This building normally requires more personnel to be employed in the terminal than in other cases. The quality of the spaces is of utmost importance.

In addition, Ro-Pax terminals are commonly fitted separately with an administration building, which generally also houses customs staff and security staff, a workshop building containing a parking/garage area for terminal tractors, crew and stations for equipment maintenance and re-fuelling. When large volumes of trucks are to be handled, a separate building is often provided for freight clearance, vehicle inspection and coach interchange. Facilities for repairing trucks, a fuel station, a restaurant/bar, WC and showers dedicated to truck drivers are also commonly provided.

6 Conclusions

This chapter provided background material regarding the technical characteristics of Ro-Ro ships and port terminals of the same type. A brief review of the technical characteristics of these ships was presented, and the main technological developments were enumerated. The conclusion is that most, if not all, innovations are related to the need for decarbonizing maritime transportation.

The chapter then presented a database of technical parameters of Ro-Ro cargo ships and Ro-Pax ships active in the EU short sea fleet, respectively with 164 and 225 ships, from 25 and 38 owners and operators. The motivation for building this database is that it allows estimating the likely technical characteristics of ships of a certain cargo capacity, as required when feasibility studies for new lines are carried out.

This database allows a number of conclusions, namely that Ro-Pax ships in the EU short sea fleet are generally older than Ro-Ro cargo ships. Ro-Ro cargo ships recorded in the database have lengths between perpendiculars between 130 m and 200 m, while Ro-Pax ships extend from 110 m to 210 m, and these size ranges cover the existing fleet. Ro-Ro cargo ships generally have higher lane lengths than Ro-Pax ships of the same size, a characteristic that results from the larger number of cargo decks in the former type of ship. Another important conclusion is that Ro-Pax service speed is higher than Ro-Ro cargo ship speed. It should be mentioned, however, that most technical characteristics show a wide dispersion, making it difficult to derive regression formulae presenting good accuracy, while lower boundaries for most variables are easy to identify. Above such lower boundaries, ships may have different values for the parameter under study, depending mostly on technical specifications and the performance required by the shipowner.

This chapter also includes a systematization of intermodal unit's characteristics in use in short sea shipping in the EU. In relation to SSS terminals, a number of key features for increasing the competitiveness of SSS was identified. These features are critical for reducing transit time and costs associated with ports. Some of the most relevant are reducing bureaucracy; ensuring uniform and clear rules on pilotage, cargo handling and stevedoring; providing flexible and round-the-clock cargo handling operations; and developing efficient maritime and land access to the port.

Finally, the chapter outlined the main technical characteristics of Ro-Ro terminals and discussed the operational practices prevailing in these facilities. The productivity levels in these terminals were indicated, and their relation with the fast turn-around time required by Ro-Ro ships was identified. Dwell times were also discussed, mentioning that dwell times are typically much lower than in container terminals. The chapter indicated that some of these Ro-Ro terminals are now developing on-dock rail terminals allowing a greater degree of integration with other modes of transportation than before, enabling for example the use of EU rail freight corridors, where available, thus fostering intermodality. This development may become critical in coming years, as some Ro-Ro operators are deploying ever larger ships which will deliver in Ro-Ro terminals hundreds of semi-trailers in a matter of a few hours.

Acknowledgements

The research presented in this chapter received support from the research project PTDC/ECI-TRA/28754/2017, financed by the Portuguese Foundation for Science and Technology (Fundação para a Ciência e Tecnologia – FCT) and is within the scope of the Strategic Research Plan of the Centre for Marine Technology and Ocean Engineering (CENTEC), financed by FCT under contract UID/Multi/00134/2020.

References

Agós, F.E. (1991), *Multi-purpose Port Terminals – Recommendations for Planning and Management*. New York: UNCTAD, United Nations.

Baltic Press (2017), *Ro-Ro & Ferry Atlas Europe. Supplement to the Monthly e-zine Harbours Review*. Gdynia, Poland: Baltic Press Ltd.

Bartlett, R. (2012), *The Valuation of Ships – Art and Science*. Marine Money's 6th Annual Korean Ship Finance Forum, Busan.

Council of the European Communities (1992), *Applying the Principle of Freedom to Provide Services to Maritime Transport Within Member States (Maritime Cabotage)*. Brussels, Belgium: Council Regulation (EEC) No. 3577/92.

DNV-GL (2018), Ferry and Ro-Ro Update.

European Commission (1999), The development of short sea shipping in Europe, COM(99) 317, Brussels, Belgium.

European Commission (2001), White paper European transport policy for 2010: Time to decide, COM(2001)370, Brussels, Belgium.

European Technology Platform Waterborne (2016), *Maritime Innovations for the 21st Century – Success Stories from EU Research*. Maritime Europe Strategy Action.

FEPORTS (2007), State of the art of short sea shipping terminals in Spain (Deliverable 2) (in Spanish), Valencia, Spain.

FSG (2002), *Ro-Pax 650*. Flensburg, Germany.

Kristensen, H.O., & Psaraftis, H. (2016), Analysis of technical data of Ro-Ro ships, report no. 02, project no. 2014–122: Mitigating and reversing the side-effects of environmental legislation on Ro-Ro shipping in Northern Europe Work, Package 2.3, July, DTU, Denmark.

Ligteringen, H. (1999), *Ports and Terminals*. TU Delft.

Lloyd's Register-Fairplay (2008), Optimar – Benchmarking strategic options for European shipping and for the European maritime transport system in the horizon, 2008–2018. Final Report.

Morales-Fusco, P. (2016), Roll on-Roll off terminals and truck freight: Improving competitiveness in a Motorways of the Seas context. PhD thesis, Facultat de Nàutica de Barcelona (FNB), Universitat Politècnica de Catalunya (UPC), Barcelona, Spain.

PIANC (2014), Masterplans for the development of existing ports. Report n° 158 Maritime Navigation Commission, Brussels, Belgium.

PLATINA (2012), Concretisation of the EC transport policy for IWT infrastructure needs on the Rhine corridor – a first approach. Report on working group on European IWT infrastructure: SWP 5.1 / D 5.11.

RECORDIT (2003), Actions to promote intermodal transport. Report of WP9 of RECORDIT Real Cost Reduction of Door-to-Door Intermodal Transport.

RINA (1992–2013), *Significant Ships of the Year*, Royal Institution of Naval Architects, London, UK.

Santos, T.A., & Guedes Soares, C. (2017a), Ship and fleet sizing in short sea shipping. *Maritime Policy & Management*, 47 (7), pp. 859–881.

Santos, T.A., & Guedes Soares, C. (2017b), Modeling of transportation demand in short sea shipping. *Maritime Economics & Logistics*, 19 (4), pp. 695–722.

Seatruck (2013), *P-Series Information*. Seatruck Ferries, United Kingdom.

Thoresen, C.A. (2014), *Port Designer's Handbook*, 4th edition. ICE Publishing, Westminster, London, United Kingdom.

TRT, MDS (2017), Gathering additional data on EU combined transport. Report for Directorate-General for Mobility and Transport, Unit D1 – Maritime Transport & Logistics, European Commission, Brussels, Belgium.

UNCTAD (1985), *Port Development – A Handbook for Planners in Developing Countries*. United Nations Conference on Trade and Development, Geneva, Switzerland.

Wijnolst, N., & Wergeland, T. (2009), *Shipping Innovation*. IOS Press BV Under the Imprint Delft University Press, Amsterdam, The Netherlands.

Part II
Quantitative methods for short sea shipping

3 Ro-Ro ship and fleet sizing in intermodal transportation

Tiago A. Santos and C. Guedes Soares

1 Introduction

The European Union (EU) has consistently promoted the competitiveness of transport chains as a means to reach the common market while still pushing for sustainability by limiting the external costs inherent to an increasing demand for transportation. Transport modes such as short sea shipping (SSS), inland waterways and freight railways can provide significant advantages while promoting these broad objectives. In fact, all shipping segments (liquid and solid bulk cargos, containerized cargos and general cargo) are included in SSS, as long as the routes connect European ports and ports of seas surrounding Europe. However, the main focus in SSS is on ferries (passenger and cargo ships), cargo roll-on/roll-off ships (cargo ro-ro ships) and container ships (cargo handled lift-on/lift-off – Lo-Lo). Ro-Ro ships are of special interest because they are characterized by faster cargo handling operations and shorter port dwell times. These factors contribute to decreased transit times compared to other ship types, especially container ships.

Short sea shipping, when compared to road transport, provides substantial advantages in terms of transportation cost (linked to economies of scale). It also allows avoiding mounting restrictions related to road transportation in Europe. On the other hand, the main shortcoming of SSS is that transit times are typically longer, and this often conflicts with just-in-time logistics strategies adopted by many shippers. These conflicts may be alleviated through the use of ro-ro ships.

Notwithstanding the fact that SSS depends on road transportation for the short final links of the transport chain, for countries on the periphery of the EU, such as Portugal and Spain, it avoids extensively using the road networks of other countries for carrying exports and imports to central and northern Europe. In fact, European countries whose road network is crossed by large quantities of trucks are increasingly regulating road haulage and applying the law very strictly: resting times, minimum wages and restrictions on cabotage. Tolls are much more common, and the same applies to restrictions to the passage of freight vehicles in the road network. Such measures aim at reducing accidents, road congestion, maintenance costs and noise and air pollution. Bad weather or social unrest (strikes, blockades) also frequently hamper the free passage of freight vehicles on EU roads and fuel prices are increasingly volatile, adding substantially to uncertainty in road transportation.

The methodology presented in this chapter contributes indirectly to mitigating these problems by providing a tool to identify corridors in which SSS is, or might be, competitive with road-based transport, thus alleviating the inconveniences indicated earlier. Different studies have conducted evaluations of the technical and economic feasibility of intermodal solutions across corridors between countries in central and northern Europe and peripheral countries, with some examples being provided in Tsamboulas et al. (2015) and Martínez-López et al. (2013, 2015). This type of study typically evaluates if a certain intermodal solution is feasible using a ship of a given size. However, in this chapter, a different approach is taken, consisting of identifying the fleet size and the cargo capacity of each ship, for a defined route, taking the perspective of the shipping company.

This chapter builds upon research undertaken by Santos and Guedes Soares (2017a), who carried out a study of demand for intermodal transportation using ro-ro ships combined with short-distance road haulage. The study was undertaken from the shipper's point of view. This means that the preferred transport solution took into consideration the overall cost and transit time, with costs calculated using the fares applied by different transport operators. Furthermore, transportation demand was estimated for various speeds and freight rates, assuming that the ship (or fleet of ships) was available and technically adequate to carry out the transportation.

This chapter uses a methodology presented by Santos and Guedes Soares (2017b) to identify the ro-ro ship cargo capacity and the size of the required fleet necessary to satisfy the estimated transportation demand. In that paper, only one port of destination in northern Europe was studied, while in this chapter several alternative ports are studied. The applied methodology allows the identification of the optimal point of operation (ship speed and freight rate), from the point of view of the shipping company. The fleet is assumed to be homogeneous, and the cost structure of the ship is systematically evaluated. An expanded version of the ship database of technical characteristics (necessary for cost assessment) used in Santos and Guedes Soares (2017b) is presented in section 4.

The methodology also applies a number of restrictions related to the specific routes (e.g. maximum ship size). The ship's technical characteristics (e.g. maximum speed) also need to be taken into account, leading to the exclusion of certain possible points of operation, as they turn out to be technically unfeasible. The economic profitability is also considered, through a balance of costs and revenue, expressed by profit before taxes over a period of one year. Thus, the methodology is useful for both economic and technical assessments of new SSS services by shipping companies. It has been implemented in a generic computer code, with all operational parameters supplied externally, making it possible to be applied in other routes.

This chapter is organized as follows. Section 2 provides a literature review on SSS studies focusing on estimating optimal ships for specific routes or simply the feasibility of certain routes. Section 3 describes the technical characteristics of cargo ro-ro ships and market conditions. Section 4 describes the methodology adopted, the numerical methods employed and how they are implemented, including a description of the database of ship characteristics used to estimate the technical parameters of the required ships for each route. Section 5 applies the methodology to three different routes in western Europe's Motorways of the Sea (MoS), enabling conclusions to be provided in section 6.

2 Literature review

The research dedicated to short sea shipping may be sub-divided into two comprehensive categories: studies on SSS policies and experiences and economic analysis of SSS competitiveness in specific routes or across specific market segments.

The first category covers general policy matters and the experiences arising from numerous intermodal transport solutions promoted under the scope of financing programmes (PACT, Marco Polo I and II, Motorways of the Sea, TEN-T). Within this first category, many papers have reviewed and analyzed the reasons for the successes and failures of SSS in the EU, namely Baird (2007), Styhre (2009), Douet and Cappuccilli (2011), Baindur and Viegas (2011), Aperte and Baird (2013), Ng et al. (2013) and Suárez-Alemán (2016). One of the conclusions of these studies is that, generally, EU-funded SSS services operate as long as the financial incentives provided by the EU support the operation. Once these incentives stop, the services disappear shortly afterwards. It is clear that research dedicated to methods that realistically evaluate the economic feasibility of these services is needed, and this chapter presents a research effort in this direction. Research in the first category has also been undertaken which analyses the experiences in other parts of the world, namely in North America and Latin America (see Brooks and Frost, 2004; Perakis and Denisis, 2008; Brooks et al., 2014).

Research presented in this chapter falls mainly within the second category of literature on SSS. This category includes substantial work devoted to evaluating SSS transport solutions, generally within the scope of intermodal transport solutions. Ricci (2003), for example, evaluates various transport corridors, including comparing costs between intermodal transport solutions and all road solutions. Tsamboulas et al. (2015) studied short and intermediate distance SSS routes using Ro-Pax ships. This study is similar to other studies, such as that of Sambracos and Maniati (2012) and Tzannatos et al. (2014), which focused on SSS routes using RoPax ships between different ports in Greece. Further works present evidence that SSS has been well studied for routes connecting to (or within) Mediterranean countries (see also Suárez-Alemán et al., 2015; Lupi et al., 2017).

The Shortsea Promotion Centre Flanders (2008) presented studies focused on northern Europe, calculating and comparing time, costs and emissions between all-road and intermodal solutions, while Trant and Riordan (2009) studied the feasibility of new services between Ireland and continental Europe. In this study, the main characteristics of the ships were fixed and the effects of variations in such variables as delays in ports, fuel price increases, road levies on trucks and time charter rate increases were analysed.

Martínez-López et al. (2013, 2015) takes SSS studies a step further by presenting an application of multi-criteria decision-making to different SSS routes between Spain and France. It concludes that routes presenting a larger potential for SSS are those between ports in Galicia and Saint-Nazaire. The authors also find that time is the most restrictive parameter for the competitiveness of intermodal transport solutions using SSS. The region of the Mediterranean and Black seas has also been studied by Martínez et al. (2013) using a similar model to evaluate the potential for SSS in that region. Galati et al. (2016) provide a study of competitiveness of SSS for a specific cargo (olive oil), while Russo et al. (2016) address competition in SSS between Ro-Ro and Lo-Lo services.

Such studies are dependent on suitable models of the cost structure of SSS and other transport modes, as reported in Sauri (2006), Janic (2007) and Ametller Malfaz (2015, 2007). In the case of Ametller Malfaz (2015, 2007), the model developed by the authors is applied in the analysis of the cost and time competitiveness of SSS in a route in the Mediterranean Sea, when compared to a fully road-based freight transport solution.

Silva and Guedes Soares (2014) take a different approach, as it is also often necessary to determine the optimal ship and fleet size for a certain forecasted freight flow, using ships of certain fixed technical characteristics. In such cases, databases of existing ships allow the determination of the most suitable ship within the existing fleet. One such database is analysed by Frouws (2013), comprising the technical characteristics of ro-ro ships, and allows the author to conclude that ships with relatively high speeds (suitable for attracting more cargo) will increase capital costs, decrease deadweight and have a larger displacement, leading to higher fuel consumption. It is very common that such ships are not economically feasible when fuel prices are high or for routes where lower speeds are more suitable. Becker et al. (2004) had already come to a similar conclusion when he considered the operation of high-speed craft in SSS. Research in fleet deployment and speed optimization of ro-ro ships has been undertaken recently (see Andersson et al., 2015; Chandraa et al., 2015), but these studies relate to pure car and truck carriers (PCTC) in deep sea routes between multiple ports, rather than SSS ships.

This literature review leads to the conclusion that few studies have evaluated the demand for SSS for various maritime freight rates and ship speeds. The same occurs regarding studies of optimal Ro-Ro ship and fleet size for the anticipated traffic. Furthermore, such studies cannot rely on a database of ro-ro ships to estimate the main characteristics, propulsion power and newbuilding costs for ships of different sizes. This chapter, in contrast, presents research in this direction.

3 Transportation demand model

3.1 Modelling of transit time

The model used in this chapter considers a transportation problem of the 'many-to-many' type. This means that it considers the transportation of cargo between multiple origin-destination pairs across Europe. These locations are defined at the level of NUTS 2 regions. The Portuguese statistics bureau (see INE, 2013) provides statistics on cargos sent by road between such regions in Portugal and European countries. These cargos could potentially be shifted to intermodal transport.

Figure 3.1 shows in detail the transport problem under consideration: competition between an intermodal voyage, which includes an SSS link between northern Portugal and a port in northern Europe, and a unimodal (road) voyage. Different ports in northern Europe will be considered in this chapter, while keeping the origin port constant.

In the intermodal solution, the transit time has several different components, the first of which is the road voyage time from the region of origin of cargo to the port:

$$T_{RegOriPort} = \frac{D_{RegOriPort}}{S_{RegOriPort}} \tag{3.1}$$

where $S_{RegOriPort}$ represents the average road speed while $D_{RegOriPort}$ represents the distance between the region of origin of cargo and the loading port. A similar

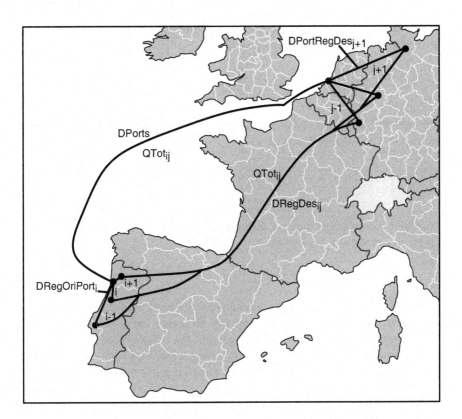

Figure 3.1 Transport problem between multiple origin and destination NUTS 2 regions.

expression allows the calculation of the time taken from destination port to region of destination of the cargo, $T_{PortRegDes}$. The time required for the resting of truck drivers in accordance with regulatory requirements is included in these time components.

In the origin and destination ports, due to cargo handling and, eventually, early arrival of cargo to the port (implying a significant dwell time), additional components of transit time arise. The cargo handling times and dwell times, indicated as $T_{OriPort}$, $T_{DesPort}$, T_{DwlOri} and T_{DwlDes}, are inputs in this model and, therefore, are specified by the user as average values. For guidance, these times are much less in ro-ro terminals than they are in container terminals (in the order of hours rather than days).

A significant component of transit time in the intermodal solution is the navigation time (T_{Nav}), which is the time necessary for the ship to complete the voyage between ports (distance is D_{Ports}). In this model, the distance between ports has been decomposed in distance travelled outside the emission control area (ECA), $D_{Ports-onECA}$; distance within the ECA, $D_{Ports-ECA}$; distance in the proximity of the destination port (D_{inPort}). Navigation occurs at a constant speed S_{Shp} except in the proximity of ports, where it is reduced to S_{port} (user specified). This last segment is necessary in order to model adequately the restricted approaches to some ports, where navigation conditions over significant distances require less speed than usual. The total navigation time is given by:

$$T_{Nav} = \frac{D_{Ports-nonECA}}{S_{Shp}} + \frac{D_{Ports-ECA}}{S_{Shp}} + \frac{D_{inPort}}{S_{Port}} \tag{3.2}$$

The total time taken by a certain cargo element in the intermodal solution, between region i and region j, will then be:

$$T_{TotInter-ij} = T_{RegOriPort-i} + T_{DwlOri} + T_{OriPort} + T_{Nav} + T_{DesPort} \\ + T_{DwlDes} + T_{PortRegDes-j} \tag{3.3}$$

Regarding the unimodal solution, the total transit time between region i and region j is much simpler and is given by:

$$T_{TotUni-ij} = T_{Regs-ij} \tag{3.4}$$

The transit time in the unimodal solutions is a function of the distance between the origin and destination regions, in kilometres. In reality, the nature of roads used, the maximum possible number of driving hours, the vehicle speed, the congestion and the weather conditions all affect the voyage time. In this model the voyage time T_{Regs} is calculated by dividing the distances D_{RdRegs} by an average road speed S_{Rd} (and adding regulatory rest times):

$$T_{Regs} = \frac{D_{RdRegs}}{S_{Rd}} \tag{3.5}$$

3.2 Modelling of costs

The cost model adopted in this study reflects the perspective of the decision maker who has to choose between a road-based solution and an intermodal solution. It is frequent today that the decision maker is not the cargo owner but rather a freight forwarder or a third-party logistics service provider (3PL), as discussed in López-Navarro (2013). The cost dimension of this choice includes pre-haulage and post-haulage costs (in the intermodal solution) and port and ship costs. Ship costs include mainly a maritime freight rate but also, due to the rising costs of fuel, a bunker adjustment factor (BAF). In some cases, the ship costs may also include cargo handling costs, where they exist.

Summarizing, when using the road-based solution, the decision maker is charged a fare by the road haulage operator for taking the cargo from A to B, subject to transit time. In the intermodal solution, a fare will be charged by the road haulage operator to take cargo to port. In addition, the shipping company will charge a freight rate per cargo unit, which under liner terms will cover all the costs including port costs, and finally a road haulage company will charge a fare for post-haulage. Finally, if the cargo unit is stored in the port terminal for more than a few days, the terminal operator may charge an additional fee.

Taking these factors into consideration, the general expression for total cost of the intermodal solution for the parcel of cargo moving from region i to region j will be:

$$C_{TotInter-ij} = C_{RdOriPort-i} + C_{OriPortCH} + C_{OriPortDW} + C_{FR} + C_{BAF} \\ + C_{DesPortCH} + C_{DesPortDW} + C_{RdPortDes-j} \quad (3.6)$$

where:

$C_{RdOriPort-i}$, $C_{RdPortDes-j}$ are the road pre- and post-haulage costs;

$C_{OriPortCH}$, $C_{DesPortCH}$ are the cargo handling costs in the origin and destination ports;

$C_{OriPortDW}$, $C_{DesPortDW}$ are the dwell time costs in the origin and destination ports;

C_{FR} is the freight rate cost; and

C_{BAF} is the bunker adjustment factor.

The total cost of the unimodal solution will be:

$$C_{TotUni-ij} = C_{RdRegs-ij} \quad (3.7)$$

where $C_{RdRegs-ij}$ are the road haulage costs, which in this case relate to the full road transport between Portugal and northern Europe.

3.3 Decision-making model

The methodology used to evaluate the demand for intermodal and unimodal transport includes systematic calculations over various combinations of freight rate C_{FR} and ship speed S_{Shp}. The total cost and transit time of both the unimodal and the intermodal solution are evaluated, for each cargo with origin in region i and destination

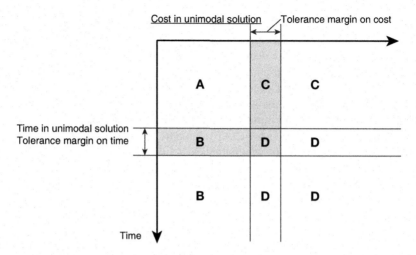

Figure 3.2 Cases in comparison of unimodal and intermodal costs and times.

in region *j*. This process is repeated for all pairs of regions (cargo elements) and also for all freight rate–ship speed pairs. For each freight rate–ship speed pair, an estimate of total transportation demand for the SSS link (and the cargo using only road) is produced by accumulating cargos flowing between various origin-destination pairs.

When comparing cost and transit time implied in each solution, a number of different situations may occur, as shown in Figure 3.2. This figure shows the levels of cost and transit time in the unimodal transport solution. It also shows that the model allows tolerances on transit time (hours) and cost (%) to be specified, leading to the shaded areas in Figure 3.2. These tolerances may be added (specified by the user at a desired level) to the unimodal levels.

When cost and transit time in the intermodal solution are less than in the unimodal transport solution, shown within area A in Figure 3.2, the intermodal transport solution is assumed to be the preferred one. This cargo element is added to the total cargo amount, $Q_{InterTot}$, that represents SSS demand. In area D, the unimodal solution is preferred, as both cost and transit time are less than those associated with the intermodal transport solution. The cargo element is added to the total cargo amount that will prefer the unimodal solution, Q_{UniTot}. For cases B and C, decision makers will face uncertainty. In this study, it is assumed that cargos inside the shaded areas will use the intermodal solution, leading to an optimistic assessment of potential intermodal cargo.

4 Ship and fleet sizing

4.1 Feasibility considerations

The size of ship (cargo capacity) and fleet necessary for an SSS route depends on the demand for cargo transportation over that route, which in turn depends on such parameters as ship speed and maritime freight rate. It is possible, however, that certain parameter pairs are not feasible due to commercial or technical reasons. These translate into restrictions (to be assessed by the shipping company) when evaluating the real feasibility of the SSS route. This chapter takes into account the following restrictions:

1 Round voyage time exceeding one week.
2 Insufficient time in port.
3 Size of required ship is too small.
4 Ship speed larger than usual service speed.
5 Severely underused propulsion power (<50% normal continuous rating (NCR)).
6 Ship needs to be smaller than maximum size allowed in ports.

The first restriction covers the case in which the speed considered for the service leads to a round voyage time, which makes a weekly service impossible. The following restriction (time in port) is needed when, although the speed is sufficient to make a weekly service possible, the remaining available time during the week is not sufficient to perform cargo handling. It is also possible that due to the small amounts of cargo estimated during the transportation demand study, the size of the required ship is too small, taking into consideration the size of ships generally used in these routes. Another possible restriction is that the speed under consideration may be too high compared to normal cargo ro-ro ship service speeds. It might also happen that the speed may be too low, leading to severely underused propulsion power (causing operational and maintenance problems). Finally, ports may pose restrictions to ship size.

These restrictions are evaluated for each maritime freight rate–ship speed pair. If the service fails in any of these restrictions, it will not be considered technically feasible. It might also occur that the revenue generated by transportation activities for a certain pair of speed and maritime freight rate is insufficient to cover the operational costs, but this is considered as an economic restriction.

4.2 Ship and fleet sizing heuristic

Transportation demand for each pair of ship speed and maritime freight rate is expressed as a weekly demand in twenty feet equivalent units (TEU) (split between imports and exports), and the revenue is calculated by multiplying the number of TEUs by the maritime freight rate. The ship or fleet of ships required is then calculated for the largest of the weekly transportation demands – import or export, thus ensuring adequate ship and fleet capacity. Capacity utilization is included as an input parameter through a 15% margin of capacity. The model considers that the ship will be as large as possible considering size restrictions arising from shipping company preferences and length, beam and draught restrictions in ports.

Ship and fleet size are calculated by the model in order to meet the weekly transportation demand with the specified utilization factor, P_{oc} (0.85 in this study).

The capacity of each ship, if indeed more than one is needed, is assumed equal for all ships. The number of ships required, denoted as N_{ships}, is iteratively increased until the required cargo capacity (in TEUs) of each ship is lower than the maximum allowable ship size:

$$C_{CAP} = \frac{\max(C_{WEXP}; C_{WIMP})}{P_{oc} N_{Ships}} \quad (3.8)$$

where C_{WEXP} and C_{WIMP} are the numbers of TEUs per week to be carried in each direction.

The following expressions give the cargo deadweights in actual (partial) loading conditions, CDW_{EXP} and CDW_{IMP}, which are smaller than the ship's full load cargo deadweight (CDW):

$$CDW_{EXP} = 14\, C_{WEXP}\, P_{mkt} \quad (3.9)$$

$$CDW_{IMP} = 14\, C_{WIMP}\, P_{mkt} \quad (3.10)$$

$$DW = 20\, C_{Ship}^{TEU} \quad (3.11)$$

The full load cargo deadweight, CDW, is calculated at 20 tonnes per TEU (maximum possible weight of a TEU container), while the cargo deadweights in partial load are calculated using an average load per TEU of 14 tonnes. A market penetration factor is also used, P_{mkt}, which is included to account for the effects of actually not having the ship running in full load. This market penetration factor accounts for the fact that the potential market may not actually be captured (initial years of a new service). In practice, it is observed that shipping companies apply lower freight rates while the market penetration is lower and after the service is firmly established they increase rates, thus improving the profitability of the operation.

4.3 Cost and revenue models

The cost model used in this study assumes that the shipping company will operate using time chartered ships (see also Trant and Riordan, 2009), thus implying that the shipping company will bear the costs of time charter contracts and all the voyage costs. Time charter rates from 2015 are used, ranging from 6000 €/day (small ships with 800 lanemetres' capacity) to 17,500 €/day (large ships with 3500 lanemetres' capacity). The total yearly cost is then:

$$C_{TC} = T/C \cdot (365 - T_{Offhire}) \cdot N_{ships} \quad (3.12)$$

where T/C stands for the time charter cost per day. $T_{offhire}$ is the number of off-hire days per year (assumed 7 days per year) and N_{ships} is the number of ships required for the fleet.

Ro-Ro ship and fleet sizing   71

The main component of voyage costs is the fuel cost. First, the propulsion power (maximum continuous rating, *MCR*) is estimated from a ship database. The service margin is applied to the *MCR* and the normal continuous rating, *NCR*, is obtained, which is used to calculate the actual propulsion power needed for each ship speed:

$$P_{Prop} = NCR \cdot \left(\frac{S}{S_{Serv}}\right)^3 \qquad (3.13)$$

where S is the speed and S_{Serv} is the service speed.

The propulsion power, P_{Prop}, is further corrected to take into account that the ship, in some conditions, will sail in lighter loading conditions. This occurs, for example, if the market penetration is low. In these cases the Admiralty coefficient, A, is used:

$$A = \frac{\Delta^{2/3} s^3}{P_{Prop}} \qquad (3.14)$$

The Admiralty coefficient is kept constant between the light loading condition and the full loading condition, allowing the calculation of the partial load propulsion power:

$$P_{PL} = \left(\frac{\Delta_{PL}}{\Delta_{FL}}\right)^{2/3} P_{Prop} \qquad (3.15)$$

On the other hand, partial load condition displacement is given by:

$$\Delta_{PL} = \Delta_{FL} - \left(CDW - \left(\frac{CDW_{EXP} + CDW_{IMP}}{2}\right)\right) \qquad (3.16)$$

where Δ_{FL} is the displacement in full load condition, *CDW* is the cargo deadweight in full load condition and CDW_{EXP} and CDW_{IMP} are the actual cargo deadweights in partial load condition (due to penetration factor). The displacement (fully loaded) is estimated from the main dimensions of the ship using a block coefficient of 0.6.

The fuel costs for propulsion per year, considering partial load, are then estimated using:

$$C_{FUELProp} = 2 \cdot \frac{D_{Port}}{S} \cdot P_{PL} \cdot SFOC_{MeIFO380} \cdot \left(\frac{365 - T_{Offhire}}{7}\right) \cdot C_{IFO380} \cdot N_{Ships} \qquad (3.17)$$

where D_{Port} is the distance between ports (nm), S is the ship speed (knots), P_{PL} is the propulsion power (kW), $SFOC_{MeIFO380}$ is the specific fuel oil consumption of the main engines (tons/kWh), C_{IFO380} is the cost per tonne for IFO380 fuel (€/ton) and N_{Ships} is the number of ships necessary in the fleet. A similar procedure is used for calculating fuel costs resulting from electrical power generation ($C_{FUELElec}$).

Additionally, the ship may need to sail through emission control areas (ECA), and in such cases the distance between ports needs to be corrected so that part of the voyage is carried out using more expensive low-sulphur (LS) fuel. The fuel consumption within the ECA is then calculated using Equation (3.17) with the necessary adjustments.

The port dues costs (payable to port authorities, generally dependent on gross tonnage of the ships) are calculated using the general formula:

$$C_{PortDues} = \left(\frac{365 - T_{Offhire}}{7}\right) \cdot (C_{PortA} + C_{PortB}) \cdot N_{Ships} \tag{3.18}$$

The values of the port dues C_{PortA} and C_{PortB} are taken from the port authority regulations.

Mooring costs and cargo handling costs depend on rates charged by port service providers. Such rates are taken as input parameters and used in the following formulae:

$$C_{moor} = C_{moorA}\left(\frac{365 - T_{Offhire}}{7}\right) N_{ships} + C_{moorB}\left(\frac{365 - T_{Offhire}}{7}\right) N_{ships} \tag{3.19}$$

$$C_{chand} = (C_{WEXP} + C_{WIMP}) C_{chandA} \left(\frac{365 - T_{Offhire}}{7}\right) N_{ships} P_{mkt}$$
$$+ (C_{WEXP} + C_{WIMP}) C_{chandB} \left(\frac{365 - T_{Offhire}}{7}\right) N_{ships} P_{mkt} \tag{3.20}$$

where C_{moorA}, C_{moorB}, C_{chandA} and C_{chandB} represent unitary rates for mooring and cargo handling as given in the regulations of service providers.

The shipping company revenue is provided by the freight rate and the bunker adjustment factor (BAF), both charged over each TEU carried on board. The BAF is considered fixed for a given route, but the freight rate is one of the variable parameters. Revenue is then given by:

$$R_{TOT} = R_{Exp} + R_{Imp} = Q_{IntExp} \cdot (Fr + BAF) + Q_{IntImp} \cdot (Fr + BAF) \tag{3.21}$$

where $QIntExp$ and $QIntImp$ are the demands for transportation (exports and imports in TEU), Fr represents the freight rate (€/TEU), BAF is the bunker adjustment factor (€/TEU).

Finally, net result is given by:

$$R_{LIQ} = R_{TOT} - C_{TC} - C_{FUELProp} - C_{FUELElec} - C_{PortDues} - C_{moor} - C_{chand} \quad (3.22)$$

4.4 Database of Ro-Ro ships

It is clear that the evaluation of suitable ship characteristics and fleet size for a given route involves in-depth knowledge of the short sea ro-ro market. This includes evaluating the technical parameters of the ship before estimating the operating and voyage costs. Such calculations need to be based on a ship database covering the ship's technical characteristics over the full range of lanemetre capacity. One such database has been developed to support the present study, which includes characteristics such as length overall, breadth, draught, gross tonnage, deadweight, propulsion power, speed and electrical power. The database includes exclusively cargo ro-ro ships of recent delivery date, operating in short sea routes around Europe. The technical data has been gathered from shipowners' and shipyards' webpages and technical shipping magazines.

The database currently includes 90 ships, some of which are representative of a set of sister vessels, implying that the sample is representative of the European fleet in this market segment and improving on the fleet database considered in Santos and Guedes Soares (2017a). The ships uniformly cover the full range of variation of ship cargo capacity expressed as lanemetre (750 m to 4000 m).

Figure 3.3 shows the lanemetre capacity of the ships as a function of the length overall. This capacity is suitable for TEU units carried on wheeled platforms, excluding any extra lanemetre capacity for light vehicles (cars)on hoistable platforms. It may be seen that some dispersion of capacities exists, but most of the ship's capacities are within 500 m of the polynomial line shown in the figure. This line is used to estimate the length overall for a given required lanemetre capacity (as determined from the transportation demand analysis). The same principle is used for deriving estimates of the other main ship characteristics.

Figure 3.4 shows the propulsion power as a function of length overall. This will be used for calculating fuel consumption. It may be seen that there is a large dispersion of data, resulting from the different service speeds for which ships may be designed. Service (design) speed is shown in Figure 3.5 and there is, in general, a range of 5 knots between different ships' service (design) speeds. As the speed is related to propulsion power by a cubic law, the required main propulsion power may be quite different, as shown in Figure 3.4. In the case of main propulsion power and service (design) speed, two polynomial lines are shown which bound approximately 90% of the data. In the determination of the ship's characteristics within the parametric calculations, the user needs to choose which of these lines to follow, meaning that they will choose to evaluate with this methodology ships with low propulsion power and, consequently, low service speed or high power (and high speed). Most shipowners nowadays tend to choose low-powered ships to limit fuel consumption.

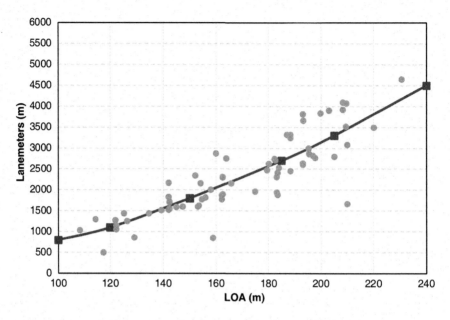

Figure 3.3 Lanemeter capacity as function of length overall for ships in the database.

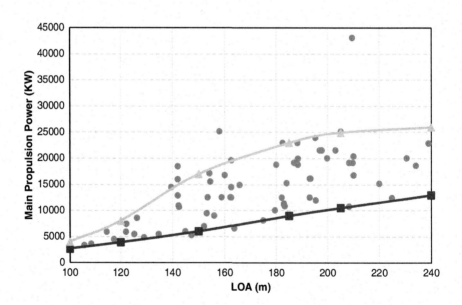

Figure 3.4 Main propulsion power installed on board ships in the database (kW).

Ro-Ro ship and fleet sizing 75

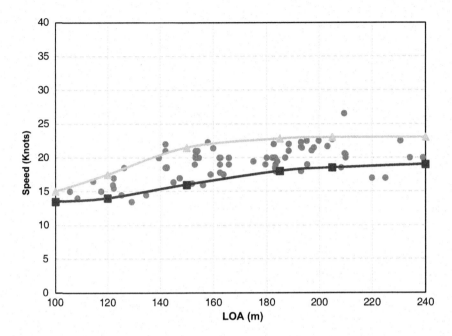

Figure 3.5 Service speed of ships included in the database.

Figure 3.6 shows the auxiliary (electrical) power installed on board as a function of length overall. It may also be seen that a wide dispersion exists. This is a consequence of the main propulsion power dispersion, as main machinery and related systems also consume significant electrical power. It also relates to other equipment installed on board, which require electrical power, such as ramps, doors and thrusters. For the same reason as for speed and main propulsion power, two polynomial lines are shown bounding approximately 90% of the auxiliary power installed on board ships in the sample. The user of this methodology will also need to choose between high or low auxiliary power and, currently, most shipowners will also take the first option. Ships with low installed propulsion and auxiliary powers will of course be more limited in their operation and less flexible in terms of possible routes (these may require high speeds not possible with a low propulsion power).

5 Application to the western Europe Motorways of the Sea

The methodologies given earlier have been implemented in computer codes, the first of which determines the intermodal transportation demand for different ship speeds and maritime freight rates. The difference between this demand and the total amount of cargo to be carried between the origin and destination NUTS 2 regions

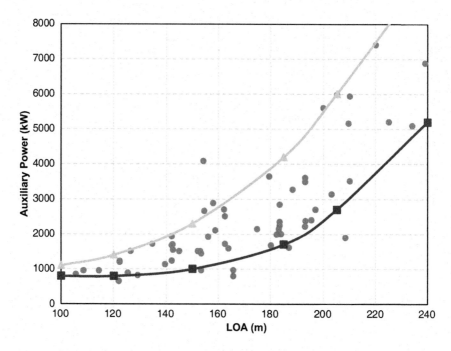

Figure 3.6 Auxiliary power installed on board ships in the database.

(an input to the code) corresponds to the demand for unimodal (road) transportation. A second code takes the intermodal demand, considers the details of the maritime route and the restrictions on ship size imposed by ports, and determines the ship size and the required number of ships for meeting the demand. It also carries out the economic analysis of the route, estimating the ship's technical characteristics and operating and voyage costs using the ro-ro ships database presented in section 4.

The working of these methodologies will be illustrated in a case study focused on the western Europe Motorways of the Sea corridor from Portugal to northern Europe. A comparison is made between three different routes bound to three different ports in northern Europe, while keeping fixed the origin port in Portugal (Leixões). The ports of destination considered in the study are Le Havre, Rotterdam and Hamburg, as shown in Figure 3.7.

Table 3.1 shows the route characteristics in terms of distance and speed used within the port areas. Port areas are those areas that present restrictions to navigation mainly related to the need to proceed at reduced speed. The speeds considered in each port are also shown in Table 3.1. The long sailing distance in the Hamburg port area is a consequence of sailing through the Elbe river estuary up to the city. In contrast, the port in Leixões is relatively small, so the sailing distance is negligible. While sailing in open sea, both outside and inside the ECAs, the speed is considered a variable, as indicated in the description of the methodology.

Ro-Ro ship and fleet sizing 77

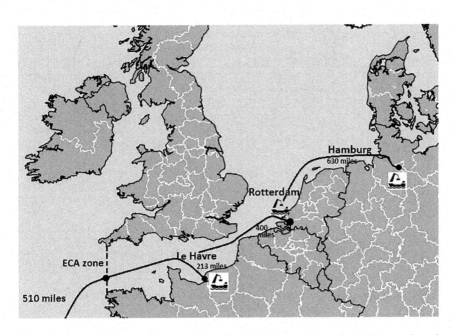

Figure 3.7 Map of the maritime routes to the three ports (with nautical distances in and out of ECA).

Table 3.1 Characteristics of the routes to the three ports.

	Le Havre	Rotterdam	Hamburg
Sailing distance outside ECA (nm)	510	510	510
Sailing distance within ECA (nm)	213	400	630
Sailing distance in port area (nm)	2	10	40
Speed limit in port area (kn)	5	10	10

Figure 3.8 shows the distribution of cargos through the northern European region situated in the area surrounding of the three ports. It may be seen that cargo is concentrated in the Benelux countries, Paris and certain cities in southern Germany. Details of the derivation of this distribution are given in Santos and Guedes Soares (2017a).

For each of the three ports, the maritime freight rate per TEU varies systematically between 200 € and 700 € in steps of 50 €. The ship's speed varies between 11 knots and 20 knots in steps of one knot. To the maritime freight rate is added the bunker adjustment factor set in this case to 27.5 € per TEU. Cargo handling costs in port terminals (of roll-on/roll-off type) are considered to be included in the maritime freight rate. Average speed in road is considered to be 65 km/h which includes an allowance for congestion in certain parts of the road network. Cost

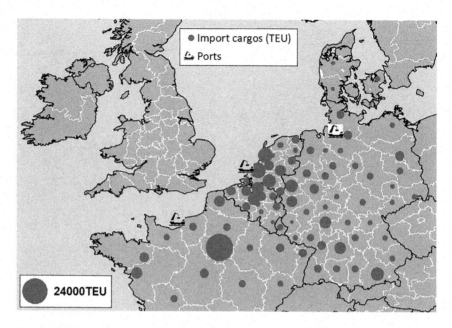

Figure 3.8 Geographical distribution of import cargos (expressed in TEUs) through NUTS 2 regions.

Source: Santos and Guedes Soares (2017a).

of road haulage is set to 0.7 €/TEU.km in Portugal, 1.5 €/TEU.km in northern Europe and 0.5 €/TEU.km for long-distance haulage. Cost calculations are done from the perspective of the user of the transport services and are carried out per TEU (a semi-trailer would correspond roughly to two TEUs).

The cargos originate (or have destinations) in the four Portuguese NUTS 2 regions. These are considered to be located at 75 km, 200 km, 325 km and 375 km from Leixões by road. Matrices are then built that include the distances by road from these regions to the different NUTS 2 regions in northern Europe, which are shown in Figure 3.8. Finally, matrices have also been derived with the distance by road from each of the three ports to the NUTS 2 regions.

The time spent by cargo in ports is dependent upon the planning of the transportation service and the time when the cargo is actually ready to be loaded in the origin. If good control exists upstream, it is possible to take advantage of the handling speed in port allowed by roll-on/roll-off operations. In many cases the shipping companies offering these regular services allow cargo to be delivered in the port terminal just a couple of hours before ship's departure. In this case study, a conservative average dwell time in port (origin and destination) of 6 hours is assumed. In fact, even in the destination port, it might well be possible that semi-trailers or containers may be picked up just a couple of hours after the ship's arrival (that is, immediately after the physical unloading of the semi-trailer or container).

Furthermore, it is assumed that loading the cargo takes on average 7 hours in Leixões and 2 hours in northern European ports, but this depends on the order by which cargo is taken on board. The criteria for choosing the road solution or the intermodal solution are total cost and transit time. This study has considered that the intermodal solution for cargo is chosen only if it is less expensive than the alternative (road). However, intermodal transportation will also be chosen if the transit time does not exceed the road transit time by 24 hours. This is reasonable for cargos which are not very urgent (exceptions are perishables and medicines) and which are not valued very highly.

Figure 3.9 shows the intermodal cargo volumes (exports) and the road cargo volumes (exports) for the various combinations of maritime freight rate and ship speed. The figure shows that the total volume of cargo transported by road is always much larger than by intermodal transport. This is because intermodal transportation is attractive only for cargo bound for/coming from NUTS 2 regions located close to the sea. For cargos with an origin/destination in NUTS 2 regions far from seaports, road transportation is preferred. Intermodal cargo is maximized for low maritime freight rates and high ship speeds (see left), leading consequently to a minimum of road cargo for the same conditions, as may be seen on the right.

Table 3.2 shows the cargo volumes conveyed by the intermodal and unimodal transport solutions for various possible ports in northern Europe. Cargo volumes conveyed by unimodal (road) transport solutions are dominant for all ports because SSS is not attractive for those NUTS 2 regions located far away from ports, as shown in Figures 3.10–3.12. In any case, Rotterdam is the port that attracts more intermodal cargo, both exports and imports. These larger volumes of cargo give some more confidence to shipping companies that ships of an appropriate size will generally present a fairly good level of utilization. Hamburg and Le Havre show lower cargo volumes, and setting up regular ro-ro services to these ports presents a larger risk for shipping companies.

Figures 3.10, 3.11 and 3.12 show the NUTS 2 regions for which the intermodal transport solution is competitive, when considering respectively the ports of Le Havre, Rotterdam and Hamburg. It may be seen that the region is continuous and located relatively near the coastline. The region served by Le Havre is much smaller than the other two because this port is closer to Portugal and maritime transport has more difficulty competing with road transportation. Rotterdam acts as a gateway to Benelux and substantial parts of western Germany. Hamburg is a good gateway to northern and eastern Germany and Denmark.

Figures 3.13 to 3.15 show the technical and financial feasibility of the three routes for various points of operation. A point of operation is financially feasible if it results in a positive net operational result, considering the ship to be fully owned (not chartered). A point of operation is technically feasible if the conditions mentioned in section 4 are simultaneously met (in the figures, the technical feasibility takes a unitary value when all conditions are met). Comparing these figures, it may be seen that the port that restricts less, from a technical point of view, the points of operation is Rotterdam. From a financial point of view (right), Le Havre leads to negative results (losses), while both Rotterdam and Hamburg

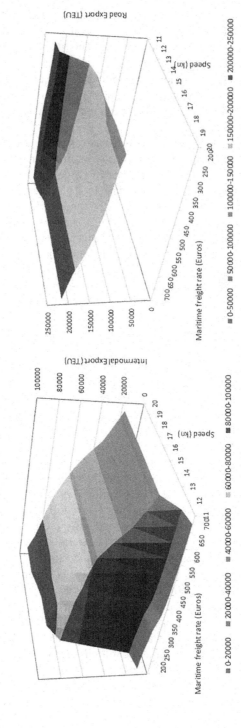

Figure 3.9 Cargo volume conveyed by intermodal and road transport solutions as function of ship speed and maritime freight rate (exports), port of Rotterdam.

Table 3.2 Cargo volumes (TEU) when using different ports.

Variable		Intermodal cargo		Road cargo	
		Exports	Imports	Exports	Imports
Hamburg	Maximum	65,909	49,037	236,180	216,698
	Minimum	0	0	170,271	167,661
Rotterdam	Maximum	92,235	107,088	236,180	216,698
	Minimum	0	0	143,945	109,610
Le Havre	Maximum	56,074	70,365	236,095	216,536
	Minimum	85	162	180,106	146,333

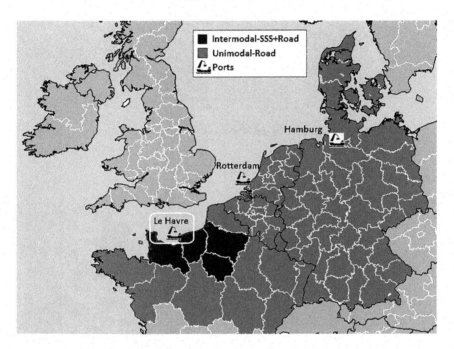

Figure 3.10 NUTS 2 regions using the intermodal transport solution through Le Havre.

allow multiple points of operation with positive results. Rotterdam presents a wider scope of points of operation with positive results.

Figure 3.16 shows the cumulative feasibility (meaning the coincidence of technical and financial feasibility) for the ports of Rotterdam and Hamburg. These points represent the possible options for a shipping company. The conclusion is that only one point is possible when using Hamburg as the port in northern Europe. This implies that the operation will be not very flexible and somewhat hazardous. Rotterdam, on the other hand, offers more feasible points of operation, providing flexibility in the operation. Speed may be varied between 14 knots and

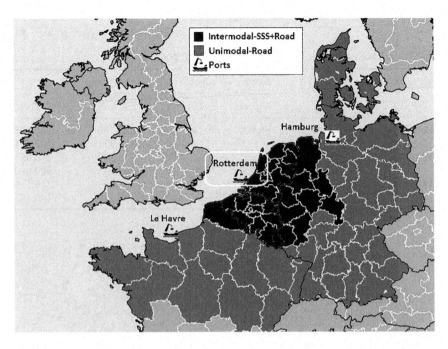

Figure 3.11 NUTS 2 regions using the intermodal transport solution through Rotterdam.

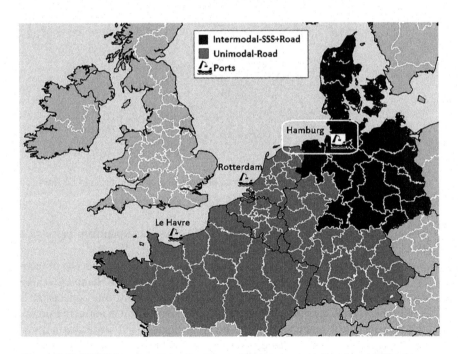

Figure 3.12 NUTS 2 regions using the intermodal transport solution through Hamburg.

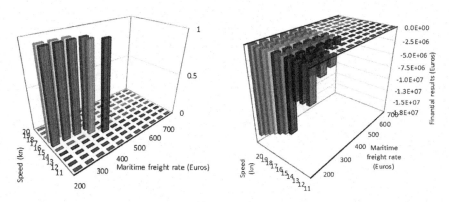

Figure 3.13 Technical and financial feasibility of points of operation for Le Havre.

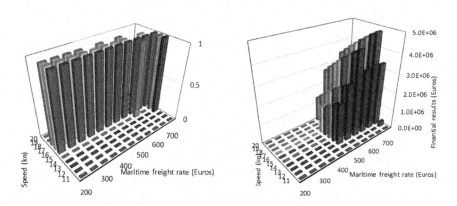

Figure 3.14 Technical and financial feasibility of points of operation for Rotterdam.

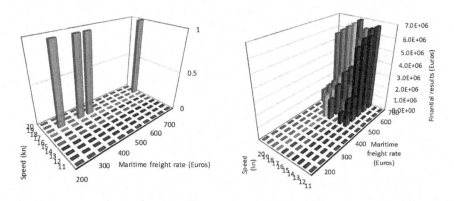

Figure 3.15 Technical and financial feasibility of points of operation for Hamburg.

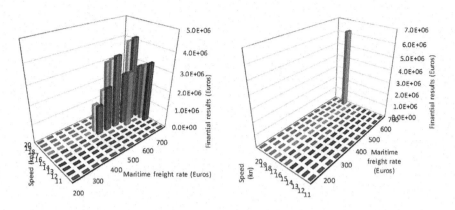

Figure 3.16 Cumulative technical and financial feasibility of points of operation for Rotterdam (left) and Hamburg (right).

18 knots, and maritime freight rates are between 450 € and 700 €. Here, flexibility means being able to introduce moderate changes in speed or pricing and still make a profit.

Table 3.3 summarizes the characteristics of the ships and the size of the fleet needed when using each port in northern Europe. The market penetration and capacity utilization are fixed, and the ECA zone is in operation and part of the route passes within it. Fuel prices are shown in the table, and their values are kept fixed within the year and are all equal for the different ports. Outside of ECA, the ship uses IFO380 and MGO (main and auxiliary power) and inside ECA it uses low-sulphur fuel. Ships with low installed main propulsion and auxiliary power have been chosen, as this is currently the option of most shipping companies.

The results indicate that for Le Havre and Hamburg, one ship is sufficient to meet the demand (cargo volumes). This demand is the one related to the optimum point of operation, not the one characterized by the highest demand for transportation. It may be seen that the ship for Le Havre has only 125.2 m in length overall, should operate at 14 knots and charges a freight rate of 400 €/TEU. It is thus a relatively small cargo ro-ro ship. However, it may also be seen that even at this 'optimum' point, the shipping company actually operates at a loss of about a million euros per year.

Regarding Hamburg, the optimum point of operation occurs at a higher speed and higher freight rate: 18 knots and 700 €/TEU. The ship is much larger (191.5 m in length overall) than the optimum ship for Le Havre. In contrast to Le Havre, the ship makes a good profit of 6.3 million € per year. Concerning Rotterdam, two ships of 174.4 m in length overall are needed to cover the demand, operating at 16 knots and charging about 650 €/TEU. Since the ships take almost a week to perform the round voyage, a fleet of two ships is required to ensure that the demand is met, rather than making two round voyages per week. Each ship makes a good

Table 3.3 Characteristics of optimum ships for the different routes.

Variable	Le Havre	Rotterdam	Hamburg
Market penetration north/south (%)	75–55	75–55	75–55
Capacity utilization (%)	85	85	85
Intermodal cargo volume (TEU, exports)	7,815	24,877	16,282
Intermodal cargo volume (TEU, imports)	4,910	32,788	19,544
Number of ships	1	2	1
Length overall (m)	125.2	174.4	191.5
Lanemeter (m)	1,238	2,596	3,095
MCR (kW)	4,261	9,134	11,313
Capacity (TEU)	177	371	442
Stacking	Single	Single	Single
Main propulsion and auxiliary power	Low	Low	Low
Crew	12	16	17
Newbuilding price per ship (million €)	21.4	29.5	32.6
IFO380 price (€/ton)	232	232	232
MGO price (€/ton)	403	403	403
LSMGO price (€/ton)	390	399	399
ULSFO price (€/ton)	370	370	370
ECA	Y	Y	Y
Speed (knots)	14	16	18
Freight rate (€/TEU)	400	650	700
Profit per ship (million €)	-1.0	4.4	6.3
Time charter rate (€/day)	7,606	13,785	15,813

profit of 4.4 million € per year, implying a total of 8.8 million € per year for the fleet of two ships.

Table 3.3 also shows the intermodal cargo volumes available for the ship in the optimum point of operation. The volumes are only a small fraction of the overall volumes of cargo exchanged between Portugal and northern European regions covered in this case study (exportation of 236,180 TEU and importation of 216,698 TEU). This is caused by two factors: first, much of the cargo is bound to inland regions for which SSS is not competitive due to the large distance from the coastline; second, the optimum point of operation from the perspective of the shipping company's economic results does not lead to maximum attractiveness of intermodal cargo.

6 Conclusions

This chapter has presented a methodology for ship and fleet sizing which comprises two steps: evaluating the potential demand for intermodal transport solutions which include short sea shipping (SSS), in routes using cargo roll-on/roll-off (ro-ro) ships; and determining the characteristics of the required cargo ro-ro ship and the fleet size needed to meet the calculated demand, while identifying the most suitable operation point.

This methodology has been applied in a case study considering three routes along the western Europe Motorways of the Sea. All routes depart from the port of Leixões in northern Portugal, and three different ports of destination in northern Europe were studied: Le Havre, Rotterdam and Hamburg. It has been concluded that the port that attracts the most intermodal cargo (the most demand for SSS) is Rotterdam. However, for all ports considered in this study, the demand depends heavily on the maritime freight rate and ship speed used by the shipping company, with lower values of freight rate and higher ship speed favouring the intermodal solution. The economic feasibility of the routes was then studied in detail, as the points of operation producing larger demands may not be feasible for shipping companies. The conclusion was that operations using Le Havre were not financially feasible (operational losses over the period of a year) and in many cases failed to attract a minimum volume of cargo (defined as that needed to fill the smallest ship size in the database). Rotterdam and Hamburg showed some combinations of ship speed and freight rate leading to positive operational results, but technical issues made some of these combinations unfeasible. Rotterdam nevertheless provides a comprehensive range of technically and financially feasible freight rate–ship speed pairs.

The set of NUTS 2 regions using intermodality around Le Havre does not extend much beyond a range of 150 km, while Rotterdam and Hamburg serve NUTS 2 regions as far as 300 km from these ports. The required fleet when using the port of Rotterdam consists of two 174 m long ro-ro ships, each making a round voyage per week (service frequency would then be twice per week). Hamburg leads to only one ship being required, albeit a slightly larger one of about 191 m in length (service frequency weekly). The best ship for Le Havre would be a small ro-ro of about 125 m in length, although it is very likely that it would operate at a loss.

These results provide useful guidance for shipping companies and governments when analysing the suitability of new short sea shipping services and developing appropriate incentive policies for such services. This study could be improved if more accurate data existed for cargo flows between NUTS 2 regions across Europe, enabling a better and more accurate characterization of the spatial distribution of cargo flows and leading to improved estimates of intermodal demand.

Acknowledgements

The research presented in this chapter received support from the research project PTDC/ECI-TRA/28754/2017, financed by the Portuguese Foundation for Science and Technology (Fundação para a Ciência e Tecnologia – FCT) and is within the scope of the Strategic Research Plan of the Centre for Marine Technology and Ocean Engineering (CENTEC), financed by FCT under contract UID/Multi/00134/2020.

References

Ametller Malfaz, X. (2007), Optimization of freight transportation through short sea shipping (in Spanish). PhD thesis, Department of Transport Engineering, Polytechnic University of Cataluña, Barcelona.

Ametller Malfaz, X. (2015), Freight transport using short sea shipping. *Journal of Shipping and Ocean Engineering*, 5, pp. 143–150.

Andersson, H., Fagerholt, K., & Hobbesland, K. (2015), Integrated maritime fleet deployment and speed optimization: Case study from RoRo shipping. *Computers & Operations Research*, 55, pp. 233–240.

Aperte, X.G., & Baird, A.J. (2013), Motorways of the sea policy in Europe. *Maritime Policy & Management*, 40 (1), pp. 10–26.

Baindur, D., & Viegas, J. (2011), Challenges to implementing motorways of the sea concept – lessons from the past. *Maritime Policy & Management*, 38 (7), pp. 673–690.

Baird, A. (2007), The economics of motorways of the seas. *Maritime Policy & Management*, 34 (4), pp. 287–310.

Becker, J.F.F., Burgess, A., & Henstra, D.A. (2004), No need for speed in short sea shipping. *Maritime Economics & Logistics*, 6 (3), pp. 236–251.

Brooks, M.R., & Frost, J.D. (2004), Short sea shipping: A Canadian perspective. *Maritime Policy & Management*, 31 (4), pp. 393–407.

Brooks, M.R., Sanchez, R.J., & Wilmsmeier, G. (2014), Developing short sea shipping in South America: Looking beyond traditional perspectives. *Ocean Yearbook Online*, 28 (1), pp. 495–525.

Chandraa, S., Fagerholt, K., & Christiansen, M. (2015), Maritime fleet deployment in ro-ro shipping under inventory constraints. *Procedia – Social and Behavioral Sciences*, 189, pp. 362–375.

Douet, M., & Cappuccilli, J.F. (2011), A review of short sea shipping in the European Union. *Journal of Transport Geography*, 19, pp. 968–976.

Frouws, J.W. (2013), Technical and economic benchmarking of existing and new ship designs. Proceedings of World Conference on Transport Research 2013, July 15–18, Rio de Janeiro, Brasil.

Galati, A., Siggia, D., Crescimanno, M., Martín-Alcalde, E., Saurí Marchán, S., & Morales-Fusco, P. (2016), Competitiveness of short sea shipping: The case of olive oil industry. *British Food Journal*, 118 (8), pp. 1914–1929.

INE (2013), Transport statistics (in Portuguese). Instituto Nacional de Estatística. Lisbon, Portugal.

Janic, M. (2007), Modelling the full costs of an intermodal and road freight transport network. *Transportation Research Part D: Transport and Environment*, 12, pp. 33–44.

López-Navarro, M. (2013), The effect of shared planning by road transport firms and shipping companies on performance in the intermodal transport chain: The case of Ro-Ro short sea shipping. *European Journal of Transport and Infrastructure Research*, 13 (1), pp. 39–55.

Lupi, M., Farina, A., Orsi, D., & Pratelli, A. (2017), The capability of motorways of the sea of being competitive against road transport: The case of the Italian mainland and Sicily. *Journal of Transport Geography*, 58, pp. 9–21.

Martínez, F., Castells, M., & Rodríguez (2013), Cost assessment simulator for transport between Mediterranean Spanish ports and the black sea. *Journal of Maritime Research*, 10 (1), pp. 31–38.

Martínez-López, A., Kronbak, J., & Jiang, L. (2013), Cost and time models for road haulage and intermodal transport using short sea shipping in the North Sea region. Proceedings of IAME 2013 Conference, July 3–5, Marseille, France.

Martínez-López, A., Munín-Doce, A., García-Alonso, L. (2015), A multi-criteria decision method for the analysis of the motorways of the Sea: The application to the case of France and Spain on the Atlantic Coast. *Maritime Policy & Management*, 42 (6), pp. 608–631.

Ng, A.K.Y, Sauri, S., & Turró, M. (2013), Short sea shipping in Europe: Issues, policies and challenges. In M. Finger & T. Holvad (eds.), *Regulating Transport in Europe*. Cheltenham: Edward Elgar, pp. 196–217.

Perakis, A.N., & Denisis, A. (2008), A survey of short sea shipping and its prospects in the USA. *Maritime Policy & Management*, 35 (6), pp. 591–614.

Ricci, A. (2003), Pricing of intermodal transport: Lessons learned from RECORDIT. *European Journal of Transport and Infrastructure Research*, 3 (4), pp. 351–370.

Russo, F., Musolino, G., & Assumma, V. (2016), Competition between ro-ro and lo-lo services in short sea shipping market: The case of Mediterranean countries. *Research in Transportation Business & Management*, 19, pp. 27–33.

Sambracos, E., & Maniati, M. (2012), Competitiveness between short sea shipping and road freight transport in mainland port connections: The case of two Greek ports. *Maritime Policy & Management*, 39 (3), pp. 321–337.

Santos, T.A., & Guedes Soares, C. (2017a), Modeling of transportation demand in Short sea shipping. *Maritime Economics & Logistics*, 19 (4), pp. 695–722.

Santos, T.A., & Guedes Soares, C. (2017b), Ship and fleet sizing in short sea shipping. *Maritime Policy & Management*, 47 (7), pp. 859–881.

Sauri, S. (2006), Cost structure in a short sea shipping line. *Journal of Maritime Research*, III (2), pp. 53–66.

Shortsea Promotion Centre Flanders (2008), The road versus shortsea "race" – Comparing both transport modes within an intermodal concept, Technical Report.

Silva, C.A., & Guedes Soares, C. (2014), Sizing a fleet of containerships for a given market. *PROMET – Traffic & Transportation*, 26 (4), pp. 333–344.

Styhre, L. (2009), Strategies for capacity utilization in short sea shipping. *Maritime Economics & Logistics*, 11 (4), pp. 418–437.

Suárez-Alemán, A. (2016), Short sea shipping in today's Europe: A critical review of maritime transport policy. *Maritime Economics & Logistics*, 18 (3), pp. 331–351.

Suárez-Alemán, A., Campos, J., & Jiménez, J.L. (2015), The economic competitiveness of short sea shipping: An empirical assessment for Spanish ports. *International Journal of Shipping and Transport Logistics*, 7 (1), pp. 42–67.

Trant, G., & Riordan, K. (2009), Feasibility of new RoRo/RoPax services between Ireland and continental Europe.

Tsambloulas, D., Lekka, A., & Rentziou, A. (2015), Development of motorways of the sea in the Adriatic region. *Maritime Policy & Management*, 42 (7), pp. 653–668.

Tzannatos, E., Papadimitriou, S., & Katsouli, A. (2014), The cost of modal shift: A short sea shipping service compared to its road alternative in Greece. *European Transport \ Transporti Europei* (56), p. 2.

4 Sustainability in short sea shipping-based intermodal transport chains

Tiago A. Santos, Mónica M. Ramalho and C. Guedes Soares

1 Introduction

The European Union (EU) transport policy has for many years now promoted intermodality and the use of transport modes which have less negative consequences for the environment, health and well-being of European citizens. The main focus has been on shifting freight transport from the road to other modes of transportation (or combinations of modes), see European Commission (1999). This is especially important as a substantial increase in road freight transport of 40% by 2030 and 80% by 2050 was forecasted by the European Commission (2011a). In parallel, the roadmap towards a single European transport area, which was outlined by the European Commission (2011b), greatly emphasizes the competitiveness and sustainability of the transport system, namely setting a 60% GHG emissions reduction target. The same reference also sets a target of reducing CO_2 emissions from maritime transport by 40% (if feasible, 50%) in 2050, compared to 2005 levels.

The rail and waterborne modes of transport, which include short sea shipping (SSS) and inland waterways (IWW), may well assist the EU in attaining these broad policy objectives. However, rail and IWW networks of most peripheral countries in the EU are not as developed as in central Europe and, in most cases, are not effectively interconnected with other regions of the EU. Simultaneously, many issues remain in terms of technical compatibility of railway lines and inland waterways in different countries. Therefore, for peripheral countries, SSS remains the most feasible alternative option, which also assists in the implementation of EU policies.

In addition, countries in central Europe have taken several measures aiming at restricting freight transportation in their road networks. The broad rationale of these policies is that freight transport (heavy goods vehicles) contribute significantly to road degradation and air pollution, leading to increased maintenance costs and health-related costs, including a significant number of fatalities arising from accidents. These further justify the development and promotion of short sea shipping.

Increasing the utilization of SSS depends on the relative performance of this mode of transportation compared to other modes. SSS is known for being cost competitive, but its transit time is generally much longer than that of road transport. Furthermore, SSS only carries cargo units between ports and relies on road transport to carry the cargo to the final destination, and this integration of different modes of transportation is sometimes prone to delays, leading to poor reliability. Also, the green reputation of SSS in comparison with road transport has been challenged by academics, see Hjelle (2010) and Kim and Van Wee (2011), due to the lagging performance of shipping in terms of reducing air pollution, for example due to the much higher sulphur content of maritime fuels in comparison with road diesel. Therefore, the external costs of short sea shipping need to be carefully monitored and compared with those of other modes of transportation.

In the EU, a broad approach to assessing the external costs of transportation has been in place for many years now (see Maibach *et al.*, 2008; Korzhenevych *et al.*, 2014; van Essen *et al.*, 2019). These references define external costs as the difference between social costs and private costs in a given activity, in this case transport, and provide a framework for its quantification in monetary terms. This quantification depends on a large number of transport network characteristics (e.g. road types) and of characteristics of the vehicles (e.g. mode, type of propulsion and fuel type).

Considering the aforementioned, it is important to develop models that assist in evaluating the potential of intermodal transport chains based in SSS, including all the dimensions of the problem: transit time and internal and external costs. This model should include all the different modes of transportation, the different types of vehicles which might be used (also the possibility of different fuel types) and a description of the physical infrastructure of existing transport networks (roads, railway lines, inland waterways, port and intermodal terminals). The main objective is to provide a tool capable of comparing the economic and social competitiveness of SSS-based transport chains with those of other intermodal and unimodal chains. This tool will also assist in providing an answer to an important research question, namely whether transport chains based on SSS still provide relatively environmentally friendly transportation.

The remainder of this chapter is organized as follows: first, a literature review on external costs of transportation and its estimation is provided, which includes the applications of these methods in various case studies. Building upon the existing methods, a subsequent section presents the numerical methods adopted in this chapter for the calculation of external costs, but also for internal costs and transit time, arising from intermodal transport operations. These methods presuppose the existence of a transport network model, which is also briefly described. This model and the numerical methods have been included in a computational tool, and its results are illustrated in a numerical results section comprising a case study dealing with intermodal transportation in Greece. This case study allows a comparison with previously published results in the open literature. A final section includes the main conclusions from this study.

2 Literature review on external costs

2.1 General

The concept of external cost arises in economics as a way to put in monetary terms the side effects of a certain activity upon a third party who did not choose to incur the effects of that activity. It is the difference between social and private (internal) cost. This concept, applied to transportation, reflects the environmental impacts (on air pollution, climate change and noise and of up- and downstream processes), accidents, congestion and infrastructure wear and tear, whose costs are not fully imputed to transport users. The concept of internalization of external costs means making transport's external effects part of the decision-making process of the transport users. This is implemented by means of taxes and charges which make users look for different, and more environmentally and socially friendly, possibilities in terms of vehicle type, vehicle utilization, transport mode or transport volume.

A set of studies on the economics of external costs in the transport sector emerged from the quest for an optimal pricing policy. In the EU context, the particular case of Dublin (Margaret *et al.*, 1997) is an early example of a study concluding that generally road travel should be taxed at a higher level, especially during peak traffic hours due to congestion costs, and that the use of clean car technologies is rewarded by lower external costs. ExternE projects, started in 1995, proposed the first systematic approach to evaluating the externalities of energy use. A bottom-up methodology was formalized under the title Impact Pathway Approach (IPA) by Friedrich and Bickel (2001) and Bickel and Friedrich (2005). It was developed to evaluate pollution effects on human health, environment, economic activities, etc. It is a step-by-step approach that helps identifying and understanding a pollutant's emissions and its sources; how these emissions spread in the atmosphere; the extent to which the population is exposed to the pollutants; and its impact on human health and other environmental damages. In the end, IPA is used to quantify these externalities using, for example, the willingness to pay for reduced health risks based on the value of statistical life (VSL).

In the light of the Eurovignette Directive (see European Parliament and Council, 1999) on road infrastructure charging, the EU commissioned the study IMPACT (Internalisation Measures and Policies for All External Cost of Transport), later reported by (Maibach *et al.*, 2008), on the internalization of external costs of transport. It recommended methods for calculating external cost figures using the best available input values and presented estimated unit values for different traffic situations in a vehicle kilometre basis for the base year of 2000. In 2011, part of the committee responsible by the IMPACT study published an update of the report in CE Delft Infras Fraunhofer ISI (2011) using 2008 as the base year. The original handbook by Maibach *et al.* (2008) has been revised and updated by Korzhenevych *et al.* (2014) and further by van Essen *et al.* (2019) and now presents the state of the art and best practice on the estimation of external costs of transport. The methodology and input and output values are explained and presented for all transport modes and at both EU and national levels, based on an extensive literature review on external cost estimation. The ready-to-use unit values provided in the 2014 study are used in this chapter to analyze the external impacts of transport on particular routes of interest, as it was the latest published report by the development date of the methodology.

Meanwhile the Marco Polo programme, dating from 2003, was active in the European Union and aimed at assisting companies shifting freight transport off the roads to other more environmentally friendly transport options. The merits of this project were measured by the difference in external costs between the transport service before and after project implementation. In Brons and Christidis (2013), the most recent external cost methodology implemented under the Marco Polo calculator, and used in the latest call for projects, is described and covers cost calculations for road, rail, inland waterways and short sea shipping, providing cost coefficients for both environmental (air pollution, noise and climate change) and socioeconomic impacts (accidents and congestion). Building upon this methodology and body of knowledge, the European Commission is currently promoting a new study on the internalization of external costs of transportation,[1] implying that the issue remains of substantial importance in achieving the sustainability goals of the EU.

2.2 Ship emissions and related external costs

The major external impacts of shipping are related to air pollution and climate change not only during navigation but also concerning up- and downstream activities (construction, maintenance and disposal of ships and vessels and port terminals). Miola *et al.* (2010) provides a useful analysis of the references for the latest methodologies, technologies and policy options for regulating air emissions from ships. It concludes that the limited availability of data has resulted in different calculation methodologies of ship emissions that are often not easy to compare. In Brons and Christidis (2013), the calculation of external costs of waterborne transport is based on different emission factors and damage costs from the ones in Korzhenevych *et al.* (2014). However, it provides useful references on the emission reduction factors of alternative fuel technologies other than low-sulphur fuel in IWW (see Table 4.1) and conventional high-sulphur fuel in SSS (Table 4.2).

The calculations from Korzhenevych *et al.* (2014) for air pollution and climate change costs for inland water transport are based on the emission factors from the STREAM (Study on Transport Emissions for All Modes) database as reported in den Boer *et al.* (2011) and emission reduction factors from Brons and Christidis (2013). Calculations by Korzhenevych *et al.* (2014), also using the emission

Table 4.1 Emission reduction factors of IWW fuel technologies for various air pollutants and CO2.

Fuel technology	NO_x	PM	SO_2	CO_2	Fuel consumption
Fuel oil (low sulphur)			Base option		
Diesel particulate filter (DPF)	–	–68%	–	–	+2%
Selective catalytic reduction (SCR)	–85%	–	–	–	–
DPF + SCR	–85%	–68%	–	–	+2%
LNG	–75%	–97%	–	–10%	–

Source: Brons and Christidis (2013).

Table 4.2 External cost correction factors per alternative fuel technology in SSS.

Fuel technology	Air pollution	Climate change
Fuel oil (high sulphur)	Base option	
Low sulphur oil	0.642	0.980
Seawater scrubbing	0.580	–
Freshwater scrubbing	0.573	–
Methanol	0.054	0.800
LNG	0.054	0.800

Source: EMSA (2010).

factors from den Boer *et al*. (2011), report the marginal air pollution and climate change costs for maritime transport differentiated per sea area according to the damage costs from the NEEDS[2] project (Preiss and Klotz, 2007).

An update of the original STREAM study was more recently published by Otten *et al*. (2017). This study reviews the emission factors of freight transport for 2014, providing solutions for direct intermodal comparison. The emissions are calculated based on the new sulphur limit of 0.1% using the most recent emission factors available from the third IMO GHG study (IMO, 2015). The NO_x emissions depend on engine type, rpm and tier category to which the engine belongs.

Based on the same emission factors for maritime shipping from IMO (2015), the EcoTransIT World (Ecological Transport Information Tool – Worldwide) was developed and available online for calculation of the environmental impact of freight transport for any route and any transport mode (EcoTransIT World Initiative (EWI), 2018).

2.3 Application studies to different transport modes

Several studies have emerged which compare short sea shipping and other transport modes services based on the calculation of external costs in Europe. The works of Sambracos and Maniati (2012), Tzannatos *et al*. (2014), Vierth *et al*. (2018), Jiang *et al*. (2010) and Fridell *et al*. (2009), just to mention a few, lead to the conclusion that the competitiveness of the sea alternative compared to the road alternative (and other modes) depends not only on the methodology used but also on several other factors, such as the world region and the distance travelled; therefore, a case-by-case analysis of the external costs is needed.

3 Methodology for costs and transit time calculation

3.1 Transport networks and services model

The transportation problem examined in this section is generally named as 'many-to-many'. In fact, the model can take a set of origins of cargo, which needs to be carried to a set of destinations. These origins and destinations are generally defined at the level of the EU NUTS 2 regions, as shown in Figure 4.1. The

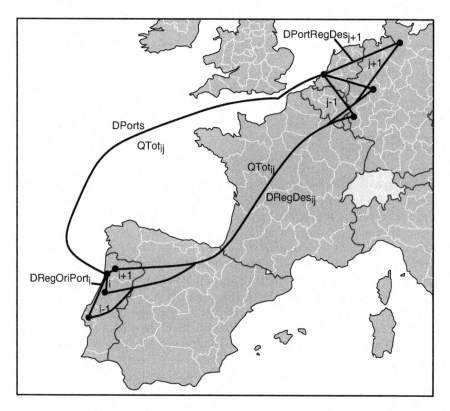

Figure 4.1 General formulation of transport problem between origin and destination NUTS 2 regions.

Source: Adapted from Santos and Guedes Soares (2017).

model considers an intermodal transport solution using an SSS service linking the two set of NUTS 2 regions, as the selected ports define the groups of regions more likely to be served by this solution. The initial and final parts of the voyage are taken over by a road haulage company (pre-carriage and post-carriage). The model also includes a fully unimodal solution, as shown in Figure 4.1, linking each pair of regions. This solution resorts to road haulage companies carrying out door-to-door transport. Other combinations of transport modes may be specified to carry cargo between origin-destination pairs, such as road-rail or road-SSS-IWW.

The decision of which transport solution to choose, for each pair of origin-destination regions, is based on two variables: transit time and cost of transportation (with or without the external costs). Numerical models, following the principles indicated in Santos and Guedes Soares (2017), for the calculation of each of these variables are presented later. Furthermore, external costs are now also estimated by the numerical model, and a more detailed model of the maritime route has been included, allowing further refinements on navigation time and a realistic modelling of external costs.

The calculation of internal costs, external costs and transit time implied by transport operations between origin-destination pairs is supported by an intermodal transport network model. This network currently consists of 3018 nodes connected by 3828 links, spread over the geographical region between Portugal and northern Europe, but also including Italy and Greece. It is an intermodal transportation network accounting for four different modes of transportation: road, rail, inland waterways and short sea/maritime shipping.

The nodes and links form an extensive database which includes relevant node-specific and link-specific characteristics, as shown in Table 4.3. Each one of the modes of transport forms a sub-network, and these sub-networks are interconnected at certain nodes: seaport terminals (sea-road-rail-IWW), intermodal terminals (IWW-rail-road). However, most nodes are simply connections between links of the same sub-network (road or rail junctions). Some nodes are actually set up in the sea, for example to delimit points where emission control areas begin or end or where the typical ship speed undergoes large variations, such as approach zones to ports.

The transport network forms the infrastructure which supports transport services. The specification of transport services is done by the user through paths. The user may specify as many paths as are necessary to describe alternative transportation services between an origin-destination pair. A path is a set of links used in succession and is specified using an ordered list of nodes. A computer code will identify the succession of links connecting the different nodes included in this list and the type (road, rail, IWW, SSS) of each link.

Table 4.3 Intermodal transportation network links definition.

Characteristic	Mode / Variable	Road	Rail	Inland Waterways	Short Sea Shipping
Type	*LinkTyp*	M – Motorway R – Main roads U – Other roads	F – Rail	I – Inland waterways	C – Container ship S – Ro-Ro
Zone	*LinkZon*	S – Suburban U – Urban R – Rural	S – Suburban U – Urban R – Rural	N/A	N/A
Country	*LinkCountry*	ISO 3166–1 Alpha-2 country code	ISO 3166–1 Alpha-2 country code	ISO 3166–1 Alpha-2 country code	NA – North East Atlantic ME – Mediterranean NS – North Sea BS – Black Sea BA – Baltic Sea
Distance	*LDist*			value in [km]	
Speed	*LSpeed*			value in [kmh]	
Congestion band	*LCong*	1–5	1–5	N/A	N/A
ECA zone	*LinkECA*	N/A	N/A	N/A	N – Outside ECA E – Inside ECA

For each path, there is also a number of definitions specific to each transport mode involved in the carriage of goods between the origin and the destination. First, a variable provides information on whether the trip takes place during the day or during the night. For trucks, the truck type, cargo capacity, gross weight, type of propulsion, EURO class, utilization factor, engine power and specific consumption and the number of axles are included. For ships (SSS), the ship type, deadweight, freight capacity (trailers), capacity utilization, type of fuel for main and auxiliary machinery, IMO emission standard, main and auxiliary engine speed rating and propulsion power and ship's design speed are included. Similar definitions are included for trains and inland waterways vessels.

3.2 Transit time model

Let us consider a set of NUTS 2 regions called O, where i denotes one of the regions belonging to O. Similarly, let us define a set D of NUTS 2 regions, with j defining an individual region belonging to this set. The two sets, O and D, may include common regions, but as the focus is on evaluating the competitiveness of short sea shipping; in practice, the two sets will not have common elements (NUTS 2 regions), as this mode of transportation is only competitive for long distances.

Transit time is evaluated for paths between the origin region i and the destination region j. A path has a total number of links denoted as *Links*. Generally, the path will consist of links of different types, except if a road transport solution is used, in which case all links are of the road type. Within each path, a transport mode will be modelled as a sub-path which goes through a number of links of the same type. The sequence of sub-paths will constitute the total path of the cargo and will be characterized by a transit time.

In the initial road-based route from the cargo's region of origin to the port (carried out by road haulage companies and often called *pre-carriage*), the time ($T_{RegOriPort-i}$) may be calculated using the following expression:

$$T_{RegOriPort-i} = \sum_{k=1}^{Lrop} \frac{D_k}{S_k} + \sum_{l=1}^{Nrop} T_l \tag{4.1}$$

where D_k and S_k represent the road distance and the average road speed in link k. It is considered that the road-based route (pre-carriage) is composed of a number *Lrop* of links. The average road speed is individually set for each link according to the type of road (motorway, rural road or urban road) and is generally some kilometres below the speed limit for trucks. The distance D_k is the real distance measured along the road considering its specific path. It may also occur that there are delays at certain nodes, which is taken into account by summing the times T_l.

A similar expression allows the calculation of the final time by road (*on-carriage*) $T_{PortRegDes-j}$, which represents the time taken for the cargo to move from the destination port to the region of destination. Both these components include the time needed for the resting of truck drivers as per Regulation (EC) No. 561/2006 (see European Parliament, 2006), which provides a common set of EU rules for maximum daily and fortnightly driving times, as well as daily and weekly minimum rest periods for all drivers of road haulage vehicles.

When the path taken by the cargo is unimodal (road only), an expression such as Equation (4.1) suffices to calculate the transit time between origin and destination. When the path is intermodal, the times $T_{RegOriPort-I}$ and $T_{PortRegDes-j}$ are to be summed to the time taken when using the main mode of transportation, be it a ship (container ship or ro-ro ship) or a train. In any of these cases, the route followed by the ship or train (a sub-path) is similarly decomposed in nodes and links, each one characterized by an average speed. The speed may be individually adjusted for each link according to the technical characteristics of a given part of the maritime route (within port, open sea, congested waters) or segment of the railway line (different segments have different maximum speeds, there are railway lines junctions).

Another reason to decompose maritime routes in individual links is the fact that certain parts of the route might be within an ECA zone and others might not. In fact, the navigation time (T_{Nav}), that is, the time necessary to complete the voyage between two ports, where the total distance is D_{Ports}, has been decomposed in a distance travelled outside the emission control area (ECA), $D_{Ports-nonECA}$; a distance within the ECA, $D_{Ports-ECA}$; and a distance in the vicinity of the origin and destination ports (total distance is D_{inPort}). The first two are covered with a constant speed S_{Shp} and the last part at a reduced speed S_{port}. This last part is necessary in order to model adequately the approaches to river ports where navigation conditions over significant distances require less speed than usual. Therefore, the total navigation time is given by:

$$T_{Nav} = \frac{D_{Ports-nonECA}}{S_{Shp}} + \frac{D_{Ports-ECA}}{S_{Shp}} + \frac{D_{inPort}}{S_{Port}} \qquad (4.2)$$

If the route inside and outside of the ECA has been decomposed in more links, the two first terms of Equation (4.2) will be converted in summations over the number of links similarly to what is done in Equation (4.1). If the ship goes through canals, nodes will be inserted at the canal entrance and exit, and a link will connect these nodes characterized by an average speed (limited by canal regulations), requiring another term to be added to Equation (4.2).

Another component of transit time arises in the origin and destination ports, due to cargo handling and, eventually, early arrival or late departure of cargo to the port (implying a dwell time, which may be even zero). In ro-ro terminals, these times are much smaller than in container terminals (in the order of hours rather than days), making this type of transportation attractive in what concerns these components of transit time. The cargo handling times and dwell times, indicated as T_{OriCh}, T_{DesCh}, T_{OriDwl} and T_{DesDwl} are inputs of the current model and, therefore, are user specified under the form of average constant values. Considering all the aforementioned, the total time taken by cargo using an intermodal solution, between region i and region j, will be:

$$T_{TotInter-ij} = T_{RegOriPort-i} + T_{OriDwl} + T_{OriCh} + T_{Nav} + T_{DesCh} + T_{DesDwl} + T_{PortRegDes-j} \quad (4.3)$$

For the unimodal solution, the total time between region i and region j will be given by:

$$T_{TotUni-ij} = \sum_{k=1}^{Links} T_{Regs-ij-k} \quad (4.4)$$

In the unimodal solution the voyage time, if taken in a simple form, is a function of the distance between the origin and destination regions. In practice, the nature of the roads, the maximum allowed number of driving hours, the speed of the vehicle, congestion and weather conditions all affect the voyage time. This variability in the voyage times T_{Regs} has been taken into account by dividing the distances D_{RdRegs} by an average road speed, S_{Rd}:

$$T_{Regs-ij} = \frac{D_{RdRegs-ij}}{S_{Rd-ij}} \quad (4.5)$$

3.3 Internal costs model

The cost and time models adopted in this study reflect the perspective of the user (decision maker) of the transport solution: a freight forwarder, a third-party logistics service provider (3PL) or a shipper, as discussed in López-Navarro (2013). The user's decision will be based mainly on the cost and time factors. Costs, in general, will include pre-carriage and on-carriage costs (intermodal solution), port costs and ship (rail) freight costs. A relatively new cost, related to the rising costs of fuel, is the bunker adjustment factor (BAF), which is also included in the model for the intermodal transport (added to the maritime freight).

From the perspective of the user of transport services, the reality he or she perceives is that in the unimodal solution the road haulage company will charge a fare for taking the cargo from A to B, subject to a certain delivery time. In the intermodal solution, a fare will be charged by the road haulage company to take the cargo to the port. The same will occur in the road segment from the destination port to the final destination region. Adding to this, the shipping company will charge a freight rate (C_{FR}) per cargo unit, which under liner terms will cover all the costs including port costs. It is useful, for the purpose of this model, to uncouple from the freight rate the terminal operator costs (basically cargo handling) and any eventual BAF related to either an increase in fuel costs or simply the need to change to another fuel type. It is usual that the freight rate includes the fuel costs, but the adjustment factor C_{BAF} is charged separately.

Considering these factors, the general expression for total cost of the intermodal solution for the parcel of cargo moving from region i to region j will be:

$$C_{TotInter-ij} = C_{RegOriPort-i} + C_{OriCh} + C_{OriDwl} + C_{FR} + C_{BAF} + C_{DesCh} + C_{DesDwl}$$
$$+ C_{RegPortDes-j} + C_{Ext-ij} \quad (4.6)$$

where:

$C_{RegPortDes-j}$, $C_{RegPortDes-j}$ are the road pre- and post-haulage costs;

C_{OriCh}, C_{DesCh} are the cargo handling costs in the origin and destination ports;

C_{OriDwl}, C_{DesDwl} are the dwell time costs in the origin and destination ports;

C_{FR} is the freight rate (maritime or rail) cost;

C_{BAF} is the bunker adjustment factor; and

C_{Ext-ij} is the external cost.

The total cost of the unimodal solution will be:

$$C_{TotUni-ij} = C_{RdRegs-ij} + C_{Ext-ij} \quad (4.7)$$

The generalized cost, C_{Gen-ij}, is then calculated as a function of total cost C_{Tot} (calculated using (4.6) or (4.7)), transit time T_{Tot} and the value of time (*VOT*) for the cargo unit:

$$C_{Gen-ij} = C_{Tot-ij} + VOT.T_{Tot-ij} \quad (4.8)$$

Generalized costs need to be calculated for both the intermodal and the unimodal solution. The value of *VOT* (in €/t.km) is the subject of much debate, and, in this chapter, has been taken from such studies as Feo *et al.* (2011) and Feo-Valero *et al.* (2011). The results of the model are sensitive to this value, namely high-value cargos will have high *VOT* and will show a preference for transport solutions with smaller transit times.

3.4 External costs model

As mentioned earlier, external costs fall in the following categories: congestion, accidents, noise, air pollution, climate change, costs of up- and downstream processes and marginal infrastructure costs. External costs are expressed as a function of marginal cost coefficients which, depending on type of cost, are expressed in euros per tonne, tonne-km or vehicle-km. In this chapter, the vehicle will be considered as roughly equivalent to a road semi-trailer or an FEU container. Depending on the ship type (Ro-Ro or container ship), the cargo unit will then be of one or the other type. The external costs are given by:

$$C_{Ext-ij} = C_{Cong-ij} + C_{Acc-ij} + C_{Noi-ij} + C_{Air-ij} + C_{CC-ij} + C_{Ud-ij} + C_{Inf-ij} \quad (4.9)$$

where the different terms are self-explanatory, but it must be taken in consideration that over a path between i and j, there will be, for example, air pollution costs arising from road, rail, IWW and maritime transportation. It may happen that the path involves only some of these transport modes, implying that some air pollution cost components will be nonexistent. Also, Korzhenevych et al. (2014) indicates that for maritime transportation (IWW and SSS) there are no accident, congestion and noise external costs.

The general formulation for calculating external costs will be exemplified below for selected cases which serve to illustrate the general principles. Let us again take a path between an origin i and a destination j, typically NUTS 2 regions. Within this path are a number of links in succession, each one denoted as k. These links may correspond to different modes of transportation. For example, the congestion cost borne in a given link k of road type, in € per vehicle, may be calculated by:

$$C_{cong-ij_{road-k}} = \frac{c_{m_{cong road}} \times d_{ijk}}{100} \tag{4.10}$$

Where d_{ijk} is the travelled distance within the link in km and the marginal coefficient $c_{m\_cong\_road}$, given in €ct/vkm, is taken from the tables provided in Korzhenevych et al. (2014). This coefficient is dependent on the type of vehicle, the link's region, road type and its congestion band:

$$c_{m\_cong\_road} = f(vehicle, region, road\ type, congestion\ band) \tag{4.11}$$

The metropolitan regions in Korzhenevych et al. (2014) are considered to refer to the suburban regions in the method's implementation. Also, the links labelled as motorways in urban areas are treated as urban main roads when choosing the most suitable cost coefficient. The congestion band of a road is defined by its volume (actual traffic flow v) to capacity (theoretical maximum traffic flow c) ratio, which may range from less than 0.25 to over 1.0, as categorized in the FORGE model (Department of Transport (2015)). As it was not possible to find information enabling a characterization of the different types of road at a European level, only the free flow band and the higher bands are chosen as the most representative. In the implementation, congestion bands 1 to 3 are considered free flow (up to v/c equal to 0.75). The links in urban and suburban areas have been assigned category 4 (near congestion) while the others are categorized as free flow. A few notoriously congested motorways in urban areas were categorized as category 5 (over capacity).

While road transportation is carried out on an individual basis (on a truck), rail, IWW and maritime transportation is carried out collectively, and the external costs need to be split by the individual cargo units. The procedure adopted for this split is exemplified in Equation (4.12), for the case of a link of rail type. The congestion cost, in € per cargo unit, is calculated by:

$$C_{cong-ij_{rail-k}} = \frac{c_{m_{cong rail}} \times d_{ijk} \times LF_{MP}}{1000 \times TraCap_{ij} \times TraUt_{ij}} \tag{4.12}$$

where the cost coefficient $c_{m\_cong\_rail}$, given in €/1000tkm, is a coefficient from Korzhenevych et al. (2014) and depends on the country of transit:

$$c_{m\_cong\_rail} = f(country) \tag{4.13}$$

When country-specific values are not available, EU average values are used. The unit costs per tonne kilometre are transformed into costs per train kilometre using the rail-specific load factors (LF_{MP}) in tonnes referred in Brons and Christidis (2013), actually based on the TREMOVE model (De Ceuster et al. (2004)). The cost is divided by the train capacity in trailers $TraCap_{ij}$ multiplied by the train capacity utilization factor $TraUt_{ij}$ in order to obtain the values per carried trailer. These variables are included in the path definition.

The climate change cost borne in a given link k of maritime transport type, in € per cargo unit, is calculated by:

$$C_{cc-ij_{mar-k}} = \frac{c_{cc\_mar} \times d_{ijk}}{SssCap_{ij} \times SssUt_{ij}} \tag{4.14}$$

The cost coefficient c_{cc_mar} given in € per ship-km and depends on the type of ship, DWT and sea region:

$$c_{cc\_mar} = f(type\ of\ ship, DWT, sea\ region) \tag{4.15}$$

The type of ship and DWT must be in the path definition. Container, Ro-Ro and Ro-Pax ships are considered to fall into the general cargo vessel type. For bulk carriers, feeder size is considered as up to 15 kt DWT, handysize from 15 kt to 40 kt and handymax greater than 40 kt. The cost is divided by the vessel's capacity in trailers $SssCap_{ij}$ multiplied by the capacity utilization factor $SssUt_{ij}$ in order to obtain the values per trailer carried on board. These variables are defined in the path definition. The central value of the carbon price used in Korzhenevych et al. (2014) is 90 € and an update of the unit costs proportional to the variation of the estimates on the carbon price is recommended.

3.5 Activity-based emissions and external costs model

The lack of consistence between external cost factors related to the different sources of air pollutant emissions, especially in the case of ships, supports in many studies the use of an activity-based methodology to calculate those costs. This alternative methodology is based on an estimate of the actual quantity of pollutant emissions in a trip through the calculation of the vehicle's fuel consumption combined with emission factors. In the end, the damage costs per quantity of pollutant are used to evaluate the external costs. This can be done for all transport modes, considering that either engine load or consumption characteristics and fuel are known and emission factors or vehicle standards are available. For the case of short sea shipping, first, the vessel's fuel consumption must be calculated;

it should include main and auxiliary engine(s) consumption. The vessel's main engine fuel consumption FC_{ME} per link, in g, can be calculated according to:

$$FC_{ME,ijk} = \frac{SFOC_{ME} \times P_{EF,ijk}}{s_{ijk}} \times d_{ijk} \qquad (4.16)$$

where P_{EF} is the effective capacity of the main engine in KW, $SFOC_{ME}$ is the specific fuel oil consumption of the main engine in g/kWh and s_{ijk} is the travel speed within the link in km/h.

The effective output at a given link speed s_{ijk}, in kW, can be estimated using the brake power–speed relation in Equation (4.17), assuming an engine load factor of 0.9 at design speed with clean hull and in calm weather. The factor 1.09 accounts for hull roughness and 1.15 for wave resistance in average conditions as per EcoTransIT World Initiative (EWI) (2018). P_{ME} is the nominal power of the main engine, in kW, and $SssSpeed_{ij}$ is the design speed of the vessel (without sea margin):

$$P_{EF,ijk} = 0.9 \times 1.09 \times 1.15 \times SssP_{ME\,ij} \times \left(\frac{s_{ijk}}{SssSpeed_{ij} \times 1.852}\right)^3 \qquad (4.17)$$

The main engine fuel oil consumption factors for engines as old as 2001 (IMO, 2015) assumed in this model are 175 g/kWh, 185 g/kWh and 195 g/kWh, for, respectively, slow-speed, medium-speed and high-speed engines.

Similarly, the fuel consumption in g of the auxiliary engines (and/or boilers) can be calculated as follows:

$$FC_{AE,ijk} = SFOC_{AE} \times P_{AE} \times \frac{d_{ijk}}{s_{ijk}} \qquad (4.18)$$

depending on the time and engine load at sea P_{AE} in kW. No emissions in port are accounted for. The engine load at sea is assumed to be 30% of engine MCR according to Whall *et al.* (2002). For auxiliary engines and boilers, the specific fuel oil consumption factor, $SFOC_{AE}$, is 225 g/kWh for medium-speed engines operating on either HFO or MDO.

Next, the amount of emissions per pollutant is obtained by multiplying the fuel consumption by the emission factors in g/g fuel:

$$g\,CO_{2,ijk} - eq = FC_{ME,ijk} \times ef_{CO-eq_2\,ME} + FC_{AE,ijk} \times ef_{CO-eq_2\,AE} \qquad (4.19)$$

$$g\,SO_{X,ijk} = FC_{ME,ijk} \times ef_{SO_X\,ME} + FC_{AE,ijk} \times ef_{SO_X\,AE} \qquad (4.20)$$

$$g\,NO_{X,ijk} = FC_{ME,ijk} \times ef_{NO_X\,ME} + FC_{AE,ijk} \times ef_{NO_X\,AE} \qquad (4.21)$$

$$g\,PM_{ijk} = FC_{ME,ijk} \times ef_{PM\,ME} + FC_{AE,ijk} \times ef_{PM\,AE} \qquad (4.22)$$

The most important air pollutants impacting human health are particulate matter (PM) (mostly fine $PM_{2.5}$ from exhaust emissions), nitrogen oxides (NO_x) and sulphur dioxides (SO_2).

The most recent emission factors available for maritime transport come from IMO (2015), differentiated by main engine and auxiliary engine, fuel type, engine rating and IMO tier for NO_x emissions. The sulphur content of HFO is assumed to be 2.51% and for MDO 0.1% according to the latest regulations. Tier 3 emission factors are deducted from Tier 1 with an 80% reduction.

Finally, the damage cost factors of exhaust emissions in €/ton of emitted pollutant differentiated per sea area from the NEEDS project (Preiss and Klotz, 2007) can be used to estimate air pollution external costs due to exhaust emissions from maritime transport $C_{air_{mar}ijk}$ € per trailer according to:

$$C_{air_{mar}ijk} = \frac{c_{ton\,SO_X} \times g\,SO_{X,ijk} + c_{ton\,NO_X} \times g\,NO_{X,ijk} + c_{ton\,PM} \times g\,PM_{ijk}}{10^6 \times SssCap_{ij} \times SssUt_{ij}} \qquad (4.23)$$

For climate change costs, the amount of emitted CO_2 equivalent gases (GHG) is multiplied by the estimate of the carbon price to calculate the climate change external costs, given in € per trailer:

$$C_{CC_{mar}ijk} = \frac{c_{ton\,CO_2} \times g\,CO_{2,ijk} - eq}{10^6 \times SssCap_{ij} \times SssUt_{ij}} \qquad (4.24)$$

For those alternative fuel technologies other than the use of MDO or HFO for which emission factors are known, the external cost reduction factors in Table 4.2 can be applied.

4 Case study

4.1 General description of the transport problem

The numerical methods given previously will now be illustrated in a case study which compares them to the results published in a paper by Tzannatos *et al.* (2014). This paper reports a study of intermodal transport (road haulage plus short sea shipping) versus unimodal transport (fully road based), along the corridor between Athens and Thessaloniki freight centres. Cargo units considered in that study are trucktainers (12 m in length), implying unaccompanied traffic. SSS is carried out using a cargo Ro-Ro ship, whose main particulars are shown in Table 4.4. The assumed cargo utilization factor of the ship is 62.5%, equivalent to carrying 200 trucktainers in each direction. At sea, the main engine operates at 80% load and the auxiliary engines at 30% load, while in port the main engine operates at 20% load for 20% of the time and is turned off for the remaining 80% of time.

Concerning the road leg associated with the intermodal transport, a five-axle EURO 5 truck is considered, and it is assumed that 55% of the distance is driven

Table 4.4 Characteristics of the modes of transportation used in the intermodal and unimodal routes.

Ro-Ro cargo ship	
Gross tonnage	32,289
Deadweight [t]	10,070
Length overall [m]	199.8
Lanemeters [m]	3830
Trailers	320
Speed average [kn]	18
Service speed [kn]	25
Propulsion power [kW]	20,070
Auxiliary power [kW]	4 × 1720
Year of construction	2003

Truck characteristics	
Chassis	5 axle
Engine MCR [kW]	365
EURO class	5

Train characteristics	
Propulsion power [kW]	2240
Capacity [FEUs]	38

Sea leg		Road Leg	
Distance [nm]	224	Distance [km]	68.7
Sailing time [h]	8.95	Speed [km/h]	55
Port time (each) [h]	3.05	Travel time [h]	1.25

Road service	
Distance [km]	504
Speed [km/h]	80
Travel time [h]	6.3

Rail service	
Distance [km]	472
Speed [km/h]	37

along a motorway. This motorway section is driven along for 40% of the overall travel time with a truck engine load of 60%, while the road section takes 60% of the overall travel time at 30% engine load. When unimodal transport is used, it is assumed that the truck engine load factor is 60% for 90% of the overall travel time, when driving along a motorway. When driving on other roads, the engine load is 30%, which takes 10% of the overall travel time.

In this chapter, a further study is carried out based on the main features of the Tzannatos et al. (2014) paper, in which it was found out that external costs were actually higher in the intermodal transport solution than in the unimodal solution for the utilization factor of 62.5%, it was decided to investigate how such a situation could be improved, using the numerical methods and route network model explained earlier. The utilization factor was set at 80% of the ship's cargo capacity, as most owners will not operate ships in routes with low utilization for long without subsidies, as experiences with the Marco Polo programme clearly indicate. A set of alternative scenarios is considered in this chapter, exploring three different sea routes, as shown in Figure 4.2. Additionally, a scenario is included which uses a freight train to take cargo units from Athens directly to Thessaloniki. A locomotive with a freight capacity of 38 FEUs, propulsion power of 2240 kW and an engine with a SFOC of 0.236 kg/kWh running with conventional fuel oil with a sulphur content of 0.005% by mass (50 ppm), similar to the one used in road transport, is considered.

In order to lower the external costs of the short sea shipping mode (Ro-Ro cargo ship), it was decided to use ports located not far from Athens but closer to Thessaloniki. The candidate ports should be located along the east coast of Greece (actually the island of Euboea), which is still not far from Athens by road but considerably shortens the sea leg of these intermodal voyages. It was found

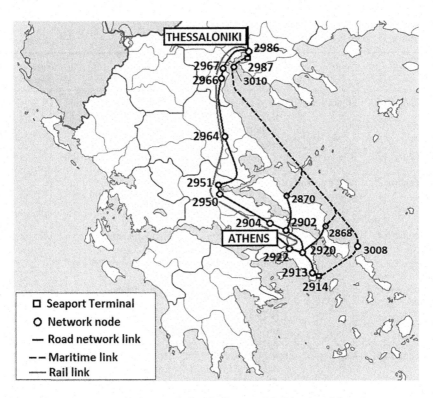

Figure 4.2 Transport networks supporting the intermodal and unimodal routes.

that this coastline does not currently possess adequate ports or roads for receiving this kind of operation. However, the little ports of Agii Apostoli and Kimasi were found to be, at least geographically speaking, adequately located for the purposes of this study. Kimasi actually is fitted with a small Ro-Ro terminal, but the road connection to the mainland is difficult, although a bridge exists to the mainland. Agii Apostoli could be accessed easily from Athens if there were a bridge or a short ferry over the South Euboean Gulf, and it is assumed, for the purpose of this study, that such a bridge exists. Assessing the cost or feasibility of such undertakings is beyond the scope of this chapter. Figure 4.2 shows in a simplified way the ports and routes used in these scenarios, namely because only a few numbered nodes are shown for easier readability. These nodes and links form a subset of a comprehensive transport network model, which covers the whole of mainland Greece.

The two first scenarios shown in Table 4.5 are identical to the ones studied by Tzannatos *et al.* (2014). In addition to these scenarios, new ones are developed using the ports of Agii Apostoli and Kimasi, which are much closer to Thessaloniki than Lavrio is, as shown in the last column of Table 4.5, and, therefore, allow ship speed to be decreased from 25 knots, which is a very high speed for a Ro-Ro

Table 4.5 Characteristics of the different scenarios studied.

Identification	Name	Description	Distances	Number of nodes
Scenario 1	Direct ferry	Ro-Ro cargo ship Lavrio-Thessaloniki + short-range road haulage	Road distance: 68 km Sea distance: 418 km	15
Scenario 2	Road direct	Long-range haulage	Road distance: 489 km	17
Scenario 3	Agii Apostoli ferry	Ro-Ro cargo ship Agii Apostoli-Thessaloniki + short-range road haulage	Road distance: 97 km Sea distance: 299 km	16
Scenario 4	Kimasi ferry	Ro-Ro cargo ship Kimasi-Thessaloniki + medium-range road haulage	Road distance: 188.5 km Sea distance: 227 km	14
Scenario 5	Kimasi ferry (ECA)	Ro-Ro cargo ship Kimasi-Thessaloniki (within ECA) + medium-range road haulage	Road distance: 188.5 km Sea distance: 227 km	14
Scenario 6	Rail	Long-haul freight train Athens (Thriasion) – Thessaloniki (Trigonos) + short-range road haulage	Road distance: 14 km Rail distance: 471.5 km	13

cargo ship and leads to very high emissions, to 19 knots, while slightly decreasing the sailing time to 8.7 hours, in the case of Agii Apostoli, and 6.7 hours, in the case of Kimasi. The use of these two ports is tested in scenarios 3 and 4, while in scenario 5 the ship's speed is further decreased to 15 knots (probably the lower limit for typical sailing speeds of Ro-Ro cargo ships in EU short sea routes) and an emission control area is put in place, implying that the ship's main engines and generators both run on low-sulphur (0.1% S) fuel. In the other scenarios, the main engines run on HFO (2.7% S) and the generators on low-sulphur MDO (0.1% S). Scenario 6 comprises the utilization of the TRAINOSE[3] railway line, which offers rail freight transport in the Athens-Thessaloniki corridor. This last scenario already runs as a competitive alternative to both sea and road freight transport in this region.

Table 4.5 also includes in the last column the number of nodes that actually defines each route. The sea legs of the routes are also decomposed in several links between nodes in order to represent the characteristics of navigation (distance and ship speed). The ship speed in the final and initial links (close to the ports) is set constant at 10 knots, while in the open sea the ship's speeds are as mentioned earlier for the different scenarios.

Table 4.6 presents the average time that the trailers spend in each port, the cargo handling costs and the storage costs. Costs for Agii Apostoli and Kimasi are the same as for Lavrio, as no values are available since these ports do not currently receive this type of traffic. Cargo handling costs are often included in the maritime freight rate, and storage costs often do not exist, as trailers spend a few hours in the seaport terminal and these costs are only charged if the trailers stay more than a couple of days in the terminal.

4.2 Transit time and transport cost

Figure 4.3 shows total transit time decomposition in the six scenarios. It may be seen that the unimodal solution (road) is the fastest solution, taking less than 7 hours, including the road pause as required by Regulation (EC) No. 561/2006. All other scenarios imply twice the transit time, about 14 hours. The ferry time decreases as the Agii Apostoli or Kimasi ports are used, even though the ship's speed was reduced to 19 knots. When the speed is further reduced to 15 knots, in scenario 5, the transit time is the highest at 14.35 hours. The main conclusion is

Table 4.6 Characteristics of the operation in seaport terminals.

Node	Lavrio	Agii Apostoli	Kimasi	Thessaloniki
	2914	2868	2870	2986
Time in port [h]	2	2	2	2
Cargo handling cost [€]	59.9	59.9	59.9	80
Storage cost [€]	0	0	0	0

108 *Tiago A. Santos et al.*

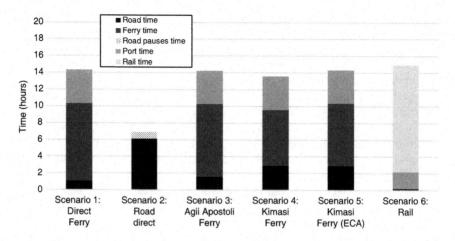

Figure 4.3 Transit time in intermodal and unimodal routes.

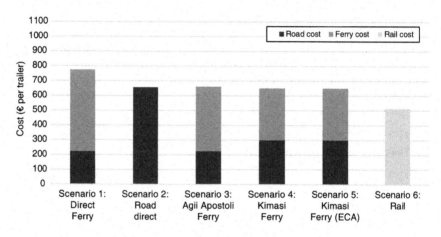

Figure 4.4 Transport cost in intermodal and unimodal routes.

that, as is well known, short sea shipping generally suffers a lack of competitiveness in terms of transit time, as ships are typically slower than trucks, ports need to be used causing a further delay and, finally, SSS is always dependent on pre-carriage and on-carriage (road) to ensure the door-to-door transport chain. The same occurs for the rail scenario, which indicates a transit time (door-to-door) slightly higher than the ro-ro scenarios.

Figure 4.4 shows the cost per trailer implied by the various scenarios. It must be stressed that the point of view adopted is that of the user of the different possible transport solutions. Therefore, such a user, be it a shipper, a forwarder or a logistics service provider, is not interested in the internal cost structure of the shipping company or of the trucking company, but rather on the total cost of the integrated door-to-door service. The cost of the ferry is in line with typical prices for ferries in Greece, depending mostly on distance.[4] Values were collected from websites for similar routes to those proposed in the scenarios for unaccompanied trailers. The road cost is in line with typical road costs in the European Union, but also taking into consideration that shorter road voyages imply a higher cost per trailer.kilometre. Port cargo handling costs are included in the ferry cost. The main conclusion from Figure 4.4 is that unimodal and intermodal door-to-door transport have similar costs. The exception is scenario 1, which uses Lavrio, for which the total cost is the highest. The figure also shows that the train option is less expensive.

4.3 Emissions and external costs

Figure 4.5 shows the air pollutant and climate change emissions for the various scenarios, calculated using the activity-based methodology detailed earlier, on a per trailer basis. It may be seen that scenario 1 is by far the worst case for all types of emissions except CO_2 emissions, which are larger in the road direct scenario. When the two other ports are used, the emissions drop severely because of the shorter distance travelled by ship and the lower speed used (19 knots). The air pollutant emissions remain much higher than those of the road direct scenario, but CO_2 is more than 40% lower than that for the road direct service. Finally, if the Kimasi port is used but the ferry runs on low-sulphur fuel only and at a reduced speed of 15 knots (due to a fictitious ECA zone in the Aegean Sea), the SO_2 and

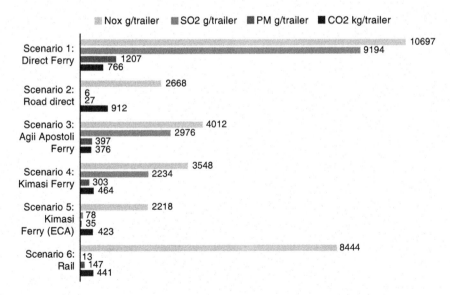

Figure 4.5 Air pollutant and climate change emissions for the various scenarios.

PM emissions are severely decreased, while NO_x decreases moderately. Overall, this last scenario's emission levels are similar to those of the road direct service, except for the level of CO_2 emissions which are decreased by the sea leg. Furthermore, the use of on-board emission abatement technologies or of cleaner fuel types would be able to make all SSS alternatives superior, concerning emissions, to the road alternative. Finally, the rail alternative is competitive in terms of CO_2, PM and SO_2 emissions but produces large quantities of NO_x.

Figure 4.6 shows the total external costs per trailer for the six different scenarios. It is evident that the situation is more evenly balanced than that seen for emissions. This is because the road direct scenario presents many more external costs related to congestion (39%), accidents, noise, infrastructure and up- and downstream costs, and these compensate for the lower emissions-related external costs. Overall, the first scenario presents the largest external costs per trailer. When measures are taken to decrease emissions, namely using the two other ports, decreasing the ship speed or using low-sulphur fuel, the external costs of the door-to-door intermodal transport solution decrease significantly and become lower than that of the road direct scenario. The rail direct scenario shows to be a competitive alternative with similar total external costs to the alternative scenarios 3 to 5. It is also possible to conclude that, in general, the external costs equal between 25% and 33% of the total transport costs shown in Figure 4.4.

In Figure 4.7, the total external cost in each scenario is shown per transport mode. It is clear that even though in scenarios 1 and 3 to 5 the sea distance is larger than the road distance, as per Table 4.5, it is the road leg of those trips which contributes greatly to the external costs. Particularly in scenario 3, the road distance is around a third of the sea distance and yet it is the largest source of costs, mostly from congestion and climate change. This result again enhances the competitiveness of sea freight transport alternatives in terms of external costs in this corridor.

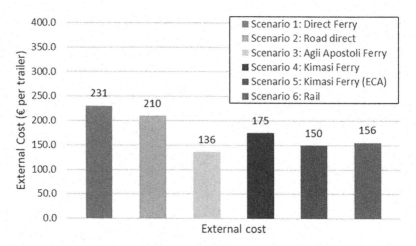

Figure 4.6 External costs comparison of the different scenarios.

Sustainability in intermodal transport 111

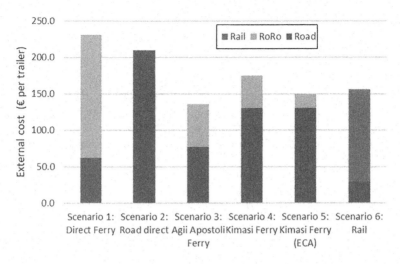

Figure 4.7 External costs comparison of the different scenarios.

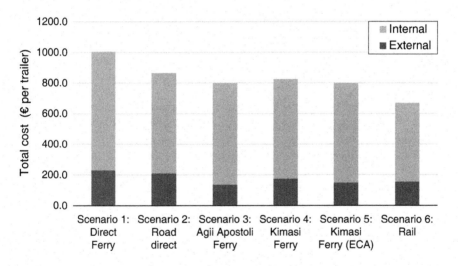

Figure 4.8 Total cost per trailer comparison of the different scenarios.

4.4 Total cost

The previous results are now combined to obtain the total cost per trailer for the different scenarios, shown in Figure 4.8. This total cost is the summation of internal costs, basically those of Figure 4.4, with the external costs shown in Figure 4.7. This means that Figure 4.8 shows the results of a full internalization of the external costs. It may be seen that in scenarios 3 to 5 the total costs per trailer are in line with those of the road direct scenario. This is obtained due to simultaneously reducing internal and external costs when compared with those of scenario 1. In any case, the rail direct scenario seems to be a competitive alternative since there is now an available railway in this corridor.

5 Conclusions

A methodology has been presented to determine transit time, transport costs, gaseous emissions and external costs in intermodal supply chains. This methodology includes an activity-based evaluation of polluting emissions for the various transport modes, with these emissions being the basis for the quantification of the related external costs. The various cost components and transit times are calculated using a detailed database of transport networks that includes road, rail and sea routes. The costs are calculated from the point of view of the user of the intermodal transport chains, rather than by looking at the detailed cost structure of the different transport service providers.

This methodology has been applied in a case study in Greece, building upon a study presented previously by Tzannatos *et al.* (2014). Various scenarios were built for different land-sea routes, ship speeds and types of fuel (lower sulphur content), aiming at improving the sustainability, but also the economic performance, of short sea shipping in the context of intermodal transport chains. The first conclusion is that direct shipping of trailers in ferries, door-to-door, from Athens to Thessaloniki with freight rates aligned with current levels in this region, appears to be not as competitive as road transportation. In addition, external costs associated with a direct ferry scenario proved to be higher than in the road transportation scenario.

An analysis has been carried out for various alternative transport options, leading to the conclusion that making the sea route shorter by using other ports allows a decrease of the ship's speed, which leads to a decrease in both the freight rate to be charged and the external costs, as less speed over smaller distances implies a much lower level of polluting emissions. In fact, it was demonstrated that direct shipping from Athens requires a very high ship speed (25 knots) leading to a very large volume of emissions, most notably of NO_x, SO_2 and PM, as compared to a fully road-based transport. However, using these alternative ports and less speed significantly decreases emissions and external costs.

The analysis also shows that if, in addition, an emission control area is in place, a further decrease of the emissions would occur and transport chains resorting to SSS (ferries) would have a level of emissions comparable with fully road-based transport. This causes fewer external costs, which in conjunction with the reduced freight rate due to a shorter sea distance leads to a significant increase in the competitiveness of SSS-based intermodal transport chains. Finally, it should be pointed out that the use of a freight rail service has an even lower total cost, so SSS needs to step up efforts to increase its commercial and environmental performance.

Finally, the results in this chapter demonstrate how this methodology, building also upon the availability of a comprehensive transport network model, may be used to obtain results which may assist shipping companies, ports and national authorities in the development and promotion of more sustainable transport chains.

Acknowledgements

The research presented in this chapter received support from the research project PTDC/ECI-TRA/28754/2017, financed by the Portuguese Foundation for Science and Technology (Fundação para a Ciência e Tecnologia – FCT) and is within the scope of the Strategic Research Plan of the Centre for Marine Technology and Ocean Engineering (CENTEC), financed by FCT under contract UID/Multi/00134/2020.

Notes

1 https://ec.europa.eu/transport/themes/logistics-and-multimodal-transport/2018-year-multimodality_en
2 NEEDS – New Energy Externalities Developments for Sustainability.
3 https://ics.trainose.gr/?lang=en
4 www.directferries.com/global and www.freightlink.co.uk/

References

Bickel, P., & Friedrich, R. (2005), *ExternE: Externalities of Energy*. Methodology 2005 Update. Luxembourg: Office for Official Publications of the European Communities.

Brons, M., & Christidis, P. (2013), *External Cost Calculator for Marco Polo Freight Transport Project Proposals*. Spain: European Union Joint Research Centre, Sevilla.

CE Delft, Infras, Fraunhofer ISI (2011), *External Costs of Transport in Europe*. Update Study for 2008. Delft: CE Delft.

De Ceuster, G., Van Herbruggen, B., Logghe, S., & Proost, S. (2004), TREMOVE 2.2 model and baseline description. Report B4–3040/2002/342069/MAR/C.1, European Commission, DG ENV, Directorate C – Environment and Health.

den Boer, E. Otten, M., & van Essen, H. (2011), STREAM international freight 2011, comparison of various transport modes on a EU scale with the STREAM database. Delft, Report 11.4377.53.

Department of Transport (2005), National Transport model FORGE – the road capacity & costs model. Research Report.

EcoTransIT World Initiative (2018), *Ecological Transport Information Tool for Worldwide Transports, Methodology and Data Update*. Berne-Hannover-Heidelberg: s.n.

EMSA (2010), The 0.1% Sulphur in fuel requirement as from 1 January 2015 in SECAs – an assessment of available impact studies and alternative means of compliance. Lisbon, Portugal.

European Commission (1999), The development of short sea shipping in Europe, COM(99) 317, Brussels, Belgium.

European Commission (2011a), Transport 2050: The major challenges, the key measures. MEMO/11/197, Brussels.

European Commission (2011b), White Paper 'Roadmap to a single European transport area – towards a competitive and resource efficient transport system'. COM(2011) 144 final. Brussels, Belgium.

European Parliament and Council (1999), Directive 1999/62/EC on the charging of heavy goods vehicles for the use of certain infrastructures.

European Parliament and Council (2006), Regulation N° 561/2006 on the Harmonization of certain social legislation relating to road transport, Strasbourg, France.

Feo, M., Espino, R., & García, L. (2011), A stated preference analysis of Spanish freight forwarders modal choice on the south-west Europe motorway of the sea. *Transport Policy*, 18 (1), pp. 60–67.

Feo-Valero, M., Garcia-Menendez, M., & Garrido-Hidalgo, R. (2011), Valuing freight transport time using transport demand modeling: A bibliographical review. *Transport Reviews*, 31 (5), pp. 625–651.

Fridell, E., Belhaj, M., Wolf, C., & Martin, J. (2009), Calculation of external costs for freight transport. *Transportation Planning and Technology*, 34 (5), pp. 413–432.

Friedrich, R., & Bickel, P. (2001), *Environmental External Costs of Transport*. Stuttgart: Springer. ISBN 978-3-642-07588-9.

Hjelle, M.H. (2010), Short sea shipping's green label at risk. *Transport Reviews: A*, 30 (5), pp. 617–640.

IMO (2015), *Third IMO GHG Study 2014 Executive Summary and Final Report*. London: International Maritime Organization.

Jiang, L., Kronbak, J., & Christensen, L.P. (2010), *External Costs of Maritime Shipping: A Voyage-based Methodology*. University of Southern Denmark (SDU), Odense, Denmark.

Kim, N.S., & Van Wee, B. (2011), Toward a better methodology for assessing CO2 emissions for intermodal and truck-only freight systems: A European case study. *International Journal of Sustainable Transportation*, 8 (3), pp. 177–201.

Korzhenevych, A., Dehnen, N., Bröcker, J., Holtkamp, M., Meier, H., Gibson, G., Varma, A., & Cox, V. (2014), Update of the handbook on external costs of transport. Report MOVE/D3/2011/571, DG-MOVE, Brussels, Belgium.

López-Navarro, M. (2013), The effect of shared planning by road transport firms and shipping companies on performance in the intermodal transport chain: The case of Ro-Ro short sea shipping. *European Journal of Transport and Infrastructure Research*, 13 (1), pp. 39–55.

Maibach, M., Schreyer, C., Sutter, D., Van Essen, H.P., Boon, B.H., Smokers, R., Schroten, A., Doll, C., Pawlowska, B., & Bak, M. (2008), Handbook on estimation of external cost in the transport sector. Version 1.1. (for the European Commission DG TREN), Delft, The Netherlands.

Margaret, O., Kieran, K.J., & Sean, M. (1997), Modeling the internalization of external costs of transport. *Transportation Research Record*, 1576, pp. 93–98.

Miola, A., Ciuffo, B., Giovine, E., & Marra, M. (2010), *Regulating Air Emissions from Ships: The State of the Art on Methodologies, Technologies and Policy Options*. s.l.: JRC European Commission. ISBN 978-92-79-17733-0.

Otten, M., Hoen, M., & den Boer, E. (2017), *STREAM Freight Transport 2016, Emissions of Freight Transport Modes*, Version 2. CE Delft, 17.4H29.10, Delft, The Netherlands.

Preiss, P., & Klotz, V. (2007), Description of updated and extended draft tools for the detailed site-dependent assessment of external costs. Technical Paper No. 7.4 – RS 1b of NEEDS Project.

Sambracos, E., & Maniati, M. (2012), Competitiveness between short sea shipping and road freight transport in mainland port connections: The case of two Greek ports. *Maritime Policy and Management*, 39 (3), pp. 321–337.

Santos, T.A., & Guedes Soares, C. (2017), Modeling of transportation demand in short sea shipping. *Maritime Economics and Logistics*, 19 (4), pp. 695–722.

Tzannatos, E., Papadimitriou, S., & Katsouli, A. (2014), The cost of modal shift: A short sea shipping service compared to its road alternative in Greece. *European Transport \ Transporti Europei* (56), paper n°2, pp. 1-20.

van Essen, H., van Wijngaarden, L., Schroten, A., Sutter, D., Bieler, C., Maffii, S., Brambilla, M., Fiorello, D., Fermi, F., Parolin, R., & El Beyrouty, K. (2019), *Handbook on the External Costs of Transport*, Version 2019. Luxembourg: Publications Office of the European Union. ISBN 978-92-79-96917-1.

Vierth, I., Sowa, V., & Cullinane, K. (2018), Evaluating the external costs of trailer transport: A comparison of sea and road. *Maritime Economics and Logistics*. https://doi.org/10.1057/s41278-018-0099-7.

Whall, C., Cooper, D., Archer, K., Twigger, L., Thurston, N., Ockwell, D., McIntyre, A., & Ritchie, A. (2002), Quantification of emissions from ships associated with ship movements between ports in the European Community. Entec UK Limited, Report to the European Commission.

5 Simulating Ro-Ro operations in the context of supply chains

Tiago A. Santos, João Escabelado, Rui Botter and C. Guedes Soares

1 Introduction

The European Union (EU) has been promoting, for many years now, the competitiveness and sustainability of supply chains as a way to enhance the development of a common market and reduce the external costs related to freight transportation. Considering this, it is well known that transport modes such as short sea shipping (SSS), inland waterways and freight railways can provide significant advantages. A sizable number of solutions related to intermodal transport has been stimulated throughout the years under different financing programmes, starting from 1992. Programmes such as PACT, Marco Polo I and II, Motorways of the Sea and TEN-T have provided funding for such innovative solutions. Intermodality has also attracted significant interest from academia, resulting in a substantial body of literature, which has reviewed all this material and interpreted the reasons for the successes and failures of intermodality and SSS in the EU, namely Baird (2007), Styhre (2009), Douet and Cappuccilli (2011), Baindur and Viegas (2011), Aperte and Baird (2013) and Ng et al. (2013).

On the practical side, it is well known that countries located in the periphery of the EU, such as Portugal and Spain, have to use the road networks of neighbouring countries for conveying their exports and imports to central and northern Europe. However, the countries in the centre of Europe are increasingly regulating road haulage (resting time, minimum wages and enforcement of cabotage protection), applying tolls and restricting the passage of freight vehicles in specific parts of the road network, thus attempting to reduce road congestion, road wear (maintenance costs), noise and pollution. In addition, poor weather conditions and social unrest (strikes, blockades) frequently delay the passage of freight vehicles on EU roads, while the volatility in fuel prices contributes to uncertain economic returns.

These circumstances add cost and uncertainty in road transportation, while increasing transit times. It is therefore important to find competitive and sustainable alternative transport solutions for supporting the development of trade between countries in the periphery and central and northern Europe. Intermodal transport solutions which include a maritime link could play a more significant role in alleviating the mounting pressures on fully road-based freight transportation, particularly if the maritime link resorts to roll-on/roll-off (Ro-Ro) ships.

Several studies have been devoted to the evaluation of the technical and economic feasibility of intermodal solutions across specific corridors between the periphery and central and northern Europe. These studies considered mainly the point of view of the decision makers for transport operations, which consider primarily transit time and cost when making their choices. However, many companies also look at other parameters (see Paixão Casaca and Marlow, 2005, 2009; Mangan et al., 2002), such as the reliability of the door-to-door intermodal transport chain, the frequency of service, the quality of service and the availability of spare capacity. It is also important to recognize that efficient Ro-Ro port terminals play a fundamental role in providing cargo handling operations which are low cost and time efficient. Considering the nature of these additional factors, often present in the mind of decision makers, simulation techniques constitute a suitable option for evaluating these door-to-door transport chains.

Accordingly, this chapter presents a simulation study of a door-to-door intermodal transport chain with multiple origins and destinations of cargo. These chains include three legs: pre-carriage (road based), short sea shipping (Ro-Ro based) and on-carriage (road based). The cargo is transhipped twice at Ro-Ro port terminals. Such study typically requires statistical data describing the operations in general, and particularly in the port terminal. A review of the literature and an inquiry to logistics companies and port terminals revealed that statistical data is scarce and confidential. For that reason, the simulation model presented in this chapter has considered data from Santos et al. (2018) for characterizing some of the operations in port terminals and is kept generic, so that any future data may be readily used to update the assessments.

This chapter is organized in the following manner. Firstly, a review of the literature on simulations of logistics operations where short sea shipping or Ro-Ro terminals are involved is presented. Second, the system to be simulated, the adopted distributions and the implementation of the simulation are presented. The simulation model is then applied in a case study, and numerical results are presented and discussed. A final section with conclusions of the study finalizes the chapter.

2 Literature review

The technical and economic feasibility of intermodal transport solutions across specific corridors between this periphery and central and northern European countries, or within specific countries, has been studied by such authors as Trant and Riordan (2009), Sambracos and Maniati (2012) and Tzannatos et al. (2014), all with the utilization of Ro-Ro ships for part of the intermodal transport. Santos and Guedes Soares (2017a, 2017b) presented two studies dedicated to the Portuguese case, considering the utilization of roll-on/roll-off (Ro-Ro) ships. In the first study, the transport demand for a transport solution that includes Ro-Ro ships and road haulage (for pre-carriage and on-carriage) was estimated for various combinations of ship speeds and freight rates, taking the perspective of the shipper (or logistics company or forwarder) and using as decision parameters the transit time and cost. In the second study, a methodology was developed to identify the Ro-Ro ship and the required fleet size necessary to meet the estimated transport demand, allowing the identification of the optimal point of operation (ship speed and freight rate), taking the point of view of the shipping company rather than the shipper.

The aforementioned studies take mainly in consideration the point of view of the shippers and shipping companies. It is important to recognize, however, that Ro-Ro services are integrated in complex and comprehensive transport chains as reported in Meersman et al. (2010). The role that efficient roll-on/roll-off port terminals play in providing cost-effective and time-efficient cargo handling operations in these fundamental intermodal nodes of supply chains has been studied by Santos et al. (2018). These authors present a case study dedicated to the operation of a short sea Ro-Ro terminal in the port of Leixões, in northern Portugal, providing statistical data valuable for modelling Ro-Ro terminal operations.

The simulation of the operation of container terminals has been carried out in an extensive number of papers in the literature, as may be seen in Angeloudis and Bell (2011). A few examples of container terminal simulations include Kia et al. (2002), Shabayek and Yeung (2002), Petering (2009) and Mathias et al. (2018). Cortés et al. (2007) extends the container terminal simulation model beyond the terminal itself to cover navigation through the estuary of a river.

The simulation of Ro-Ro terminals or of intermodal transport chains (including a Ro-Ro service) is much less covered. Some of the available studies in this field are those of Keceli et al. (2013) and Oznan et al. (2016), both specifically dealing with the simulation of Ro-Ro terminals. Pelícia et al. (2016) present a simple simulation model for a Ro-Ro service between Manaus and São Paulo (Brazil).

Examples of other related studies include those of Chen and Chen (2004) and Liu and Zhang (2009), dealing with the design of the layout and processes of Ro-Ro terminals that handle cars, but these terminals are significantly different from those used for handling freight (in trucks or in containers on wheeled platforms). Finally, Zhang et al. (2009a, 2009b) consider the specific process of yard operations in the same type of terminals. Overall, research in the field of simulation of Ro-Ro terminals, especially when integrated in door-to-door intermodal transport chains, still requires further development.

3 Simulation model

3.1 General description of the transport problem

As mentioned in the previous section, simulation models of door-to-door intermodal transport chains are largely absent in the literature but could be used to assess the reliability and other parameters of these chains. One such model presented in this chapter considers typical transport operations of a logistics company that needs to send general cargo (in containerized form) from northern Portugal to northern France. This company has a set of customers (exporting companies) in Portugal (from which the company collects cargo), and these customers send cargo to typical locations in northern France. The cargo unit will be considered equivalent to a full truckload or a 40-foot container. Currently, the mentioned logistics company uses roads to carry the cargo, but it is experiencing increasing problems in using the EU road system, due to the restrictions mentioned previously.

The logistics company is now studying the possibility of using a Ro-Ro cargo liner service, currently in operation between a port in Portugal and a port in France. In addition, it would have to use a fleet of trucks in Portugal to take the containers to the port and the same in France (respectively pre-carriage and on-carriage). The ship can only carry containers on top of wheeled platforms or semi-trailers, as is typically the case for Ro-Ro cargo ships, implying that this will be, in any case, unaccompanied transport.

The company is, however, resisting using this Ro-Ro line as, in general, short sea shipping experiences problems with reliability and this might produce unacceptable delays in cargo delivery. The company usually accepts contracts with time windows for delivery in different locations. Therefore, it needs to estimate the number of failed deliveries per year when using the intermodal solution, in order to compare the numbers with its extensive experience in using the fully unimodal road-based solution. The reliability of the intermodal or unimodal transport solutions need to be evaluated under the influence of several unpredictabilities, which will be enumerated and characterized using probability distributions in the next sections.

3.2 Logistics company operation

The simulation model comprises the full intermodal supply chain between a set of locations in one country and a set of locations in another country. As mentioned, the problem takes the perspective of a logistics company that has a set of customers (exporting companies) located in different locations around the port of Leixões (fitted with a Ro-Ro terminal). The destinations of cargos are located away from these origins and are not far from a second port (Le Havre), also fitted with a Ro-Ro terminal. A shipping company is providing a regular maritime connection between these ports using Ro-Ro cargo ships, as shown in Figure 5.1. The origins and destinations of cargo form clusters in both extremes connected by this regular line, as they are located across well-defined port hinterlands.

The logistics company operates a fleet of trucks in the origin region and another fleet of trucks in the destination region. The companies also use the necessary drivers, which will carry out their work while respecting the driving time legal restrictions according to the EU regulations (see European Parliament and Council, 2006) for freight transport (daily rests and weekly rests). The number of trucks in the company's fleet (and also the number of drivers) is fixed, and if no truck and driver are available for grabbing the cargo in the origin, it is necessary to wait for available resources. The equipment waits at the company's facilities in Portugal and at the port of Le Havre for the booking to take place. The orders (bookings) 'wait' in a queue sorted according to the number of remaining days until the start of the time window for delivering in the destination area. This reflects the 'criticality' of the booking process. The transportation has to start around 3 days before the beginning of the time window for delivering in order to ensure successful delivery.

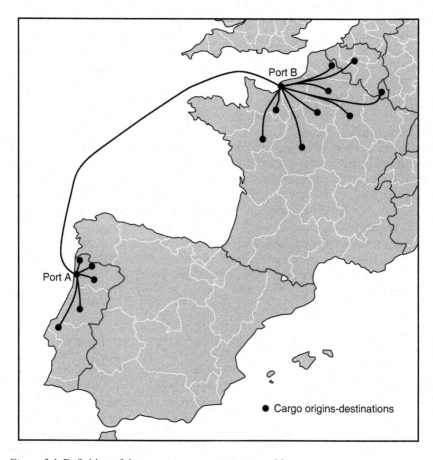

Figure 5.1 Definition of the many-to-many transport problem.

There is a total of six cities of origin where cargos are generated and six cities of delivery destination. The system is set to generate 2400 cargo units per year, and the distribution (number) of cargos (full container loads) to be carried between the origin and destination area, per year, is fixed for each origin-destination (O-D) pair, see Figure 5.2. The number of cargo units may be easily changed in the model, but the general criteria in deciding the distribution of cargo units has been to specify larger volumes for O-D pairs which include Paris or Luxembourg, where large Portuguese communities reside.

The occurrence of bookings throughout each month is, however, uncertain. There is also a seasonality effect with a peak in the autumn (September to November). In these 3 months, 45% of the annual cargo is carried, while in the other three quarters of the year it is carried the remaining 55%. Bookings of cargo are not controllable in terms of time of delivery and destination of cargo. Once they have

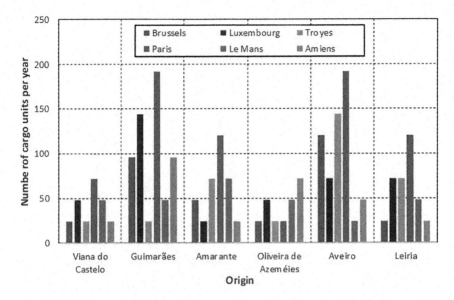

Figure 5.2 Distribution of cargo units to be carried between origin-destination pairs.

been accepted by the commercial department (outside the scope of the simulation), the cargos should be delivered within the delivery window.

The origins of cargo in the area of origin are six cities at known distances from the port. As can be seen in Figure 5.3, two different speed distributions are used, one for intermodal road transport and another one for unimodal (fully road-based) transport, with 75.7 km/h and 77.6 km/h of average speed respectively. The reason for the slightly lower speed in intermodal transportation (pre-carriage and on-carriage) is because congestion normally exists in the access to ports and the speed distribution tends towards smaller values.

Cargos have a time window for delivery (characterized by day and time of beginning and end, separated by 48 hours) at the destination cities and are characterized by a booking date, which is the departing point for carrying out the transportation. The bookings accepted by the logistics company occur with a random distribution (user specified) between the fourth day and the ninth day before the beginning of the delivery window in destination, as shown in Figure 5.4. Containers may be delivered in the terminal from 2 days and up to 3 hours before ship departure. In the destination port the cargo may be picked up after a number of hours, which is variable and uncertain (minimum 3 hours and up to 9 hours after ship arrival, with uniform distribution) from the ship's arrival. When a cargo unit is in port ready to be picked up, the truck will pick up the ones that are more delayed.

Upon delivery of the cargo (container) in the port or in the cargo's final destination, the truck returns to the company's facilities in the region (located not far

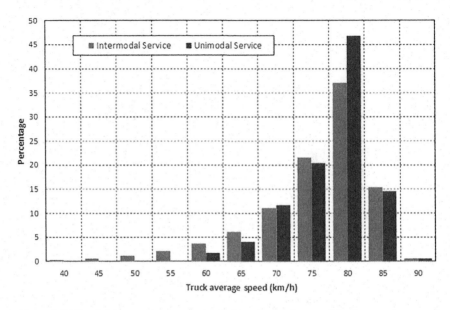

Figure 5.3 Distribution of average truck speed in intermodal (pre-carriage and on-carriage) and unimodal (long-distance haulage) transport.

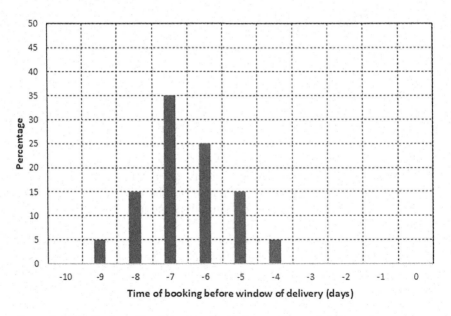

Figure 5.4 Distribution of booking times in relation to contracted delivery time.

from each port). After every 5000 km travelled, each truck goes out of service for 24 hours in order to perform cleaning and maintenance activities. Then the resource should be set as available for further use. The fleets in the two regions are set at a given specified level before the simulation.

3.3 Port and shipping line operation

Uncertainties considered in the simulation model also cover certain aspects of the operation at the port terminal and the ship. First, the port (and consequently the terminal) is closed due to bad weather two times per year of one day each, which occur according to a random distribution over the period between November and March, presented in Figure 5.5. The ship is inoperative two days per year (off-hire for technical reasons), and this event will occur randomly (uniform distribution) over the year. Strikes in the port occur twice per year also randomly (uniform distribution) over the year. This implies no departures will happen over these days (bad weather or strike) if the days coincide with ship departure days. The containers will have to wait for the ship to be ready to sail (the ship departs one day later than scheduled day). Bad weather and strikes are only known 24 hours in advance, so it is not possible to plan for these events. When an off-hire event (due to technical reasons) happens, it is only known right at departure time and corresponds to last minute technical problems.

The port (terminal) gates are only open between 6:00 AM and 12:00 PM, as is the case in most ports, so if trucks arrive outside this time period they must wait. Nevertheless, the system is designed to predict the time of arrivals so that

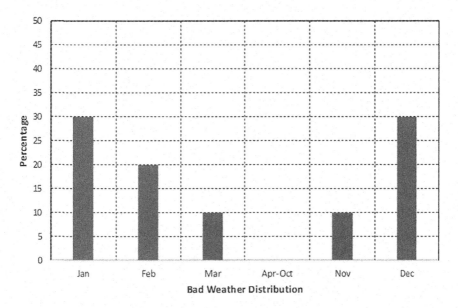

Figure 5.5 Distribution of bad weather occurrences over the year.

the trucks only start the voyage when it is expected that they will arrive within the port opening hours. The ship departs from port according to a set schedule: fixed day and time of departure. The model allows a weekly frequency or multiple departures per week, always at fixed days and hours. However, in practice, the ship is frequently delayed according to a random distribution (departure time uncertain), with a distribution as shown in Figure 5.6. This distribution is asymmetric, and it considers that the ship only departs after the time scheduled, never before. Seasonality has an effect upon this distribution (more delays in autumn, which is the peak season) and, from September to November, it changes into the one presented in Figure 5.6.

The loading process is carried out using the terminal's own fleet of tugmasters, which tow the wheeled platforms (mafis) with the stacked containers or the semi-trailers into the ship's cargo spaces. The ship generally accepts last minute cargo up to 3 hours before departure time (truck needs to arrive at least 3 hours before departure time). In autumn (September to November), the ship is generally full and 90% of the time is not able to take last minute bookings (cargos). During the rest of the year, the ship is able to take last minute bookings 90% of the time. Last minute bookings mean bookings made in the day (24 hours) before the scheduled departure time. Time delay between trying to book space in the ship and the booking time in the logistics company is fixed at 6 hours.

The ship's service speed is generally 15 knots but, in reality, it is uncertain, according to the distributions shown in Figure 5.7. The distributions vary according to the season of the year. This variability in ship speed leads to variations in

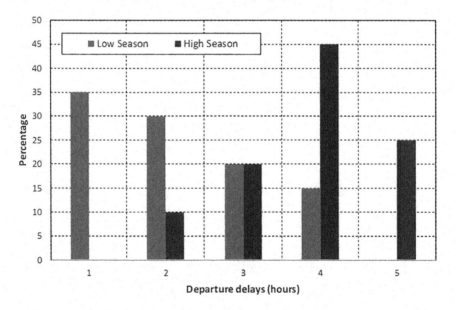

Figure 5.6 Distribution of delays in departure time from port.

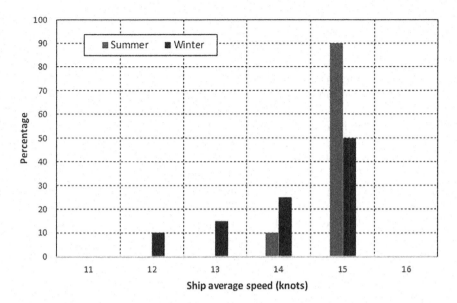

Figure 5.7 Distribution of average ship speed in summer and winter.

the sailing time between ports. The values adopted for these distributions are in line with the operational practices of a regular service currently in operation.

3.4 Logistics company costs

The simulation model allows the cost calculation of the logistics company when using this intermodal solution. The cost structure of the logistics company is composed of its internal costs due to the operation of a fleet of trucks with the corresponding drivers. Complete costs of these fleets are considered to be the capital costs, fuel costs, tolls, insurance, driver wages, maintenance and road circulation taxes, following the values given in Tzannatos *et al*. (2014) and Sambracos and Maniati (2012). The fleet of trucks is fixed in each simulation, but the effects of variations in its size in terms of costs and reliability of the transport solution may be evaluated.

The ship costs incurred by the logistics company take the form of a freight rate per container, charged per voyage, plus a bunker adjustment factor (BAF) indexed to marine fuel cost. The late delivery of cargo in destination cities has associated penalties of a fixed amount of 400 € per day of delay. The anticipated delivery is not possible, making it necessary for the truck to wait in the port of destination before taking to the road on time to deliver the cargo unit within the delivery window.

3.5 Summary of uncertainties and performance indicators

Considering the description of the operations in previous sections, the uncertainties involved in this simulation model are:

- Ship departure time (delays in departing for some hours);
- Availability of cargo space in the ship (especially in high season);
- Bad weather in ports (closing down the ports for some days in winter);
- Bad weather in road (closing down certain links for some days in winter);
- Ship technical off-hire (breakdowns);
- Port and terminal strikes;
- Ship speed (decrease in speed in winter time, especially);
- Time between customer bookings and the beginning of the delivery window in destination;
- Spatial and temporal distribution of actual bookings;
- Distribution of bookings throughout the year (seasonality);
- Road speed (defined on a link-by-link basis, with rush hour in certain links); and
- Unavailability of trucks (mechanical failures).

The performance indicators which are to be measured while simulating the system, or calculated based on the simulation results, are the following:

- Reliability of the transport solution expressed as number of late deliveries in destination cities per year;
- Total cost of logistics company operation per year, split between fixed and variable costs;
- Average transit time per origin-destination pair per year; and
- Average occupancy of the truck fleets during the 24 hours upon ship arrival.

3.6 Implementation of the problem

The problem described in the previous section has been modelled using the discrete event simulation software ARENA. Altiok and Melamed (2007) describe the main principles of modelling using this particular software, while Figure 5.8 represents summarily the general layout of the simulation model, that is, the sequence of events from cargo generation to delivery at destination.

Firstly, the cargo is generated using uniform distributions, which are different depending on the season (peak in autumn months). Once cargo units are generated, the origin-destination pairs (represented by cities) are assigned and the system has to foresee if each cargo unit can be admitted for the intermodal transport, in other words, if it will be delivered within the delivery time window by the intermodal option. To do so, it must be predicted how long it will take to deliver each cargo to the final destination. This prediction consists in calculating the many waiting times, resting breaks and travel times of each mode of transport along the

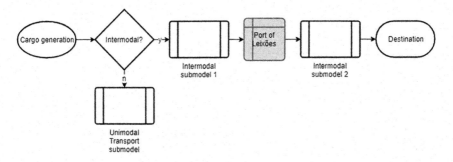

Figure 5.8 General layout of the simulation model.

process, using average delays, expected number of breaks necessary and average speeds. After predicting how long the delivery will take, there are some conditions that must be satisfied, in the following order:

1   If the estimated delivery date is within the delivery time window (delivery date set plus 48 h).
2   If cargo generated 24 hours before ship departure can be accepted. This decision is made following the 'last minute cargo' distributions mentioned in section 3.3.
3   If it can be predicted that cargo will arrive at the port when it is still closed, the cargo waits in the origin to call the truck. If the cargo is generated more than 48 hours before ship departure, the cargo waits to call the truck in order to avoid port storage fees.

Only if these three conditions are satisfied, the truck is requested to pick the cargo up at the cargo origin and deliver it in the port of Leixões. Otherwise, if one or more conditions are not satisfied, the cargo cannot be accepted for intermodal transport and it will be automatically referred for unimodal transport (road transport only).

In case intermodal transport may be used, the model goes through Intermodal Sub-model 1, the port of Leixões and, then, Intermodal Sub-model 2, which includes the port of Le Havre and subsequent on-carriage operations to the final cargo destination, as shown in Figure 5.8.

Once the cargo has been admitted for intermodal transport, it enters Intermodal Sub-model 1, which is represented in Figure 5.9. To pick the cargo up, it is necessary that a truck and a driver are available. If so, the truck speed is assigned and the voyage to the cargo origin starts. When the truck arrives, the cargo unit and the truck are merged and the voyage to the port of Leixões starts immediately. When at the port, if the port is closed, the truck waits until it opens. Otherwise, the cargo unit is unmerged and stored at the port. The truck goes to the truck park immediately, unless it is necessary to perform maintenance or cleaning activities,

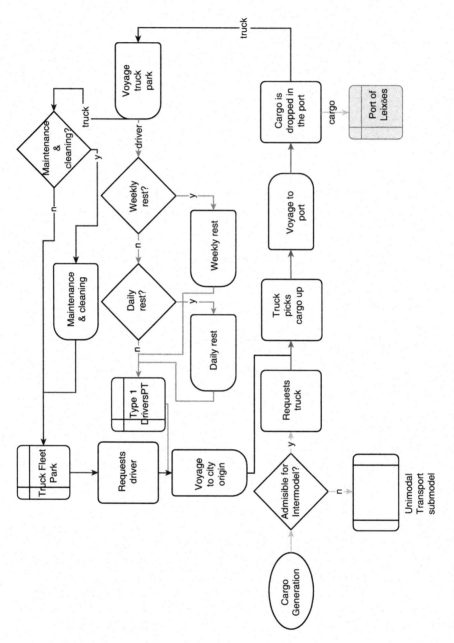

Figure 5.9 General layout of Intermodal Sub-model 1.

and the driver is set as available again, after the daily or weekly rest breaks, if necessary, to take one. When another cargo unit is generated in the system, the same procedure is repeated.

When the ship arrives in the port of origin, Intermodal Sub-model 2 is initiated. Figure 5.10 shows the details of this sub-model. All cargo units in the port are assumed ready to be loaded in the ship when it arrives. The ship arrival is scheduled for once every 7 days, which means that the ship is set to arrive always at the same hour of the same day of the week (fixed schedule).

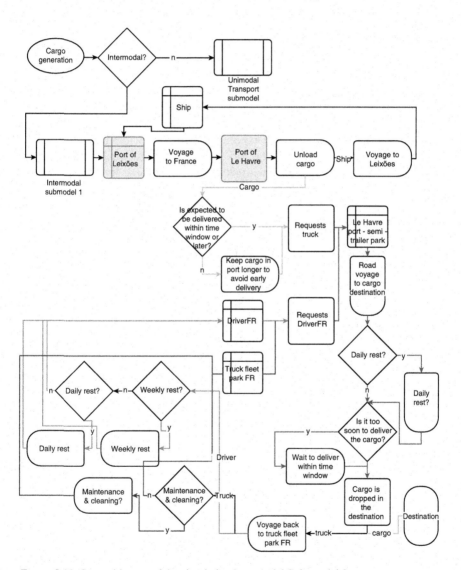

Figure 5.10 General layout of the simulation Intermodal Sub-model 2.

The uncertainties are the actual ship departure from port, since it depends on the departure delay (as per Figure 5.6), the possibility of bad weather occurring (as per Figure 5.5), the possibility of ship technical off-hire (technical failures) and the possibility of port strike events. If one or more events occur, the ship is kept from loading and consequently the trip will be delayed longer than departure delay. When the departure is possible, the ship speed is calculated from its random distribution, the ship and the cargo units are merged, and the voyage starts after the departure delays.

When the ship arrives at the port of Le Havre, the port might be closed, and there are also possibilities of strike and bad weather events. If one or more of those events occur, the ship waits to get in the port. After ship berthing, due to logistic and bureaucracy matters, it takes 3 hours for the first cargo unit to be unloaded and to be picked up. After those 3 hours, the remaining cargo units get ready to be picked up at a uniform rate throughout 6 hours, making up a total of 9 hours necessary to get all cargo ready to ship by road, since ship arrival to the port.

Unloaded cargo units are sorted by shipping priority, making it possible that cargo is unloaded later but actually is shipped from port first. The truck is requested to pick up a cargo only if it is not expected to deliver it before the delivery date, otherwise the cargo is stored at the park longer. When the truck is requested, if there is also a driver available, the truck speed is calculated from the respective random distribution and the voyage immediately starts. If necessary, the driver will stop to take a daily rest on his or her way to destination or on the way back, which means that the daily rests may affect the time of deliveries. Similar to what happens in the end of Intermodal Sub-model 1, when the truck and driver come back, the truck goes to the truck park immediately, unless it is necessary to perform maintenance or cleaning activities and the driver is set as available again, after the daily or weekly rest breaks. When another cargo unit requests a truck, the same procedure is repeated.

4 Case study

The general characteristics of the transport problem, as well as the uncertainties affecting it, have already been described in section 3. In complement to that information, Figure 5.11 shows the locations of the assumed origins of cargos in northern Portugal. Figure 5.12 shows the destinations of cargos in northern France, Belgium and Luxembourg. These figures also show the distances by road between the cargo origins and destinations, the ports of loading and unloading and the location of the truck parking used by the company in Portugal (vicinity of Leixões) and France (vicinity of Le Havre). The volumes of cargo that flow between each origin-destination pair have been shown in Figure 5.2.

In this study, the results of the simulation model are presented for a case in which the logistics company is using a combination of the intermodal and unimodal solutions. The latter is used when the company identifies that the cargo will arrive too late at the destination if it uses the intermodal solution. This basically occurs because the ship service has a weekly schedule and when cargos

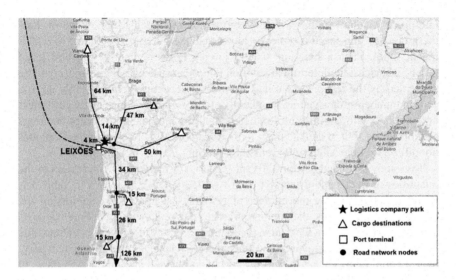

Figure 5.11 Location of cargo origins in Portugal, loading port (Leixões) and logistics company truck park.

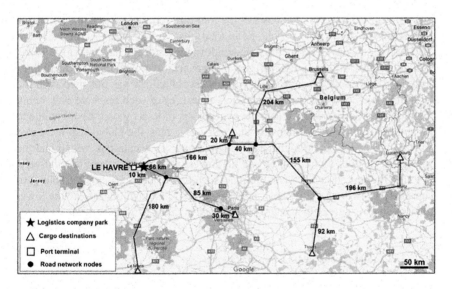

Figure 5.12 Location of cargo destinations in northern France, unloading port (Le Havre) and logistics company park.

are booked at short notice. Sometimes it is not possible to forward it using the intermodal solution so that it is delivered within the specified time window. Furthermore, the ship speed is typically lower than the truck speed, leading to higher transit times. Such a situation, that is, having to use unimodal transport (road based) instead of the intermodal solution (ship) because of lack of time, could be prevented by the company if it had a policy of accepting bookings only up to a certain number of days before the actual delivery window. Since many customers now operate with just-in-time strategies, it seems reasonable to accept bookings at short notice, but to deviate them to the road when it is likely that the ship does not offer a feasible solution for making it on time.

This study is carried out for different scenarios, which differ with respect to the quantities of trucks and drivers of each type (resources), as shown in Table 5.1. Reducing or increasing the number of resources changes the reliability of the transport system, that is, the number of cargos delivered within the time windows changes. Since there is a fee paid to the customer for day of delivery out of the time window, the total cost may increase when there is a large number of late deliveries.

The simulations are set to start on 7 May and have a duration of 365 days. In order to get reliable results for each scenario, it was observed that with 20 iterations the system is perfectly stabilized, that is, the calculations computed for the reliability obtained would not change significantly with further iterations. Figure 5.13 shows the reliability obtained depending on the number of iterations and supports this conclusion.

Figure 5.14 shows the total costs of the four different scenarios and the number of days of late deliveries of each one in total, that is, if one cargo unit arrived to the destination 4 days beyond the time window, it counts as 4 days of late delivery.

It can be observed in Figure 5.14 that the scenarios corresponding to the highest global costs are scenarios 1 and 4. The lowest reliability was obtained with the conditions of scenario 1, which had such quantities of each resource that, being comparatively low, it could create the expectation of lower global cost, but due to the number of days of late delivery and respective fees, the global cost increased substantially. The second higher global cost occurs in scenario 4, which had the highest quantity of each resource and the lowest number of days of late delivery, although the investment in resources was such that resulted in higher global cost. The scenarios with lower global costs are scenarios 3 and 4, but despite the lower quantities of resources in scenario 2, the higher number of days of late delivery

Table 5.1 Definition of scenarios for simulations.

	Scenario 1	Scenario 2	Scenario 3	Scenario 4
Intermodal Drivers PT	8	8	8	8
Unimodal Drivers	14	14	17	20
Intermodal Drivers FR	11	10	11	15
Trucks PT	15	16	18	20
Trucks FR	8	8	9	12

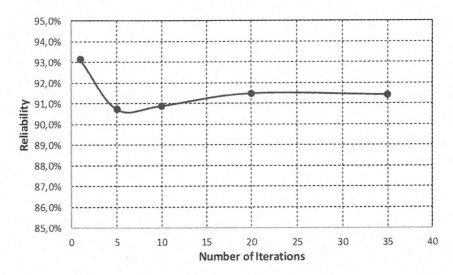

Figure 5.13 Average reliability as a function of the number of iterations.

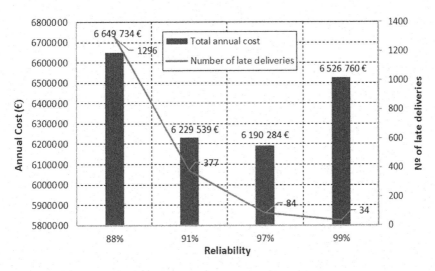

Figure 5.14 Annual cost of the system and number of late deliveries corresponding to different reliability levels.

increased the global cost, making scenario 3 the one with lower cost. Therefore, scenario 3 has neither the lowest investment in resources nor the lowest number of days of late delivery, but is the one with lowest global cost. It can thus be considered that the best cost-benefit relation is found for scenario 3, which also leads to highly reliable deliveries.

Figures 5.15 and 5.16 show the occupancies of trucks based in Portugal and in France. It can be noted that the peak of occupancy occurs during the high season (from September to November), since the number of cargo units almost triples in this period. Figure 5.15 shows a constant oscillation of around 40% every time of the year. This oscillation is due to the resting time of drivers, the 24-hour break for truck maintenance and cleaning and the requirement that cargo units are only delivered in the port of Leixões 48 hours before ship departure. The last one causes a big variation in the occupancy every week, since all cargo generated during the 5 days after a ship departure is on hold at its origin facility until 48 hours before the next ship departure. In the low season, the number of drivers and trucks is substantially higher than required, but the critical period is in the high season, thus the fleets' size were dimensioned with this period in consideration.

In Figure 5.16, similarly to what happens with the trucks in Portugal, an occupation peak in the high season is clearly noticeable. It also presents a more or less constant oscillation but of larger amplitude. This oscillation is because all cargo units to be shipped from the port of Le Havre to the final destination come

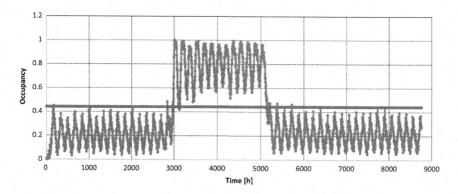

Figure 5.15 Occupancy of the truck fleet in Portugal.

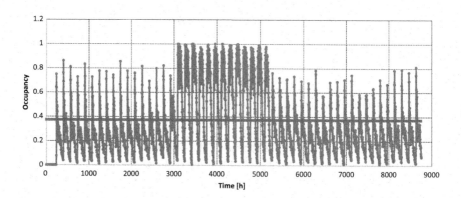

Figure 5.16 Occupancy of the truck fleet in France.

together, every week, and so there are brief periods when there is no cargo to ship; when the ship arrives, the demand for trucks increases sharply and suddenly.

Table 5.2 shows, for each scenario, that having different quantities of trucks and drivers changes the average occupancy of each resource throughout the year.

The simulation results presented hereafter relate to levels of reliability of the intermodal solution of approximately 88%, 91%, 97% and 99% of cargo units delivered within the delivery window. Table 5.3 shows, for these levels of reliability on a yearly basis, the size of the truck fleets in Portugal and France, number of drivers in Portugal and in France, number of cargos deviated to the road, number of intermodal cargos that arrived within the delivery window, number of road cargos that arrived within the delivery window, average occupancy of the truck fleets during the days before ship departure (during the 24 hours before the opening of the 2 days' free time in the port of Leixões), average occupancy of the truck fleet in France during the 24 hours after ship arrival, average number of cargo units on board the ship per week, total values of the penalties paid for late delivery (intermodal and road), total value of the transport costs for all the cargos, average transit time between Guimarães and Paris by road and average transit time between Guimarães and Paris by ship.

Analyzing the results in Table 5.3, it is possible to observe that the percentage of cargo forwarded using the intermodal solution is quite high and approximately constant despite the scenarios. That happens because the system is set to give priority to the intermodal solution, that is, it only forwards cargo units using the unimodal solution if there is no intermodal cargo to be delivered in the port. This decision, when there are not enough resources to attend all needs, impairs the unimodal solution, avoiding as far as possible any delay in intermodal transport. The reason for that decision is that unimodal transport occupies its resources for much longer when compared with the intermodal one. Giving priority to the intermodal solution allows shipping more cargo units with fewer resources. In scenario 4, the unimodal reliability is much higher than in the other scenarios, since the number of trucks and drivers is much larger. Nevertheless, its reliability is not as high as the intermodal one due to the same reason: priority of resources for the intermodal solution. However, if the quantities of unimodal drivers and trucks were even higher, the reliability would be approximately 100%. Such a scenario was not considered since it would not be realistic, regarding the high costs it would represent.

Table 5.2 Trucks and driver's occupancy (fraction of full occupancy) form the various scenarios.

	Scenario 1	Scenario 2	Scenario 3	Scenario 4
Intermodal Drivers PT	0.10	0.10	0.11	0.10
Unimodal Drivers	0.35	0.33	0.35	0.24
Intermodal Drivers FR	0.25	0.38	0.28	0.18
Trucks PT	0.44	0.39	0.44	0.32
Trucks FR	0.37	0.38	0.37	0.24

Table 5.3 Characteristics and results of the transport system for different levels of reliability.

	Scenario 1	Scenario 2	Scenario 3	Scenario 4
Intermodal Drivers PT	8	8	8	8
Unimodal Drivers	14	14	17	20
Intermodal Drivers FR	11	10	11	15
Trucks PT	15	16	18	20
Trucks FR	8	8	9	12
% Intermodal	76.7%	77.7%	77.4%	77.3%
Intermodal Reliability	97.7%	96.7%	98.1%	98.9%
% Unimodal	23.3%	22.3%	22.6%	22.7%
Unimodal Reliability	54.5%	72.9%	92.3%	98.0%
Total Reliability	87.7%	91.3%	96.8%	98.7%
High season occupancy of trucks PT 72 h before ship departure	0.84	0.78	0.61	0.46
High season occupancy of trucks FR 24 h after ship arrival	0.97	0.92	0.89	0.78
Average number or cargos on board per week	35	36	36	36
Total late delivery penalties [Unimodal]	500,940 €	125,220 €	20,520 €	4880 €
Total late delivery penalties [Intermodal]	17,460 €	25,460 €	14,440 €	8820 €
Total transport costs	6,649,734 €	6,229,539 €	6,190,284 €	6,526,760 €
Average transit time Guimarães-Paris [Intermodal]	175 h	178 h	174 h	172 h
Minimum transit time Guimarães-Paris [Intermodal]	91 h	90 h	92 h	92 h
Average transit time Guimarães-Paris [Unimodal]	106 h	60 h	44 h	38 h
Minimum transit time Guimarães-Paris [Unimodal]	33 h	33 h	33 h	33 h

Table 5.4 shows the detailed results for the yearly costs of the transport system, separated between costs with the unimodal solution and costs with the intermodal solution. The fixed costs are directly proportional to the number of resources (trucks and drivers), so lower quantities of resources correspond to lower fixed costs. Tolling, fuel, lubricant and tire replacement costs are represented in the unimodal solution, since it uses much more the truck than the intermodal solution, in which the truck is only used during pre-carriage and on-carriage. On the other hand, the intermodal solution has the significant extra cost of ship transportation, although it turns out to be less expensive than the unimodal one.

Table 5.4 Detailed costs of the intermodal and unimodal operations.

			Scenario 1	Scenario 2	Scenario 3	Scenario 4
Intermodal	Fixed Costs	Annualized capital investment	77,951 €	79,728 €	89,299 €	114,645 €
		Driver's annual cost	480,396 €	455,112 €	480,396 €	581,532 €
		Other fixed costs	67,814 €	69,359 €	77,686 €	99,736 €
		Maintenance	19,975 €	20,430 €	22,883 €	29,377 €
	Variable Costs	Tolling PT	50,779 €	51,373 €	50,968 €	50,771 €
		Tolling FR	253,485 €	257,465 €	255,680 €	255,142 €
		Fuel	830,363 €	842,259 €	833,096 €	834,403 €
		Lubricants	148,279 €	150,403 €	148,767 €	149,000 €
		Tire replacement	148,279 €	150,403 €	148,767 €	149,000 €
		Ship transport (maritime freight)	1 362,713 €	1,380,563 €	1,371,788 €	1,369,838 €
		Late delivery fines	17,460 €	25,460 €	13,460 €	8,820 €
Unimodal	Fixed Costs	Annualized capital investment	101,564 €	107,592 €	121,436 €	135,115 €
		Driver's annual cost	420,000 €	420,000 €	429,828 €	600,000 €
		Other fixed costs	88,356 €	93,601 €	105,644 €	117,544 €
		Maintenance	26,025 €	27,570 €	31,117 €	34,623 €
	Variable Costs	Tolling Portugal	20,737 €	19,884 €	20,079 €	20,120 €
		Tolling Spain	35,315 €	33,903 €	34,233 €	34,274 €
		Tolling France	222,647 €	213,500 €	214,929 €	215,250 €
		Fuel	1,309,116 €	1,256,842 €	1,267,434 €	1,269,350 €
		Lubricants	233,771 €	224,436 €	226,327 €	226,670 €
		Tire replacement	233,771 €	224,436 €	226,327 €	226,670 €
		Late delivery fines	500,940 €	125 220 €	20,140 €	4,880 €
Total Annual Cost			6,649,734 €	6,229,539 €	6,190,284 €	6,526,760 €

5 Conclusions and recommendations

This chapter has presented a discrete event simulation model of intermodal transportation in supply chains, using ro-ro ships for the short sea shipping leg of the transport operations. The model includes the possibility of still resorting to road transportation when it is clear that the intermodal solution will lead to a late delivery. This model has been implemented using a commercial software package and applied to the analysis of transport operations of a generic logistics company, between Portugal and northern France, Belgium and Luxembourg.

The objective of the simulation is to quantify the reliability of intermodal transportation when the truck fleets (in both geographical areas) and the number of drivers engaged in road haulage operations are varied. Costs implied by such intermodal operations are also quantified. The main uncertainties affecting the two transport solutions have been included in the simulation model. The demand for transportation over a period of one year is fixed for a variety of origin-destination pairs, but time of occurrence of actual customer bookings is uncertain and affected by seasonality effects.

The model results show that it is possible to use the model to quantify the truck and driver numbers necessary to attain specified levels of reliability of transport operations (in this case study, between 88% and 99%). Under the assumptions of the current model, the minimum total cost of the system occurred for a fleet of 18 trucks in Portugal (used for both unimodal and intermodal transport) and 9 trucks in France. Truck drivers need to number 8 for intermodal transport in Portugal, 17 for unimodal transport and 11 for intermodal transport in France. This corresponds to a significant total reliability level of 97% at a cost of 6.19 million euros. It then needs to be ascertained, from the perspective of the logistics company, if this reliability level is indeed acceptable for the customers of the logistics company (shippers of cargo).

The simulation model also allows an analysis of the impact of different set-up details and parameters in the numerical results. For example, it was also expected that full road transport would be more reliable than the intermodal, but under the conditions set, it was not. Also, with a smaller delivery time window, the reliability of the intermodal solution would likely decrease substantially, since the time of arrival is much more spread out within the time window than in the unimodal solution.

A number of recommendations for further studies may be made, including the expansion of the simulation model to include the complete simulation of fully road-based transport operations. This would enable the comparison of both types of operation: intermodal versus unimodal. The effects of increasing the ship's service frequency could also be assessed. Finally, it would be interesting to obtain real data from logistics companies and port and terminal operators, enabling a fine-tuning of the distributions used to characterize the uncertainties or, indeed, the upgrading of the model with other uncertainties suggested by practice.

Acknowledgements

The research presented in this chapter received support from the research project PTDC/ECI-TRA/28754/2017, financed by the Portuguese Foundation for Science and Technology (Fundação para a Ciência e Tecnologia – FCT) and is within the scope of the Strategic Research Plan of the Centre for Marine Technology and Ocean Engineering (CENTEC), financed by FCT under contract UID/Multi/00134/2020.

References

Altiok, T., & Melamed, B. (2007), *Simulation Modeling and Analysis with Arena*. Burlington: Academic Press.

Angeloudis, P., & Bell, M.G.H. (2011), A review of container terminal simulation models. *Maritime Policy & Management*, 38, pp. 523–540.

Aperte, X.G., & Baird, A.J. (2013), Motorways of the sea policy in Europe. *Maritime Policy & Management*, 40 (1), pp. 10–26.

Baindur, D., & Viegas, J. (2011), Challenges to implementing motorways of the sea concept – lessons from the past. *Maritime Policy & Management*, 38 (7), pp. 673–690.

Baird, A. (2007), The economics of motorways of the seas. *Maritime Policy and Management*, 34 (4), pp. 287–310.

Chen, Y., & Chen, C. (2004), Design principle for the handling process and plan layout of commercial automobile Ro/Ro terminal. *Port & Motorway Engineering* (3), pp. 21–23.

Cortés, P., Muñuzuri, J., Nicolás Ibáñez, J., & Guadix, J. (2007), Simulation of freight traffic in the Seville inland port. *Simulation Modelling Practice and Theory*, 15, pp. 256–271.

Douet, M., & Cappuccilli, J.F. (2011), A review of short sea shipping in the European Union. *Journal of Transport Geography*, 19, pp. 968–976.

European Parliament and Council (2006), Regulation (EC) No. 561/2006 of 15 March 2006 on the harmonisation of certain social legislation relating to road transport.

Keceli, Y., Aksoy, S., & Aydogdu, V. (2013), A simulation model for decision support in Ro-Ro terminal operations. *International Journal of Logistics Systems and Management*, 15 (4), pp. 338–358.

Kia, M., Shayan, E., & Ghotb, F. (2002), Investigation of port capacity under a new approach by computer simulation. *Computers & Industrial Engineering*, 42 (2–4), pp. 533–540.

Liu, H., & Zhang, Z. (2009), Enlightenment concerning design of modern specialized automobile Ro/Ro wharf. *Port & Motorway Engineering* (10), pp. 91–93.

Mangan, J., Lalwani, C., & Gardner, B. (2002), Modelling port/ferry choice in Ro-Ro freight transportation. *International Journal of Transport Management*, 1 (1), pp. 15–28.

Mathias, N.A.S., Santos, T.A., & Guedes Soares, C. (2018), Analysis of a new container terminal using simulation approach. In C. Guedes Soares & T.A. Santos (eds.), *Progress in Maritime Engineering and Technology*. London: Taylor & Francis Group, pp. 43–52.

Meersman, H., Van De Voorde, E., & Vanelslander, T. (2010), Port competition revisited. *Review of Business and Economics*, 55 (2), pp. 210–233.

Ng, A.K.Y, Sauri, S., & Turró, M. (2013), Short sea shipping in Europe: Issues, policies and challenges. In M. Finger & T. Holvad (eds.), *Regulating Transport in Europe*. Cheltenham: Edward Elgar, pp. 196–217.

Oznan, E.D., Nas, S., & Guler, N. (2016), Capacity analysis of Ro-Ro terminals by using simulation modelling method. *The Asian Journal of Shipping and Logistics*, 32 (3), pp. 139–147.

Paixão Casaca, A.C., & Marlow, P.B. (2005), The competitiveness of short sea shipping in multimodal logistics supply chains: Service attributes. *Maritime Policy and Management*, 32 (4), pp. 363–382.

Paixão Casaca, A.C., & Marlow, P.B. (2009), Logistics strategies for short sea shipping operating as part of multimodal transport chains. *Maritime Policy and Management*, 36 (1), pp. 1–19.

Pelícia, R.S., Pelo, M.A.P., Galdi da Silva, M., Botter, R.C., & Pereira, N.N. (2016), Feasibility study of MOS in Brazil using roll-on/roll-off vessels between Manaus and São Paulo. In C. Guedes Soares & T.A. Santos (eds.), *Maritime Technology and Engineering 3*, vol. 1. London: Taylor & Francis Group, pp. 105–115.

Petering, M.E.H. (2009), Effect of block width and storage yard layout on marine container terminal performance. *Transportation Research Part E: Logistics and Transportation Review*, 45 (4), pp. 591–610.

Sambracos, E., & Maniati, M. (2012), Competitiveness between short sea shipping and road freight transport in mainland port connections; the case of two Greek ports. *Maritime Policy and Management*, 39 (3), pp. 321–337.

Santos, T.A., & Guedes Soares, C. (2017a), Modeling of transportation demand in short sea shipping. *Maritime Economics and Logistics*, 19 (4), pp. 695–722.

Santos, T.A., & Guedes Soares, C. (2017b), Ship and fleet sizing in short sea shipping. *Maritime Policy and Management*, 47 (7), pp. 859–881.

Santos, T.A., Guedes Soares, C., & Botter, R.C. (2018), Characterizing the operation of a roll-on roll-off short sea shipping service. In C. Guedes Soares & T.A. Santos (eds.), *Progress in Maritime Engineering and Technology*. London: Taylor & Francis Group, pp. 77–88.

Shabayek, A.A., & Yeung, W.W. (2002), A simulation model for the Kwai Chung container terminals in Hong Kong. *European Journal of Operational Research*, 140 (1), pp. 1–11.

Styhre, L. (2009), Strategies for capacity utilisation in short sea shipping. *Maritime Economics & Logistics*, 11 (4), pp. 418–437.

Trant, G., & Riordan, K. (2009), Feasibility of New RoRo/RoPax Services between Ireland and continental Europe.

Tzannatos, E., Papadimitriou, S., & Katsouli, A. (2014), The cost of modal shift: A short sea shipping service compared to its road alternative in Greece. *European Transport \ Transporti Europei* (56), p. 2.

Zhang, L., Zhang, Z., Li, W., & Gao, H. (2009a), Research on the yard operation in automobile Ro-Ro terminals. *Logistics Technology* (12), pp. 5–6.

Zhang, Y., Zhang, L., Li, W., & Yan, X. (2009b), Research of intelligent decision of vehicle slot of automobile Ro-Ro terminal yard. *Journal of Highway and Transportation Research and Development*, 26 (S1), pp. 27–33.

6 Multi-criteria decision method applied to Motorways of the Sea

Alba Martínez-López and Lourdes Trujillo

1 Introduction

Since the end of the 1990s, the European Transport Policy, through successive White Papers on Transport, supported the development of intermodal chains through short sea shipping (SSS) as a strategic measure to mitigate the negative effects of the intra-community transport of commodities (pollution, congestion, noise, bottlenecks, etc.) for European citizens.

Even though the initial aims remained over time (alleviating congestion and the pressure on bottlenecks in the European road and rail networks through a modal shift), the suggested transport alternative was finally consolidated in a wider concept (White Paper on Transport 2001): the Motorways of the Sea – MoS – (Commission of the European Communities, 2001). Thus, the MoS not only made reference to the seaborne stretches of transport chains but also involved their integration into 'door-to-door' transport by considering the necessary services for the modal shift in ports. The MoS suggest wider benefits by improving administrative procedures among maritime regions, environmental performance, modal shift operations, etc. Since then, numerous milestones in the evolution of the MoS concept can be highlighted; however, one of the most significant supports in the European Union (EU) context was its inclusion (through maritime corridors, Project 21 of the recommendations of the 'Van Miert' group in 2003) in the Trans-European Transport Network (TEN-T) by the European Commission (Revision of TEN-T guidelines 2004 – Decision No. 884/2004). Despite explicit support for the MoS, it is widely recognized that the development of the intermodal chains through MoS in the EU did not meet the initial expectations. This reality has motived a large debate in the EU that has driven not only an exhaustive revision report about MoS results (European Commission, 2017) but also a careful *Detailed Implementation Plan* (*DIP*) provided by the European Coordinator for MoS in 2018 (Simpson, 2018).

The MoS reports concluded that there was a need for a more holistic approach covering the whole freight logistics chain to enhance intermodality. In that sense, the ports in MoS should be not just start and end nodes for the corridors (current configuration of the TEN-T Core Network Corridors – Regulation (EU) No. 1315/2013–) but also linking hubs between corridors (maritime and land legs).

This recommendation must be also accompanied by reflection about the current port classifications (core and comprehensive ports in the current TEN-T Network – Regulation (EU) No. 1315/2013–) and their consequences. Many peripheral regions and islands of the European Union have been not only excluded from the network planning and transport maps of the TEN-T, but they were also largely absent from the projects funded from MoS funding programmes due to a deficient definition of the ports included in the TEN-T. Consequently, there is a consensus about the need to extend the current TEN-T corridors by reconsidering the actual port eligibility criteria (with high difficulties to be applied across all ports with great contextual varieties).

Given this need, this chapter proposes a method able to identify the ports that form the most suitable maritime route (MoS) to articulate intermodal chains that are competitive against the road alternative. The proposed method is made of two steps. The first identifies, through a multi-criteria decision matrix, the most suitable maritime route to establish an MoS that enables the intermodal chains to have the highest success possibilities versus the trucking alternative. In turn, the second step provides knowledge about the risk assumed when a decision is made from the quantitative results obtained in the first stage through a sensitivity analysis applied to the matrix. This also permits identifying the most relevant variables on the success of the intermodality. Even though the method was developed from a European need, its easy adaptation to other realities through a change in the problem's approach (new targets) allows wide utility.

The remainder of this chapter is organized as follows. After the introduction, section 2 provides details about the structure of the method and its calculation process. Sections 3 and 4 introduce particular applications to real-life cases in the European context and outside of the European framework. In the last section, the method is adapted to the specific needs of the new framework. The aim of these sections is not just to improve comprehension of the method but also to show its delocalized utility. Finally, section 5 draws global conclusions and potentials for the method proposed.

2 Numerical method

2.1 Quantitative assessment of transport alternatives

The first step of the method provides a quantitative assessment of the possibilities of intermodality success through different MoS alternatives. This involves evaluating the performance of the door-to-door transport chain; in other words, the entire intermodal chain must be analyzed from the loader standpoint. Considering this assumption, a multi-criteria decision method is applied where the time and cost attributes (evaluation criteria) are analyzed for the intermodal chains versus trucking. With this application, a three-dimensional matrix will be obtained in such a way that it provides final evaluation information through dimensionless port indexes.

The method introduced is based on 'many-to-many' transport networks (Daganzo, 2005); this involves the combination of several capillary hauls on land and just one trunk haul (the seaborne transport) for the intermodal chains (see Figure 6.1). Thus, this configuration involves the combination of several *nodes* (final origins or destinations for the loads) on land and pairs of *hubs* (consolidation centres for the cargo). The method assumes nodes are the endpoints of the chains on land and hubs correspond to the ports that make up the MoS (trunk haul, see Figure 6.1). To optimize method performance, the number and localization of the nodes and hubs are deterministic and discrete. Even though the modal choice for short-distance transport is based on multiple criteria (see for example Cullinane and Toy, 2000; García-Menendez and Feo-Valero, 2009), most authors agree that the time and the cost invested in the service are decisive selection criteria.

Assuming this reality, both attributes are evaluated for the whole chain (see Figure 6.1) through normalized indexes by considering both transport alternatives (*i*): cost index (see Equation 6.1) and time index (see Equation 6.2).

$$I^C_{ihjkn} = 1 - \frac{Cost_{ihjkn}}{\sum_{i=1}^{2} Cost_{ihjkn}} \qquad \sum_{i=1}^{2} I^C_{ihjkn} = 1 \qquad (6.1)$$

$$I^T_{ihjk} = 1 - \frac{Time_{ihjk}}{\sum_{i=1}^{2} Time_{ihjk}} \qquad \sum_{i=1}^{2} I^T_{ihjk} = 1 \qquad (6.2)$$

The closer the index value is to one, the more interest the decision maker has in that transport mode compared to the alternative. In other words, index values close to one involve lower times and costs compared to the other transport mode. According to Equations (6.1) and (6.2), the index assessment is carried out for every possible transportation route between each pair of nodes (*h* and *j*, see Figure 6.1) and through all alternative ports (*k*) able to articulate MoS with

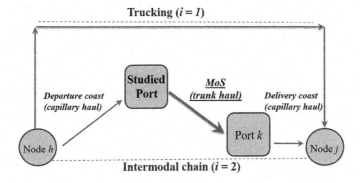

Figure 6.1 The 'many-to-many' model applied to study transport alternatives.

the studied port ('one-to-one' network approach). The index calculation requires considering the following issues for a complete evaluation:

- Transport analysis is just one direction; this involves every candidate port of the departure coast (see Figure 6.1) being assessed by analyzing the performance of the whole chain through all possible connections (MoS) with ports on the delivery coast ($K=\{1,2,\ldots k\}$).
- The same fleet (technical and operative features) will operate in all possible MoS and just two transport alternatives are evaluated, trucking and intermodal chain through MoS ($i = 1$ and 2).
- All nodes ($H = \{1,2,\ldots h\}$ and $J = \{1,2,\ldots j\}$) have an associated probability for sending (γ_h) and receiving (α_j) cargo to and from the rest of the nodes. Despite the fact that the characteristics of every framework must address the calculation of those probabilities, a population criterion can be assumed as a first approach (see Equations 6.3 and 6.4), since the SMEs (small and medium enterprises that are the main loaders for freight short transport in Europe (Van Oort and Stam, 2005)) are located in the main population centres.

$$\alpha_j = \frac{Population_j}{\sum_j population_j} \qquad \sum_j \alpha j = 1 \quad \forall j \in J \qquad (6.3)$$

$$\gamma_h = \frac{Population_h}{\sum_h Population_h} \qquad \sum_h \gamma_h = 1 \quad \forall h \in H \qquad (6.4)$$

The method considers that the cost indexes (see Equation 6.1) must analyze the possible route performances during a time period in the past. In this way, every year of the range ($N = \{1,2,\ldots n\}$) will have an associated weighting factor (see Equation 6.5) in relation to the yearly cargo volume (in tonnes) moved between each pair of ports (pattern traffic evolution).

$$\beta_n = \frac{Volume_n}{\sum_n Volume_n} \qquad \sum_n \beta n = 1 \quad \forall n \in N \qquad (6.5)$$

Equations (6.6) and (6.7) define relevance indexes (*RI*). These are indicators whose values are a result of simple index aggregation (see Equations 6.1 and 6.2).

$$RI_{ikn}^C = \sum_h \sum_j (\gamma_h \times (I_{ihjkn}^C \times \alpha_j)) \qquad \forall h \in H; \forall j \in J \qquad (6.6)$$

$$RI_{ik}^T = \sum_h \sum_j (\gamma_h \times (I_{ihjk}^T \times \alpha_j)) \qquad \forall h \in H; \forall j \in J \qquad (6.7)$$

In this way, evaluation through relevance indexes overtakes the one-to-one approach to provide wider information about the selection probability (based on the competitiveness in terms of time and cost) for a transport mode (*i*) against its competitor by taking into account all the possible endpoints of the route (many-to-many transport model, see Figure 6.1) and the configuration of the route (every MoS alternative defined by the studied port and a *k* port). In turn, Equations (6.8) and (6.9) show the different indexes of relevance (*DIR*). These indexes widen the evaluation by showing the advantage in terms of time (DIR^T_k) and cost (DIR^C_{kn}) of the intermodal option against trucking.

$$DIR^T_k = RI^T_{2k} - RI^T_{1k} \tag{6.8}$$

$$DIR^C_{kn} = \left(RI^c_{2kn} - RI^c_{1kn}\right) \times \beta_n \tag{6.9}$$

To support decision-making about the most suitable MoS and identify chains with the highest possibilities of success (main target), one unique indicator (port index PI_k) should be developed for every candidate port (*k*). This index must be able to reflect the competitiveness of the intermodal chain articulated through one MoS against the road alternative. Indeed, this information can be provided by the difference index of relevance in terms of time (DIR^T_k, see Equation 6.8). However, this does not occur for the difference index of relevance in terms of cost (DIR^C_{kn}, see Equation 6.9) since the latter is dependent on the analysis year (*n*). Consequently, Equations (6.10) and (6.11) show the port indexes in terms of time (PI^T_k) and cost (PI^C_k), where the latter collects the assessment of the whole time range (*N* = {1,2,... *n*}).

$$PI^T_k = DIR^T_k \tag{6.10}$$

$$PI^C_k = \sum_n \left(DIR^C_{kn}\right) \quad \forall n \in N \tag{6.11}$$

2.2 Sensitivity and risk analysis

While analysis of the multi-criteria decision matrix, defined in the first step, can quantify the performance of the chains involving different MoS, this matrix is built from a static scenario (for a particular moment). This involves considering that many inputs for the matrix will vary over the estimation time through forecasts for further scenarios ($\forall n \in N$). This fact, along with unknown variable estimation, leads to an assumed risk level on the results obtained from the first step. Thus, to determine the risk assumed with the decisions made in the first step, a sensitivity analysis is proposed for the port index values (Equations 6.10 and 6.11).

This analysis first involves identifying the main risk inputs considered in the matrix construction. Afterwards, through modifications of the values of these variables, several scenarios must be assessed. To avoid optimistic or pessimistic approaches (generation of static scenarios), the Monte Carlo method is suggested, since this method permits evaluating the port indexes through variations in the values of all necessary variables for simultaneous calculation (probability distributions are initially defined for those variables). As a result of this application, Monte Carlo analysis offers a probability distribution for the port indexes in the intermodal chains. Thus, through port index evaluation as good estimators of these distributions, the risk assumed with the decisions made from the first step can be determined (reliability). To measure the goodness level of the port indexes as estimators of their distributions (centred, consistent and efficient estimator), the following features must be considered:

- The bias: evaluated as the difference between the distribution mean and the base case (initial value for the port indexes from the first step).
- The consistency: determined as the distance between the most probable value in the distribution and the base case. The consistency rises with proximity.
- The efficiency: defined through the coefficient of variability. In this way, it is inversely proportional to the standard deviation.

While the identification of the risky variables is highly dependent on the framework, the following inputs often are key variables on the construction of the multi-criteria decision matrix:

- The port index in terms of time: population factors (α_h and α_j), the loading/unloading speed in port, waiting times in port, the truck speed and the vessel speed.
- The port index in terms of cost: population factors (α_h and α_j), the weighting factor for the recorded annual volume of traffic between the connected regions (βn), the road transport cost per km and the freight cost per transport unit. For this latter variable, assessing the fuel separately from the rest of the costs is recommended (for SSS the bunkering costs represent approximately 48% of the total freight costs, this is followed by the port costs, 28%, and the crew costs, 11% (Martínez-López et al., 2016)).

3 Application case to the European context

3.1 General

The most demanding requirements (reliability, frequency, scheduling) for freight traffic are imposed by food and perishable goods transport. Thus, despite the unpredictable consequences of Brexit in the EU context, the North Sea Region (NSR) was selected as a representative application case for the European context. The intensive roll-on/roll-off (ro-ro) traffic for food and perishable goods between the UK and the European continent (Food Port Project, 2013, Work Package 5: Market knowledge) indicates that the NSR will remain one of the busiest maritime areas of the world.

Rosyth port in Scotland was selected as the *studied port* due to the DFDS Seaways (Det Forenede Dampskibs-Selskab Seaways) decision in 2018 to finish the unique ro-ro maritime route between Scotland and continental Europe:

Rosyth-Zeebrugge (Belgium). In this way, this application case analyzes whether this maritime route was the most suitable for the intermodal chains, taking into account its competitiveness during the last four operation years of the service, from 2014 to 2017 ($N = \{1,2,...,4\}$). In this manner, the analysis completes the findings of the Food Port Project about this corridor (Food Port Project, 2014, Work Package 3: Corridor 1 – Rosyth-Zeebrugge ferry service) and it follows one of the recommendations from the Transport Research Institute of Edinburg (Food Port Project, 2014) to enhance the revision of ports involved in the service.

From the Food Port Project findings (Work Package 5: Market knowledge, 2013), the main food goods moved from Scotland are fish, whisky and retail and their main destinations are Germany, France and the Benelux zone (these regions were also identified as the main export destinations of Scotland in 2017: National Statics publication for Scotland, 2019). Consequently, one node per country was selected as an endpoint of the network in the continental coast ($J = \{1,2,3\}$, see Figure 6.1 and Table 6.1), Cologne, Lille and Amsterdam (with population weighting factors: α_j; $\forall j \in J$, see Table 6.2).

Regarding the hubs of the network (see Table 6.2), the studied port was Rosyth, and the candidate ports to establish an MoS ($K = \{1,2,3\}$) were Zeebrugge (Belgium), Rotterdam (Netherlands) and Bremerhaven (Germany). All these ports are collected as 'core ports' in the TEN-T (Regulation (EU) No. 1315/2013).

Table 6.1 Information about the trucking between Scotland and the European continent.

Scottish cities (h)	European cities (j)	Road distances (km)
Glasgow	Cologne	1219
	Lille	916
	Amsterdam	1170
Aberdeen	Cologne	1434
	Lille	1131
	Amsterdam	1384
Edinburgh	Cologne	1215
	Lille	912
	Amsterdam	1166

Table 6.2 Information about the capillary hauls in European continent and trunk hauls.

Continental Ports (k)		Zeebrugge		Rotterdam		Bremerhaven	
α_j (population ratio)	Continental nodes (j)	Road distance from the port to node (km)	Maritime distance from Rosyth (km)	Road distance from the port to the node (km)	Maritime distance from Rosyth (km)	Road distance from the port to the node (km)	Maritime distance from Rosyth (km)
27.61%	Cologne	305	750	255	728	378	843
31.50%	Lille	90		229		599	
40.89%	Amsterdam	262		78		354	

148 Alba Martínez-López and Lourdes Trujillo

Table 6.3 Information about the capillary hauls in Scotland.

a_h (population ratio) (%)	Road distance from the Rosyth port to cities (km)	Scottish nodes (h)
45.56	63	Glasgow
16.79	184	Aberdeen
37.65	23	Edinburgh

While all continental nodes are recognized as core nodes in the TEN-T (Regulation (EU) No. 1315/2013), only two Scottish nodes ($H = \{1,2,3\}$, Glasgow, Aberdeen and Edinburgh), Edinburg and Glasgow, are currently collected in the TEN-T as core nodes (weighting factors: a_h; $\forall h \in H$, see Table 6.3).

It is remarkable that the closest port to the continental nodes (*j*), Rotterdam, also articulates the shortest intermodal chain (971 km average distance, 25% by land) followed by Zeebrugge (1038 km, 28% by land) and Bremerhaven (1349 km, 37% by land).

3.2 Quantification of the port indexes

Even though the method permits a wide analysis of the competitiveness of every possible MoS by considering the particular conditions of every port involved, to simplify the application case, identical operative features were assumed for all ports. In this manner, the competitiveness analysis was carried out under identical conditions; this led to an assessment essentially based on the geographical chain obtained through different MoS. These results permitted the identification of which ports had the best conditions for the MoS and how far their current performances were from the assumed ones. Thus, the assumptions for the application case were:

- For all MoS, the technical features of the vessel *Finlandia Seaways*, which was operating between Zeebrugge and Rosyth up to 2018, were considered. This is a ro-ro vessel with GT = 11,530 t, 20 knots service speed and a cargo capacity of 1899 lanemetres (approximately 117 trailers) offering a service frequency of three departures per week in each direction.
- The trucks considered for the freight transport were five-axle trucks (refrigerated and articulated vehicle as in directive 96/53/CE). This involves 12.5-meter length and 24 tonnes for the maximum net weight.
- An average speed of eight trailers/(driver × hour) (one driver per 19 trucks; Martínez-López et al., 2015) was assumed for every port as an initial value for the loading/unloading ratio. Additionally, one hour was also considered in Rosyth for steaming time from/to the open sea (Food Port Project, 2014).
- European legislation was considered to determine the time invested in the trucking: maximum permitted speed for heavy goods vehicles (the majority of the EU member states determines a maximum speed of 80 km/h using speed

limiters, directive 92/6/EEC, 92/24/EEC, 2004/11/EC, Regulation 165/2014) and the minimum rest periods for the drivers (Regulation 561/2006 of European Parliament).
- A unitary cost for road transport (euro/km) was estimated for every studied year (2014–2017, 1339, 1290, 1230, 1323 €/km respectively) from the Observatory of Road Freight Transport Costs (Ministry of Public Works of the Government of Spain 2014, 2015, 2016 and 2017).
- The port dues were assumed identical for every port (identical conditions evaluation); in this way the freight cost will vary only with maritime distance on the MoS. The calculation equations published in 2015 about the freight costs for the NSR (Martínez-López et al., 2015) were considered and updated for every year of the range.

Figure 6.2 shows the port indexes in terms of time (PI^T_k) and cost (PI^C_k). All indexes are positives for the MoS through Zeebrugge and Rotterdam; this involves

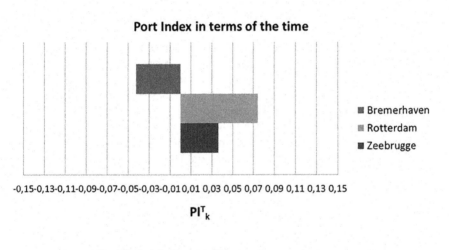

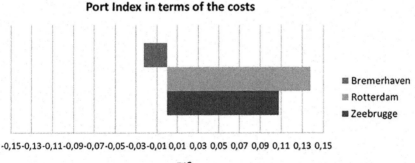

Figure 6.2 Port indexes in terms of time (PI^T_k) and cost (PI^C_k) for the intermodality through Rosyth port.

a favourable situation for intermodality. However, the situation changes when the intermodal chain is articulated through Bremerhaven. Paying attention to the absolute values reached in the analysis for both port indexes (in time and costs), the MoS with the highest possibility to offer a competitive alternative to trucking is Rosyth-Rotterdam. Indeed, the greatest advantage for intermodality is based on costs (as expected), with time being the most limiting parameter for competitiveness (Figure 6.2).

Despite the higher competitiveness of the intermodal chains through Rotterdam (under ideal conditions) over trucking (positive port indexes in terms of time and cost – see Figure 6.2), the results obtained in this quantitative analysis also confirm the convenience of exploring alternative continental ports for an MoS between Scotland and continental Europe (Food Port Project, 2014).

The quantitative step permits further analysis based on the convenience of one transport mode versus another for every pair of nodes (see Equations 6.1 and 6.2; when the value of the indexes is greater than 0.5 the advantage is to that transport mode). From this analysis, one relevant finding can be drawn, the competitiveness of the intermodal chains is based not just on the land distance from/to the boarding port (common praxis for the boarding port choice), but also on the configuration of the total network in comparison to trucking. Thus, despite the proximity of Lille to Zeebrugge (90 km, see Table 6.2), both transport alternatives proved to be equally competitive in terms of time for service from Glasgow to Lille through MoS Rosyth-Zeebrugge ($I^T_{1121} = I^T_{2121} = 0.5$, see Table 6.4). The opposite occurs for transport between Glasgow and Cologne through the same MoS. In this latter case, Cologne is the farthest node from the Zeebrugge port (305 km, see Table 6.2); despite this, the intermodal option shows an advantage over trucking in terms of time ($I^T_{1111} = 0.49$; $I^T_{2121} = 0.51$, see Table 6.4).

Table 6.4 Port index in terms of time for the application case in Europe.

Studied Ports (k)		Zeebrugge		Rotterdam		Bremerhaven	
Transport alternatives (i)		Truck	MoS	Truck	MoS	Truck	MoS
Scottish nodes (h)	Continental nodes (j)	I^T_{1hj1}	I^T_{2hj1}	I^T_{1hj2}	I^T_{2hj2}	I^T_{1hj3}	I^T_{2hj3}
Glasgow	Cologne	0.49	0.51	0.47	0.53	0.52	0.48
	Lille	0.50	0.50	0.50	0.50	0.57	0.43
	Amsterdam	0.49	0.51	0.46	0.54	0.52	0.48
Aberdeen	Cologne	0.39	0.61	0.38	0.62	0.42	0.58
	Lille	0.49	0.51	0.49	0.51	0.56	0.44
	Amsterdam	0.39	0.61	0.36	0.64	0.42	0.58
Edinburgh	Cologne	0.49	0.51	0.47	0.53	0.51	0.49
	Lille	0.50	0.50	0.50	0.50	0.57	0.43
	Amsterdam	0.49	0.51	0.45	0.55	0.52	0.48

3.3 Sensitivity and risk analysis

To determine the risk assumed with the decisions made from the quantitative analysis (first step), the multi-criteria decision matrix previously built (in the first step) is evaluated through Monte Carlo simulations in this second step of the method. This permits an assessment of the results by considering different working scenarios that are the result of modifying the values of the risk variables in the matrix (their values were estimated or forecasted in the first step). For this application case (Scotland–continental Europe), all generated scenarios belong to the past (2014–2017; $N = \{1,2,\ldots,4\}$), consequently all values for the variables are already known; however, the consulted sources involved a risk (diverse formats). For this reason, triangular probability distributions were assumed for all variables with a variation range of 20% between the most and the least probable values.

Figure 6.3 shows the probability distribution shapes obtained from the Monte Carlo simulations for both port indexes (2,000,000 tests with a 100% certainty level).[1] According to the results, all the resulting probability distribution shapes are very similar for both port indexes regardless of the continental port choice and fit beta distributions. For the port index in terms of the time (PI_k^T), this homogenous behaviour is mainly due to the geographical location of the ports and, consequently, to a similar configuration of the transport networks (relative weight of the transport modes in the intermodal solution and the road distance for the unimodal solution).

A further understanding of this reality can be reached from the sensitivity analysis (see Table 6.5).

The two most influential parameters on the port index in terms of time (PI_k^T) for all ports (see Table 6.5) were the truck speed (negative influence on the index) and the vessel speed (positive influence). The time invested in the road transport is a stepped function (Sandberg-Hanssen et al., 2012) that is strongly affected not just by the truck speed but also by Regulation 561/2006, which determines a driver's maximum continuous driving hours per day. In this way, depending on the network configuration, small modifications of truck speed could significantly modify the time invested in trucking (a difference of one day's travel). This is not appreciated in the current application case (see Figure 6.3), where the most influential variables have a similar relative weighting on the variance (see Table 6.5). This justifies the stability shown in the distributions obtained in the simulations (see Figure 6.3).

Likewise, the probability distributions obtained for the port index in terms of costs (PI_k^C) have proved to be very stable by fitting beta theoretical distributions (see Figure 6.3) as well. In this case, a clear prevalence of road costs (negative) over the rest of the inputs indicates a low capacity to modify the expected results (controllable variables). Even though the values obtained in the sensitivity analysis are similar for all ports (see Table 6.5), Bremerhaven port has shown particular sensitivity to the configuration of the transport network in the continent (population of continental nodes, 12.51%) by reducing the relative weight of the road cost

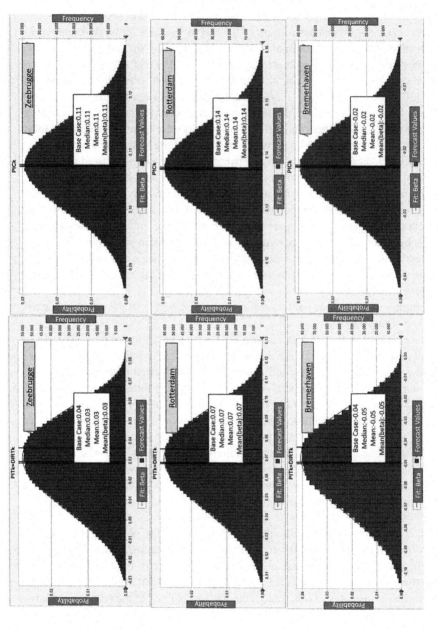

Figure 6.3 Probability distributions of the port indexes for the case of Scotland–continental Europe, obtained using Monte Carlo simulations in terms of time PI^T_k (top) and costs PI^C_k (bottom).

Table 6.5 Contribution of the inputs to the variance of the port index distributions.

Contribution to the variance IP_k^T				Contribution to the variance IP_k^C			
Assumptions	BEZEE*	NLRTM	DEBRV	Assumptions	BEZEE	NLRTM	DEBRV
Truck speed (km/h)	52.56%	50.25%	50.60%	Road cost (€/km)	86.92%	81.27%	75.15%
Vessel speed (kn)	45.44%	47.39%	47.37%	Freight costs bunkering	12.56%	11.54%	11.93%
Loading/ unloading speed (unids/h)	1.86%	2.03%	1.48%	Freight costs without bunkering	0.08%	0.08%	0.06%
Population of Scottish nodes	0.10%	0.09%	0.14%	Population of Scottish nodes	0.13%	0.12%	0.10%
Population of continental nodes	0.03%	0.23%	0.41%	Population of continental nodes	0.06%	6.77%	12.51%
				Yearly cargo volume (tonnes)	0.25%	0.22%	0.24%

Note: * indicates international seaport names: BEZEE (Zeebrugge), NLRTM (Rotterdam) and DEBRV (Bremerhaven).

(75.15%). This is due to the long land stretches in its intermodal chains (37%) compared to the chains using the other candidate ports (25% through Rotterdam and 28% through Zeebrugge). Despite the low relevance obtained for node population (relative distribution of the load among the nodes), Lille has been the most influential continental node in all cases and for both indexes (PI_k^T and PI_k^C).

Table 6.6 shows the statistic results obtained for the probability distributions of the Monte Carlo simulations (see Figure 6.3). The bias taken in the port selection according to the quantitative values reached is low in all cases (the difference between the distribution means and the index values); therefore, the port indexes have proven to be centred estimators. In addition, the port indexes are consistent estimators since the distance between the most probable value and the base case is also low in all cases (see Figure 6.3). Nevertheless, the performance of port indexes is not so homogenous among ports when their efficiency is evaluated. Paying attention to the coefficient of variability (Table 6.2), dispersion is relevant for the port index in terms of the time, reaching a maximum level for the distribution through Zeebrugge and a minimum through Rotterdam.

As a conclusion of this analysis, the port indexes have proven to be good estimators (centred, consistent and efficient estimators) in terms of the costs for all MoS evaluated. This means that the decisions made by considering the quantitative values reached in the first step are reliable. However, the time port indexes are shown as low-efficiency estimators, especially for analysis of the routes through Zeebrugge. Therefore, decisions taken based on time port index values should be taken with precaution.

Table 6.6 Statistical results from the Monte Carlo simulations.

Statistics	PI_k^T			PI_k^C		
	BEZEE*	NLRTM	DEBRV	BEZEE	NLRTM	DEBRV
Base Case: Value PI_k^T or PI_k^C	0.04	0.07	−0.04	0.11	0.14	−0.02
Mean	0.03	0.07	−0.05	0.11	0.14	−0.02
Median	0.03	0.07	−0.05	0.11	0.14	−0.02
Standard Deviation	0.02	0.02	0.02	0.01	0.01	0.01
Coeff. of Variability	0.7365	0.3218	−0.3926	0.0704	0.0586	−0.2982
/Mean-Base Case/	0.01	0.00	0.01	0.00	0.00	0.00

Note: * indicates international seaport names: BEZEE (Zeebrugge), NLRTM (Rotterdam) and DEBRV (Bremerhaven).

As a main finding of this application case, Rotterdam could be the most suitable continental port to establish an MoS with Rosyth. Aside from reaching the best quantitative results (first step), the high risk assumed by Zeebrugge's index in terms of the time and its greater dependence on road attributes (non-controllable inputs see Table 6.5) leads to Rotterdam having a preferential position as a port choice.

4 Application case to eastern Africa

4.1 General

While in all contexts, the intermodality through MoS attempts to reduce road use for door-to-door transport, its motivation is highly dependent on the region analyzed. Thus, the lack of a complete road connection among all possible nodes is the main reason for eastern Africa's interest in intermodality through SSS. This fact, along with the elevated costs for building and maintaining land corridors with significant costs for border crossings and taking into account the size of the economics of this region (Haralambides et al., 2011), drives the consideration of intermodality with a seaborne stretch as a suitable solution to transport commodities among the eastern African countries. Therefore, unlike the case of Europe, evaluation of the relative competitiveness between modal transport alternatives is not suitable in this framework, since trucking is not often an option, forcing a modification of the initial approach.

Since the articulation of intermodal chains is highly dependent on the port's feasibility to be a load consolidation centre and this capacity is not ensured in this application case, the route analysis should be focused on port performance in this role. Consequently, the analysis of the eastern African ports should prioritize studying the combined performance of the port services for SSS traffic (facilities, effectiveness of cargo handling systems, cargo dwell time, ship turnaround time and port duties) with their capillary hauls (mainly conditioned by the location of the port with respect to the nodes). This involves a modification on the transport

Multi-criteria decision method applied 155

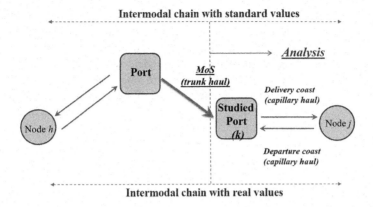

Figure 6.4 The 'one-to-many' model applied for eastern Africa application.

network's configuration regarding the initial suggestion of the method (many-to-many model, see Figure 6.1). Figure 6.4 shows the redefinition of the transport network for this application case ('one-to-many' transport model) where the importance of the landlocked countries in the port hinterlands is collected.

As a consequence of the foregoing, the initial method was modified to provide information about the ports with the intention to cover two priority targets for this region, the identification of weak points of the ports, like consolidation centres of the load inside the intermodal chains, and how far from standard their performance is in that role.

Even though the difficulty of finding reliable historical data about port operations limited the analysis to a unique year, which, therefore, eliminated a variable ($N = \{1,2,\ldots n\}$), a new analysis variable was introduced, the kind of vessels suitable for SSS ($Q = \{1,2,3\}$): container ships, Ro-Ro ships and Ro-Pax ships. This offered a wider analysis for the identification of weak points in port performance.

To simplify port comparison in the region, a unique port indicator was provided for the performance assessment, the port index (PI_k). The adapted method assumes an identical relevance for all kinds of compatible fleets for SSS (see Equations 6.13 and 6.14) and for both attributes of time and cost (see Equation 6.12). In this way, both port indexes (PI_k^T and PI_k^C) are integrated into just one (PI_k).

$$PI_k = \frac{1}{2}*\left(PI^T_{\ k}+PI^C_{\ k}\right); \tag{6.12}$$

$$PI^T_{\ k} = 1/3*\sum_{q=1}^{3} PI^T_{\ kq}; \qquad \forall q \in Q \tag{6.13}$$

$$PI^C_{\ k} = 1/3*\sum_{q=1}^{3} PI^C_{\ kq}; \qquad \forall q \in Q \tag{6.14}$$

As was said before, due to the particulars of the studied region, the port indexes integrate the comparison between port performance (with real information about the ports and their hinterlands) and a standard performance instead of a comparison between transport modes (see Figure 6.4). Consequently, Equations (6.15)–(6.18) collect the adaptation of the initial method to the eastern African case where the superscript 's' represents the standard values. Thus, the closer the port index (PI_k) is to one, the higher competitiveness of the port for intermodal chains.

$$I^C_{jkq} = 1 - \frac{Cost_{jkq}}{Cost_{jkq} + Cost^S_{jkq}} \qquad (6.15)$$

$$I^T_{jkq} = 1 - \frac{Time_{jk}}{Time_{jkq} + Time^S_{jkq}} \qquad (6.16)$$

$$PI^C_{kq} = RI^C_{kq} = \sum_j \left(I^C_{jkq} \times \alpha_j \right) \qquad \forall j \in J \qquad (6.17)$$

$$PI^T_{kq} = RI^T_{kq} = \sum_j \left(I^T_{jkq} \times \alpha_j \right) \qquad \forall j \in J \qquad (6.18)$$

As can be seen in Figure 6.4, aside from the capillary hauls performance and the port activities on land (loading process, one-stop centre clearance time and truck processing, etc.), the modified method also analyzes the maritime operations whose realization is managed by the port, such as the pilot, towing and anchoring services. In addition, the ship actual waiting time (the waiting time for the ship from its arrival at the fairway buoy to the pilot on boarding) is also included in the analysis. Since the method does not consider the whole trunk haul (the maritime route, see Figure 6.4) in the intermodal analysis, the studied port is coincident with the candidate port (k). In this case, three ports were selected as *studied ports* $(K = \{1,2,3\})$ due to their activity volume: Djibouti (in the north), Mombasa (in the centre) and Durban (in the south). The node selection for every studied port $(J = \{1,2,3\}$, see Figure 6.4) took into account that, while the coastal countries in eastern Africa exclusively use their own ports, the landlocked countries use several ports (Haralambides et al., 2011) by overlapping the port hinterlands. The selected nodes (population weighting factors: α_j; $\forall j \in J$) are:

- Djibouti: Djibouti, Addis Ababa (Ethiopia) and Dire Dawa (Ethiopia);
- Mombasa (Kenya): Nairobi (Kenya), Yuba (South Sudan) and Kampala (Uganda); and
- Durban (South Africa): Johannesburg-Pretoria-Ekurhuleni (South Africa), Harare (Zimbabwe) and Gaborone (Botswana).

The obtained transport networks show the following average distances for the hinterlands: Djibouti: 656 km, Mombasa: 781 km and Durban: 869 km. To carry out the simulations, 2017 data (Martínez-López et al., 2019) were considered.

Table 6.7 Technical features for standard vessels operating under SSS conditions.

Features	Feeder	Ro-ro	Ro-Pax
Gross tonnage (GT)	10,585	15,224	41,700
Volume (m³)	35,000	51,730	137,728
Cargo units	1036 TEUs	105 trucks	173 trucks
Vessel speed VB (kn)	19.3	19.5	21
Reference vessel	*Conmar Bay* (IMO: 9458975)	*La Surprise* (IMO: 9198719)	*MV Pont-Aven* (IMO: 9268708)

In turn, the technical features of the trucks used for the European case were applied to the eastern African case, and the technical features assumed for the vessels in all simulations are those collected in Table 6.7. Finally, the standard values for the calculations (see Equations 6.15 and 6.16) were assumed from a medium-size European port with MoS activity: the port of Vigo (Vigo-St. Nazaire).

4.2 Port index calculations

According to the aggregated results (see Figure 6.5), no studied port reaches the standard performance as a consolidation centre for loads ($PI_k < 0.5$). However, the closest performance to European standards is Mombasa, followed by Durban and Djibouti. Paying attention to the results achieved in terms of the time and costs (see Figure 6.5), the eastern African ports exceed the European standards in terms of cost ($PI_k^C > 0.5$) but this does not occur in terms of time ($PI_k^T < 0.5$).

From an analysis of the detailed information about the port index in terms of time (see Table 6.8), the road performance for capillary hauls is mainly responsible for these low values. Moreover, general findings can be drawn from the port performance as well, owing to the elevated transit and queue times in the ports (one-stop centre clearance time and truck processing); the cargo handling berth productivity was not as relevant as expected in the port times (see 1.2.1 in Table 6.8).

The remarkable deviation for the time invested in the maritime operations (point 1.1.2 in Table 6.8) compared to the European standards is mainly due to the inclusion of the ship's actual waiting times (pre-berthing times) in this item.

Table 6.9 outlines further information about the contributions of different items to the port index in terms of cost. Information about tugging and loading services is not shown since the first is not required for the European standard (SSS traffic) and the second is not carried out by port drivers in Ro-Pax vessels. As in the time performance, in all ports, the influence of the road determines the sense of the intermodality in terms of cost compared to the standard European port. Focusing the attention on the contribution of the ports (maritime stretch, see Table 6.9), it can be concluded that the cost deviation in the seaborne leg is dependent on the kind of vessel. The main reason is the tariff structure for the ports, which directly relates the gross tonnage (or the volume) of the vessels with the charges. This structure severely penalizes the rolled cargo vessels with a low ratio of occupation for the cargo volume.

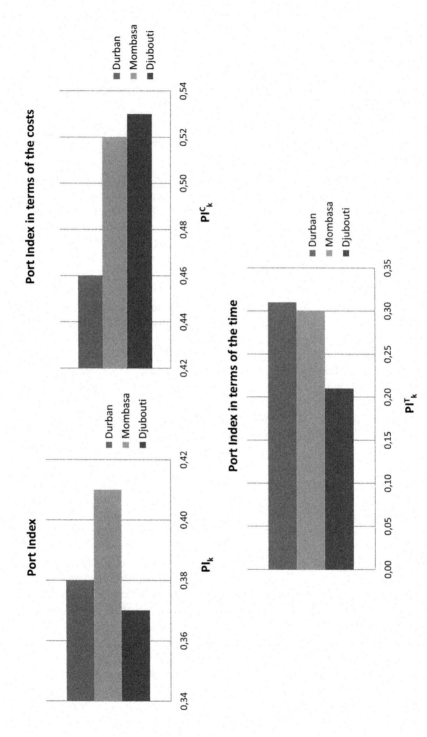

Figure 6.5 Port indexes (PI_k), port indexes in terms of time (PI^T_k) and cost (PI^C_k) for the eastern African ports.

Table 6.8 Disaggregation of the port index in terms of time for the eastern African ports.

		Container (PI^T_{k1})	Ro-Ro (PI^T_{k2})	Ro-Pax (PI^T_{k3})	PI^T_k
1. Intermodal transport (h)	Djibouti (k = 1)	0.22	0.21	0.21	0.21
	Mombasa (k = 2)	0.33	0.30	0.30	0.31
	Durban (k = 3)	0.32	0.30	0.30	0.31
1.1 Time invested in the land stretches (h)	Djibouti (k = 1)	0.06	0.06	0.06	0.06
	Mombasa (k = 2)	0.13	0.13	0.13	0.13
	Durban (k = 3)	0.16	0.16	0.16	0.16
1.2 Time invested in maritime stretch (h)	Djibouti (k = 1)	0.28	0.28	0.27	0.27
	Mombasa (k = 2)	0.39	0.43	0.41	0.41
	Durban (k = 3)	0.40	0.39	0.38	0.39
1.2.1 Port Times (h)	Djibouti (k = 1)	0.29	0.28	0.28	0.28
	Mombasa (k = 2)	0.40	0.45	0.43	0.43
	Durban (k = 3)	0.44	0.43	0.43	0.43
1.1.2 Maritime operations (h)	Djibouti (k = 1)	0.05	0.05	0.05	0.05
	Mombasa (k = 2)	0.08	0.08	0.08	0.08
	Durban (k = 3)	0.03	0.03	0.03	0.03

Table 6.9 Disaggregation of the port index in terms of cost for the eastern African ports.

		Container (PI^C_{k1})	Ro-Ro (PI^C_{k2})	Ro-Pax (PI^C_{k3})	PI^C_k
1. Intermodal transport ($)	Djibouti (k = 1)	0.54	0.52	0.53	0.53
	Mombasa (k = 2)	0.53	0.51	0.51	0.52
	Durban (k = 3)	0.46	0.45	0.46	0.46
1.1 Costs of the land stretches ($/t)	Djibouti (k = 1)	0.54	0.54	0.54	0.54
	Mombasa (k = 2)	0.54	0.54	0.54	0.54
	Durban (k = 3)	0.47	0.47	0.47	0.47
1.2 Cost of the maritime stretch ($)	Djibouti (k = 1)	0.50	0.45	0.39	0.45
	Mombasa (k = 2)	0.47	0.37	0.26	0.36
	Durban (k = 3)	0.40	0.37	0.35	0.37
1.2.1 The ship duty ($/t)	Djibouti (k = 1)	0.74	0.42	0.44	0.54
	Mombasa (k = 2)	0.59	0.20	0.20	0.33
	Durban (k = 3)	0.63	0.25	0.25	0.37
1.2.2 The load duty ($/t)	Djibouti (k = 1)	0.49	0.40	0.40	0.43
	Mombasa (k = 2)	0.29	0.27	0.30	0.29
	Durban (k = 3)	0.23	0.34	0.40	0.32
1.2.2 The pilot duty ($/t)	Djibouti (k = 1)	0.63	0.53	0.32	0.49
	Mombasa (k = 2)	0.43	0.35	0.16	0.31
	Durban (k = 3)	0.36	0.35	0.32	0.34
1.2.4 The tug services ($/t)	Djibouti (k = 1)	—	—	—	—
	Mombasa (k = 2)	—	—	—	—
	Durban (k = 3)	—	—	—	—
1.2.5 The mooring services ($/t)	Djibouti (k = 1)	0.57	0.57	0.44	0.49
	Mombasa (k = 2)	0.44	0.38	0.32	0.38
	Durban (k = 3)	0.81	0.77	0.72	0.76
1.2.6 The loading services ($/t)	Djibouti (k = 1)	0.50	0.50	—	0.50
	Mombasa (k = 2)	0.55	0.47	—	0.51
	Durban (k = 3)	0.49	0.41	—	0.45

This issue is partially resolved in the European standard port by means of joining this charge to the port time of the vessel (highly influenced by the loading time). In this regard, Djibouti introduces the most adequate tariff structure to the features of the SSS transport, consequently its port index value in terms of costs is the highest (see Table 6.9 and Figure 6.5).

5 Conclusions

The performance of the intermodal chains though MoS has been under analysis in the last years. Reports and studies have shown several possible improvement points for the MoS articulation. Among them, the role of the ports arises as a concerning issue. This fact has motivated the need to review the choice criteria for the ports involved in TEN-T, their classification and, consequently, their convenience within the scope of MoS. This chapter attempts to contribute to port evaluation by offering a multi-criteria decision method able to analyze the opportunities for the success of the entire intermodal chain through different MoS versus the trucking alternative. The method proposes a many-to-many transport network and provides a quantitative and qualitative analysis. The first step ranks the candidate ports for the establishment of an MoS in according to the time and cost attributes. The qualitative evaluation determines the reliability of the decision made from the first analysis.

Thus, from the application of the method to the European case, the following conclusions can be drawn: even though Rosyth-Zeebrugge articulated competitive intermodal chains regarding trucking, the results obtained in terms of time assumed a significant risk. To this regard, the MoS Rosyth-Rotterdam offered better quantitative and qualitative results for the intermodal chains between Scotland and the European continent. Consequently, the convenience of assessing alternative continental ports beyond Zeebrugge for an MoS between Scotland and continental Europe has been confirmed. Likewise, the results also confirm the possible mistake assumed when the boarding port is uniquely chosen by considering the land distance between the node and the port.

Even though the method's utility has been proven through a European application case (Scotland–continental Europe), the potential of the method exceeds the European context. This chapter includes the application of the first step of the method (quantitative analysis) to the eastern African region. This latter application case has required adaptation of the initial method to both the needs and reality (constraints) of the region. In such a way, the method is modified by offering a unique port index in order to evaluate the port performance as a consolidation centre for the load in the intermodal chains. Among the analyzed ports in this application case, the Mombasa port proved to be the closest one to the standard reference. In all cases, the road performance was the most influent variable on the results obtained. However, the results also revealed as an essential improvement point the pre-berthing waiting times (especially in Djibouti) and the lack of suitability of the port due to the particular conditions of the SSS fleet, with low cargo ratios.

Note

1 The certainty level involves the percentage of values in the variation range compared to all values obtained through the simulation.

References

Commission of the European Communities (2001), White paper: European transport policy for 2010: Time to decide, Brussels

Council of the European Union (1992), Council directive 92/6/EEC of 10 February 1992 on the installation and use of speed limitation devices for certain categories of motor vehicles in the Community. Official Journal of the European Communities L 57/27 of 2 March 1992.

Council of the European Union (1992), Council directive 92/24/EEC of 31 March 1992 relating to speed limitation devices or similar speed limitation on-board systems of certain categories of motor vehicles. Official Journal of the European Communities L 129/154 of 14 May 1992.

Council of the European Union (1996), Council directive 96/53/EC of 25 July 1996 laying down for certain road vehicles circulating within the community the maximum authorized dimensions in national and international traffic and the maximum authorized weights in international traffic. Official Journal of the European Communities L 235/59 of 17 September 1996.

Cullinane, K., & Toy, N. (2000), Identifying influential attributes in freight route/mode choice decisions: A content analysis. *Transportation Research Part E: Logistics and Transportation Review*, 36 (1), pp. 41–53.

Daganzo, C. (2005), *Logistic Systems Analysis*. Berlin: Springer.

European Commission (2017), Motorways of the sea: An ex-post evaluation on the development of the concept from 2001 and possible ways forward. Directorate-General for Mobility and Transport (DG MOVE).

European Parliament and Council (2004), Decision no 884/2004/EC of the European parliament and of the council of 29 April 2004 amending decision no 1692/96/EC on community guidelines for the development of the trans-European transport network. Official Journal of the European Union L 167 of 30 April 2004.

European Parliament and Council (2004), Directive 2004/11/EC of the European parliament and of the council of 11 February 2004 amending council directive 92/24/EEC relating to speed limitation devices or similar speed limitation on-board systems of certain categories of motor vehicles. Official Journal of the European Union L 44/19 of 14 February 2004.

European Parliament and Council (2006), Regulation (EC) No. 561/2006 of the European parliament and of the council of 15 March 2006 on the harmonisation of certain social legislation relating to road transport and amending council regulations (EEC) no 3821/85 and (EC) no 2135/98 and repealing council regulation (EEC) no 3820/85. Official Journal of the European Union L 102/1 of 11 April 2006.

European Parliament and Council (2013), Regulation (EU) No. 1315/2013 of the European parliament and the council of 11 December 2013 on Union guidelines for the development of the trans-European transport network and repealing decision no 661/2010/EU. Official Journal of the European Union L 348/1 of 20 December 2013.

European Parliament and Council (2014), Regulation (EU) no 165/2014 of the European parliament and of the council of 4 February 2014 on tachographs in road transport, repealing Council Regulation (EEC) no 3821/85 on recording equipment in road transport and amending Regulation (EC) No. 561/2006 of the European parliament and of the council on the harmonisation of certain social legislation relating to road transport. Official Journal of the European Union L 60/1 of 28 February 2014.

Food Port Project (2013), Work package 5: Market knowledge. Available at http://archive.northsearegion.eu/ivb/projects/details/&tid=129.

Food Port Project (2014), Work package 3: Corridor 1 – Rosyth-Zeebrugge ferry service. Available at http://archive.northsearegion.eu/files/repository/20141211142353_WP3_1_Cor1_Rosyth_Zeebrugge_ferry_service_Report_Motorways_of_Seas_Options_Aug_2014_Food_Port_North_Sea_Rgion_Programme.pdf

García-Menendez, L., & Feo-Valero, M. (2009), European common transport policy and short sea shipping: -Empirical evidence based on modal choice models. *Transport Reviews*, 29 (2), pp. 239–259.

Haralambides, H., Veldman, S., Van Drunen, K., & Liu, M. (2011), Determinants of a regional port-centric logistics hub: The case of East-Africa. *Maritime Economics and Logistics*, 13 (1), pp. 78–97.

Martínez-López, A., Caamaño, P., & Míguez, M. (2016), Influence of external costs on the optimisation of container fleets by operating under motorways of the sea conditions. *International Journal of Shipping and Transport Logistics*, 8 (6), pp. 653–686.

Martínez-López, A., Kronbak, J., & Jiang, L. (2015), Cost and time models for the evaluation of intermodal chains by using short sea shipping in the North Sea Region: The Rosyth-Zeebrugge route. *International Journal of Shipping and Transport Logistics*, 7 (4), pp. 494–520.

Martínez-López, A., Trujillo, L., Chica, M. (2019), Assessment of the feasibility of the Eastern African ports to articulate intermodal chains through Short Sea Shipping. *IAME 2019 Conference, June 25th–28th, Athens, Greece.*

Ministry of Public Works of the Government of Spain (2014), Observatory of road freight transport costs, January, Madrid.

Ministry of Public Works of the government of Spain (2015), Observatory of road freight transport costs, January, Madrid.

Ministry of Public Works of the Government of Spain (2016), Observatory of road freight transport costs, January, Madrid.

Ministry of Public Works of the Government of Spain (2017), Observatory of road freight transport costs, January, Madrid.

Sandberg-Hanssen, T., Andreas-Marthisen, T., & Jorgensen, F. (2012), Generalized transport costs in intermodal freight transport. *Social and Behavioural Sciences*, Special Issue: Proceedings of EWGT2012–15th Meeting of the EURO Working Group on Transportation, September, Paris, Vol. 54, pp. 189–200.

Scottish Government (2019), Export statistics Scotland 2017. National Statics publication for Scotland.

Simpson, B. (2018), Motorways of the sea: Detailed implementation plan of the European coordinator. Mobility and Transport, European Commission.

Van Oort, F., & Stam, E. (2005), Agglomeration economies and entrepreneurship: Testing for spatial externalities in the Dutch ICT industry. *Max Planck Institute for Research into Economics Systems Discussion Papers on Entrepreneurship, Growth and Public Policy*, No. 0905.

7 The economic impact of tourism on the Motorways of the Sea Nantes–Gijón

José F. Baños Pino, Luis Valdés Peláez, Eduardo Del Valle Tuero and Emma Zapico Fernández

1 Introduction

The notion of the so-called Motorways of the Sea (MoS) was mentioned for the first time in the White Paper on Transport published by the European Union (see European Commission, 2001). In that document, the relevance of sea transport is highlighted as a key factor for sustainable development, and more specifically, for establishing connections between outlying regions, thus decreasing the environmental impact of road transport and traffic congestion on particular routes.

In the last few years, MoS, primarily intended for freight transportation, have also become a popular means of transport for tourists wishing to travel to certain holiday destinations. Furthermore, the technical characteristics of roll-on/roll-off (Ro-Ro) ships make them suitable both for tourists travelling in their own vehicles as well as for foot passengers. This new concept became more than evident in the MoS approved in 2009, which saw the opening in September 2010 of a connection between El Musel Port in Gijón (Spain) and Nantes-St Nazaire Harbour in France. One year after the line began operating, in September 2011, more than 34,000 tourists had benefitted from this service, with the added value that they would not necessarily limit their sightseeing to the cities located at the ports of call but would venture to other locations further away.

Despite several years of successful service, in 2014 the line stopped operating once the financial support ended. Since then there has been a growing interest by the firm Baleària for the reopening of the line. They have already made a proposal, and negotiations between the different governments and the company are currently underway.

Although the European Union does not currently provide funding for MoS, the EU programme 'Connecting Europe' has granted aid to the aforementioned company in order to convert the engines of five of its vessels to liquefied natural gas (LNG), with one of these ferries poised to connect Gijón and Nantes-St Nazaire.

It is expected that by the end of 2020 or early 2021, the shipping company Baleària will re-establish the ferry line service. Therefore, one of the main aims of this study is to determine in a tourist context the economic effects of re-establishing the MoS and its viability, given the size of the new vessel put into service as well as the journey frequencies, and, additionally, compare them with cruise activity in the port of Gijón. Consequently, this chapter will focus on the use by tourists of one of the western European MoS. This is an aspect little discussed in the literature, since most of the works have focused on studying MoS characteristics from the perspective of freight transport (Martínez-López et al., 2015; Seoane et al., 2017; Santos and Soares, 2017); Baños et al. (2018) is one of the few exceptions.

The structure of this chapter is as follows. Section 2 reviews the principal characteristics of the MoS Nantes–Gijón. In section 3 a descriptive analysis of touristic demand of the MoS is performed, while an econometric estimation of the determinants of the tourist expenditure incurred in Asturias by users of the MoS is presented in section 4. The study of its economic impact, together with the main results obtained, appear in section 5. Finally, in section 6, the most relevant conclusions reached and their implications for economic policy are highlighted.

2 The Motorways of the Sea Gijón–Nantes

The MoS Gijón–Nantes came into operation on 9 September 2010, and it was conceived both for freight and passenger transport. Its main objective was to decongest trans-Pyrenees roads through three weekly connections from both harbours with approximately 14 hours' journey time, covering 274 nautical miles.

However, despite the favourable results obtained in terms of traffic, the end of the subsidy, together with a lack of promotion and the commissioning of a new MoS in Vigo, caused LD Lines to cancel its activity between Nantes and Gijón on 16 September 2014 (see Figure 7.1).

Four years after the closure of the MoS Nantes–Gijón the European Union approved, with the support of the Gijón Port Authority, the project of the shipping company Baleària to revive the line. Baleària is one of the principal Spanish shipping companies in freight and passenger transport, with a major presence in the Mediterranean.

Sicilia is the name of the vessel which will cover the Gijón–Nantes line, a Ro-Pax with accommodation capacity for 950 passengers in their cabins or reclining seats, almost double that of the previous vessel, the *Norman Atlantic*[1] with a capacity of 500 passengers. Likewise, the *Sicilia* has 2000 lanemetres which allow loading 100 trucks, an inferior load capacity to that of the *Norman Atlantic* which permits 120 trucks. The vessel has a breadth of 25.6 metres, has an overall length of 186 metres and is equipped with two 9450 kW engines (each).

Due to growing concern within the EU about the use of more sustainable fuels, the reduction of the noise generated by ships and the price of fuel, the reopening of this MoS will be dependent on the shipping company's LNG retrofits for the ferry which will sail in the Gijón–Nantes line. Specifically, through a global project called 'LNGHIVE2 Vessels demand: Green market and smart links – LNG solutions for smart maritime links in Spanish core ports', the shipping company will receive a maximum contribution of 11,797,424 euros from the European Union in order to retrofit five Ro-Pax vessels and adapt them to the use of LNG, instead of fuel oil. Total eligible costs are calculated to be around 58,987,122 euros, which implies that EU support represents 20% of the latter amount.

Thus, it is now essential to strengthen the environmental consideration of the new proposal. To do this, Vallejo-Pinto et al. (2019) analyze the emissions of the

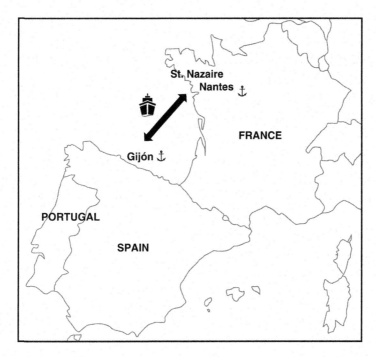

Figure 7.1 MoS Gijón–Nantes.
Source: Author's own elaboration.

Table 7.1 Motorways of the Sea (MoS) timetables.

Gijón–Nantes				*Nantes–Gijón*			
Departures		*Arrivals*		*Departures*		*Arrivals*	
Day	Hour	Day	Hour	Day	Hour	Day	Hour
Sunday	15:00	Monday	06:00	Monday	19:00	Tuesday	11:30
Tuesday	19:00	Wednesday	11:30	Wednesday	19:00	Thursday	11:30
Thursday	19:00	Friday	11:30	Friday	23:00	Saturday	14:00

Source: Author's own elaboration from Port Authority of Gijón.

previous LD Line vessel that operated the MoS in comparison with road freight transport. They conclude that environmental gains depend crucially on the type of itineraries. Nevertheless, the use of LNG as fuel instead of diesel would clearly prove more environmentally friendly.

The period for modernizing the ship concludes in December 2020, and consequently, it is expected that the reinstatement of the line will be effective by the middle of 2021. Additionally, it is necessary to install an LNG loading facility for ships in the docks of Gijón port. Table 7.1 shows weekly services offered by the

166 *José F. Baños Pino et al.*

previous line. It is expected that the new timetable will be similar, as previous experience demonstrates that these schedules are those that best fit with real traffic.

3 Descriptive analysis of transportation demand of the MoS Gijón–Nantes

The data used in this study were collected from a survey carried out by the authors between July and November 2013. We have used information for a total of 924 valid face-to-face interviews with MoS users. It should be noted that the target population were Spanish or foreigners who used this MoS to travel to Europe, as well as those European tourists who returned to their country of origin after their stay in Spain. Line users who are resident in Asturias were not included in the analysis in order to concentrate on the economic impact of inbound tourism.

3.1 Seasonality

Monthly data for the Gijón–Nantes line based on the survey of 2013 is plotted in Figure 7.2 and reveals a strong seasonality concentrated during the summer months (June to August) and with an annual peak in August, for passengers travelling with a private vehicle. Furthermore, from April onwards it seems that user numbers start to increase in a sustained way. However, this tendency reverts in September when the numbers for this passenger type decrease, seeing an appreciable drop in October.

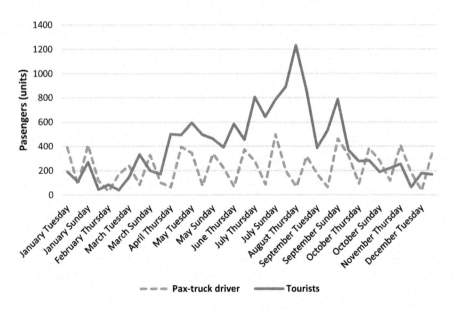

Figure 7.2 MoS Gijón–Nantes passenger traffic in 2013.

Source: Author's own elaboration from Port Authority of Gijón.

Foot passengers cover a small proportion of total users. However, it is in May and July when the highest number of this group of travellers is reached. As in the previous case, it can be corroborated by the existence of a seasonal trend.

In the case of transport professionals, the tendency remains more or less stable, although there is a decrease in the influx for July and August, which recovers in September albeit with a minimum registered in December.

The number of passengers travelling with private vehicles in May and June from Nantes to Gijón is similar to the previous case (Figure 7.1). However, in contrast, in the Gijón–Nantes route the sustained growth does not commence until May. Maximum values are achieved in the main summer months: June, July and August. This group sees a moderate decline in September, which becomes more pronounced in October and November.

The number of foot passengers is even lower than that for the Gijón–Nantes line. Maximum values are reached in March, June and September, which makes the task of defining an arrival pattern for this group slightly ambiguous. With reference to transport professionals, the months with the highest concentration of travellers are January, March and November.

3.2 Attributes of passengers

Based on the information obtained from interviews of holidaymakers who used the MoS Gijón–Nantes, a descriptive analysis is presented with the main attributes that define the tourists who used the line during the year 2013. As can be seen

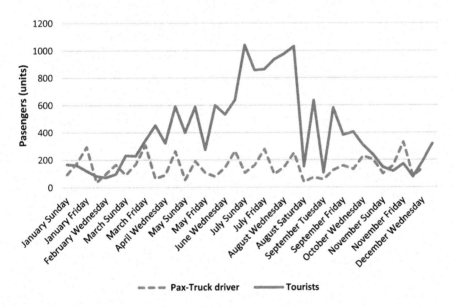

Figure 7.3 MoS Nantes–Gijón passenger traffic in 2013.
Source: Author's own elaboration from Port Authority of Gijón.

in the map labelled 'Tourists' in Figure 7.4, the vast majority of this type of users of the MoS Gijón–Nantes were French. Specifically, 76.6% of the total number of tourists surveyed came from France; in other words, more than three-quarters of the total number of individuals interviewed. The number of French tourists was followed by Spanish, but at a distance, since the latter represent only 12.1%. The remaining nationalities are less frequent, coming from Belgium (4.2%), The Netherlands (2.3%), United Kingdom (1.6%), Portugal (1.4%), Germany (0.97%) and Ireland (0.54%). The percentage of tourists from Switzerland and Sweden does not exceed 0.5%.

In the case of professional freight transport, differences exist with respect to tourist movements. Figure 7.4 shows that the main diagonally positioned user-flows are composed by the following countries: France (31.9%), Portugal (29.3%), Spain (20.7%) and Germany (8.1%). In fact, this diagonal congregates 90% of the total flows generated by transport professionals. Other countries with fewer users are Belgium with 3.8%, The Netherlands with 3.6% and United Kingdom with 1.4%. As in the previous case, there are other nationalities with scarcer frequencies such as Ireland (0.62%), Denmark (0.29%), Luxembourg (0.14%) and Poland (0.05%). Note that in this grouping we have also excluded truck drivers who reside in Asturias.

In terms of age distribution, the predominant cluster is those aged between 46 and 65, which represents almost half of the total. It is followed by those aged 36 to 45, with 30.6%. The age group from 18 to 35 and that of those over 65 years old are the least frequent, accounting for 11.1% and 10.9% respectively. Consequently, middle-aged adults are those most likely to use this means of transport to travel.

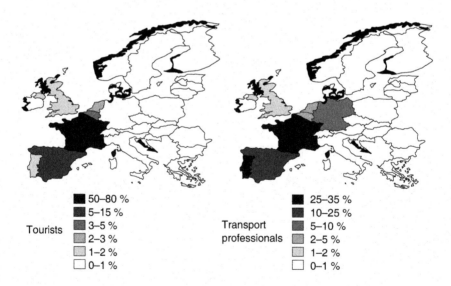

Figure 7.4 Users of MoS Gijón–Nantes.

Source: Author's own elaboration from Port Authority of Gijón.

Regarding education level, 59.8% of those interviewed said they have university studies and, in addition, 2.0% had a master's or doctorate degree. Moreover, 16.8% had professional training and 15.2% had secondary school studies. It is noteworthy that only 6.2% of the passengers surveyed stated that they had only primary studies.

Almost half of those interviewed stated that they were employees (49.4%). Likewise, almost a quarter was civil servants or public sector employees, 19.2% were retired and only 1.8% self-employed. The least frequent responses were students, managers, directive staff and independent professionals, accounting for 5.7% of the total.

Finally, almost half of those interviewed (45.2%) stated that they had a monthly family income of between three thousand and five thousand euros. Those whose income is less than three thousand euros per month represent 35.2% of the total. The income interval between five thousand and seven thousand euros and that of over seven thousand euros are less frequent, 11.9% and 7.7% respectively.

3.3 Holiday destination of tourists using the route

In order to present the results relating to the holiday destination, we consider three different user groups. The first refers to foreigners returning home after having finished their holidays in Spain. The second group are Spaniards who start their holidays in Europe, and the third considers foreigners embarking on their holiday (mainly of Portuguese nationality).

Table 7.2 shows the final holiday destination zones for foreigners returning to their countries, of which the three most frequent are Asturias with 35.2%, Galicia with 18.9% and Portugal with 17.9%. These are followed by other destinations of northern Spain including the Basque Country and Cantabria. Less frequent destinations were the south of Spain – Ruta de la Plata with 3.7%, on a tour of Spain with 1.3% or North Africa with 0.3%.

Table 7.2 Final holiday destination of inbound tourism in Spain.

Destination	Percentage (%)
Asturias	35.2
Galicia	18.9
Portugal	17.9
Cantabria and Basque Country	9.7
Inland Spain	4.4
Southern Spain – Ruta de la Plata (Silver Road)	3.7
Spain (inland) and Portugal	3.5
Galicia and Portugal	2.8
Tour for Spain	1.3
France	1.3
Mediterranean (Catalonia and Levante)	0.8
North Africa	0.3

Source: Author's own elaboration.

Table 7.3 Final holiday destination of outbound Spanish tourism.

Final destination	Percentage (%)
France	85.3
Benelux	6.0
Germany	1.7
United Kingdom	1.7
Other Europeans	5.3

Source: Author's own elaboration.

The most popular destination among Spaniards who used the MoS to go on holiday to Europe is undoubtedly France (85.3%), as indicated in Table 7.3. On the other hand, 6% travelled to the Netherlands or Belgium and 1.7% travelled to Germany or the United Kingdom; those going to other European countries accounted for 5.3% of the total. These included destinations such as Iceland, Ireland or Russia. Finally, regarding foreign passengers who use the MoS to go on holiday (mainly Portuguese nationals), the preferred destination was France with 76.9%.

4 Semiparametric estimation results

In order to examine the determinants of the individual tourist expenditure of MoS users in Asturias (TEM henceforth), this section estimates the relationship between the reported TEM and certain explanatory variables grouped into two categories: socio-demographic characteristics of the passengers (gender, age, income levels, country of residence) and trip-related features (choosing Asturias as the holiday destination, vehicle type, previous experience in the MoS transport). The descriptive analysis revealed the existence in the sample of a high proportion (17%) of null observations in the dependent variable (of the 924 valid responses, 157 indicated zero expenditure).

Due to this fact, it is well known that the econometric analysis requires using alternative methods to the ordinary least squares (OLS). Consequently, in this study the tobit model (Tobin, 1958) was the basic analytical tool chosen to deal with the censored nature of the distribution of tourist passengers' expenditure. More precisely, we employ symmetrically censored least squares (SCLS) to estimate the tobit model, a semiparametric technique suggested by Powell (1986). This semiparametric specification produces consistent and robust estimators when correcting the heteroscedasticity and non-normality problems that are usually found in the tobit model estimated by maximum likelihood (Chay and Powell, 2001).

The TEM transformed logarithmically is used as the dependent variable in the empirical application. In terms of the explanatory variables used in the regressions, all of them are discrete or dummy variables which represent individual characteristics or travel-related features, so that a value unit signifies belonging to a particular category. Definitions and sample statistics of our explanatory variables are summarized in Table 7.4.

Economic impact of tourism on Nantes–Gijón 171

Table 7.4 Definitions and sample statistics of the explanatory variables.

Variables	Definitions	Mean	Standard deviation
Gender	Dummy variable. Takes the value 1 if the tourist is a male	0.71	0.45
Aged 45–65	Dummy variable. Takes the value 1 if the age of the tourist is between 45 and 65 years	0.47	0.49
Aged >65	Dummy variable. Takes the value 1 if the age of the tourist is older than 65 years	0.11	0.31
Medium income	Dummy variable. Takes the value 1 if the monthly income of the tourist is between 2,000 € and 4,000 €	0.44	0.49
High income	Dummy variable. Takes the value 1 if the monthly income of the tourist is over than 4,000 €	0.19	0.38
ESP	Dummy variable. Takes the value 1 if the tourist resides in Spain	0.12	0.32
BEL	Dummy variable. Takes the value 1 if the tourist resides in Belgium	0.04	0.20
NLD	Dummy variable. Takes the value 1 if the tourist resides in The Netherlands	0.02	0.15
PRT	Dummy variable. Takes the value 1 if the tourist resides in Portugal	0.01	0.11
D_Asturias	Dummy variable. Takes the value 1 if Asturias is the holiday destination	0.44	0.49
Motor home	Dummy variable. Takes the value 1 if the tourist travelled by motor home	0.12	0.32
Other vehicle	Dummy variable. Takes the value 1 if the tourist travelled on foot or by bike	0.06	0.23
Experience	Dummy variable. Takes the value 1 if the tourist has had previous experience in the MoS transport	0.03	0.16

Source: Author's own elaboration.

We have estimated the semiparametric censored regression model using the Stata SCLS programme developed by Santos Silva (2012). The results of the SCLS estimation are shown in Table 7.5, and it can be appreciated that seven of the explanatory variables are statistically significant. The positive sign of the gender coefficient suggests that male tourists tend to increase their levels of consumption in relation to female ones. It has also been detected that being over the age of 45 positively affects levels of consumption, when compared to younger tourists. Likewise, nationality also explains the different expenditure patterns. Taking as a reference the tourists of French nationality, it turns out that Spanish, Belgian or Dutch nationals show a greater tendency to touristic consumption in Asturias. Also, as was expected, the fact that Asturias is the holiday destination positively affects consumption. On the other hand, the individual's income, the experience in MoS transport and the type of vehicle used to travel have no influence on the level of expenditure.

Table 7.5 Semiparametric estimation results of the tobit model.

Variables	Coefficients	t-values
Constant	1.3997	6.95***
Gender	0.3103	2.41**
Aged 45–65	0.3096	2.56**
Aged >65	0.6701	2.96***
Medium income	−0.0936	−0.69
High income	−0.0190	−0.11
ESP	0.3932	2.18**
BEL	1.3936	5.48***
NLD	0.7254	2.51**
PRT	0.5495	1.10
D_Asturias	2.6929	18.22***
Motor home	−0.1017	−0.57
Other vehicle	0.2132	0.99
Experience	0.4532	1.46

Source: Author's own elaboration.

Note: *, ** and *** indicate statistical significance at 10%, 5% and 1%, respectively.

Table 7.6 Marginal effects of the semiparametric tobit model.

Variables	Marginal effects (€)
Gender	1.3639
Aged 45–65	1.3628
Aged >65	1.9544
ESP	1.4817
BEL	4.0293
NLD	2.0654
D_Asturias	14.7746

Source: Author's own elaboration.

Finally, the marginal effects computed for each of the statistically significant variables are presented in Table 7.6. These marginal effects are expressed in euro in order to facilitate their interpretation. It should be noted that passengers' expenditure will increase by 14.8 euros if the tourist has chosen Asturias as the main destination. We have also obtained that passengers over 65 years old will spend almost 3 euros more than those under 45. Furthermore, and taking France as the reference for a country of residence, the marginal effects obtained indicate that a traveller from Belgium will spend 5.5 euros more and a Dutch tourist will spend 2.5 euros more.

5 The economic impact on the regional economy

Different methodological tools have been applied in the literature for estimating the economic impact of tourism: cost-benefit analysis, tourism satellite accounts, computable general equilibrium models or multipliers derived from input-output (I-O) tables. I-O analysis (Fletcher, 1989, 1994; Crompton *et al.*, 2001; Tyrrell and Johnston, 2001; Frechtling, 2010; Song *et al.*, 2012) is the methodology that has prevailed in the literature until now, but it is known to suffer from various limitations.

Firstly, the methodology requires the acceptance of some very restrictive assumptions used to simplify economic behaviour, for example assuming constant technical coefficients (Briassouilis, 1991) or considering the demand and production functions as maintaining fixed proportions (Leontief's technologies). These assumptions therefore imply that input (output) prices remain unchanged in relative terms, something which is not necessarily the case, with prices varying as a result of changes in the demand for tourism (Dwyer *et al.*, 2000). The consequences derived from not allowing the replacement of those factors which have experienced a price increase over time for other relatively cheaper ones will obviously be more relevant the greater the difference between the price structure on the I-O table creation date and the date on which the impact of tourism is analyzed.

Furthermore, the I-O approach is susceptible to other weaknesses, such as the assumption of freely available factors. This would imply that whatever the moment in time, supply is able to totally absorb changes in demand. Hence, the effects of any increased demand in tourism for an economy as a whole would always prove to be positive in an I-O framework, whereas reality would require researching into the possible negative effects derived from the expulsion effect onto other economic sectors through the resource and factor flows towards those involving tourist-related activities (Blake and Sinclair, 2003; Dwyer *et al.*, 2003). This expulsion effect will depend on the excess capacity of the tourism-related industry involved, the characteristics of the labour market or the possible modifications of the economy's true exchange relationship. In sum, I-O analysis tends to overestimate impacts (Dwyer *et al.*, 2004; Polo *et al.*, 2008). These consequences are even more important for the analysis of a tourist boom, bearing in mind the subsequent change it would cause in the economy's productive structure or for the study of special events.

It would then be necessary to acknowledge that I-O models are not the most appropriate for analyzing the economic impacts of tourism in large areas or multiregions, and using computable general equilibrium models (CGE) seems more adequate for this purpose. However, in the case of small regions, it may be considered that no relevant restrictions exist as to the offer of inputs, as long as the economy is open to external factors. Additionally, it may be assumed that relative prices are set outside these small economies. Under these circumstances and bearing in mind that these regions do not usually have a CGE reference model, the construction of which is very costly, it may be justified to use the I-O model, since the advantages of its use would probably outweigh the disadvantages (Dwyer *et al.*, 2004; Polo *et al.*, 2008). For this reason, in order to estimate the effects of the MoS on the economy of Asturias, this is the analytical tool chosen.

Applied to tourism, these I-O models use the estimated expenditure of visitors to assess direct impacts, which are then adjusted to local conditions in order to reflect the circulation of said expenditure in the local economy. Therefore, in this study the I-O analysis was applied, taking as a starting point the measurement of tourist expenditure for all MoS users. The basic idea of the model is that an increase in tourism expenditure which is satisfied serves to generate an increase in activity (direct effect) for the first-level suppliers of this demand (shops, restaurants, etc.) who in turn generate a spin-off effect with their own suppliers (food, beverages, etc.) and so on, generating rounds of economic transactions which constitute indirect effects. However, the impacts of domestic tourism expenditure do not end with these two effects, as they generate an increase in the income of domestic economies through salaries, which translates into increased private spending, creating a new cycle of effects known as induced.

The I-O model allows the quantification of the indirect and induced effects produced on each activity sector through an increase in tourism demand, by identifying the total feedback effects that are generated in the economic system. This recognizes the fact that the effects of demand are not only direct but that they are further transmitted to other branches of activity through the network of dominant interrelations. Finally, the total economic impact is the addition of the direct, indirect and induced effects.

Indirect and induced effects can be calculated by the equation:

$$X = \left(I - A^R\right)^{-1} Y \qquad (7.1)$$

where X is the vector of the production of each sector, I is the identity matrix and A^R is the matrix of regional technical coefficients. If vector Y stands for tourist expenditure, then X would represent the direct and indirect production that such expenditure generates in the region through the network of its productive sectors. However, if Y measures the demand from the region's economic agents due to an increase in income as a consequence of previous direct or indirect impacts, then X would represent the effects induced by tourism activities.

Using the I-O tables, if we divide the value added of each sector (VA_i) by the value of the production generated by each sector (X_i), we obtain the sectorial value added coefficients (α_i):

$$\alpha_i = VA_i / X_i \qquad (7.2)$$

As with the regional technical coefficients, we assume that these value-added coefficients remain constant. Solving for X_i in Equation (7.2) and substituting into Equation (7.1), we obtain the following matrix expression for value-added:

$$VA = A_{VA}\left(I - A^R\right)^{-1} Y \qquad (7.3)$$

where VA is the value-added vector to be calculated and A_{VA} is a matrix whose diagonal elements are the sectorial technical coefficients of the added values, taken from the Asturian I-O tables and whose off-diagonal elements are zeros.

To calculate the induced impacts we analyze the basis of the gross salaries and wages generated from the direct and indirect effects. In this manner, we can determine the percentage that the economy, on the whole, devotes to private consumption, taking into consideration the information provided by the regional accounts. Once the value for that variable has been established, its disaggregation by sector (vector Y, corresponding to private consumption) will be carried out by means of a similar disaggregation but this time applied to private consumption within the region.

Hence, in this chapter, an I-O model based on the Asturian I-O tables for 2015, being the latest available (SADEI, 2019), has been used to estimate the tourism economic impact of the MoS on the regional economy. The main variable employed to estimate the economic impact of tourism will be gross value added (GVA). But in this context it should be pointed out that the economic impact is not limited to the GVA and could also be measured by alternative indicators such as turnover, employment, wages and salaries or gross operating surplus, assuming of course stability in the proportional relationships between these regional productions and said magnitudes.

As mentioned previously, we have estimated the total expenditure of tourists in 2013 via face-to-face interviews. More precisely during that year, the 17,976 users of the MoS Gijón–Nantes engaged in individual average spending of 98.6 euros in Asturias. The forecast we propose for 2021 (the expected date for re-establishing the MoS) is based on an update of this tourist expenditure, taking into consideration the information collected by the Tourist Information System of Asturias (SITA). The latter quantified an average annual growth of tourism expenditure per capita over the past few years of circa 2.25%. Applying this growth rate from 2013 onwards would result in an increase to 118 euros for the average individual tourist expenditure of MoS users.

Moreover, we are going to assume that the passenger load factor of the ferry line service will be similar to those for 2013. Figure 7.5 depicts this monthly percentage of tourist occupation, varying between a value of more than 80% in August and roughly 9% in November, with an average value of 30%. Multiplying this occupation rate by the capacity of transporting passengers on the new ferry, the resultant number of MoS tourists would reach the figure of 34,154 passengers per annum. Accordingly, total tourist expenditure could be expected to amount to 4,031,778 euros in 2021.

The port taxes charged by the port of Gijón (in the form of embarkation charges per passenger and vehicle) must be added to this figure, thereby increasing total expenditure to 4,272,482 euros. However, the spending incurred by crew members or vessel-related expenditure (fuel bunkering, mooring rates, pilotage charges, ship maintenance, etc.) are not included as tourist spending, but are instead allocated to goods transport expenditure.

Table 7.7 summarizes amounts spent by visitors on four categories for goods and services. Similarly to 2013, purchases of food products and sundry purchases would account for more than half of tourism expenditure (51%) followed by restaurant services and hotels (45%).

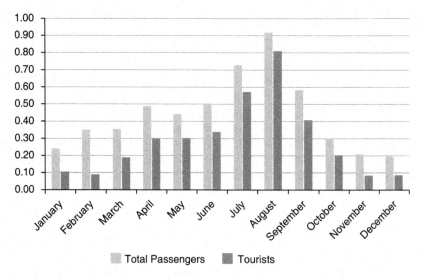

Figure 7.5 Passenger load factor (%) MoS Gijón–Nantes.
Source: Author's own elaboration from Port Authority of Gijón.

Table 7.7 Expected tourism expenditure by category and sector of activity (€).

Category of Expenditure	Sector of Activity	Expenditure
Purchases of food products and sundry purchases	Trading and repairs	2,108,124
Hotel and restaurant services	Hotels, restaurants and cafes	1,854,937
Passenger embarkation charges	Transport	240,705
Sundry activities	Other services	68,717
Total		**4,272,482**

Source: Author's own elaboration from Asturian 2015 I-O.

The application of this expenditure vector enables us to quantify the expected economic impact generated by the MoS Nantes–Gijón tourism passengers in Asturias, in terms of GVA, and Table 7.8 shows the breakdown, in terms of sectors of activity and types of effect. As observed, in 2021 the expected direct effects would amount to 2,375,741 euros; indirect effects to 1,024,530; and induced ones to 636,906 euros. Hence, the expected total effect on the GVA of Asturias from this activity would total 4,037,177 euros (current). In turn, Table 7.9 shows the economic impact of tourism in Asturias in terms of expected employment for different sectors. For 2021, the creation of 92 jobs (full time equivalent, FTE) in total is estimated, mostly in service-related industries, broken down into 64 direct, 16 indirect and 12 induced jobs, respectively.

Table 7.8 Expected economic impacts in terms of GVA (€) of MoS Gijón–Nantes, 2021.

Sector of Activity	Direct	Indirect	Induced	Total
1 Agriculture and fisheries	–	15,888	6,639	22,527
2 Extraction industries	–	10,443	3,166	13,609
3 Food, beverages and tobacco	–	33,329	8,482	41,811
4 Other manufacturing	–	10,708	3,643	14,351
5 Metallurgy	–	3,390	947	4,337
6 Transformation of metals	–	11,688	2,574	14,262
7 Energy and water	–	96,997	29,321	126,318
8 Construction	–	41,729	12,964	54,693
9 Trading and repairs	1,237,006	140,485	101,511	1,479,002
10 Transport	121,587	83,248	19,926	224,762
11 Hotels, restaurants and cafes	970,207	10,085	91,122	1,071,414
12 Financial services, information and communication	–	111,234	53,548	164,782
13 Business services	–	422,182	219,465	641,647
14 Health and social services	–	15,261	41,148	56,410
15 Other services	46,941	17,861	42,449	107,252
TOTAL	2,375,741	1,024,530	636,906	4,037,177

Source: Author's own elaboration from Asturian 2015 I-O.

Table 7.9 Expected economic impacts in terms of employment (FTE) of MoS Gijón–Nantes, 2021.

Sector of Activity	Direct	Indirect	Induced	Total
8 Construction	–	1	–	1
9 Trading and repairs	36	5	3	44
10 Transport	2	2	–	4
11 Hotels, restaurants and cafes	23	1	2	26
12 Financial services, information and communication	–	1	1	2
13 Business services	–	5	3	8
14 Health and social services	–	–	1	1
15 Other services	3	1	2	6
TOTAL	64	16	12	92

Source: Author's own elaboration from Asturian 2015 I-O.

Although the figure of 4 million euros mentioned earlier is not excessive, it represents practically 100% of the annual governmental aid granted by Spain to the MoS during the period 2011–2014, which can give an idea of the important contribution made by tourism expenditure. Therefore, we believe that performing a timely valuation of tourist activity as a complement to the principal function of the MoS could justify the provision of some form of public aid during the initial years of operation, until a line is able to reach a level of maturity and objective profitability. From an aesthetic point of view, whilst it is true that in terms of the on-board services offered the MoS is not the same as a cruise, which is obviously much more sophisticated and oriented to vacation enjoyment, it still remains attractive as a mode of transport compared to the road alternative, given the savings in journey time, overall safety and rest and comfort available.

6 Conclusions

Motorways of the Sea (MoS), which also include regular ferry lines connecting ports in different countries within the EU, were conceived as the most competitive and sustainable alternative to the transport of goods by road, the latter transport mode entailing severe external costs (congestion, emission of pollutants, accidents, etc.). In this sense, in 2010 the connection between Nantes and Gijón was approved by the European Commission, in an attempt to capture a significant amount of truck traffic between the north of Portugal, Spain and France and thus alleviate congestion in the Pyrenees area. However, the increase in the number of passengers who use the ferries for leisure purposes and the existence of marked seasonality with important peaks of demand in July and August highlight their potential use for tourism.

Despite the promising results obtained by the MoS, in September 2014 the shipping company responsible for operating this route considered the traffic volumes insufficient and unilaterally decided to cancel the line. It is expected that during 2021 another shipping company, Baleària, specialized in both passenger and freight transport, will reopen the ferry service connecting the port of Nantes-St Nazaire and Gijón. Thus, in this chapter, we have attempted to analyze the economic importance of this means of transport in terms of tourism development. In this context, one of the main aims of the research is to study the viability of re-establishing the MoS by evaluating its economic effects on tourism, based on new factors such as the increased size of the new vessel put into service (providing a greater capacity to carry passengers) and more frequent trips.

To that end, firstly a descriptive analysis is undertaken of the profile for the typical MoS user, based on a survey carried out during 2013 for 924 tourists who used the line. Findings indicate the predominance of French users, aged between 36 and 65, with a high level of education. Likewise, there are a large number of Spaniards, non-residents in Asturias, who use the MoS to visit a European country, mainly France. Other countries of residence for tourists, such as Belgium, Holland and the United Kingdom, represent smaller percentages.

Secondly, a symmetrically censored least squares regression model is applied to estimate the determinants of the individual tourist expenditure of MoS users in Asturias. With a view to explaining the level of passenger expenditure two factors are important: certain socio-demographic characteristics amongst tourists (gender, age or country of residence) and trip-related variables, such as choosing Asturias as the holiday destination.

Thirdly, the study evaluates the expected economic effect on Asturias (the region to which the port of Gijón belongs) of future MoS usage by tourists in 2021 when the line will potentially be reopened. To that end, an I-O analysis is performed under the assumption that the new line will maintain both the frequencies of 2013 and the same passenger load factor. The results obtained place the annual impact in terms of gross added value at a little over 4 million euros, representing the creation of 92 full-time jobs.

The results related to economic impact can be compared with another more sophisticated activity of marine passenger transport, namely cruises. Hence, in 2021, the expected total tourist expenditure by holidaymaker users of the MoS (4,031,718 euros) would be equivalent to that made by 91,000 cruise liner users who disembark in the port of Gijón. Also, if we consider a cruise liner with a capacity of 4300 passengers, it would be necessary for 21 ships bearing those characteristics to call in at the port of Gijón to obtain an economic impact similar to that obtained by the tourist activity of the MoS. It should be pointed out that currently 17 cruise ships are predicted to call in at the port of Gijón, with an average capacity of 1100 passengers, figures which fall well short of the previous hypothesis. In this sense, the fact that the new concessionaire has great experience in the transport of tourists could increase the potential of the line for this use without overlooking, however, its fundamental function for goods transport.

It is also important to highlight that over the 4 years during which LD Lines, the previous shipping line, operated, both the Spanish and French governments made annual contributions of three and a half million euros each. As can be appreciated, this amount is vastly lower than the creation of wealth that could be obtained from the tourist use of the MoS.

Finally, the new ship destined to run the line will use LNG as fuel, which implies very important environmental advantages in comparison with the previous situation of the MoS, eliminating any doubts about its environmental viability.

Note

1 Previously to the *Norman Atlantic*, two other Ro-Pax ships were used on this route: the *Norman Bridge* and the *Norman Asturias*.

References

Baños, J.F., Valdés, L., Del Valle, E., & Zapico, E. (2018), Economic importance of the motorways of the sea for tourism: The experience of the route Nantes-Gijón. *Maritime Economics & Logistics*, 20 (2), pp. 300–320.

Blake, A., & Sinclair, M.T. (2003), Tourism crisis management US response to September 11'. *Annals of Tourism Research*, 30 (4), pp. 813–832.

Briassouilis, H. (1991), Methodological issues: Tourism input-output analysis. *Annals of Tourism Research*, 18, pp. 435–449.

Chay, K.Y., & Powell, J.L. (2001), Semiparametric censored regression models. *Journal of Economic Perspectives*, 15 (4), pp. 29–42.

Crompton, J., Lee, S., & Shuster, T. (2001), A guide for undertaking economic impact studies: The Springfest example. *Journal of Travel Research*, 40 (1), pp. 79–87.

Dwyer, L., Forsyth, P., Madden, J.J., & Spurr, R. (2000), Economics impacts of inbound tourism under different assumptions regarding the macroeconomy. *Current Issues in Tourism*, 3 (4), pp. 325–363.

Dwyer, L., Forsyth, P., & Spurr, R. (2004), Evaluating tourism's economic effects: New and old approaches. *Tourism Management*, 25 (3), pp. 307–317.

Dwyer, L., Forsyth, P., Spurr, R., & Van Ho, T. (2003), Tourism's contribution to a state economy: A multi-regional general equilibrium analysis. *Tourism Economics*, 9 (4), pp. 431–448.

European Commission (2001), White paper European transport policy for 2010: Time to decide. Office for Official Publication of the European Communities, Luxembourg.

Fletcher, J.E. (1989), Input-Output analysis and tourism impact studies. *Annals of Tourism Research*, 16, pp. 514–529.

Fletcher, J.E. (1994), Input-output analysis. In S. Witt & L. Moutinho (eds.), *Tourism Marketing and Management Handbook*. New York: Prentice-Hall.

Frechtling, D. (2010), The tourism satellite account: A primer. *Annals of Tourism Research*, 37 (1), pp. 136–153.

Freire-Seoane, M.J., González-Laxe, F., & Pais-Montes, C. (2017), Short sea shipping in the Atlantic Arc: A spatial shift-share approach. *International Journal of Shipping and Transport Logistics*, 9, pp. 323–370.

Martínez-López, A., Munín-Doce, A., & García-Alonso, L. (2015), A multi-criteria decision method for the analysis of the Motorways of the Sea: The application to the case of France and Spain on the Atlantic Coast. *Maritime Policy and Management: The Flagship Journal of International Shipping and Port Research*, 42 (6), pp. 608–631.

Polo, C., Ramos, V., Rey-Maquieira, J., Tugores, M., & Valle, E. (2008), The potential effects of a change in the distribution of tourism expenditure on employment. *Tourism Economics*, 14 (4), pp. 709–725.

Powell, J.L. (1986), Symmetrically trimmed least squares estimation for Tobit models. *Econometrica*, 54, pp. 1435–1460.

SADEI (2019), Marco input-output de Asturias. Oviedo, Spain.

Santos, T.A., & Soares, C.G. (2017), Modelling transportation demand in short sea shipping. *Maritime Economics & Logistics*, 19 (4), pp. 695–722.

Santos Silva, J. (2012), SCLS: Stata module to perform symmetrically censored least squares. Boston College Department of Economics.

Song, H., Dwyer, L., Li, G., & Cao, Z. (2012), Tourism economics research: A review and assessment. *Annals of Tourism Research*, 39 (3), pp. 1653–1682.

Tobin, J. (1958), Estimation of relationships for limited dependent variables. *Econometrica*, 26 (1), pp. 24–36.

Tyrrell, T., & Johnston, R. (2001), A framework for assessing direct economic impacts of tourism events: Distinguishing origins, destinations, and causes of expenditures. *Journal of Travel Research*, 40 (1), pp. 94–100.

Vallejo-Pinto, J.A., Garcia-Alonso, L., Álvarez-Fernández, R., & Mateo-Mantecón, I. (2019), *Iso-emission map*: A proposal to compare the environmental friendliness of short sea shipping *vs* road transport. *Transportation Research Part D*, 67, pp. 596–609.

Part III
Regional studies on short sea shipping

8 Ro-Ro short sea shipping and Motorways of the Sea

Evolutionary patterns of road hauliers' operating strategies

Miguel Ángel López-Navarro

1 Introduction

Concerns about the environmental impacts of transport have become an issue of growing importance in recent years, at both institutional and academic levels (European Commission, 2011, 2016; European Environmental Agency, 2013; Larson et al., 2013; Cristea et al., 2013; Llano et al., 2018). These concerns are exacerbated by the consideration that if patterns of global trade continue as forecast, the volume of international freight transport will have quadrupled by 2050, with a resulting 290% increase in CO_2 emissions deriving from it by that year (OECD/ITF, 2015). The transport industry's high contribution to greenhouse gas emissions calls for changes in the current behaviour of companies, from mere compliance with environmental regulations to adopting a more proactive attitude to their environmental strategies. Nevertheless, this attitude should not be limited to achieving greater energy efficiency by using fewer resources and reducing emissions with the most conventional transport modes. It also extends to the use of alternative modes, or a combination of modes (intermodality), in order to achieve greater environmental sustainability.

In designing policies for sustainable mobility, specifically in the context of intermodal transport, interest in the development of short sea shipping (SSS) has come to the fore in the last decade and has led to numerous studies on this subject in different geographical regions, although most of the research has been carried out in Europe (see, for example, Baird, 2007; Gouvernal et al., 2010; López-Navarro et al., 2011a, 2011b; Christodoulou et al., 2019; Michaelides et al., 2019). In a context characterized by a rising flow in the exchange of products and services, the European Union (EU) considers SSS as a priority in moving towards sustainable mobility. Under the explicit assumption that the current transport system is not sustainable and requires changes, the EU highlights intermodality as a strategy to be promoted. In this endeavour, SSS would be prioritized in the design of the European sustainable mobility policy. It would complement road transport, which, although it is characteristically flexible and highly competitive (Sternberg et al., 2013; Ellram and Golicic, 2015), generates considerable negative externalities, both in environmental terms and in road congestion, noise, accidents, etc.

With regard to the SSS context, although the results achieved to date are not in line with the initial expectations and the financing initiatives designed to promote it (European Court of Auditors, 2013), the EU has prioritized a programme based on the so-called Motorways of the Sea (MoS) (European Parliament, 2014). These are maritime corridors or SSS lines known for their competitiveness, efficiency and speed, and with them the EU hopes to close the gap between supply and demand, providing intermodal services that can compete with door-to-door transport by road. As noted in a recent document from the European Commission (2018:6–7), MoS is considered 'a maritime pillar of the Connecting Europe Facility and intends to connect the prioritised transport corridors in the EU as well as support industry in capturing the latest technological developments in the maritime sector'.

One of the barriers traditionally associated with the development of SSS in general, and MoS in particular, is that cooperation between stakeholders has not always been optimal (European Parliament, 2014). As stated in that document,

> Motorways of the Sea are part of complex supply chains that neither start nor end at seaports. Short sea shipping is in many (if not all) cases one of various different transport modes within a chain, and a number of stakeholders are represented within these chains from shipper to end customer. The MoS projects need to consider the integrated supply chain so that they are 'connected' to other 'shackles' in the chains and are not standalone projects.
>
> (European Parliament, 2014:11)

Cooperation between all the agents in the transport chain is, therefore, a decisive factor when it comes to improving the response of intermodal transport to the needs of shippers, as opposed to the all-road option (López-Navarro, 2011a, 2013b; Morales-Fusco et al., 2012; Christodoulou et al., 2019).

One of the key players in the development of roll-on/roll-off (Ro-Ro) SSS and, by extension, of the MoS, are the road hauliers (Rodríguez, 2012; López-Navarro, 2014). With regard to these agents, most of literature has focused on determining the conditions favouring modal shift (see, for example, Bergantino and Bolis, 2004, 2008; Brooks and Trifts, 2008; Puckett et al., 2011). However, past research has paid little attention to the operational strategies of road hauliers and to the challenges facing these firms when changing the all-road operative model to the intermodal transport option. Some exceptions are the studies of Torbianelli (2000), López-Navarro et al. (2011a, 2011b), López-Navarro (2013a, 2013b) and Morales-Fusco et al. (2012, 2018).

This chapter focuses on road hauliers and Ro-Ro SSS as a direct alternative to all-road transport. By taking this approach, we are excluding the 'captive' maritime market where Ro-Ro traffic does not compete with road transport. Taking as a reference both a broader investigation into the efficiency of Spanish road hauliers and a previous study of Ro-Ro SSS between Spain and Italy (López-Navarro et al., 2011b), two objectives are proposed in this study:

a   To evaluate how road hauliers perceive the benefits of this intermodal alternative as compared to all-road transport.
b   To analyze, with reference to the companies that participated in the earlier study, the evolution in their behaviour in using this mode of transport. The

aim is to examine the changes over time in the operational strategies of these companies because of their experience in the use of Ro-Ro SSS, but also in response to the actions of the shipping companies in the period considered.

The chapter is structured as follows. In the next section we analyze the two possible operating strategies for road hauliers – accompanied versus unaccompanied transport – in an attempt to determine their characteristics, the factors that condition their use and their theoretical pattern of evolution. We then describe the methodology and present the results. Finally, we detail the main implications of the results and highlight the conclusions.

2 Ro-Ro shipping and short sea Motorways of the Sea: road hauliers as a key player

In recent years, a vast literature has grown up around SSS and MoS. Apart from the studies on institutional and regulatory issues (Douet and Cappuccilli, 2011; Gese and Baird, 2013), a significant body of literature has been developed from the perspective of shipping industry and the infrastructures through which they operate (see, for example, Paixão and Marlow, 2002; Santos and Guedes Soares, 2017; Michaelides et al., 2019), in order to analyze the main barriers that hinder the use of SSS and to define proposals that might extend its use. While this research is necessary and relevant, it must also be recognized that the literature has devoted less attention to the user companies.

In response to this latter question, some studies have taken the perspective of shippers (see, for example, Brooks and Trifts, 2008; Puckett et al., 2011; Pérez-Mesa et al., 2010). Other authors have approached the subject from the perspective of freight forwarders, logistics service providers or road hauliers (see, for example, Bergantino and Bolis, 2004, 2008; Feo et al., 2011; López-Navarro et al., 2011a, 2011b, 2013a, 2013b). In general, regardless of the approach taken, these studies analyze how certain attributes that have traditionally been used to characterize transport (costs, transit times, frequency of service or service reliability) affect the modal shift from the all-road to the intermodal transport option. Also of note are several recent works that explore the importance of environmental issues in the decision to consider Ro-Ro SSS and MoS (Hjelle, 2010; Hjelle and Fridell, 2012; López-Navarro, 2014). In fact, intermodal solutions are explicitly identified as one of the elements associated with sustainable transport that logistics operators can offer their customers (Martinsen and Huge-Brodin, 2010; Martinsen and Björklund, 2012).

It is important to identify who takes the decision to use an intermodal transport system through Ro-Ro SSS, rather than the all-road traditional option, because it can help to determine possible actions or incentives that will encourage its use. Logistics service providers/road hauliers are, in our opinion, the key players in determining whether to use intermodal solutions in Ro-Ro SSS or MoS. In fact, Ro-Ro transport is the main focus of the MoS (Paixão and Marlow, 2007; Baindur and Viegas, 2012), which have been highlighted by the EU as part of the Trans-European Transport Network (TEN-T) and constitute the core of European policy on SSS. Using semi-trailers allows shorter delivery times, an advantage that is particularly relevant in a context of increasingly widespread just-in-time operations. As Woxenius and Bergqvist (2011) note, following Schramm (2006), the success of intermodal transport chains depends greatly on which agent acts as the coordinator and how well the operations are integrated. These authors highlight that whereas shipping companies, their agents or specialized sea forwarders take on the coordinating role in container transport, road transport firms or road-based forwarders predominate in the organization of transport chains involving semi-trailers. Douet and Cappuccilli (2011) also outline the potential of Ro-Ro SSS shipping, in a context where road hauliers are the backbone of the intermodal transport chain.

Nevertheless, according to Gouvernal et al. (2010) and López-Navarro et al. (2011b, 2013a), road hauliers may be reluctant to use intermodal transport, since their business model is largely organized around road transport, for which they have their own transportation networks. Using SSS and MoS entails significant adjustments and changes in the company, which may be a hindrance to the more widespread use of intermodal solutions (López-Navarro, 2013a). Similarly, Eng-Larsson and Kohn (2012), in reference to rail intermodality, point out that logistics providers are unwilling to invest in rail transport capacity, which conflicts with their own considerable road transport networks.

The literature addressing the issue of modal shift by road hauliers does not usually examine the question of the organizational adjustments required to facilitate intermodal transport. Few studies have paid attention to how these firms organize their business model and define their strategies when operating in the context of Ro-Ro SSS and MoS. Some exceptions are the works of Torbianelli (2000), De Solere (2007), Desiderio et al. (2008), López-Navarro et al. (2011a, 2011b, 2013a, 2013b) and Morales-Fusco et al. (2018). There are two strategies, defined as operating modes (López-Navarro, 2013a) or as business models (Morales-Fusco et al., 2018), that road hauliers can follow to organize their Ro-Ro SSS operations: (1) accompanied transport (semi-trailers are shipped together with their tractor units and drivers travel on board as passengers); (2) unaccompanied transport (only semi-trailers board the vessels).

Unaccompanied transport is a more advanced and committed stage in adopting the Ro-Ro SSS option. As López-Navarro (2013a: 377) noted,

> the unaccompanied transport option constitutes, in principle, the most favourable in economic and sustainable terms – loading the whole truck takes up more space on board and involves higher costs resulting from inactive tractor units and drivers. . . . Furthermore, by not shipping tractors, space would be freed up to board more semi-trailers, and it would also help to reduce emissions per tonne transported. Consequently, the use of unaccompanied transport is a more sustainable option. However, unaccompanied transport involves greater organisational restrictions.

More specifically, López-Navarro (2013a) identified five key areas of change in developing a transitional process to use Ro-Ro SSS, especially where unaccompanied transport is involved (Table 8.1): (1) restructuring of the fleet, resulting from

Table 8.1 Main challenges in the process of change from all-road transport to unaccompanied Ro-Ro short sea shipping.

Dimension	Observations	
Organization of haulage and fleet restructuring	Outsourced haulage	The firm's fleet is entirely made up of semi-trailers (it must sell its tractor units and use the services of independent hauliers, generally drivers with just one vehicle – owner-operators)
		The optimal number of semi-trailers per tractor unit will depend on pre- and post-haulage distances
		Savings in capital investments for tractor units
		Internal haulage option is preferred because it favours coordination
	Internal haulage	In addition to semi-trailers, the firm also have tractor units for haulage (it must sell some of its tractor units because fewer of them will be needed in unaccompanied SSS than in international all-road transport)
		Cooperation agreements with local hauliers are usual in haulage activity at destination
	Road haulier has to assess whether more semi-trailers are necessary, since their rotation in the maritime operation may be slightly lower than in the all-road alternative	
Restructuring of the driving staff	The firm must reduce its driving staff – wholly or partially, depending on the option chosen to organize haulage activity – and modify the contract conditions of those who remain in it (only national routes)	Possible occurrence of workplace disputes in case of redundancies
		Salary savings for the company
		Less driver discretion (more control by the company)
Changes in operating model and development of coordination capabilities	The road haulier must adapt its operating model when using maritime transport – the services of the shipping company. It must become familiar with new documentation and administrative procedures, and also with port operations	
	The road haulier must coordinate the turnaround cycle in each port through efficient management of haulage operations, including new players when haulage is outsourced or when cooperation agreements with local hauliers are established (*capabilities to efficiently coordinate its equipment/ capabilities to coordinate the intermodal transport chain as a whole*)	
Improving commercial capacity at destination	The firm must intensify its commercial activity, especially at destination, to achieve return cargos within the port's hinterland and minimize empty returns (*commercial capabilities*)	
	To increase its commercial capacity, the firm can establish cooperation agreements with local firms at the other end of the SSS line, and new skills should be developed in this field (*capabilities to manage cooperation relationships*)	
Establishing an adequate infrastructure to organize haulage in the destination country	Own subsidiary	Although the firm does not have tractor units at destination (outsourced haulage), it must have an adequate infrastructure that allows it to coordinate haulage operations efficiently
		When the firm has tractor units and drivers at destination a more sophisticated infrastructure is needed to manage its own resources
	Cooperation agreements	Joint ventures with local hauliers. The joint venture coordinates the haulage operations
		Cooperation agreements with local hauliers (whose tractor units are used). The local partner coordinates the haulage operations
		Cooperation agreements with local hauliers are a relevant factor in unaccompanied transport. They allow the adequate coordination of post-haulage through use of partner' equipment, as well as improving the commercial capability to secure return cargos

Source: López-Navarro (2013a).

the need for more semi-trailers and fewer tractor units; (2) restructuring of the driving staff, as a result of changes in the fleet; (3) changes in the business model, associated with port operations and the management of the cycles in each port; (4) improvement of commercial capacities at the destination; and (5) establishment of an adequate infrastructure to organize shipments at the destination. Such elements can represent serious obstacles to road hauliers' use of Ro-Ro SSS in its most efficient mode: unaccompanied transport.

Taking into account the arguments presented earlier, we propose the following two hypotheses regarding the evolution in companies' patterns of use of Ro-Ro SSS:

a   Given the growing competitive pressure on road freight transport in recent years (rising fuel and toll prices, tighter restrictions on driving times, etc.) and increasing institutional support for intermodal transport, it can be expected that companies which were using Ro-Ro SSS at time t_0 will have intensified their use at time t_1.

b   Given that unaccompanied transport is more profitable than accompanied transport, it is expected that the companies that were using accompanied transport in the context of Ro-Ro SSS at time t_0 will have evolved towards unaccompanied transport at time t_1. The significant organizational adjustments required by this operating strategy may lead companies to start their Ro-Ro SSS activities using the accompanied mode, but once they are familiar with intermodal operations they may increase their use of unaccompanied transport in pursuit of higher profits.

3 Methodology

This work is part of a larger project on the efficiency of Spanish international road hauliers, carried out in 2014. The target population was, in the first instance, the member companies of ASTIC (Spanish Association of International Road Transport Companies). A total of 76 road hauliers responded to the questionnaire sent to them (one section was designed to evaluate how these firms perceived the benefits of SSS as compared to all-road transport). Of these, only 29 used SSS (38.15%). The survey also asked 'non-user' companies to evaluate the SSS option from the perspective of potential users if they had the necessary information to do so. A total of seven 'non-user' companies provided this assessment.

Additionally, an attempt was made to gather information about the use of SSS from those companies that were not included in the aforementioned sample but that had participated in a study on Ro-Ro SSS carried out in 2007 (López-Navarro, 2011b). The aim was to perform a longitudinal analysis of their behavioural patterns in using this intermodal solution. Responses to this earlier study were received from 81 international road hauliers, which used the Ro-Ro SSS lines between Spain and Italy (41 Spanish, three Portuguese and 37 Italian). In the present investigation, and for cost reasons, only the Spanish, Portuguese and Italian companies that had a delegation in Spain (a total of seven) were considered; in this case the survey was addressed to the Spanish subsidiary. Taking into account these restrictions, the number of companies considered in this new investigation fell from 81 to 51. Seven of the companies that participated in this new study were members of ASTIC and were therefore included in the aforementioned population (one of these firms operated with SSS but no longer used the lines between Spain and Italy). Regarding the other 44 companies considered, 18 participated in the study (one of which also did not use the Ro-Ro SSS between Spain and Italy), 11 were no longer active, 13 did not answer because they no longer used SSS and considered that they did not have sufficient criteria to assess the issues raised, and two decided not to participate.

Based on those numbers, this study allows us to assess the perceptions of using Ro-Ro SSS, as an alternative to the all-road option, provided by 47 companies that used any of the following lines (all of them with at least two weekly departures): Barcelona-Genoa, Barcelona-Rome, Valencia/Barcelona-Livorno/Savona, Valencia-Salerno, Gijón–Nantes, Bilbao-Zeebrugge, Bilbao/Santander-Portsmouth/Plymouth. However, as mentioned previously, to compare the evolution of their operating strategies, information was only available from 23 companies which made use of the Ro-Ro SSS lines between Spain and Italy.

The data in Table 8.2 show that these companies operated with an average of 139.68 tractor units (including both the units owned by the company and those of regular collaborators, giving a measure of the number of vehicles the company usually operates with) and 183.08 semi-trailers; these figures are significantly higher than the sector average. Furthermore, these are companies with a strong international orientation, as reflected in an average of 68.52% of their total transport operations dedicated to international transport.

The average number of semi-trailers shipped/loaded by the companies is 36.6 units per week. However, these data require a more detailed analysis. It should be taken into account that 17 companies (36.2%) shipped fewer than five semi-trailers per week; 18 companies (38.3%) shipped between five and 20 semi-trailers; eight companies (17%) shipped between 21 and 100 semi-trailers; and only four companies (8.5%) shipped more than 100 semi-trailers per week.

Furthermore, the road hauliers claimed responsibility for the decision to use Ro-Ro SSS in 94.25% of the shipments (Table 8.3), whereas only 5.75% of the shipments actually responded to the requirements of the shipper. These figures support the notion we outlined in the previous section that road hauliers are the agents that actually coordinate the intermodal transport chains in the SSS

Table 8.2 Road hauliers' characteristics (*n* = 47).

Characteristics	Average values
Tractor fleet (units)	139.68
Semi-trailer fleet (units)	183.08
International transport (% of total transport)	68.52
Semi-trailers loaded (per week)	36.60

Table 8.3 Agent responsible for the decision to use Ro-Ro SSS ($n = 47$).

Agent responsible	Percentage of total shipments (average values)
The client (the shipper)	5.75
The road haulier	94.25

semi-trailer segment (as opposed to the containers). Road hauliers therefore play a predominant role in the development of this mode of transport, which is a key commitment in the EU's sustainable mobility policy.

4 Results

Table 8.4 shows the road hauliers' perceptions of Ro-Ro SSS in comparative terms regarding the all-road transport option, differentiating between 'users' and 'non-users' (the latter being companies that, despite not using Ro-Ro SSS, considered they had relevant information to evaluate it). Non-use could be linked to a poorer evaluation of this intermodal transport option in terms of the main defining attributes of transport (cost, transit time, etc.), as well as the inertia derived from the use of the all-road option and the possible reluctance to make organizational adjustments to operate efficiently through Ro-Ro SSS. Specifically, companies were asked to assess, in comparison with the unimodal road option, the Ro-Ro SSS line they used the most (or the one they could potentially use in the case of non-user companies).

The results of Table 8.4 show that when the traditional parameters associated with transport (cost and transit time) are considered, road hauliers that use Ro-Ro SSS value it as the most favourable option (the values are greater than 3 on a 5-point Likert scale). Although the transit time is considered to be one of the weaknesses of SSS, the value of this dimension may have been conditioned by the fact that approximately one third of the companies analyzed (15 out of 47) assessed the Barcelona-Rome SSS line because it was the one they used the most. This line, operated by Ro-Pax ships and which also provides passenger transport, has a very favourable transit time (evaluated by road haulier users as 4.33). If we exclude these companies, the average score for this dimension falls to 3.15, a value that is still favourable to SSS but very close to the midpoint on the measurement scale.

A more favourable assessment is also given for safety, understood as the absence of damage to cargo and equipment and, especially, environmental impact. On the other hand, user companies give intermodal transport lower scores for both operational and document complexity. Intermodal freight transport is logically more complex than unimodal transport by road, given that various actors are responsible for organizing and controlling each part of the transport chain. Intermodality demands coordination, and agents need to make an effort to integrate their operations within the framework of the transport chain (Caris et al.,

Table 8.4 Ro-Ro SSS vs all-road transport (road hauliers' assessments).

Parameter[1]	Users (n = 47)	Non-users (n = 7)	Difference
Cost	3.21	2.71	0.50
Time of journey	3.53	2.42	1.11
Safety (no damage to cargo/equipment)	3.42	3.00	0.42
Operational complexity	2.78	2.42	0.36
Administrative and documental complexity	2.78	2.42	0.36
Environmental impact	3.93	3.71	0.22

1 Parameters were measured on a 5-point Likert scale (1 = the intermodal transport option is much worse; 5 = the intermodal transport option is much better).

2008; López-Navarro, 2011b, 2013b; Morales-Fusco et al., 2012; Christodoulou et al., 2019).

Comparisons of the assessments made by the 'user' and 'non-user' companies should be made with the appropriate reservations due to the low number of responses from 'non-users'. According to this comparison, the 'non-users' assess all the parameters more negatively. These results reveal certain negative prejudices about Ro-Ro SSS by non-users, which undoubtedly constitute a barrier to its adoption. This finding supports the idea that although transport companies are one of the key players in the development of Ro-Ro SSS, their reluctance to use this mode of transport for their semi-trailers is well known. This reluctance, beyond the negative prejudices noted earlier, may be due to the inherent adjustments to operating strategies that firms must make when switching to Ro-Ro SSS (Gouvernal et al., 2010; López-Navarro, 2013a). However, in an economic and institutional context favourable to the use of intermodal transport, road hauliers must make the effort to integrate into intermodal transport chains. In addition, if their purpose is to operate more consistently in this field using the most efficient option – unaccompanied transportation – they must introduce changes in their business model in order to achieve maximum efficiency and profitability.

We now turn to the main research question in this study, namely the analysis of the evolution of the road hauliers' operating strategies in the use of Ro-Ro SSS. To this end, we conduct a comparative analysis with the results of the previous study carried out in 2007, which should allow us to identify certain patterns of behaviour in companies' use of this mode of transport. Our initial hypotheses were as follows: (a) given the growing competitive pressure on road freight transport in recent years and increasing institutional support for intermodal transport, it can be expected that companies which were using Ro-Ro SSS at time t_0 will have intensified their use at time t_1; (b) given that unaccompanied transport is more profitable than accompanied transport, it is expected that the companies that were using the accompanied transport in the context of Ro-Ro SSS at time t_0 will have evolved towards unaccompanied transport at the time t_1.

Our comparative analysis of the results of the 2007 study and the present investigation can only be made for the SSS lines between Spain and Italy, given that this was the geographical scope of the first study. In the 2007 study the following Ro-Ro SSS lines were considered: Barcelona-Genoa (operated by the Grandi Navi Veloci shipping company), Tarragona-Livorno (operated by the Suardíaz shipping company) and Barcelona-Rome, Valencia-Livorno and Valencia-Salerno (operated by the Grimaldi shipping company). At the time of the current study the scenario was slightly different, as the Tarragona-Livorno line was no longer operational, the Barcelona-Genoa line, although operational, had reduced its frequency to two weekly departures, and the Valencia-Livorno line operated as a circular Valencia-Barcelona-Livorno-Savona line with three weekly departures. Also, at the beginning of 2014, the Grimaldi shipping company extended its independent departures from Barcelona and Valencia to Livorno and Savona and increased the frequencies of this route, thus corroborating this company's commitment to Ro-Ro SSS and the MoS in the Mediterranean Sea.

Given these changes and the possible cargo transfers that may have occurred between the different SSS lines, we consider it appropriate to analyze the evolution of shipments by the two shipping companies that operated at the time of the second study: Grandi Navi Veloci and Grimaldi. The evolution in terms of the continuity of the road hauliers' use of Ro-Ro SSS and their shipments is shown in Tables 8.5 and 8.6. The results highlight the impact, in the case of the Barcelona-Genoa line (operated by Grandi Navi Veloci), of the reduction in frequency from six weekly departures to only two in the period between the two studies. Thus, of the 26 companies considered that used this line in 2007, only three continued to operate through it in 2014 (the total variation in the number of weekly shipments

Table 8.5 Road hauliers' evolution (2007–2014).

Shipping company	Road hauliers that operated with the shipping company in 2007	Road hauliers that operate with the shipping company in 2014	Road hauliers that stopped operating in the period analyzed	Road hauliers that started operating in the period analyzed	Road hauliers that continued to operate in the period analyzed	Variation (semi-trailers loaded per week)
Grimaldi	27	23	10	6[b]	17	+ 685.97
Grandi Navi Veloci	26	3[a]	23	0	3	− 462.56

(a) The three companies that currently use the Ro-Ro SSS line operated by Grandi Navi Veloci also use some of the Ro-Ro SSS lines operated by Grimaldi.
(b) These are companies that in 2007 used the Ro-Ro SSS line operated by Grandi Navi Veloci.

Table 8.6 Variation in the number of semi-trailers loaded per week considering only the road hauliers that continue using Ro-Ro SSS ($n = 23$).

	2007	2014
Semi-trailers loaded per week (average values)	40.14	60.06

shows a negative balance of 462.56 units). In contrast, in the case of the lines operated by Grimaldi, the overall situation evolved favourably (the variation in the number of shipments had a positive balance of 685.97 weekly units for the road hauliers considered in the study).

The first of our hypotheses is not easy to interpret in light of the events that have taken place during the period under analysis. Of the 51 companies from which we tried to collect information in the two moments of time considered, and as we have indicated in the methodology section, 11 were no longer active, 13 did not answer because they no longer used SSS and two were in the end not considered because, although they used the SSS, they no longer operated the lines between Spain and Italy (in addition to two others who decided not to participate). The reduction in the number of departures in the case of the Ro-Ro SSS line operated by the company Grandi Navi Veloci, but also the effects of the economic crisis, may have influenced these figures. However, and regarding the behaviour of the companies that continued using the SSS in the period under analysis, to a certain extent the results support the hypothesis proposed; that is, they show a positive evolution in the use of Ro-Ro SSS through the increase in the number of weekly shipments. However, the data on average are misleading, since the relevant increases are associated with just five companies that significantly increased their shipments, and more specifically in the unaccompanied transport mode. These companies represent 83.8% of the shipments (of the 23 companies considered) and together they have increased by 575.4 units the weekly shipments in the period analyzed. Of the other companies analyzed, only four had increased numbers of shipments. These results show a market that is evolving towards greater concentration.

Finally, and with regard to the second of the hypotheses proposed (the accompanied vs. unaccompanied transport operating strategy), no relevant transfer to the second option seems to be observed over time as a consequence of the experience accumulated in the use of Ro-Ro SSS. The five most relevant user companies mentioned earlier used unaccompanied transport almost exclusively, whereas the remaining 18 road hauliers mainly followed the accompanied transport strategy, the same pattern as in 2007. This finding reveals the difficulty of shifting from a model of accompanied transport, with fewer necessary organizational adjustments, to the unaccompanied transport model, which requires more substantial changes to operate.

5 Conclusions

Within the framework of the EU transport policy, the promotion of SSS, and especially the MoS, constitutes one of the basic pillars of action to achieve sustainable mobility. However, despite significant investments through various European programmes, the outcomes do not seem to align with the proposed objectives.

The present study was developed from the perspective of one of the key actors in consolidating this intermodal option: road hauliers. The research makes several contributions; firstly, that road haulier companies are the main agents in the decision to use Ro-Ro SSS, as compared to potential demands from the shippers themselves. This conclusion reinforces previous claims in the literature that road hauliers are the key players in coordinating the intermodal transport chain with regard to semi-trailers and can guide public administrations in their decisions when offering incentives to promote the development of Ro-Ro SSS.

Secondly, our analysis of user companies' perceptions of Ro-Ro SSS versus all-road transport reveals that when the traditional parameters associated with transport are considered – cost or transit times – user road hauliers evaluate the intermodal option more favourably. This more favourable assessment also applies to safety and especially environmental impact. Although some studies note that SSS is not always the best choice in environmental terms (Hjelle, 2010; Vanherle and Delhaye, 2010; López-Navarro, 2014), there is a widespread tendency in the professional field to emphasize the environmental advantages of SSS. This is shown, for example, in the technical training days provided by the Spanish Association for the Promotion of SSS to promote this mode of transport.

Notwithstanding these positive assessments related to intermodal transport, when we refer to issues associated with complexity (both operational and administrative) Ro-Ro SSS users assess this option in less favourable terms than unimodal road transport. The administrative complexity involved in SSS calls for decisions at the political EU level to streamline these procedures. As for operational complexity, the results show that the increased number of agents involved in the transport chain makes intermodal transport more complex and strengthens the calls for greater collaboration among them. In fact, this lack of collaboration appears as one of the major problems in a relatively recent study requested by the European Parliament's Committee on Transport and Tourism (European Parliament, 2014). Although the reality confirms the difficulties in adequately optimizing intermodal transport chains, it is necessary to seek cooperation among the different agents in order to offer shippers the best logistics solutions according to their needs, in terms of both economic competitiveness and environmental sustainability.

Thirdly, the more negative perceptions of Ro-Ro SSS by the 'non-users', as opposed to the 'users', especially in some relatively objective parameters (such as cost or transit times, with values below the midpoint on the measurement scale in the case of non-users), may be reflecting certain information barriers to non-users' conceptions of Ro-Ro SSS. The future lines of action defined in the report requested by the European Parliament's Committee on Transport and Tourism, referred to earlier, identify the need to raise awareness about the opportunities offered by the MoS through an active campaign targeting all stakeholders, not only ports and port authorities, and state that many of the logistics actors are still unaware of their benefits. The report explicitly states that the provision of information on SSS and the MoS should be extended to other interested parties, such as intermodal transport operators, logistics service providers and shippers, which would help potential partners to reflect jointly on possible services and projects.

Finally, our analysis of the behaviour patterns of the road hauliers' use of Ro-Ro SSS, the main objective of the study, reveals that:

a   Although the number of shipments increased in the analyzed period, it has not been possible to verify a firm commitment by the companies analyzed to intensify their use. The fact that during the period considered one of the two shipping companies (NGV) substantially reduced the frequency of weekly departures (from six to two) in the line it operates has meant that most of the road hauliers using that line ceased to use Ro-Ro SSS. Although there has been a rise in the total number of shipments between Spain and Italy by the companies analyzed as a result of the improvement of the services of the other shipping company considered (Grimaldi), this development has gone hand in hand with a limited number of larger road hauliers. These road haulier companies have developed a business model based on unaccompanied transport and in close collaboration with the shipping company, so they are benefiting from significant market share increases. The rest of the companies have experienced marginal variations in terms of the number of shipments.

b Taking into account the two points in time considered, in contrast to what might be expected, we observed no significant transition from an accompanied to an unaccompanied transport operating strategy among the companies analyzed. Apart from the road hauliers that have most benefited from the increase in the number of shipments and that already followed an unaccompanied transport model in 2007, the accompanied transport mode still prevails in the rest of the companies that continue to use Ro-Ro SSS. Considering the greater advantages associated with unaccompanied transport, this finding highlights the difficulties involved in the process of transition towards this operating strategy.

Apart from the importance of the aspects linked to the characteristic parameters of Ro-Ro SSS lines, the results point to the relevance of the road hauliers' business model or operating strategy when using Ro-Ro SSS and the MoS, as well as their collaborative relationships with the shipping companies.

The present study is not without limitations. Firstly, the research was based on a small number of companies, which is especially noticeable in our comparison of 'user' and 'non-user' perceptions of Ro-Ro SSS. Secondly, the analysis of the behavioural patterns in the road hauliers' operational strategies within the framework of Ro-Ro SSS are limited to the context of Spain and Italy and to the companies that participated in the study carried out in 2007. However, it is our understanding that these limitations do not undermine the results of the present investigation.

References

Baindur, D., & Viegas, J.M. (2012), Success factors for developing viable motorways of the sea projects in Europe. *Logistics Research*, 4 (3–4), pp. 137–145.

Baird, A.J. (2007), The economics of motorways of the sea. *Maritime Policy & Management*, 34 (4), pp. 287–310.

Bergantino, A.A., & Bolis, S. (2004), An analysis of maritime Ro-Ro fright transport service attributes through adaptive state preferences: An application to a sample of freight forwarders. *European Transport*, 25–26, pp. 33–51.

Bergantino, A.S., & Bolis, S. (2008), Monetary values of transport service attributes: Land versus maritime ro-ro transport. An application using adaptive stated preferences. *Maritime Policy & Management*, 35 (2), pp. 159–174.

Brooks, M.R., & Trifts, V. (2008), Short sea shipping in North America: Understanding the requirements of Atlantic Canadian shippers. *Maritime Policy & Management*, 35 (2), pp. 145–158.

Caris, A., Macharis, C., & Janssens, G.K. (2008), Planning problems in intermodal freight transport: Accomplishments and prospects. *Transportation Planning and Technology*, 31 (3), pp. 277–302.

Christodoulou, A., Raza, Z., & Woxenius, J. (2019), The integration of RoRo shipping in sustainable intermodal transport chains: The case of a North European RoRo service. *Sustainability*, 11, pp. 2422.

Cristea, A., Hummels, D., Puzzello, L., & Avetisyan, M. (2013), Trade and the greenhouse gas emissions from international freight transport. *Journal of Environmental Economics and Management*, 65 (1), pp. 153–173.

Desiderio, M., Reffet, F., Potier, M., Le Bourhis, P., & De Solere, R. (2008), Motorways of the sea and rolling highways: From the users' point of view. Paper presented at the European Transport Conference, Association for European Transport.

De Solere, R. (2007), Study of relevance criteria governing long-distance unaccompanied road transport. The choice for sustainable development. Paper presented at the 23rd PIARC World Road Congress, 15–21 September, Paris.

Douet, M., & Cappuccilli, J.F. (2011), A review of short sea shipping policy in the European Union. *Journal of Transport Geography*, 19 (4), pp. 968–976.

Ellram, L.M., & Golicic, S.L. (2015), Adopting environmental transportation practices. *Transportation Journal*, 54 (1), pp. 55–88.

Eng-Larsson, F., & Kohn, C. (2012), Modal shift for greener logistics – the shipper's perspective. *International Journal of Physical Distribution & Logistics Management*, 42 (1), pp. 36–59.

European Commission (2011), White paper – Roadmap to a single European transport area – towards a competitive and resource efficient transport system. Available at https://ec.europa.eu/transport/themes/strategies/2011_white_paper_en (accessed 14 May 2019).

European Commission (2016), A European strategy for low-emission mobility. Available at https://eur-lex.europa.eu/resource.html?uri=cellar:e44d3c21-531e-11e6-89bd-01aa75ed71a1.0002.02/DOC_1&format=PDF (accessed 14 May 2019).

European Commission (2018), Motorways of the sea. Detailed implementation plan of the European coordinator Brian Simpson, April. Available at https://ec.europa.eu/transport/sites/transport/files/101_web_final_ii_mos_dip_2018.pdf (accessed 14 May 2019); www.eea.europa.eu/publications/road-user-charges-for-vehicles (accessed 14 May 2019).

European Court of Auditors (2013), Have the Marco Polo programmes been effective in shifting traffic from the road? Special Report n° 3, Luxembourg. Available at https://publications.europa.eu/en/publication-detail/-/publication/b00ba421-8036-44fd-9654-ba17199dadd8/language-en (accessed 14 May 2019).

European Environment Agency (2013), Road user charges for heavy goods vehicles (HGV). Technical Report N° 1/2013.

European Parliament (2014), Improving the concept of motorways of the sea. Directorate-general for internal policies policy department B: Structural and cohesion policies.

Available at www.europarl.europa.eu/RegData/etudes/STUD/2014/540330/IPOL_STU(2014)540330_EN.pdf (accessed 14 May 2019).
Feo, M., Espino, R., & Garcia, L. (2011), An stated preference analysis of Spanish freight forwarders modal choice on the south-west Europe motorway of the sea. *Transport Policy*, 18 (1), pp. 60–67.
Gese, X., & Baird, A.J. (2013), Motorways of the sea policy in Europe. *Maritime Policy & Management*, 40 (1), pp. 10–26.
Gouvernal, E., Slack, B., & Franc, P. (2010), Short sea and deep sea shipping markets in France. *Journal of Transport Geography*, 18 (1), pp. 97–103.
Hjelle, H.M. (2010), Short sea shipping's green label at risk. *Transport Reviews*, 30 (5), pp. 617–640.
Hjelle, H.M., & Fridell, E. (2012), When is short sea shipping environmentally competitive? In J. Oosthuizen (Ed.) *Environmental Health-Emerging Issues and Practice* (pp. 3–20). Rijeka, Croatia: IntechOpen.
Larson, P.D., Elias, A., & Viafara, J. (2013), Toward sustainable trucking: Reducing emissions and fuel consumption. *Transportation Journal*, 52 (1), pp. 108–120.
Llano, C., Pérez-Balsalobre, S., & Pérez-García, J. (2018), Greenhouse gas emissions from intra-national freight transport: Measurement and scenarios for greater sustainability in Spain. *Sustainability*, 10 (7), pp. 1–33.
López-Navarro, M.Á. (2013a), Unaccompanied transport as a strategy for international road hauliers in Ro-Ro short sea shipping. *Maritime Economics & Logistics*, 15 (3), pp. 374–394.
López-Navarro, M.Á. (2013b), The effect of shared planning by road transport firms and shipping companies on performance in the intermodal transport chain: The case of Ro-Ro short sea shipping. *European Journal of Transport and Infrastructure Research*, 31 (1), pp. 39–55.
López-Navarro, M.Á. (2014), Environmental factors and intermodal freight transportation: Analysis of the decision bases in the case of Spanish motorways of the sea. *Sustainability*, 6 (3), pp. 1544–1566.
López-Navarro, M.Á., Moliner-Tena, M.Á., & Rodríguez-Artola, R.M. (2011a), Long-term orientation of international road transport firms in their relationship with shipping companies: The case of short sea shipping. *Transportation Journal*, 50 (4), pp. 346–369.
López-Navarro, M.Á., Moliner-Tena, M.A., Rodríguez-Artola, R.M., & Sánchez, J. (2011b), Accompanied versus unaccompanied transport in short sea shipping between Spain and Italy: An analysis from transport road firms perspective. *Transport Reviews*, 31 (4), pp. 425–444.
Martinsen, U., & Björklund, M. (2012), Matches and gaps in the green logistics market. *International Journal of Physical Distribution & Logistics Management*, 42 (6), pp. 562–583.
Martinsen, U., & Huge-Brodin, M. (2010), Greening the offerings of logistics service providers. Proceeding of the 22nd Annual NOFOMA Conference, June 10–11, Kolding, Denmark, pp. 969–984.
Michaelides, M.P., Herodotou, H., Lind, M., & Watson, R.T. (2019), Port-2-Port communication enhancing short sea shipping performance: The case study of Cyprus and the eastern Mediterranean. *Sustainability*, 11 (7), pp. 1–22.
Morales-Fusco, P., Grau, M., & Saurí, S. (2018), Effects of RoPax shipping line strategies on freight price and transporter's choice. Policy implications for promoting MoS. *Transport Policy*, 67, pp. 67–76.

Morales-Fusco, P., Saurí, S., & Lago, A. (2012), Potential freight distribution improvements using motorways of the sea. *Journal of Transport Geography*, 24, pp. 1–11.

OECD/ITF (2015), ITF transport Outlook 2015, OECD Publishing/ITF. Available at www.oecd.org/environment/itf-transport-outlook-2015-9789282107782-en.htm (accessed 14 May 2019).

Paixão Casaca, A.C., & Marlow, P.B. (2002), Strengths and weaknesses of short sea shipping. *Marine Policy*, 26 (3), pp. 167–178.

Paixão Casaca, A.C., & Marlow, P.B. (2007), The impact of the trans-European transport networks on the development of short sea shipping. *Maritime Economics & Logistics*, 9 (4), pp. 302–323.

Pérez-Mesa, J.C., Céspedes-Lorente, J.J., & Andújar, J.A.S. (2010), Feasibility study for a Motorway of the Sea (MoS) between Spain and France: Application to the transportation of perishable cargo. *Transport Reviews*, 30 (4), pp. 451–471.

Puckett, S.M., Hensher, D.A., Brooks, M.R., & Trifts, V. (2011), Preferences for alternative short sea shipping opportunities. *Transportation Research Part E*, 47, pp. 182–189.

Rodríguez, A. (2012), El transporte marítimo de corta distancia y las autopistas del mar. *Papeles de economía española*, 131, pp. 268–247.

Santos, T.A., & Guedes Soares, C. (2017), Methodology for ro-ro ship and fleet sizing with application to short sea shipping. *Maritime Policy & Management*, 44 (7), pp. 859–881.

Schramm, H.J. (2006), Governance of multimodal transport chains: A brokerage roles approach. Proceedings of the Logistics Research Network Annual Conference. Newcastle, 6–8 September.

Sternberg, H., Germann, T., & Klaas-Wissing, T. (2013), Who controls the fleet? Initial insights into road freight transport planning and control from an industrial network perspective. *International Journal of Logistics Research and Applications*, 16 (6), pp. 493–505.

Torbianelli, V.A. (2000), When the road controls the sea: A case study of Ro-Ro transport in the Mediterranean. *Maritime Policy and Management*, 27 (4), pp. 375–389.

Vanherle, K., & Delhaye, E. (2010), Road versus short sea shipping: Comparing emissions and external costs. Proceedings of the International Association of Maritime Economists, July, Lisbon, Portugal, pp. 7–9.

Woxenius, J., & Bergqvist, R. (2011), Comparing maritime containers and semi-trailers in the context of hinterland transport by rail. *Journal of Transport Geography*, 19 (4), pp. 680–688.

9 The competitiveness of Motorways of the Sea

A case study in Italy

Marino Lupi, Alessandro Farina and Antonio Pratelli

1 Introduction

Motorways of the Sea (MoS) are Ro-Ro and Ro-Pax short sea shipping (SSS) services with specific characteristics: they have to be viable, regular, frequent, high quality, reliable and integrated in door-to-door logistics chains. MoS were proposed in the 2001 White Paper on the European transport policy (European Commission, 2001) and have then become one of the priority projects of the Trans-European Transport Network (TEN-T) programme (European Parliament, 2004). They are aimed at setting up a valid alternative to all-road transport and integrating inland transport, especially where geographical constraints exist. The European Commission strongly supports the development of MoS as a valid alternative to the all-road mode. According to the 2011 White Paper (European Commission, 2011), road transport is no longer sustainable: high CO_2 emissions are registered and the increase in road congestion requires the construction of new roads.

A study by Grimaldi for the European Climate Change Programme, cited in the 2001 White Paper (European Commission, 2001: 42), demonstrated that, on any given link, the intermodal option based on SSS produced 2.5 times less pollution, in the form of CO_2 emissions, than the all-road option. A comparison analysis for the Genoa (IT)-Preston (UK) corridor points out that the external cost of a 40-feet container is about 0.14 euro/km for SSS compared to 0.24 euro/km for all-road transport (Black *et al.* 2003, tab. 4.23:73). In Denisis (2009), it is calculated that, in the US, the external cost of MoS is, on the average, 0.0319 $/ton-mi, while the external cost of all-road transport is, on the average, 0.0647 $/ton-mi. External costs are calculated from air pollution, climate change, noise, congestion and accidents.

Some studies have been carried out on the competitiveness of MoS against all-road transport, for example Ng (2009). MoS still have to overcome several shortcomings: to carry out an integrated door-to-door service, they require the 'collaboration' of the road or rail mode for collection and delivery and a network of well-located inland terminals. Nowadays the efficiency of ports, seaside port services and landside port services, that is, port-hinterland connections, is still too low: as shown in Fusco *et al.* (2012), this can badly affect the competitiveness of intermodal transport. The most critical aspect regards the complexity of administrative procedures in ports, which leads to high transit times and, therefore, to a severe decrease of the efficiency of MoS services. A lot of effort still has to be done, in both Italy and Europe, in order to achieve a considerable modal shift from road to MoS. Indeed, in Italy in 2016, MoS accounted for about 6% of road freight traffic, while in the EU-28, the situation is even worse: MoS accounted for only 1.7% of road freight traffic according to Eurostat (2019). On the other hand, the EU would have a wide potentiality for the development of MoS, because it has a coastline of 67,000 km and has between 60% and 70% of its industrial and production centres located within 150–200 km off the coast.

In this chapter, firstly, the evolution of Motorways of the Sea services offered at Italian ports is analyzed. Detailed research on MoS routes calling at Italian ports in 2015 has been carried out. Within MoS routes, the main characteristics of Ro-Pax services (which serve not only freight vehicles, but also passenger ones) and cargo only Ro-Ro services (which carry only freight vehicles) are identified. In the following, we will refer to this last type of routes as 'cargo Ro-Ro'.

Subsequently, the evolution of MoS routes is studied, and in particular Italian MoS routes in 2015 are compared with those in the years 2008, 2010 and 2012. This study highlights two main aspects. Firstly, the great majority of MoS routes in Italy are Ro-Pax ones: cargo Ro-Ro routes are only 31% of the total. Secondly, from 2008 to 2015, route frequencies have decreased, while the number of port calls in each route has increased. More recent data about Italian MoS routes were collected in March 2019; this research is currently ongoing, therefore only aggregated results for the year 2019 are presented in this chapter. Regarding the number of routes and frequencies per week, 2019 data register the opposite trend, as both have increased from 2015 to 2019; however, 2019 values are still below those of 2012.

The capability of cargo Ro-Ro and Ro-Pax routes of being competitive against all-road transport has also been studied. Both cargo Ro-Ro and Ro-Pax routes, currently, show several problems related to their competitiveness against all-road mode: Ro-Pax routes are not reliable and cargo Ro-Ro routes are not fast and frequent; consequently, they neither fulfil essential requirements for MoS services. As reported at the beginning of this introduction, MoS services must be viable, regular, frequent, high quality, reliable and integrated in door-to-door logistic chains.

This chapter also presents a quantitative analysis on the competitiveness of intermodal transport, based on MoS, in comparison with all-road transport. This analysis, described in section 3, concerns the intermodal alternative, based on MoS, against the all-road mode in the Ligurian Sea coastal region. This region shows a relevant freight transport demand and several road and rail mobility problems due to road congestion. Moreover, the territory orography makes it difficult, and costly, to build new roads or to improve existing ones. As a result, a modal shift of at least some part of freight traffic, from all-road to intermodal transport, is desirable. Nevertheless, the distances among coastal cities are low, often much lower than the break-even distances of intermodal transport reported in literature.

In the first phase of this analysis, the alternative to the all-road mode consisting of the MoS routes currently in operation has been studied. A detailed network model (road and MoS) has been developed to compare monetary costs and travel times for the two alternatives: all-road and intermodal transport based on MoS. Currently, intermodal transport is far from convenient, from the point of view of both monetary costs and travel times. Indeed, direct MoS connections between these ports do not exist: all MoS alternatives actually require the use of two routes in succession, with interchange in Corsica. In addition, the arrival time of the first route does not coincide with the departure time of the second service, and no fare integration exists.

Several improvement scenarios have been studied. In the first scenario, a fare integration between the two routes composing the MoS alternative has been introduced. In the second scenario, the two current routes (e.g. Leghorn–Bastia and Bastia–Nice) are joined into a single route (e.g. Leghorn–Bastia–Nice) to reduce travel times. Finally, in the third scenario, the development of completely new MoS routes has been studied: this scenario requires greater investments than do the previous ones but is the best in terms of competitiveness of intermodal transport against all-road transport.

2 Motorways of the Sea routes in Italy

2.1 Italian Motorways of the Sea routes in 2015

In this section, an analysis has been performed on Motorways of the Sea routes to/from Italian ports. This study distinguishes between Ro-Pax services (i.e. routes which serve not only freight vehicles but also passenger ones) and cargo Ro-Ro services (which carry only freight vehicles). Data have been recorded from July to October 2015. This choice is due to the high seasonality effects of Ro-Pax services during the year: several routes reduce their frequencies, or register no departures at all, during low season periods. The months of July and August are high season, September can be considered as a transition period, while October is low season. As a result, the most significant data are those of July and August (high season) and October (low season).

The total number of cargo Ro-Ro routes (national and international) is 30; these routes are managed by 7 shipping companies, with 69 departures per week, and connect 14 Italian ports and 10 non-Italian ports. The number of departures per week is always the same in the period of study, because there is no variability in cargo Ro-Ro departures from high season to low season periods.

The total number of Ro-Pax routes (domestic and international) is 61 in high season and 47 in low season, with 339 departures per week in high season and 200 departures per week in low season. They are managed by 23 shipping companies and connect 41 ports in high season and 40 in low season: 22 (high season) and 21 (low season) Italian and 19 non-Italian ports.

Routes are reported extensively in the appendix of Lupi *et al.* (2017a). The most frequent routes are those which connect the Italian mainland with the islands or the two sides of the Adriatic Sea. The most frequent domestic routes are Leghorn–Olbia and Napoli–Palermo, which connect the Italian mainland with the islands of Sardinia and Sicily. Among international routes, the most frequent ones are Pozzallo–Malta, which is the shortest route to reach Malta from Italy, and the routes connecting Adriatic ports to Greece.

The port connected to the highest number of destinations (national and international) is Genoa, with 13 destinations, while Leghorn is connected to 12 destinations. The port which registers the highest number of departures per week is Leghorn, with 75 departures per week (national and international) in July and August (high season), 68 in September and 48 in October (low season).

The collected data show that the majority of MoS routes are Ro-Pax. In high season (July and August), only 33% of routes are cargo Ro-Ro, against 67% of Ro-Pax. In low season (October), the percentage of Ro-Pax routes is slightly less: 39% of routes are cargo Ro-Ro, against 61% of Ro-Pax routes. Moreover, cargo Ro-Ro departures per week are 17% of the total departures per week in high season (July and August) and around 28% in October (low season). Ro-Pax departures instead are 83% of the total in high season and around 72% in low season. As far as the number of port calls is concerned, in general, cargo Ro-Ro routes cross a greater number of ports. Indeed, about 70% of Ro-Pax routes, but only about 37% of cargo Ro-Ro routes, is point to point. About 23%–25% (low season) of Ro-Pax routes cross three ports, while 43% of cargo Ro-Ro routes cross three ports. Finally, while 20% of cargo Ro-Ro routes cross more than three ports, only about 3%–4% of Ro-Pax routes crosses more than three ports. The shape of cargo Ro-Ro and Ro-Pax routes is generally different: a cargo Ro-Ro route may perform a long path, for example connecting Savona and Genoa with Catania and Bari, in order to achieve a higher load factor of the ship, while a Ro-Pax route usually stops at intermediate ports only if their geographical position is along the route. For example, the Ro-Pax route Venice–Ancona–Igoumenitsa–Patras calls at the ports of Ancona and Igoumenitsa because they are along the route between Venice and Patras.

2.2 Cargo Ro-Ro and Ro-Pax services and the competition of Motorways of the Sea against all-road transport

To understand whether cargo Ro-Ro or Ro-Pax routes can be competitive against all-road transport, road hauliers, operating between the Italian mainland and Sicily, were interviewed about the main aspects which influence their choice between intermodal transport, based on MoS, and all-road (see Lupi et al., 2017c). The interviewed firms reported that monetary costs (in particular ticket costs), travel times and route frequencies are always the most important characteristics of a competitive MoS route. But road hauliers reported that the reliability of MoS routes is another essential factor: a change in route schedules or the unavailability of some services because the ship is full is perceived very badly.

Ro-Pax routes register higher frequencies and lower travel times (because they call at a lower number of ports) than cargo Ro-Ro routes do. On the other hand, Ro-Pax routes lack in reliability. Indeed, while in low season Ro-Pax ships have a low load factor, in high season they are almost full. As a result, it often happens that commercial vehicles are not able to make the reservation for the desired ship departure, because it is already full, and have to postpone their departure, for example to the day after. This occurs quite often because usually passengers (and their cars) are able to make their reservation a long time in advance (therefore they usually find an available space on the ship), while it is not the same for freight vehicles. This results in a lack of reliability, which is not acceptable for MoS services in competition with all-road ones. Therefore, to allow passengers and cargo to share the same ship is not a good solution for increasing competition of intermodal transport. On the other hand, it is clear that this choice is made by MoS operators in order to maximize their revenues.

In synthesis, both cargo Ro-Ro and Ro-Pax services are inadequate to offer a competitive alternative against all-road freight transport. Ro-Pax routes perform well regarding frequencies and travel times but badly as far as reliability is concerned. On the other hand, cargo Ro-Ro services perform well as far as the reliability of the service is concerned but badly regarding travel times and frequencies.

2.3 The development of Motorways of the Sea from 2008 to 2015 and the trend after 2015

Italian MoS routes that operated in 2015 were compared with those in 2008, 2010 and 2012. The collected data refer to February 2008, March 2010 and November 2012. These routes have been reported in detail in Danesi *et al.* (2008, 2010) and Lupi and Farina (2014). The data have been collected in low season periods. Actually, the analysis of the years 2008–2012 did not aim at distinguishing between cargo Ro-Ro and Ro-Pax routes and at analyzing their differences, therefore the seasonality of Ro-Pax routes was not of concern. In addition, while cargo Ro-Ro routes keep the same frequencies during the year, in high season Ro-Pax routes are not reliable, because some departures are unavailable for booking because the ship is full. This was the reason why the survey in previous years has been performed only in low season periods. In addition, cargo Ro-Ro and Ro-Pax routes for 2015 are considered together in the comparison, because in the previous years cargo Ro-Ro and Ro-Pax routes were not distinguished. These data have also been compared with the newest ones, collected in March 2019, which is again a low season period.

The results of the comparison are shown in Tables 9.1 and 9.2. All these data show an evolution towards longer routes, calling at a greater number of ports.

Table 9.1 Synthesis of the comparison among 2008, 2010, 2012, 2015 (low and high season) and 2019 data.

	n° departures by week						n° routes					
	2008 l.s.	2010 l.s.	2012 l.s.	2015 l.s.	2015 h.s.	2019 l.s.	2008 l.s.	2010 l.s.	2012 l.s.	2015 l.s.	2015 h.s.	2019 l.s.
Domestic	169	174	166	109	164	165	28	32	35	29	33	37
International	245	250	241	156	244	141	50	45	46	48	58	44
Total	414	424	407	265	408	306	77	77	91	77	91	81

Table 9.2 Number of routes calling at a given number of ports in 2008, 2010, 2012, 2015 (low and high season) and 2019.

Route typology	n° routes						percentage of routes					
	2008 l.s.	2010 l.s.	2012 l.s.	2015 l.s.	2015 h.s.	2019 l.s.	2008 l.s.	2010 l.s.	2012 l.s.	2015 l.s.	2015 h.s.	2019 l.s.
Point-to-point	73	67	63	43	55	51	94.8	86.8	69.2	55.8	60.4	62.9
Connecting 3 ports	4	10	19	26	28	22	5.2	13.2	20.9	33.8	30.7	27.2
Connecting more than 3 ports	0	0	9	8	8	8	0	0	9.9	10.4	8.8	9.9
Total	77	77	91	77	91	81	100	100	100	100	100	100

As a result, the route length increases, but also travel times increase and average speeds decrease. Consequently, the competitiveness with all-road transport decreases. This is particularly evident when the low season of 2015 is considered. In Table 9.1, the number of routes and the route frequencies, in the years under analysis, are reported. The number of routes and route frequencies have been distinguished in domestic, international and total (i.e. domestic and international). In this table, and also in Table 9.2, 'l.s.' represents 'low season' and 'h.s.' represents 'high season'.

From the comparison, a severe decrease in the departures per week can be observed from 2012 to 2015, although this trend already existed from 2010 to 2012. In addition, the variability of weekly frequencies between high and low season in 2015 is also relevant: 408 in high season and 265 in low season. As regards the number of routes, an initial increase from 2008 to 2012 could be observed, but the number of routes registers a decrease from 2012 to 2015. An explanation of this phenomenon could be that operators try to maximize the revenues and put in operation only routes with a high load factor of ships: therefore, in low season when the transport demand is lower, some routes are not operated and the route frequencies are highly reduced. In addition, it can be observed that some routes, from 2012 to 2015, have been joined: for example, the routes Genoa–Palermo and Leghorn–Palermo have been joined in a route Genoa–Leghorn–Palermo–Genoa. This choice has been made by MoS operators in order to serve more markets by a single route, because, in this way, the load factor of ships could be further increased.

Furthermore, as shown in Table 9.2, from 2008 to 2015, MoS routes became longer and called at a higher number of ports. In 2008, around 95% of routes were point-to-point; in 2015, only 60% of routes were point-to-point in high season, while in low season they were only 56%.

After 2015, the trend changed. From 2015 to 2019, an increase in frequencies per week has taken place, from 265 in 2015 (low season) to 306 in 2019 (low season). However, this increase is completely due to domestic routes, because frequencies of international routes have slightly reduced. Moreover, it must be underlined that 2019 frequencies are still much lower than those registered in 2008, 2010 and 2012. The number of routes has also increased, from 77 in 2015 to 81 in 2019; but in 2012 the number of routes was 91. The number of ports crossed by each route grew from 2008 to 2015 but then decreased from 2015 to 2019, because some new point-to-point routes, in competition against all-road transport, have been established.

After 2015, MoS operators have been trying to develop MoS routes which try to fulfil some of the requirements of MoS routes: frequency, travel time (fast), and integration in door-to-door logistics chains. This is in particular the strategy of the Grimaldi MoS operator. Indeed, already before 2015, Grimaldi was the most important MoS operator in Italy, followed by Tirrenia; but now Tirrenia has strongly decreased its market, the Grimaldi market has peaked, and the gap between Grimaldi and the other MoS operators has strongly increased.

3 The competitiveness of Motorways of the Sea in the Ligurian area

3.1 Characteristics of the selected Motorways of the Sea

An exploration of prospects of developing competitive MoS routes fulfilling the requirements of MoS is carried out in this section for a specific region, the Ligurian Sea coastal area. The ports taken into account are Civitavecchia, Leghorn, Genoa, Savona, Nice, Toulon and Marseilles. This case study is very interesting because the distances among ports are very low and generally are lower than the break-even distance values reported in literature; but the area is highly populated and the existing motorways are narrow, tortuous and very congested. Moreover, an important bridge of the A10 Ligurian motorway collapsed in August 2018 and the only alternative way crosses the city centre of Genoa. As a result, a modal shift of at least a part of freight traffic, from road to MoS, should be desirable.

Break-even distance values for intermodal transport based on MoS are generally very high. Martinez-Lopez *et al.* (2015:610) report, for MoS routes along the Atlantic coast, a break-even distance between 800 and 1400 km (according to the typology of freight transported and to the pre- and post-haulage distances); the same values are reported in the study of EMMA (1999), while Olivella Puig *et al.* (2004:308) report a break-even distance between 1000 and 1300 km. In European Parliament (1999), a break-even distance of 1380 km for intermodal transport based on MoS has been proposed; in the work by Jiang *et al.* (1999), a break-even distance of 1400 km has been suggested; in West MoS (2008), a break-even distance of 1000 km has been considered. These distances are considerably greater than those among ports of the Ligurian coast.

MoS routes in the study are related to October 2015. These are generally Ro-Pax routes, which show relevant changes in the frequencies due to seasonality. Therefore, the last week of October has been taken into account to determine the route

206 *Marino Lupi et al.*

frequencies to use in the study, because this week is the farthest from the high season period. The routes operated in the study area are reported in Table 9.3. The analysis shows that there is no direct MoS connection between pairs of cities of the mainland: it is always necessary to cross the port of Sardinia or Corsica, where the tractor and trailer must be disembarked from the first ship and embarked on the second.

Considering the current MoS routes supplied (see Table 9.3), the following could be observed:

- Civitavecchia is connected to Genoa only via Olbia;
- Leghorn is connected, via Bastia, to Savona, Nice, Toulon and Marseilles.

Therefore the following MoS connections were excluded:

- Civitavecchia–Genoa, because calling at Olbia means, from a geographical point of view, lengthening the path significantly.
- Leghorn–Savona, because it is necessary to change the ship at Bastia, therefore to cross the border between Italy and France twice: this, added to the short distances between Leghorn and Savona, makes the intermodal alternative not competitive.

As a result, in the analysis of the current situation, the following paths were considered:

- Leghorn–Bastia–Nice (and vice versa) with 4 services per week,
- Leghorn–Bastia–Toulon (and vice versa) with 7 services per week,
- Leghorn–Bastia–Marseilles (and vice versa) with 5 services per week from Leghorn to Marseilles and 7 vice versa.

Table 9.3 Characteristics of MoS routes in operation in the Ligurian area (data refer to the last week of October 2015).

Connection		Operator	Frequency per week
Civitavecchia	Arbatax	Tirrenia	2
Civitavecchia	Olbia	Tirrenia	7
Leghorn	Bastia	Sardinia/Corsica Ferries	7
Leghorn	Golfo Aranci	Sardinia/Corsica Ferries	7
Leghorn	Olbia	Moby Lines	7
Genoa	Porto Torres	Tirrenia	7
Genoa	Olbia	Tirrenia, Moby Lines	3
Savona	Bastia	Sardinia/Corsica Ferries	4
Bastia	Nice	Sardinia/Corsica Ferries	4
Bastia	Toulon	Sardinia/Corsica Ferries	9
Ajaccio	Toulon	Sardinia/Corsica Ferries	9
Ajaccio	Marseilles	SNCM, La Méridionale	7
Bastia	Marseilles	SNCM, La Méridionale	5 from Bastia to Marseilles, 7 vice versa

Source: Ramspa website, MoS operators' websites.

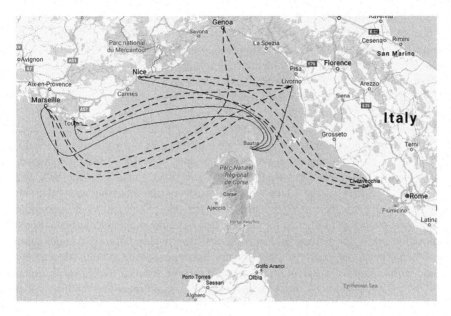

Figure 9.1 The existing routes considered in the research (solid lines) and the proposed new routes (dashed lines).

Therefore, the following three O-D pairs were considered: Leghorn–Nice, Leghorn–Toulon and Leghorn–Marseilles. The existing MoS connections taken into account in the research, that is Leghorn–Bastia, Bastia–Nice, Bastia–Toulon and Bastia–Marseilles, are reported as solid lines in Figure 9.1. The figure shows also in dashed lines the proposed routes, which will be described in section 3.4.3.

Regarding all-road transport, it has been considered a path, between each of the three O-D pairs previously reported, which crosses the motorways of the Ligurian area: A12 and A10 in Italy, A8 in France. Paths having both origin and destination in French cities, for example Nice–Marseilles, Toulon–Marseilles and Nice–Toulon, have been excluded, because they fall outside the purpose of the research; in addition, these O-D pairs are too close for intermodal transport to be competitive.

It must be underlined that in 2015, when the research was performed, the bridge of the A10 motorway was still in operation; now, travel times of road transport have increased by 15–30 minutes, depending on the hour of the day; but in the morning peak hour they can increase by 45 minutes.

3.2 Calculation of the monetary cost, the travel time and the generalized cost of paths for all-road and intermodal accompanied transportation

For each path linking the O-D pairs considered, the monetary cost, the travel time and the generalized cost have been determined, taking into account two transport modes: all-road and intermodal accompanied. An intermodal network model has been developed. The intermodal network model has been represented through a graph: origin and destination cities, ports, motorway exits and crossings have been represented through nodes; motorway and highway portions and MoS routes have been represented through links. For the monetary cost calculation, an IVECO Stralis AS 46 Eco, five axes, has been considered. In the case of intermodal unaccompanied transport, a 12.5-metre-long semi-trailer has been considered.

Generalized cost has been calculated by adding to the monetary cost the monetized transit time, that is, the transit time multiplied by the value of time (VoT). There is high disagreement in the literature about the VoT of freight transport. For the all-road mode, De Jong (2004) propose several values for the VoT, one for each freight typology, which are often also very different from each other; an average value for them is 6.33 € per tonne per hour. For road–MoS intermodal transport (which is of interest for our research), Bergantino and Bolis (2004) proposed in 2004, for national and international transport in Italy, an average value of 0.65 € per tonne per hour; but the same authors proposed in 2008 (Bergantino and Bolis, 2008), for Italian international transport, a much higher value, equal to 3.71 € per tonne per hour. A more recent VoT, again regarding the intermodal transport road–MoS, has been proposed by Feo et al. (2011), and it is equal to 6.82 €/h, considering shipments of 15 t. Therefore, a VoT equal to 0.455 € per tonne per hour is obtained: this last VoT has been used in this research for the calculation of the generalized cost.

3.2.1 Travel time of an intermodal path

The travel time of an intermodal path is composed of:

- waiting time, at the origin port, for the first ship ('frequency delay');
- embarkation time, at the origin port, on the first ship;
- voyage time on the first ship;
- disembarkation time, at the intermediate port, from the first ship;
- waiting time for the second ship at the intermediate port;
- embarkation time, at the intermediate port, on the second ship;
- voyage time on the second ship;
- disembarkation time, at the destination port, from the second ship.

In the improvement scenarios, the connection between each O-D pair is performed by a single route, which calls at the intermediate port. In this case, the travel time of an intermodal path is composed of:

- waiting time, at the origin port, for the ship ('frequency delay');
- embarkation time at the origin port;
- voyage time, which comprises also the stop time at the intermediate port;
- disembarkation time at the destination port.

The voyage times have been collected from MoS operators' websites. The waiting time for the following ship, at the intermediate port, has been calculated according to the routes' timetables. The 'frequency delay' is a quantity which takes into account the frequency of the MoS route and the fact that the maritime service is not always available at the time desired by the customer. It has been determined according to the research of Ghobrial and Kanafani (1995), performed for air transport, but adapting its results to maritime transport. Further details are reported in Lupi et al. (2017c).

As regards the time for embarking and disembarking the tractor and the semi-trailer, in accompanied transport, it was considered, as suggested in Russo (2005), that the articulated lorry must arrive at the Ro-Ro terminal at least 1.5 hours before the departure of the ship and that the time necessary for disembarking it from the ship is equal to around half an hour. Therefore, the total embarkation and disembarkation time, in accompanied transport, has been assumed equal to 2 hours.

In the case of unaccompanied transport, it is necessary to bring the semi-trailer to the terminal at least 2 hours before the departure; in addition, usually semi-trailers are the last to be disembarked, therefore a disembarkation time of 1 hour for unaccompanied transport could be assumed. As a result, the total embarkation and disembarkation time has been assumed equal to 3 hours.

3.2.2 Monetary cost of an intermodal path

The monetary cost of an intermodal path is composed of:

- ticket price, which also comprises the cost for the driver cabin (only accompanied transport) and for embarking and disembarking the semi-trailer (only unaccompanied transport);
- cost of the driver.

The ticket price has been determined analyzing MoS operators' websites; if this information was unavailable, MoS operators or maritime agencies were interviewed. The ticket price has been determined for a 16.5-metre-long articulated lorry and for only one driver in case of accompanied transport, and for a 12.5-metre-long semi-trailer in case of unaccompanied transport.

The driver cost comprises:

- driver cost for embarking/disembarking the vehicle;
- cost of the working hours lost by the driver on board and at the intermediate port while waiting for the following ship (considered only in accompanied transport).

The cost of the driver for embarking and disembarking operations has been determined considering the full cost: i.e. 26 €/h (comprising salary, taxes and pension contributions), as it was proposed in Il Sole 24 Ore (2011). In accompanied transport, 1 working hour for embarkation and 0.5 working hours for disembarkation have been considered, as proposed in Russo (2005). In unaccompanied transport it has been considered the working time to deliver and to pick up the semi-trailer at the terminal; in this case, 0.5 working hours for both embarkation and disembarkation have been taken into account (Russo, 2005).

The working hours lost by the driver on board, or waiting for the following ship, have been taken into account only in accompanied transport. These hours have been calculated according to the European Regulation No. 561/2006 (European Parliament, 2006), which regulates the drive and rest times of truck drivers. Indeed, some hours spent by the driver on board or waiting at the intermediate port could be considered as rest hours, therefore they are not paid, but if the voyage plus the waiting time at the intermediate port are greater than 11 hours, not all of these hours could be considered as rest hours. A reduced cost for the driver, equal to 17.60 €/h (Rossi and Rubino, 2009), could be taken into consideration for the lost working hours, because during the voyage or while waiting for the following ship, the driver does not work.

3.2.3 Travel time of a road link

For each road link, the length and the speed have been determined. Distances have been collected from road maps. The speed has been calculated according to the characteristics of the link (e.g. urban road, motorway, etc.) and to the typology of vehicle taken into account. For motorways and rural highways, it was considered the maximum allowed speed for a five-axis truck and trailer: 80 km/h in motorways and multilane highways and 70 km/h in two-lane highways. We took into consideration lower speeds for motorways and highways characterized by high congestion or tortuous geometry. We calculated the speed of urban links according to the characteristics of each link: road typology, level of congestion, existence of traffic lights and existence of singularities which increase the transit time.

The total travel time, in each road path, has been increased by the driver rest hours. The maximum possible working hours are calculated according to European Regulation No. 561/2006, in particular: after a 4-hour 30-minute driving period, the driver must stop driving for at least 45 minutes; the daily working period must consist of maximum 10 hours; the daily rest time must be at least 9 hours (reduced daily rest time) or 11 hours (regular daily rest time): we considered an average daily rest time of 10 hours.

3.2.4 Monetary cost of a road link

The monetary cost of a road link is equal to the sum of the following:

- Cost of the driver: equal to the number of hours driven (rest hours are not included) multiplied by the full hourly cost of the driver (26 €/h).
- Cost of the motorway ticket: calculated from the following websites: www.autostrade.it in Italy and www.autoroutes.fr in France.

- Fuel cost: calculated according to the average speed, the slope and the degree of tortuosity of the link.
- 'Other costs': amortization, taxes and insurance, lubricants, tyres, maintenance: collected, according to the typology of vehicle (IVECO Stralis AS 46 Eco, five axes), from specialized magazines; in this research, Vado e Torno (2012) has been considered.

3.3 Comparison of monetary costs and travel times between all-road and intermodal accompanied transport in the current situation

For each intermodal path, based on MoS, the monetary cost, the travel time and the generalized cost have been determined. In Table 9.4, the comparison between all-road and intermodal transport is reported. The difference in percentage between monetary and generalized costs of all-road and intermodal transport is calculated as follows:

$$\frac{\text{intermodal cost} - \text{'all-road' cost}}{\text{'all-road' cost}} \% \qquad (9.1)$$

The results reported in Table 9.4 clearly show that an intermodal alternative currently exists, but it is not convenient in terms of monetary and generalized costs and of travel times. The difference in percentage has been calculated as reported in Equation (9.1). Positive differences, in percentage, among costs point out that the intermodal alternative is worse than the all-road one; negative differences point out that the intermodal transport alternative is better than the all-road one.

3.4 Improvement scenarios

The lack of competitiveness of intermodal transport is mainly because, among the ports considered, it does not exist as a single service or route connecting the origin and destination ports without transhipment at an intermediate port. The need for changing the ship in Bastia results in high travel times and costs: the two routes do not coincide in Bastia, and it is necessary to pay for two different tickets. In addition, the necessity of crossing the port of Bastia increases the distances of the intermodal transport: for example, in the case of the path Leghorn–Nice, the distance of the intermodal transport is less than that of the all-road mode by only 5% (Table 9.4).

In order to overcome this situation, several proposals for improvement have been studied. In all improvement scenarios, the introduction of the Ecobonus has been considered. The Ecobonus provides a discount in the ticket price between 20% and 30%; this study uses a reduction by 25% of the ticket price. The first two improvement scenarios (M1 and M2) still consider calling at the port of Bastia, while the M3 scenario studies the establishment of new point-to-point routes (direct routes) from origin to destination ports without intermediate calls.

Table 9.4 Comparison, in terms of monetary cost, travel time, generalized cost and distance, between the all-road and the intermodal alternatives.

Path	all-road				Intermodal					% diff. monetary cost	% diff. generalized cost
	Monetary cost (€)	Travel time (hh:mm)	Generalized cost (€)	Distance (km)	n° services per week	Monetary cost (€)	Travel time (hh:mm)	Generalized cost (€)	Distance (km)		
Leghorn–Nice	765	05:45	804	372	4	1099	35:05	1338	354	43.66%	66.42%
Nice–Leghorn	765	05:45	804	372	4	1071	32:45	1294	354	40.00%	60.95%
Leghorn–Toulon	1078	07:35	1130	521	7	1186	26:10	1364	468	10.02%	20.71%
Toulon–Leghorn	1078	07:35	1130	521	7	1186	23:30	1346	468	10.02%	19.12%
Leghorn–Marseilles	1191	08:10	1247	576	5	1359	28:52	1556	542	14.11%	24.78%
Marseilles–Leghorn	1191	08:10	1247	576	7	1359	25:50	1535	542	14.11%	23.10%

M2 and M3 scenarios comprise also the unaccompanied intermodal transport. The unaccompanied intermodal transport was not considered in the first scenario (M1). Indeed, the unaccompanied transport would require not only the handling of the semi-trailer at the initial and final terminals, but also the presence of some personnel to look after the semi-trailer, since it is disembarked from the first ship until it is embarked on the second ship. The unaccompanied transport has been taken into account for the improvement scenarios M2 and M3, which do not require the transhipment of the road vehicle at an intermediate port; therefore, in these cases, it is not necessary to look after the road vehicle at the port.

In more detail, the improvement scenarios taken into account are the following:

M1: Fares integration: it is possible to make a single ticket (with a minor cost per t-km) for the service between the O-D port pairs; this service is still composed of two separate routes calling at Bastia, performed by two different ships, although only one ticket is used.

M2: Merging of the two routes, necessary to connect each O-D pair, in a single route: for example, merging the routes Leghorn–Bastia and Bastia–Nice in a single route Leghorn–Bastia–Nice. As a result, it is possible to reach Nice from Leghorn using the same ship, but contemporarily, the transport demand to/from Bastia is satisfied. This leads to a high benefit in terms not only of ticket cost but also of travel time. In addition, this improves connections between Leghorn and Nice without the necessity to provide a new point-to-point route, which is a more sizeable investment than the fusion of the existing routes.

M3: This improvement scenario regards the establishment of new point-to-point (direct) routes connecting the ports of the Ligurian coast without any intermediate stop. In this case, the investment is greater than those in the two previous improvement scenarios.

3.4.1 Scenario M1: fare integration

This improvement scenario (M1) considers maintaining routes and timetables at the current status but using a single ticket for the two routes in the intermodal path. For example, in the path Leghorn–Nice, it would be no longer necessary to purchase two tickets, Leghorn–Bastia and Bastia–Nice, but only one ticket would be purchased, whose price is calculated considering the connection Leghorn–Nice (through Bastia) as if it were composed of only one route.

For this improvement scenario, it was necessary to determine a relation which allows to calculate the ticket price as a function of the route length. Several relations have been studied in Lupi *et al.* (2017b), section 6.1. The relation which provided the best results has been the following:

$$p = k + m\, l \qquad (9.2)$$

where:
p is ticket price (€);
l is route length (km); and

k and m are coefficients, respectively intercept point and slope of the regression line. These coefficients have been determined through linear regression and are respectively $k = 230.28$ €; $m = 0.85$ €/km.

This M1 improvement scenario reduces only monetary costs and not times of intermodal transport. Therefore, while monetary costs reduce significantly, times do not change. As a result, generalized costs also show an improvement, but not a significant one, and only in four cases out of six is the generalized cost of the intermodal transport less than the all-road one. This is due to the long travel times of intermodal transport: in the path Leghorn–Nice (and vice versa), the waiting time in Bastia is so high that the generalized cost of intermodal transport is still greater than that of the all-road mode.

3.4.2 Scenario M2: merging of the existing routes in longer routes calling at the port of Bastia

This section reports the improvement in travel times, monetary costs and generalized costs after the merging of the routes (M2 improvement scenario) Leghorn–Bastia, Bastia–Nice, Bastia–Toulon and Bastia–Marseilles (and vice versa) into the routes Leghorn–Nice, Leghorn–Toulon and Leghorn–Marseilles (and vice versa). All these routes have an intermediate stop in Bastia. In order to decrease, as much as possible, the travel time of the intermodal alternative, the duration of the ship call at Bastia is reduced to the minimum.

The benefit of this improvement scenario does not concern only travel times but also monetary costs. Indeed, the transhipment of the tractor and semi-trailer at the intermediate port, from one ship to another, is no longer necessary, because the origin and the destination of the intermodal transport are connected through only one ship. Therefore, it is no longer necessary to look after the vehicle at the intermediate port. As a result, the unaccompanied intermodal transport alternative has also become feasible.

A model which allows forecasting the ticket price for unaccompanied transport has also been developed. The calibration of this model, performed through linear regression, is described in Lupi et al. (2017b), section 6.2. The ticket price of unaccompanied transport, p_{unacc}, can be calculated as follows:

$$p_{unacc} = 170.96 + 0.71\,l \tag{9.3}$$

where l is the route length (km). A dwell time in Bastia equal to 3 hours has been hypothesized: 3 hours is the time required to load and unload the vehicle for the unaccompanied transport mode, which requires more time. In addition, the frequency of all routes has been set equal to 7 services per week (i.e. one departure per day) as suggested by road hauliers. The travel time between Leghorn and Nice is reduced to 18 hours in accompanied transport and to 19 hours in unaccompanied transport. The travel time between Leghorn and Toulon is reduced to 22 h 20 min for accompanied transport and to 23 h 20 min for unaccompanied transport.

In addition, a route between Civitavecchia and Marseilles has also been introduced: indeed the distance between these two ports by the all-road mode is over 800 km, and this is in favour of intermodal transport. This route has an intermediate call at Bastia (with a dwell time, in Bastia, equal to 3 hours as for the other routes), and its travel time is equal to 28 hours for accompanied transport and to 29 hours for unaccompanied transport. The call at Bastia has been introduced, because a path Civitavecchia–Marseilles via Bastia is much shorter, from the geographical point of view, than a path via Olbia.

The results for this improvement scenario are reported in Table 9.5 and are compared with those of all-road transport. The differences in percentage have been calculated as reported in Equation (9.1) and are related to the differences between intermodal accompanied transport and all-road mode and to the differences between intermodal unaccompanied transport and all-road mode.

Table 9.5 shows that intermodal transport, considering only travel times, is not yet competitive, although the situation has improved, especially as regards the O-D pair Civitavecchia–Marseilles. But it must be underlined that, for this O-D pair, the travel time of all-road mode is high because of the daily rest time of the driver. Considering instead the monetary cost, the intermodal transport is always

Table 9.5 Comparison, in terms of monetary cost, travel time, generalized cost and distance, between the all-road and the intermodal accompanied and unaccompanied alternatives, for the improvement scenario M2.

Origin		Leghorn	Leghorn	Leghorn	Civitavecchia
Destination		Nice	Toulon	Marseilles	Marseilles
Via (intermediate port)		Bastia	Bastia	Bastia	Bastia
All-road	monetary cost (€)	765	1078	1191	1622
	travel time (hh:mm)	05:45	07:35	08:10	20:35
	generalized cost (€)	804.2	1129.7	1246.7	1762.3
	distance (km)	372	521	576	815
Intermodal accompanied	monetary cost (€)	508.2	662.1	747.6	871.3
	travel time (with frequency delay)	18:00	22:20	24:20	28:02
	generalized cost (€)	631	814.4	913.6	1062.5
	distance (km)	354	468	542	627
% difference monetary cost accompanied/all-road		−33.6%	−38.6%	−37.2%	−46.3%
% difference generalized cost accompanied/all-road		−21.6%	−27.9%	−26.7%	−39.7%
Intermodal unaccompanied	monetary cost (€)	363.1	427.6	469.5	518.2
	travel time (with frequency delay)	19:00	23:20	25:20	29:02
	generalized cost (€)	492.7	586.8	642.3	716.2
	distance (km)	354	468	542	627
% difference monetary cost unaccompanied / all-road		−52.5%	−60.3%	−60.6%	−68.1%
% difference generalized cost unaccompanied / all-road		−38.7%	−48.1%	−48.5%	−59.4%

more favourable than all-road, particularly in the unaccompanied case. In addition, the generalized cost is lower for intermodal transport, but in a lower percentage than the monetary cost, because it takes into account travel times.

3.4.3 Scenario M3: establishment of completely new routes between pairs of ports of the Ligurian coast

The establishment of new point-to-point routes between pairs of ports of the Ligurian coast was analyzed. Because of the geographical conformation of the coast and the existing connections among ports, the development of six new point-to-point routes was hypothesized:

- Civitavecchia–Nice (7 services per week),
- Civitavecchia–Toulon (7 services per week),
- Civitavecchia–Marseilles (7 services per week),
- Leghorn–Nice (7 services per week),
- Leghorn–Toulon (7 services per week),
- Leghorn–Marseilles (7 services per week),

as well as a route calling at three ports: Civitavecchia–Genoa–Marseilles. This is a single route, without transhipment in Genoa: freight having origin in Civitavecchia and destination in Marseilles stays on the same ship. This route has been compared to all-road transport both as a single route and as two separate routes: Civitavecchia–Genoa and Genoa–Marseilles. All these routes are reported, in dashed line, in Figure 9.1.

There are substantially two reasons that the route Civitavecchia–Marseilles via Genoa has been considered both as a single route and as two separate routes. Firstly, the transport demand considered in this route does not have only origin or destination in Civitavecchia or Marseilles but also in Genoa. Therefore, it is necessary to also know costs (monetary and generalized) and travel times between Genoa and Civitavecchia and between Genoa and Marseilles. Secondly, the possibility exists that one of the two parts of the route registers a low demand, for example the route Genoa–Marseilles, therefore it may be decided to keep in operation only the route part which registers the highest demand, for example the route Civitavecchia–Genoa.

The results, in terms of monetary cost, travel time and generalized cost, deriving from the development of these new routes are shown in Tables 9.6 (regarding accompanied transport) and 9.7 (regarding unaccompanied transport).

In this scenario, travel times have reduced significantly. Monetary costs have also decreased, especially because the voyage is shorter; therefore, drivers loose a smaller number of working hours. Distances have also reduced; indeed, it is no longer necessary to cross the port of Bastia, which had increased the length of the path substantially. The most competitive routes are Leghorn–Toulon, Leghorn–Marseilles and those to/from Civitavecchia, because they are the longest routes: the ticket price per km is lower; moreover the voyage is longer, therefore the

Table 9.6 Comparison between all-road and intermodal accompanied transport in the M3 scenario.

Origin	Destination	Via (intermediate port)	All-road monetary cost (€)	Travel time (hh:mm)	generalized cost (€)	Distance (km)	Intermodal (accompanied) monetary cost (€)	Travel time (with frequency delay)	generalized cost (€)	Distance (km)	% difference monetary cost	% difference generalized cost
Leghorn	Nice	direct	765	05:45	804.2	372	390.0	12:49	477.4	245	−49.02%	−40.64%
Leghorn	Toulon	direct	1078	07:35	1129.7	521	498.0	16:48	612.6	372	−53.80%	−45.77%
Leghorn	Marseilles	direct	1191	08:10	1246.7	576	598.7	19:23	730.9	458	−49.73%	−41.37%
Civitavecchia	Nice	direct	1202	09:20	1265.6	610	547.7	18:05	671.0	415	−54.43%	−46.98%
Civitavecchia	Toulon	direct	1510	12:00	1591.8	760	689.3	21:43	837.5	523	−54.35%	−47.39%
Civitavecchia	Marseilles	direct	1621	20:35	1762.3	815	781.3	24:05	945.5	589	−51.83%	−46.35%
Civitavecchia	Marseilles	Genoa	1621	20:35	1762.3	815	1077.5	33:20	1304.9	752	−33.57%	−25.96%
Civitavecchia	Genoa	direct	810	07:06	857.5	425	513.0	17:11	630.2	370	−36.59%	−26.51%
Genoa	Marseilles	direct	811	06:06	852.6	395	550.2	18:09	674.0	382	−32.16%	−20.96%

effects of loading/unloading times on the total of the voyage time are less; finally, the travel times of the all-road mode in the Civitavecchia–Marseilles path are higher, because of the increased daily rest time of the driver.

A route which could satisfy quite a high transport demand is Civitavecchia–Marseilles via Genoa:

- Civitavecchia is the port of Rome and therefore collects the transport demand to/from Latium;
- Genoa is connected with Milan and Turin and therefore registers a high intermodal transport demand;
- Marseilles is in a favourable position to reach Lyon and Paris.

In addition, this route allows avoiding some roads which are highly congested, especially in summer, and which do not have a high level of safety:

- Between Tarquinia (just in the north of Civitavecchia) and Grosseto, there is no motorway, but there is a highway (partially a multi-lane one and partially a two-lane one) showing geometrical and traffic characteristics not adequate for long-distance heavy traffic. Moreover, the A12 motorway between Viareggio and Genoa is congested, particularly during summer.
- The route portion Genoa–Marseilles allows avoiding the A10 motorway, which is highly congested, especially in summer. Moreover, this motorway is currently interrupted at its beginning, in correspondence to the 'Morandi' bridge; therefore, it is necessary to cross the city of Genoa to avoid this interruption.

The route has a dwell time of 3 hours in Genoa, which is the amount of time strictly necessary for boarding and disembarking the vehicle (to/from the ship) for the unaccompanied intermodal transport which requires more time.

For this route, the same frequency of the other routes proposed is hypothesized: one departure per day. A greater frequency, for example two departures per day, halves the frequency delay, but this does not lead to relevant benefits, because in any case the time for embarking and disembarking is 2 hours for accompanied transport and 3 hours for unaccompanied transport. In addition, road hauliers reported that for them it is necessary to have at least one departure per day, especially in the evening: the driver can spend the night travelling by sea, therefore driving and rest times are optimized.

4 Conclusions

In this chapter, firstly, an analysis of the development of Italian MoS routes has been carried out. Italian MoS routes in the year 2015 have been studied, distinguishing between Ro-Pax routes, carrying both passengers and freight, and cargo Ro-Ro routes. These routes have been compared with those registered in the years 2008, 2010 and 2012. This analysis has shown that cargo Ro-Ro routes

Table 9.7 Comparison between all-road and intermodal unaccompanied transport in the M3 scenario.

Origin	Destination	Via (intermediate port)	All-road monetary cost (€)	All-road Travel time (hh:mm)	All-road generalized cost (€)	All-road Distance (km)	Intermodal (unaccompanied) monetary cost (€)	Intermodal Travel time (with frequency delay)	Intermodal generalized cost (€)	Intermodal Distance (km)	% difference monetary cost	% difference generalized cost
Leghorn	Nice	direct	765	05:45	804.2	372	301.4	13:49	395.7	245	−60.60%	−50.80%
Leghorn	Toulon	direct	1078	07:35	1129.7	521	372.2	17:48	493.6	372	−65.48%	−56.31%
Leghorn	Marseilles	direct	1191	08:10	1246.7	576	418.0	20:23	557.1	458	−64.90%	−55.32%
Civita-vecchia	Nice	direct	1202	09:20	1265.6	610	394.8	19:05	524.9	415	−67.15%	−58.52%
Civita-vecchia	Toulon	direct	1510	12:00	1591.8	760	459.3	22:43	614.2	523	−69.58%	−61.41%
Civita-vecchia	Marseilles	direct	1621	20:35	1762.3	815	501.2	25:05	672.2	589	−69.10%	−61.86%
Civita-vecchia	Marseilles	Genoa	1621	20:35	1762.3	815	612.1	34:20	846.3	752	−62.26%	−51.98%
Civita-vecchia	Genoa	direct	810	07:06	857.5	425	379.0	18:11	503.0	370	−53.16%	−41.34%
Genoa	Marseilles	direct	811	06:06	852.6	395	395.9	19:09	526.5	382	−51.18%	−38.25%

and Ro-Pax routes have different characteristics. The majority of Italian MoS routes are Ro-Pax ones. Cargo Ro-Ro routes have been developed in order to maximize the operator's revenues by calling at several ports, therefore serving several markets, although this results in worse service because of higher travel times. Ro-Pax routes are, generally, shorter and call at a lower number of ports. Furthermore, while cargo Ro-Ro routes maintain almost the same frequencies during the year, Ro-Pax routes highly reduce their frequencies from high season to low season periods. In addition, Ro-Pax routes in high season are not reliable: ships are usually almost completely full; therefore, it is difficult for truck drivers to find an available slot. The high travel times and low frequencies registered by cargo Ro-Ro routes decrease their competitiveness against all-road transport; on the other hand, the low reliability shown by Ro-Pax routes badly affects their competitiveness against all-road transport.

A comparison of routes between 2015 and 2019 has shown that some investments have been done, especially by the Grimaldi operator, to increase the competitiveness of MoS routes. New fast point-to-point routes, connecting pairs of ports of the Italian mainland, in competition with all-road transport, have been established. Moreover, MoS operators are investing also in routes connecting the Italian islands to the mainland, in particular on those routes well integrated in door-to-door logistics chains.

This chapter has also quantitatively analyzed the competitiveness of MoS routes in the Ligurian coastal area. In this case study, on one hand, the low distances are not in favour of intermodal transport, but on the other hand, because of the high level of congestion of existing road infrastructures, the shift of a quota of freight transport demand from the all-road mode to intermodal transport, based on MoS, is desirable.

Currently, various Motorways of the Sea routes are in operation in the coastal area of the Ligurian Sea, but they are not competitive. On the other hand, the proposed improvement scenarios, particularly the development of completely new point-to-point routes (M3), lead to lower monetary and generalized costs of intermodal transport than those of the all-road mode. However, travel times of intermodal transport remain substantially higher. In order to increase the competitiveness of the intermodal alternative, based on MoS, it is necessary to reduce, as much as possible, not only monetary costs but also travel times.

In general, in order to improve the competitiveness of the intermodal alternative, it is necessary not only to optimize the supply of MoS routes, but also to adopt measures aimed at disincentivizing all-road transport. In particular, it is necessary to internalize the external costs of road transport. But the measures currently adopted, for example fuel taxes, are non-punctual measures, therefore their outcome often is not a modal shift towards more sustainable transport modes but simply an increase of transport costs. Indeed, it is necessary to penalize not road transport in general, but only road transport between those O-D pairs which have an efficient intermodal alternative. In this field, rewarding measures such as the Ecobonus could have a positive effect. Alternatively, a penalty could be introduced to heavy trucks using the Ligurian road infrastructures, and, at the same time, a reward to heavy trucks making use of the MoS, after the introduction of efficient services.

This study of competitiveness of MoS routes in the Ligurian coast area shows also that, if the intermodal transport is optimized, it is possible to obtain a break-even distance which, at least from the point of view of monetary costs, is much lower than the break-even distances reported in literature. Indeed, this study has shown that it is possible to obtain the break-even of the monetary cost also with a distance, of the all-road mode, equal to 372 km. But it must be underlined that such a small break-even distance resulted because, in the case study, the road parts of the intermodal transport are not present. The road parts of the intermodal transport could be very expensive, in terms of €/tkm (or €/TEU-km), as reported in Hanssen *et al.* (2012).

Finally, the research carried out on competitiveness of MoS routes in the Ligurian coast area has clearly shown that it is relatively easy to act on the intermodal transport costs. It is instead more difficult to act on travel times, because, if the intermodal paths are short, the embarkation and disembarkation times are relevant; but it is possible to obtain relevant improvements if the call times at the intermediate ports are reduced to a minimum or if point-to-point routes, which have low travel times, are developed.

References

Bergantino, A.S., & Bolis, S. (2004), An analysis of maritime ro-ro freight transport service attributes through adaptive stated preference: An application to a sample of freight forwarders. *European Transport \ Trasporti Europei*, 25–26, pp. 33–51.

Bergantino, A.S., & Bolis, S. (2008), Monetary value of transport service attributes: Land versus maritime ro-ro transport. An application using adaptive stated preferences. *Maritime Policy and Management*, 35 (2), pp. 159–174.

Black, I., Seaton, R., Ricci, A., & Enei, R. (2003), RECORDIT (Real Cost Reduction of Door-to-Door Intermodal Transport) Final Report: Actions to Promote Intermodal Transport.

Danesi, A., Farina, A., & Lupi, M. (2010), A comparative analysis of Lo-Lo and Ro-Ro short sea shipping networks in Italy. Proceedings of 13th International Conference of Transport Science, ICTS 2010, University of Ljubljana, Faculty of Maritime Studies and Transport, pp. 1–11.

Danesi, A., Lepori, C., & Lupi, M. (2008), The Italian motorways of the Sea system: Current situation, policies and prospects. Proceedings of 11th International Conference of Transport Science, ICTS 2008, University of Ljubljana, Faculty of Maritime Studies and Transport.

De Jong, G. (2004), Main survey into the value of time in freight transport by road. Technical Report. Rand Europe.

Denisis, A. (2009), An economic feasibility study of short sea shipping including the estimation of externalities with fuzzy logic. PhD thesis, University of Michigan.

EMMA (1999), European marine motorways, the potential for transferring freight from road to high-speed sea transport system, IV framework programme of the European Commission.

European Commission (2001), European transport policy for 2010: Time to decide, White Paper, European Commission, Brussels.

European Commission (2011), Roadmap to a single European transport area – towards a competitive and resource efficient transport system, White Paper, European Commission, Brussels.

European Parliament (1999), The development of short sea shipping in Europe: A dynamic alternative in a sustainable transport chain. Second Two-yearly Progress Report, European Parliament, Brussels.

European Parliament (2004), Decision no 884/2004/EC of the European parliament and of the council of 29 April 2004 amending decision no 1692/96/EC on community guidelines for the development of the trans-European transport network. Official Journal of European Union L 167, European Parliament, Brussels.

European Parliament (2006), Regulation no 561/2006 of the European parliament and of the council of 15 March 2006 on the harmonisation of certain social legislation relating to road transport and amending council regulations (EEC) no 3821/85 and (EC) No. 2135/98 and repealing council regulation (EEC) no 3820/85. Official Journal of the European Union L 102/1, European Parliament, Brussels.

Eurostat (2019), Transport statistics database. Available at https://ec.europa.eu/eurostat/data/database (accessed May 2019).

Feo, M., Espino, R., & Garcia, L. (2011), A stated preference analysis of Spanish freight forwarders modal choice on the south-west Europe Motorway of the Sea. *Transport Policy*, 18 (1), pp. 60–67.

Fusco, P.M., Sauri, S., & Lago, A. (2012), Potential freight distribution improvements using motorways of the sea. *Journal of Transport Geography*, 24, pp. 1–11.

Ghobrial, A., & Kanafani, A. (1995), Future of airline hubbed networks: Some policy implications. *Journal of Transportation Engineering*, 121 (2), pp. 124–134.

Hanssen, T.E.S., Mathisen, T.A., & Jørgensen, F. (2012), Generalized transport costs in intermodal freight transport. *Procedia – Social and Behavioral Sciences*, 54, pp. 189–200.

Il Sole 24 Ore (2011), Lordo, netto e costo del lavoro – Ccnl Trasporto, logistica e spedizione merci, Il Sole 24 Ore, n. 9 of 25 February 2011, pp. 92–93.

Jiang, F., Johnson, P., & Calzada, C. (1999), Freight demand characteristics and mode choice: An analysis of the results of modeling with disaggregate revealed preference data. *Journal of Transportation and Statics*, 2 (2), pp. 149–158.

Lupi, M., & Farina, A. (2014), The development of the Italian Motorways of the Sea network in the years 2008–2012. In M. Losa & T. Papagiannakis (eds.), *Sustainability, Eco-Efficiency and Conservation in Transportation Infrastructure Asset Management*. Boca Raton (US): CRC Press, Taylor and Francis Group, pp. 765–775.

Lupi, M., Farina, A., Pratelli, A., & Bellucci, L. (2017a), An analysis of the Italian ro-ro and ro-pax network in the years 2008–2015. *Transport Problems*, 12, Special Edition, pp. 127–140.

Lupi, M., Farina, A., Pilato, F., & Pratelli, A. (2017b), An analysis on the potential motorways of the sea alternative to "all-road" transport in the Ligurian-Northern Tyrrhenian area. *Ingegneria Ferroviaria*, 72 (12), pp. 953–984.

Lupi, M., Farina, A., Orsi, D., & Pratelli, A. (2017c), The capability of motorways of the sea of being competitive against road transport: The case of the Italian mainland and Sicily. *Journal of Transport Geography*, 58, pp. 9–21.

Martinez-Lopez, A., Munin-Doce, A., & Garcia-Alonso, L. (2015), A multi-criteria decision method for the analysis of the motorways of the sea: The application to the case of France and Spain on the Atlantic Coast. *Maritime Policy and Management*, 42 (6), pp. 608–631.

Ng, A.K.Y. (2009), Competitiveness of short sea shipping and the role of port: The case of North Europe. *Maritime Policy & Management*, 36 (4), pp. 337–352.

Olivella Puig, J., Martínez De Osés, F., & Castells i Sanabra, M. (2004), Intermodalidad Entre España Y Europa, El Proyecto INECEU [Intermodality between Spain and Europe, the INECEU project], University of Cataluña.

Rossi, D., & Rubino, S. (2009), Autostrade del Mare: Modellazione ed analisi della competitività rispetto al trasporto stradale. Master thesis, University of Genoa.

Russo, F. (2005), *Sistemi di trasporto merci. Approcci quantitativi per il supporto alle decisioni di pianificazione strategica tattica ed operativa a scala nazionale*. Milano: FrancoAngeli.

Vado e Torno (2012), *Costi di Esercizio. Supplemento al n. 6/2012 di Vado e Torno*. Milano: Vado e Torno srl.

West MoS (Western Europe Sea Transport and Motorway of the Sea) (2008), *Consolidated report*. Brussels: European Commission, Trans European Transport Networks Budget.

Websites

Motorways of the Sea website, viewed March 2019:
www.ramspa.it
Motorways of the Sea operators websites, viewed March 2019:
www.anekitalia.com/
www.carontetourist.it/v2.6_it/
http://www2.gnv.it/
www.grimaldi-lines.com/
www.jadrolinija.hr/
www.messinaline.it/
www.minoan.it/index.shtml
www.moby.it/
http://montenegrolines.com/
www.corsica-ferries.it/
www.snav.it/
www.tirrenia.it/merci/
www.lameridionale.com/it/rubrique/le-nostre-traversate-26.html
www.sncm.it/

10 The cost of modal shift
The case of Greece

Evangelos Sambracos and Marina Maniati

1 Introduction

According to current published data, the modal share of freight transport in EU-28 (total tonne kilometres) was 50.9% for roads, 33.3% for shipping, 11.6% for railways, 4.2% for inland waterways and 0.1% for air, showing that road transport still dominates compared to other means of transport. Over the last 30 years or so, the growth of intra-continental trade – with road transport carrying most of the freight in the EU – and also the growing number of transport inefficiencies linked to pollution, congestion, operational costs and accidents (Seungjin *et al.*, 2019:1) have rendered it necessary to search for new ways to address the issue of competition (Snaddon, 2001:376, Sambracos and Maniati, 2012:322). In the EU and elsewhere in the developed world, policymakers are starting to view short sea shipping (SSS) as a potentially viable alternative transport mode (EU, 2008; Gertjan and Wiegmans, 2018:1, Medda and Trujillo, 2009). According to the European Commission, the 'Motorways of the Sea' could become the mode that will replace long-distance road transport (Baird, 2007:288). Under the Marco Polo programme, which the EU Commission has supported for many years, subsidies for SSS were provided with a view to shifting as much freight traffic as possible from roads to other transport modes. Medium-sized ports and vessel operators could also benefit from SSS, as indicated by the fact that, in certain cases, using maritime routes has already replaced other transport modes due to its potential for achieving lower operational costs (Ng, 2009:338; Grammenos, 2013:415; Celen and Kalkan, 2018:70). It should be mentioned that relevant studies concerning the cross-price demand elasticity show that it is usually higher than one, meaning that a hike in road transport costs would trigger a proportionately higher demand for SSS (Lobe, 2001:13). It should also be noted, however, that the modal shift from road to sea presupposes the existence of a well-connected port network providing quick and efficient services (Paixao and Marlow, 2007:306).

Overall, the research has emphasized predominantly the increase of transport supply in order to cover the transport demand more efficiently. However, because externalities concerning the pricing were not taken into account, this has made the market more favourable for road transport.

Figure 10.1 Ports of Eleusis and Patras – road and sea transport.

In this chapter, we examine seaborne transport, as an alternative to the road shipment of cargos, through a distance of about 250 km, as shown in Figure 10.1. Of course, there are cases where rail transport may be competitive to both road and sea freight transport. However, in the case of the Attica-Patras corridor, no available railway line offers cargo transport, and the lack of terminals qualifying for semi-trailer or container handling makes the comparison of train transport not applicable in our case. Thus, the seaborne connection between Patras[1] (a major Greek import-export area) and West Attica[2] (the biggest Greek industrial centre close to West Athens) via the Corinth Canal provides an appropriate case study, as private costs and revenues, as well as externalities, have to be considered to both identify and estimate the factors that can make such modes more competitive in comparison to road transport (Sambracos and Maniati, 2012:322; Paixao and Marlow, 2002:168; Ametller, 2015:149) (Figure 10.1). Finally, the relevant discussion assumes major significance within the framework of the broad promotion of sea transport in European transport.

2 General methodology approach

To calculate the total costs (both private and social) involved in the sea and road transport alternatives for the Attica-Patras route, we employ data of cargo volumes and types to help us identify the potential market share and at the same time consider the existing opportunities for shifting parts of cargo traffic towards seaborne routes.

Furthermore, we endeavour to (1) accurately evaluate the size, kind and general specifications of a Ro-Ro ship typical cargo and (2) identify potential ports and seaborne alternatives while taking into account the region's geographical/physical peculiarities, such as the Corinth Canal, with a view to compiling a list of the minimum technical characteristics that the typical ship used in each resulting maritime leg should dispose (Sambracos, 2003:177).

In order to justify the competitiveness between sea and road transport, the structure and procedures of the supply chain from Attica to Italy (and vice versa), upon which this chapter is based, are described as follows:

a   The freight is loaded on trucks with detachable trailers, which will be stored in dedicated areas at the Eleusis port;
b   Once the vessel arrives at the port, the operator loads the trailers using own tractors; and
c   Upon arrival at the Patras port, the trailers are unloaded and the freight either stored in specialized storage areas pending the arrival of the next available ship or directly transhipped to vessels sailing to Italy, where it will be reloaded to private trucks (cargo consignee) until it reaches its final destination. Classical assessment methodologies are then employed to determine to what extent sea transport on the Attica-Patras and Patras-Attica routes can emerge as a competitive and viable alternative, while taking into consideration the demand and technical characteristics recorded for the said routes and examining a wide range of financing possibilities.

For the purposes of our analysis, costs (either in case of road or SSS freight transport) are classified in the following categories (Stopford, 1997:160):

1   Operating costs, which constitute the expenses involved in the day-to-day running of each mode, are estimated based on the following relationship:

$$OC_{tm} = M_{tm} + ST_{tm} + MN_{tm} + I_{tm} + AD_{tm} \tag{10.1}$$

where OC is the operating costs; M denotes either the manning cost for the Ro-Ro or the driver cost for the truck; ST is the supply cost for stores in both modes; MN is the routine repair and maintenance cost for both the Ro-Ro and the truck; I is the relevant insurance cost; and AD refers to the relevant administration cost for both modes.

2   Voyage costs that are associated with a particular voyage and include items such as fuel, fees and canal dues. The principal components of the voyage costs are:

$$VC_{tm} = FC_{tm} + D_{tm} + TP_{tm} \tag{10.2}$$

where VC is the voyage costs; FC is the fuel costs, lubricants and auxiliaries for both road and SSS transport; D refers to the port, light and canal dues in case of the Ro-Ro, and to the relevant tolls in case of the truck; and TP denotes the tugs and pilotage cost that concerns only the SSS transport. Especially for SSS transport, the main cost category is fuel costs (per hour cruising), which is estimated based on the relationship:

$$C = aNQP \tag{10.3}$$

where *a* denotes the real horse power capacity of the engine; *N* denotes the horse power of main engines; *Q* refers to the specific fuel consumption of propulsion engines; and *P* is the price of fuel.

3 Periodic maintenance costs, which are incurred either per annum or especially for the Ro-Ro when it is dry-docked for major repairs, usually at the time of its special survey.

4 Capital costs and repayments, depending on the way each mode is financed.

In order to develop a common financial estimation plan, the annual depreciation is also determined by the following formula:

$$D = \frac{P-S}{L} \tag{10.4}$$

where *D* stands for annual depreciation; *P* denotes the purchase value of each mode; *S* denotes the salvage value of each mode (especially in case of SSS); and *L* denotes the lifespan of each mode's operation.

Furthermore, economic feasibility of individual investment projects is evaluated through the use of two criteria, namely the NPV (net present value) and the IRR (internal rate of return). The former is calculated using:

$$NPV = \sum_{t=0}^{n} \frac{CFI_t - CFO_t}{(1+i)^t}, t \in \{0,1,...,n\} \tag{10.5}$$

In Equation (10.5), *CFI* stands for indexed cash flow inputs and *CFO* for indexed cash flow outputs. The *IRR* is then defined as the interest rate so that *NPV* equals zero. Thus:

$$NPV = f(i): IRR+ \to IRR; f(IRR) = 0 \tag{10.6}$$

Differences in external costs applying to sea and road transport are calculated by taking into account known data relating to accident and environmental costs (Perakis and Denisis, 2008:591; Aminuddin, 2015:229), potential climate change impact factors as well as potential damages to nature and the landscape. Based on the welfare-theory approach (Maibach et al., 2008), the aforementioned costs need to be considered as external costs incurring from a specific transport mode. The unit values set out in the EU Handbook on external costs of transport (Korzhenevych et al., 2014) form the basis for the estimations presented in this chapter.

3 Case study: the connection between Patras and Eleusis Port

3.1 Transport demand

Despite its drop during the previous decade, believed to arise primarily from the economic crisis, there is considerable evidence that transport demand can justify the creation of an economically viable seaborne leg of transportation connecting the port of Patras and that of Eleusis in West Attica (see Figure 10.2). According to the data supplied by the authorities of the ports in question, large volumes of the eastbound cargo arriving at Attica are destined for consumption or transhipment (Sambracos, 2003:176). Even though the transport demand data along the examined routes are currently unavailable, the fact that the study adopts a comparative approach through its examination of two different modes of transport means that we can still draw reliable conclusions. In addition, due to the type of cargo traffic habitually transported between Attica and Patras, the sea transport alternative may emerge as economically viable even if perishable goods were taken out of the equation. Cargo types easily transported via sea, such as 'Livestock Products' (5% of the total cargo volume) or 'Grouped Cargos' (54%) represent a much higher percentage of the eastbound traffic as compared to cargo types that are better suited for road transport, for example 'Minerals and related products' or 'Food and Beverages' (COMTRADE, 2018).

3.2 Port infrastructure

As concerns port infrastructure, the quay length of the Patras port amounts to approximately 3000 m, while its docks are between 8.5 and 10.5 m deep. The port can serve ships weighing up to 25,000 tonnes and measuring up to 220 m and is equipped with warehouses covering an 8000 m^2 surface, while cargo can also be stored outdoors in an 80,000 m^2 area. Finally, seven gates serving as entry and exit points are spread along the coast. The Eleusis port, on the other hand, covers a 50,000 m^2 surface and can handle up to 500,000 tonnes in cargo traffic. Approximately 500 ships call on the port every year, which are served along a total quay length of 1037 m and a dock area covering 24,000 m^2, with dock depth ranging

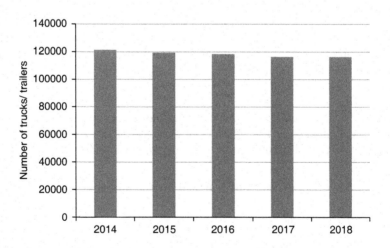

Figure 10.2 Loaded/unloaded trucks/trailers at the port of Patras.
Source: Patras Port Authority.

between 8.5 and 10.5 m. The Eleusis region is an area of significant commercial and industrial activity, home to many industrial units of high capitalization. Furthermore, the port is located near major road and railway infrastructure, providing it with a competitive edge and rendering it an excellent base for various types of trade flows, leading also to increased demand for transport services.

3.3 Vessel and truck characteristics

Taking into account the factors of demand, market capacity and the limitations related to the transport network, it is estimated that a standard 6500 GT Ro-Ro (no more than 110 m long, with two decks, a maximum 17 m beam and 4 m draught) that can carry 60 trucks measuring 15 m in length and 2.5 m in width would be the optimal vessel for the route. The Ro-Ro should perform two trips on a daily basis, one in each direction. The two-engine (4500 hp each) Ro-Ro should have an 18-person crew[3] and an operational speed ranging between 14 and 17 knots,[4] in order for the seaborne route between Patras and Eleusis to present a competitive advantage and emerge as a more efficient alternative as compared to road transport.

Since the purpose of comparing different transport modes is to evaluate the potential for SSS, in this chapter the type of vehicle considered for use on the examined routes is an articulated truck with detachable trailers, with a weight of 7.5 tonnes for the actual vehicle and 7 tonnes for the platform and a cargo capacity of up to 28–29 tonnes. Furthermore, since the nature of the cargo determines the type of trailer to be used (though in the majority of cases the function, size and intended use does not present significant variations), the analysis presented in the next section uses a closed trailer for general cargo in pallets as a standard reference unit. Based on the distance of the Attica-Patras route (220 km), the maximum speed limits as well as the actual average speed (85 km/h and 80 km/h respectively), the duration of a single trip (one way) is estimated at 3 hours.

4 Financial results

4.1 Annual cost estimation results

Concerning road transport, the estimation of costs is based on the following assumptions and categories (Forkenbrock, 1999:505; Janic, 2007:33):

Road transport cost of acquisition. A vehicle's acquisition cost is affected by the number of years it has been in circulation, as well as its technical characteristics and manufacturing details. Our calculations are based on the assumption that the cost for a new vehicle is €90,000 and for a second-hand one €50,000.

Road transport operating cost. The operating costs of road transport provided by a new truck include M, driver's basic salary (approximately €1,800[5] per month for payroll and employee's and employer's social security contributions); *ST*, €1,100 on average per annum; *MN*, cost for technical surveying according to existing legislation (€100 per annum cost for each vehicle) and maintenance cost (€4,000 per vehicle per year); *I*, insurance premiums (€350 per vehicle per semester) and general insurance cost for cargo (€1,000 per vehicle per year); and *AD*, communication, handling, etc. (€100 per vehicle per month), as well vehicle state fees (€925 per vehicle per year). The aforementioned assumptions are modified in the case of operating a 5-year-old truck: *M*, driver's basic salary and *AD* costs remain the same, whereas *ST* equals to €1,133 on average per annum; *MN* cost is €4,182 per vehicle per year; and *I* cost is €1,721 per year.

Road transport voyage cost. The cost for road transport includes the following: *FC*, (a) fuel costs, for the calculation of which we have assumed that trucks will travel with an 80 km/h speed on average and that vehicles consume from 1 L per 3 km to 1 L per 2.8 km, depending on whether they are new or second-hand, with a normalized fuel price at €1.25 per litre and (b) lubricants, priced at €40 for every 10,000 km; and *D*, tolls, expected to incur a €70 cost per one-way journey.

Table 10.1 shows the total operating and voyage costs per annum for operating a transport service between Attica and Patras (assuming 320 round trips per year), with different figures given for new and second-hand trucks. The cost per round trip for a new truck is calculated at €420.61 while the respective figure for a second-hand truck is €434.07.

Sea transport cost, on the other hand, can be broken into the following categories (Musso and Marchese, 2002:280).

Sea transport capital cost. For the purposes of this study, capital cost arises from the purchase of new or second-hand Ro-Ro ships. In scenario 1, which

Table 10.1 Annual operational and voyage cost for road transport (one truck, Athens–Patras–Athens, first year).

	New Truck	Second-hand Truck
OC: Operating Cost (€)		
M: Driver's basic salary	21,539	21,539
ST: Stores	1,100	1,122
MN: Maintenance	4,100	4,182
I: Insurance	1,700	1,714
AD: Administration	2,125	2,125
Subtotal 1	30,564	30,682
VC: Voyage Cost (€)		
FC: Fuel Cost and Lubricants	59,230	63,420
D: Tolls	44,800	44,800
Subtotal 2	104,030	108,220
Total (1+2)	134,594	138,902

includes the acquisition of a new vessel, the total capital cost is expected to be €13,000,000, while in scenario 2 (second-hand Ro-Ro) the cost is estimated at €10,000,000[6] (Maibach *et al.*, 2008). In both cases, cash flow capital is assumed to amount to approximately 4/12 of the total operating expenses.

Sea transport operating cost. This is categorised as follows: (1) *M*, costs related to manning, for the calculation of which the effective collective bargaining agreements as well as a 2.5% growth rate of wages per annum are weighed in; (2) *ST*, amounting to an average €20,000 in scenario 1 and €22,000 in scenario 2 (second-hand Ro-Ro) on a yearly basis, with an increase of 1% per annum; (3) *MN*, maintenance and repair costs, which are related to the vessel's size, type and years of service and estimated on the basis of rate and the vessel's initial capital cost. For example, a new Ro-Ro is estimated to cost 0.9% of its construction value in maintenance and repair for the first 5 years, 1.20% for the next 5 years, 1.5% between its 11th and 15th years of service and 2% between its 16th and 20th years; (4) *I*, the cost of insurance is also calculated as a percentage of the initial capital cost, set at 1.0% of the value of the Ro-Ro with an annual increase of 1%; and (5) *AD*, costs related to administration and office maintenance (capital paid for renting spaces, office supplies, etc.), expected to incur expenses amounting to €40,000 per annum, while the yearly costs for hiring staff are estimated at €60,000, to which an increase of 3.5% per year is added.

Sea transport voyage cost. The estimation of these costs rests upon the following series of assumptions:

1 *FC* constitutes the main voyage cost, with the propulsion engines having a power rating (a) at approximately 0.85; a horsepower (N) equalling 9000 hp; specific fuel consumption (Q) estimated at 0.08 and 0.085 kg/hph respectively depending on whether the Ro-Ro will be new or second-hand; and the fuel price (P) defined at €0.53 per kg/hph (€530 per tonne) for the 5-month period from January to May 2019. An average of 10.6 tonnes of fuel per round-trip is estimated to be consumed if a new Ro-Ro is deployed, while the equivalent figure for a second-hand Ro-Ro is defined at 11.3 tonnes. Furthermore, while the ship remains at the port, it is assumed to consume 15% of its habitual sea fuel consumption (Kadir *et al.*, 2017:2). As concerns lubricant costs, *FC*, since these are proportionally related to fuel costs they are estimated as a percentage of the latter, namely 10%, with an increase of 2% per annum.

Thus, if a new ship is deployed, the total fuel cost per year (calculated on the basis of 5569 cruise hours per year) is defined at €1,806,361, while the fuel cost for every cruise hour is estimated at €324.36. This figure will rise to €405.45 if fuel consumption while the Ro-Ro is at the port and lubricant costs are also factored in. In the case of a second-hand ship, the corresponding figures will be €1,919,258 total fuel costs per year; €344.63 cost fuel per hour, and €430.79 with the inclusion of lubricants and consumption while anchored at port.

2 *D* refers to port charges paid to the ports of Patras and Eleusis. At the port of Patras, anchorage fees are at €14.70 per 1000 GT, berth fees at €79.75 per 330 m and mooring fees at €26.58; at the port of Eleusis, the respective dues are as follows: €3.00 per 1000 GT, €33 per 330 m and €10.89. Thus, the total costs incurred for port charges in both ports for the estimated 640 yearly port calls is defined at €169,773. Furthermore, there are the charges for the Corinth Canal crossings, which are calculated based on the prices set by the canal management at €1,731,200 per annum, with a 1% increase per year.

3 *TP* refers to tugs and pilotage costs, also calculated according to the prices set by the Corinth Canal management as well as the relevant market prices at the two ports. These amount to €1,614,720.

Based on the aforementioned assumptions, Table 10.2 shows the route's annual round trip operating and voyage costs. These are calculated at €18,042.64 for scenario 1 and €18,483.64 for scenario 2.

Considering the annual costs of both road and sea transport as presented in Tables 10.1 and 10.2, we conclude that the seaborne route alternative accrues annual costs that correspond to 50 trailers travelling on the Patras to Attica and Attica to Patras route for 320 round trips per year. The annual costs of seaborne trade correspond to the total cost required for operating approximately 50 trailers, which make 320 round trips per year each, on the route Patras–Attica–Patras. Moreover, taking into account an average load per truck of 7.5 tonnes, the aforementioned trailers will be able to move 240,000 tonnes of cargo if the vehicles travel at their maximum capacity both to and from their point of departure, while the Ro-Ro can transport up to 288,000 tonnes on 38,400 trailers. It is therefore evident that the total cargo that can be transported on the alternative seaborne route is significantly higher than the one 50 trailers could transport for the same cost.

Table 10.2 Ro-Ro annual operational and voyage cost (line Patras–Eleusis, first year).

	New Ro-Ro	Second-hand Ro-Ro
OC: Operating Cost (€)		
M: Manning Cost	504,067	504,067
ST: Stores	20,000	22,000
MN: Maintenance	117,000	156,000
I: Insurance	130,000	189,800
AD: Administration	100,000	100,000
Subtotal 1	871,067	971,867
VC: Voyage Cost (€)		
FC: Fuel Cost and Lubricants	2,257,951	2,399,072
D: Port and canal dues	1,900,973	1,900,973
TP: Tugs and pilotage	1,614,720	1,614,720
Subtotal 2	5,773,644	5,914,765
Total (1+2)	6,644,711	6,886,632

4.2 Revenue evaluation results

The estimated revenue is measured at fair value of the payment that will be received and represents the income from the sale of services of maritime or road transport. As for the maritime transport, one of the basic assumptions is that revenues gravely depend on the relevant market share, that is, the cargo volume available for this kind of transport (market penetration rate). This figure is estimated at 400,000 tonnes on a yearly basis for the Athens-Patra route. If a standard ship making a round trip on the Athens-Patras line carries trucks with a cargo capacity of 7.5 tonnes (in line with the corresponding assumption in the analysis or road transport), then the cargo volume transported per round trip amounts to 540 tonnes, considering a rate of capacity utilization of 60%. The Ro-Ro vessel that has been selected for the purposes of this study can carry a total of 60 such trucks, while the corresponding market share appears to be large enough to justify, from an economic point of view, the operation of the line.

Total revenue of sea transport is calculated based on 2019 prices. In order for the seaborne route to compete with road transport, the maximum fare of a unit transported via sea is considered to be equal to the equivalent road transport operating and total cost (Table 10.1) standardized on per day/round trip basis (320 days – trips of trucks). The operating costs have been calculated based on the equivalent costs applying for road transport on the Patras-Athens route (Table 10.1). Therefore, since the fares charged for truck transportation are subject to limitations, we have developed different scenarios concerning the vessel's utilization rates and transportation charges.

Considering the aforementioned, the basic assumptions for generated revenue can be summarized in the following way:

a   Freight rate amounts to €420.61 for each truck or trailer making a two-way journey;
b   Capacity utilization is calculated at an average rate of 60% (72 trucks/trailers on a round trip, 36 trucks/trailers in each direction);
c   The line runs without disruption for 320 days per year; and
d   The market expansion rate is approximately 2.5% per year.

The relevant results are shown in Tables 10.1 and 10.2.

4.3 Financial evaluation results

For the scenarios presented in our study and for the estimation of the annual depreciation cost, the operation life of the Ro-Ro is defined to be 25 years. At the end of this period, we estimate the salvage value of the ship following its demolition, which we calculate on the basis of the current market scrap price (tonnes of steel). Considering that the proportion of GT and extracted steel (in tonnes) is equal to 1/2, the final amount of steel is equal to 4000 tonnes. If the average price of steel is at €380 per tonne, we calculate that the ship will have a salvage value amounting to €1,520,000.[7]

The investment will be covered by shipowner's own funds and/or by another private investor and by funds secured through loans at an interest rate of 5%, which will need to be paid back within 10 years. Concerning the total value of funds secured via loans, we consider alternative scenarios, with loans covering 70%, 50% and, finally, 30% of the ship's acquisition value. Furthermore, a discount rate is factored into our calculations, based on the benchmark interbank offer rate (e.g. LIBOR, EURIBOR), as well as a premium intended to account for the loan's repayment period and cover risks potentially resulting from the endeavour (ranging between 1%–4% and depending on the terms of the loan).

Cash flow analysis for different scenarios of financial leverage results based on NPV and IRR are presented in Table 10.3, proving that the investment is profitable in both cases (new build and second-hand Ro-Ro).

As concerns the break-even point in the cases of using both a new and a second-hand Ro-Ro, our analysis shows that the freight rate equals to €288.40 and €294.13 per unit transported[8] respectively for every transported unit (Figures 10.2 and 10.3).

The amounts in Figure 10.3 are below the €420.61 threshold level, which is the maximum freight the shipping company can charge to be compete with the equivalent rate for road transport (based on its total annual cost divided by the assumed capacity transported). Considering the aforementioned, it emerges that the operation of the line is an economically viable solution involving considerable profits for its operator. Furthermore, the level of capacity utilization equals 5123 and 5260 trailers per year if a new Ro-Ro vessel is deployed and 3264 trailers if the ship purchased had previous years of service. Taking into account the fact that the Ro-Ro has a maximum carrying capacity of 38,400 trucks, our conclusion is that a company that will operate the line based on a price discriminatory policy can secure considerably larger profit margins.

Moreover, a sensitivity analysis also included in this study examines different scenarios with a view to determining the risk premium that would best reflect the risks the company could potentially be exposed to as a result of operating the vessel in the examined line. The scenarios we elaborated are as follows:

- Scenario 1: The price of fuel increases by 10%.
- Scenario 2: The cost of capital increases by 10%.

Table 10.3 Cash flows analysis results for Ro-Ro (line Patras–Eleusis–Patras).

% of equity in the capital cost	New build		Second-hand	
	NPV	IRR	NPV	IRR
30%	€16,520,381	13.02%	€19,796,019	16.67%
50%	€16,103,526	12.75%	€19,571,559	16.48%
70%	€15,686,671	12.49%	€19,347,098	16.28%

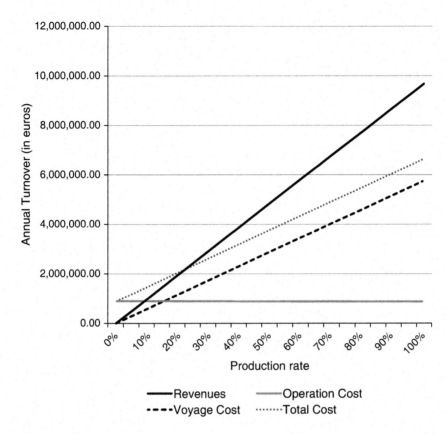

Figure 10.3 Break-even point analysis results for a new-built Ro-Ro (line Patras–Eleusis–Patras).

In both scenarios, we assume that only 30% of capital cost is covered through the company's own funds; in other words, the worst-case scenario. Regarding scenario 1, a 10% hike in fuel costs causes also the freight to increase to €260.4 in the case of a new Ro-Ro and to €267.10 if there were previous years of service. Furthermore, the trailers used for round trips in a year would be 5437 and 5617 respectively. As a result, costs are still significantly lower than at the road transport threshold level, now increased to €420.61 because of the increase in the price of fuel, while transport capacity via the seaborne route continues to have a competitive advantage over the road transport alternative. Concerning scenario 2, the 10% increase in the capital cost also results in higher freight, which is defined at a minimum of €250.60 for a new Ro-Ro and at €256.70 for a second-hand one, while the minimum capacity utilization is set at 5269 and 5404 trailers respectively. It is therefore evident that in this case too the seaborne route maintains its comparative advantage despite the rise in the cost of capital.

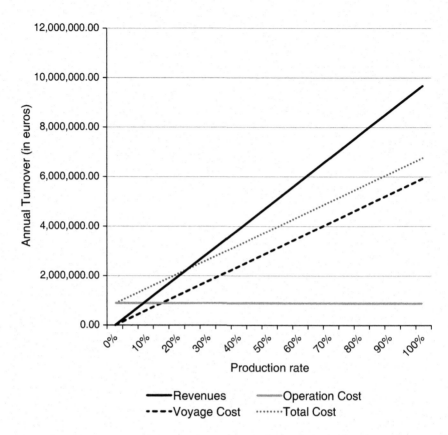

Figure 10.4 Break-even point analysis results for a second-hand Ro-Ro (line Patras–Eleusis–Patras).

Table 10.4 Sensitivity analysis for Ro-Ro (line Patras–Eleusis–Patras).

30% of equity in the capital cost	New build		Second-hand	
	NPV	IRR	NPV	IRR
10% Increase of Fuel Cost	€13,447,550	11.49%	€16,968,032	14.99%
10% Increase of Capital Cost	€13,235,169	10.92%	€17,023,582	14.20%

Sensitivity analysis proves that the operation of a line linking the port of Patras to that of Eleusis is a viable investment, even if the aforementioned scenarios materialize. We will now examine the external factors affecting road and sea transport, with a view to establishing the many advantages of the latter over the former.

5 External cost estimation results

Table 10.5 presents the unit values that are used per external cost component for both road and sea freight transport between Patras and Eleusis based on the EU Handbook on estimation of external costs in the transport sector (2014) (Korzhenevych et al., 2014).

Thus, the marginal costs for air pollution for both road and sea freight transport are €9.3 ct/veh-km[9] (Euro-0 Class) and €240/ves-km.[10] Furthermore, to generate comparable external cost estimates of accidents involving road transport, unit values (marginal costs) for accidents for different network types in € ct/veh-km are used.[11] For Greece, the relevant values are €1.3 ct/veh-km for urban roads, €0.9 ct/veh-km for motorways and €1.3 ct/veh-km for other roads. Accidents in maritime and inland waterways are almost zero. Noise costs, which depend closely on population density, are estimated in € per 1000 vkm[12] and are taken into account for thin traffic situations during daytime. Under this category, there are no available data for sea freight transport. As for external cost estimation due to climate change estimation, based on GHGs relevant for both road and sea transport, it is evaluated at the central value for CO_2: €90/tonne. Congestion external cost estimation for road transport is based on the FORGE model used in the National Transport Model of the UK, DfT (2009), while there are no relevant data for sea transport. Nature and landscape external cost is estimated as per 1000 EUR/km. For road transport, there is a differentiation between historic network and motorways extension, while for SSS transport, external costs of single accidents may be extremely high (e.g. oil spills), although such events are fortunately rare today.

Based on the estimated unit values presented in Table 10.5, the relevant external cost for both road and sea freight transport per round trip and tonne for the Patras–Eleusis–Patras round trip is presented in Table 10.6. More specifically, in order to estimate the accurate external cost for both road and sea transport, we multiply the prices presented in Table 10.5 with the distance Patras – Eleusis – Patras (440 km and 481 vessel km for road and sea transport respectively). Then, the results are divided with the transported volume for the whole round trip (15 tn and 540 tn for road and sea transport respectively). The externalities of sea transport are considerably lower compared to road freight transport, especially as far as the categories 'accidents', 'noise' and 'congestion'

Table 10.5 Marginal external costs for road and sea freight transport (line Patras–Eleusis–Patras).

Cost component	Road freight transport (€ ct/veh-km)	Sea freight transport (€ ves-km)
Accidents	0.9	0
Air pollution	9.3	240
Noise	1.5	N/A
Climate change	5.6	141
Congestion	7.0	N/A
Nature and Landscape	1.2	92

Table 10.6 External costs per round trip and tonne (Patras–Eleusis–Patras).

Cost component	Road freight transport (€/tn)	Sea freight transport (€/tn)
Accidents	0.26	0.00
Air pollution	2.73	2.14
Noise	0.44	N/A
Climate change	1.64	1.26
Congestion	2.05	N/A
Nature and Landscape	0.35	0.82
Total	**7.47**	**4.22**

(per tonne transported) are concerned, since sea transport is clearly superior in these categories. Note also the superior performance of sea transport in air pollution and climate change categories, also because the truck considered is Euro-0 class.

6 Conclusion

Both financial and socioeconomic analysis show that SSS between Patras and Eleusis is significantly more competitive than the road alternative and may contribute to the adoption of a greener multimodal freight transport system, as the internalization of externalities conveys a truer picture of the costs and benefits involved, demonstrating the superiority of SSS (to the road alternative). More specifically, the growth of heavy road transport and related environmental cost (air pollution, congestion and accidents) are amongst the main socioeconomic problems that SSS promotion policies may address. SSS policies should promote the provision of many transportation and logistics routing choices for various stakeholders, in order to encourage currently underdeveloped seaports to be further developed. Relevant policies need also to promote an efficient logistics transport system in order to get industrial/city centres close to the main waterways.

The last may counterbalance the main advantage of road transport of door-to-door or warehouse-to-warehouse delivery, contributing to the reduction of carriage, loading and unloading cost. Furthermore, the road transport alternative has the advantages of speed and flexibility (Goel, 2009:50), enabling it to ensure 'just-in-time' delivery. This is an increasingly important factor, since the bulk cargo load is much higher than general cargo. In addition, road transport emerges as a better mode in cases where there are limitations in the network and infrastructure.

Another disadvantage of seaborne routes are the delays that often occur due to increased port traffic causing congestion. As the loading, unloading and handling of cargo is often subject to longer waiting periods, undertaking investments to improve existing infrastructure and services at the two ports may be a valuable first step to increase interest in SSS. A second step that would also boost the attractiveness of SSS is the construction of an efficient road network connecting mainland ports to urban areas of interest, so that the consignee can be guaranteed to receive the cargo 'just in time'.

It should also be noted that ports are simply part of a longer supply chain that serves all modes of transport, thus rendering it possible to compare Ro-Ro vessel to highways and railway lines. For that reason, transport equivalence measures need to be put into effect to lift the obstacles and to direct state funds towards the building of new ships. In that way, a fairer competition would be put in place between sea transport investments and road or railway investments, which have been receiving substantial financial support on both a local and a European level. It is through a combination of adopting the appropriate investment strategies and policy initiatives that sea shipping could improve its share as compared to other transport modes.

Notes

1 Port of Patras.
2 Port of Eleusis.
3 Greek maritime law for this type of ship requires that the 18-person crew is allocated as follows: deck, nine persons; engineering department, six persons; stewards, three persons.
4 The port of Patras is approximately 130 nm far from Eleusis. Therefore, a vessel sailing at a speed of 17 knots on an average is estimated to complete a one-way journey within 7.65 h, while the round trip is estimated at 15 h. If the operational speed is reduced to 14 knots, the journey times will rise to 9.3 and 18.6 h respectively.
5 The accurate prices based on which the total cost is estimated are €1,127.70 for payroll and €667.24 for both employee's and employer's social security contributions per month.
6 Second-hand Ro-Ro vessels are priced only a little lower than new ones, since the former present the advantage of being immediately available. The fact that a new Ro-Ro may take up to 2 years to build is a factor of great significance during a ship purchase decision.
7 Given that the market scrap prices vary significantly, a vessel's demolition value is also a variable amount. In this chapter, we have used the 2019 scrap value as the basis for our calculation.
8 The total amount of units transported is based on the basic assumptions that (a) the average rate of capacity utilization is 60% (72 trucks/trailers on a round trip, 36 trucks/trailers per each way) and (b) the scheduled service is offered on an undisrupted basis of 320 days/year. The break-even point, where the total expenses equal total revenues, is then divided with the total units transported.
9 veh-km, vehicle-kilometre: 1 kilometre travelled by a single vehicle; €ct per vessel-km; max: marginal costs per vessel-km upstream, air pollutants in harbour areas are complicated to allocate. The values provided are from 2008, since there is lack of values in 2014 EU Handbook.
10 ves-km: 1 kilometre travelled by a single vessel (1 km = 0.539956 nm).
11 Road transport, Handbook on estimation of external costs in the transport sector, Level of externality depends on the treatment of individual self-induced accidents (individual or collective risk); insurance covers compensation of victims (excluding value of life). Sea freight transport: impact assessment on the internalization of external costs, difference between driver (operator) and victims. Insurance covers parts of compensation of victims (excluding value of life).
12 Road transport, values from CE Delft *et al.* (2011), updated to price level of 2010.

References

Ametller, X. (2015), Freight transport using short sea shipping. *Journal of Shipping and Ocean Engineering*, 5, pp. 143–150.

Aminuddin, Md. Arof (2015), Determinants for a feasible short sea shipping: Lessons from Europe for ASEAN. *Asian Social Science*, 11 (15), pp. 229–238.

Baird, A. (2007), The economics of motorways of the sea. *Maritime Policy & Management*, 34 (4), pp. 287–310.

Çelen, A., & Kalkan, E. (2018), Analysis of intermodal and intramodal competition in freight transport market between Turkey and Europe. *Gazi İktisat ve İşletme Dergisi*, 4 (2), pp. 67–86.

Delft, Infras, Fraunhofer ISI (2011), External Costs of Transport in Europe – Update study for 2008. CE Delft, Delft, NL (CE-publications are available from www.cedelft.eu)

DfT (2009). *National Transport Model – High Level Overview*. UK Government: Department for Transport (DfT), London, UK.

EU 2008. Impact assessment on the internalisation of external costs, {COM(2008) 435}, {COM(2008) 436}, {SEC(2008) 2209}.

Forkenbrock, D.J. (1999), External costs of intercity truck freight transportation. *Transportation Research Part A*, 33, pp. 505–526.

Gertjan, V.D.B, & Wiegmans, B. (2018), Short sea shipping: A statistical analysis of influencing factors on SSS in European countries. *Journal of Shipping and Trade*, 3 (6), pp. 1–20.

Goel, A. (2009), A roadmap for sustainable freight transport. In F. Heyde, A. Lohne, & C. Tammer Shaker (eds.), *Methods of Multi-criteria Decision Theory and Applications*, pp. 47–56. https://pdfs.semanticscholar.org/ad19/48e958551366d3c061fd94340c08a2a52367.pdf?_ga=2.267454030.1383259067.1579536426-162938255.1562239535

Grammenos, C. (2013), *The Handbook of Maritime Economics and Business*. Abingdon: Taylor and Francis, pp. 415–421.

Janic, M. (2007), Modelling the full costs of an intermodal and road freight transport network. *Transportation Research Part D*, 12 (1), pp. 33–44.

Kadir, M., Güler, A., Mısırlıoğlu, T., & Meng, W. (Reviewing Editor) (2017), A new method for calculating fuel consumption and displacement of a ship in maritime transport. *Cogent Engineering*, 4 (1), pp. 1–7.

Korzhenevych, A., Dehnen, N., (DIW econ), Bröcker, J., Holtkamp, M., Meier, H., (CAU), Gibson, G., Varma, A., & Cox, V., (Ricardo-AEA) (2014), *Update of the Handbook on External Costs of Transport Final Report*, MOVE/D3/2011/571.

Lobe, P. (2001), UNITE, case studies 7J – Mohring effects for freight transport. UNITE (UNIfication of accounts and marginal costs for Transport Efficiency), Working Funded by 5th Framework RTD Programme. ITS, University of Leeds, Brussels, pp. 1–34.

Maibach, M., Schreyer, C., Sutter, D., Van Essen, H.P., Boon, H., Smokers, R., Schroten, A., Doll, C., Pawlowska, B., & Bak, M. (2008), Handbook on estimation of external costs in the transport sector. Report Produced Within the Study Internalisation Measures and Policies for All external Cost of Transport (IMPACT).

Medda, F., & Trujillo, L. (2009), When is short sea shipping an alternative to land transport? Special World Bank Report. *Critical Issues in Port and Maritime Sector*, 1, pp. 1–48.

Musso, E., & Marchese, U. (2002), Economics of short sea shipping. In C. Th Grammenos (ed.), *The Handbook of Maritime Economics and Business*. London: Lloyd's of London Press, pp. 280–304.

Ng, A.K.Y. (2009), Competitiveness of short sea shipping and the role of port: The case of North Europe. *Maritime Policy & Management*, 36 (4), pp. 337–352.

Paixao, A.C., & Marlow, P.B. (2002), Strengths and weaknesses of short sea shipping. *Marine Policy*, 26, pp. 167–178.

Paixao, A.C., & Marlow, P.B. (2007), The impact of the trans-European transport networks on the development of short sea shipping. *Maritime Economics & Logistics*, 9, pp. 302–323.

Perakis, N.A., & Denisis, A. (2008), A survey of short sea shipping and its prospects in the USA. *Journal of Maritime Policy and Management*, 35 (6), pp. 591–614.

Sambracos, E. (2003), Market analysis and pricing policies for sea canals: The case of the Greek Corinth Canal. *Journal of Maritime Policy and Management*, 30 (2), pp. 175–190.

Sambracos, E., & Maniati, M., (2012), Competitiveness between short sea shipping and road freight transport in mainland port connections: The case of two Greek ports. *Maritime Policy & Management*, 39 (3), pp. 321–337.

Seungjin, S., Hong-Seung, R., & Sung Ho, H. (2019), Characteristics analysis of freight mode choice model according to the introduction of a new freight transport system. *Sustainability*, 11, pp. 1–13.

Snaddon, D.R. (2001), Competition in transportation – a literature analysis. *Technovation*, 21 (6), pp. 375–383.

Stopford, M. (1997), *Maritime Economics*, 2nd edition. London: Routledge, pp. 160–170.

United Nations COMTRADE 2018 database on international trade. https://comtrade.un.org/data. Data extracted on 25 May 2019.

11 Short sea shipping in the Association of Southeast Asian Nations

Aminuddin Md Arof and Amayrol Zakaria

1 Introduction

The Association of Southeast Asian Nations (ASEAN) was established in 1967 with the objectives of accelerating economic growth, fostering social progress and promoting regional peace and stability through joint endeavours and equal partnership between regional countries. All the ten countries of the Southeast Asian region are members of ASEAN except for East Timor. Gaining independence in 2002, East Timor has been given observer status to the regional body. In 2014, intra-ASEAN trade amounted to USD 608 billion, which was about a quarter of ASEAN's total international trade (Ministry of International Trade & Industry, 2015). Similarly, China, ASEAN's immediate neighbour, has continued to become their biggest trading partner with a trade value of USD 600 billion in 2018 (Beh, 2019). Geographically, the region can be divided into mainland Southeast Asia and archipelagic Southeast Asia (ASEA). Due to the semi-archipelagic nature of this region and the intensity of their trade involvement within the region and with their immediate neighbours, it can easily be surmised that short sea shipping (SSS) is an imperative rather than an alternative to ensure smooth trading activities.

Mostly, there is no strict definition of SSS. Some definitions consider the types of vessels used, types of cargo or passenger transported, and geography or distance. In fact, Medda and Trujillo (2010) opine that there is no agreement on a common definition of SSS amongst experts. Similarly, Douet and Cappuccilli (2011) maintain that an unambiguous and concise definition of SSS does not exist. One of the earliest definitions of SSS is that of Balduini (1982), who defines it as 'a maritime transport between ports of a nation as well as between a nation's port and the ports of adjacent countries'.

Although the concept of SSS is a European one, the economic development goals of the ASEAN cannot be accomplished without a local form of SSS, particularly in its Ro-Ro form. For example, in the ASEAN leaders' meeting of 28 October 2010, it was declared that in order to achieve an ASEAN community by 2015, the regional association should ensure that systematic efforts are taken to improve connectivity within the various national borders, among the ASEAN countries, and between the member countries and the extra-regional countries

(ASEAN, 2011). They simultaneously declared the adoption of the Master Plan on ASEAN Connectivity (MPAC) in an effort to enhance national and regional physical, institutional and people-to-people linkages that has been entrusted with seven key strategies. The key strategies, among others, emphasize the successful construction of an ASEAN Highway Network (AHN) and a Singapore-Kunming Rail Link (SKRL) and the formation of an 'integrated, efficient and competitive maritime transport system' (ASEAN, 2011:38). According to ASEAN, this is in line with their objective of developing an integrated and well-functioning intermodal transport while at the same time addressing the problems caused by environmental degradation and pollution (ASEAN, 2011). In support of the formation of an 'integrated, efficient and competitive maritime transport system', one of ASEAN's key actions is the establishment of reliable and efficient shipping routes, which will connect mainland and archipelagic Southeast Asia. Having been amazed by the success of the Philippines Nautical Highway (PNH) system that has demonstrated significant benefits in terms of the lowering of transport costs and growth of the regional market through the utilization of Ro-Ro ships, ASEAN members have agreed to establish a Ro-Ro policy as one of the important means for enhancing intra-ASEAN connectivity (ASEAN, 2011). Due to the slow progress of the action plans laid down in the MPAC, ASEAN leaders have subsequently launched MPAC 2025 to reinforce their desire to achieve a seamless and integrated ASEAN community (ASEAN, 2016).

Among others, this chapter will discuss the current situation on domestic SSS in ASEA. This will be followed by the feasibility study on ASEAN Ro-Ro SSS and the current situation of international SSS in the ASEAN. Before the conclusion, the focus of this chapter will be on the development and testing of a decision-making model for interstate SSS in this region.

2 Current situation of domestic SSS in ASEA

ASEA comprises Indonesia, the Philippines, the eastern part of Malaysia and Brunei Darussalam (see Figure 11.1). The eastern part of Malaysia and Brunei Darussalam together with the province of Kalimantan in Indonesia are co-located on the island of Borneo. This sub-region is dominated by two biggest archipelagic nations of the world – Indonesia and the Philippines.

At present, most of the SSS involving Ro-Ro and passenger transportation are dedicated to intra-state connections. Most regional interstate SSS operations involve the movement of cargo using feeder container vessels connecting the hub ports of Singapore, Port Klang, Port Tanjung Pelepas (PTP) and Laem Chabang with other smaller ports within the region. Other intra-regional shipping connections include bulk carriers, product tankers and offshore support vessels.

Indonesia, as the largest ASEAN country as well as the largest archipelagic nation in the world, is a country of about 13,600 islands with more than 253 million inhabitants. Its main inter-island network is highly dependent on maritime transport, which also involves Ro-Ro vessels. Their Ro-Ro services are split between two authorities under the Ministry of Transport. The first is

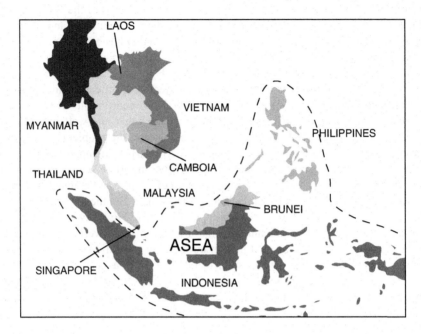

Figure 11.1 The ASEA.
Source: Adapted from aseanup.com.

the Directorate General of Land Transportation (DGLT), which has been the initial authority for Ro-Ro service since 1981, and the second is the Directorate General of Sea Transportation (DGST), which is the given authority for long-distance ferry services (JICA, 2013). Under DGST, SSS ferry services are divided into state-owned shipping companies represented by PT PELNI and PT ASDP Indonesia Ferry, or Persero, which jointly operate four Ro-Ro vessels out of a total of 29 vessels. In addition, seven private shipping companies operate 23 Ro-Ro vessels for open sea crossings (JICA, 2013). Persero operates another 98 Ro-Ro vessels, with 103 more Ro-Ro vessels being operated by the private sector under the DGLT authority serving 144 routes, of which 78 are considered active (JICA, 2013). As the Indonesian government started providing subsidies to pioneer shipping services in the 1970s based on a constitutional obligation, several incentives have been provided to private operators in order to ensure a feasible SSS service (JICA, 2013). Among the incentives are a special franchise for ferry operators that ensure no direct competition with other direct shipping services and the differentiation between subsidy route and commercial route that is opened to free market competition (JICA, 2013). Among the problems encountered by Ro-Ro operators in Indonesia are low tariffs, especially for short-distance services, which are set by the governments and which make it impossible to upgrade to bigger vessels due to limited port capacity. Additional problems involve no fixed schedule for long-distance service due to fluctuation of demand; dedicated Ro-Ro terminals are only available at ASDP ports, meaning that Ro-Ro vessels have to use the cargo wharf alternately with cargo vessels in other ports; and insufficient parking space for vehicles in most ports (JICA, 2013).

Before the Philippines' Ro-Ro policy was introduced in 2003, the leading method of shipping was the lift-on/lift-off (Lo-Lo) and conventional liner system (ADB, 2010). In the Lo-Lo system, goods are shipped in containers and loaded or discharged by using cargo-handling gears fitted on board ships or those belonging to the ports. After its inception in 2003, the Ro-Ro system has transformed the landscape of the Philippines maritime sector. For instance, a Ro-Ro service called 2GO has been portrayed as a simpler and improved service, which allows shippers control over their cargo movements. This subsequently led to a reduction in costs and faster delivery lead time. The 2GO service was reported to have reduced transport and freight logistics activities from nine steps with the Lo-Lo service to just three steps. It also managed to reduce delivery time from an average of 9 days to just 3 days (ADB, 2010). This has resulted in a speedy growth in the freight handled on the Ro-Ro networks. For instance, there has been an increase in rolling cargo traffic to 419,740 vehicles in 2008 from just 254,029 in 2003. Similarly, passenger traffic has seen an increase to 3 million in 2008 along the Western Nautical Highway alone from a mere 1.86 million in 2003 (ADB, 2010). Figure 11.2 shows the layout of the Philippines Nautical Highways.

Besides Indonesia and the Philippines, most domestic Ro-Ro and passenger ferry services in the other ASEAN states mainly involve connections between the mainland and their outlying islands. Among others, domestic Ro-Ro services are available from Penang to Butterworth, Kuala Perlis to Langkawi, and Menumbok to Labuan in Malaysia. In other mainland Southeast Asian countries, the availability of their domestic Ro-Ro services is not significant. However, there are interstate Ro-Ro services connecting the port of Muara in Brunei Darussalam with Labuan and Menumbok in the eastern part of Malaysia. Similarly, a Ro-Ro ferry service connecting Singapore and Tanjung Belungkor in the southern part of peninsular Malaysia was introduced in 2001 but was terminated in 2006 due to poor demand.

3 Feasibility study on ASEAN Ro-Ro SSS

A feasibility study on interstate ASEAN Ro-Ro connections was performed by the Japanese International Cooperation Agency (JICA) on behalf of the ASEAN governments in 2012. In the study, eight potential interstate Ro-Ro shipping routes connecting five countries were examined. The ASEAN countries involved were Brunei Darussalam, Indonesia, Malaysia, Philippines and Thailand. During the field survey in the first half of 2012, the JICA team visited five national capitals and 17 port cities, and 212 respondents were consulted or interviewed. Based on the study, only five routes were recommended for a more detailed examination due to various factors, as presented in Figure 11.3 and Table 11.1.

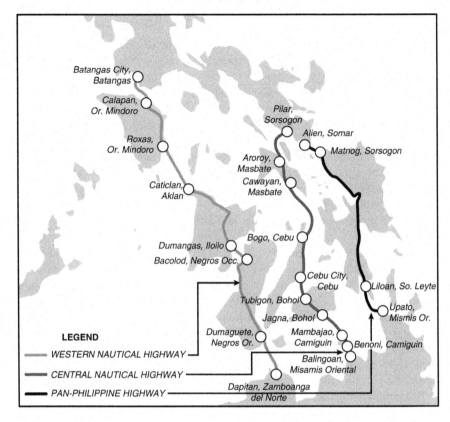

Figure 11.2 The Philippines Nautical Highways.
Source: Adapted from ADB (2010).

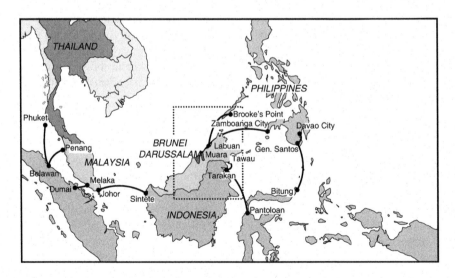

Figure 11.3 The routes covered by JICA's feasibility study.
Source: Adapted from JICA (2013).

For the column on available infrastructure in Table 11.1, 'A' signifies the availability of an international Ro-Ro terminal. 'B' indicates that Ro-Ro terminal is available without customs, immigration, quarantine and security (CIQS) facilities, 'C' signifies that a Ro-Ro terminal is not available, while 'D' indicates that the designated port is not suitable to handle Ro-Ro vessels, as in the case of Sintete and Brooke's Point. In summary, Table 11.1 shows that there is no ideal candidate route that has been rated triple-A in terms of demand and infrastructure readiness. Nevertheless, two Malacca Strait crossing routes seem to be viable, since existing traffic along the two routes was observed. In fact, currently there is a daily service between Melaka and Dumai, whilst there used to be a thrice-weekly service between Belawan and Penang until around 2008 before it was terminated. In spite of the available traffic, the Malaysian ports of Melaka and Penang were rated poorly in term of Ro-Ro infrastructure, whilst the Indonesian ports of Belawan and Dumai need to upgrade their Ro-Ro terminals with CIQS facilities to meet international standards. The Davao/General Santos or Gensan (Philippines)–Bitung (Indonesia) route was rated third in the survey where existing traffic was observed on part of the route. Cross-border trading was generally done using traditional boats, which is popularly known as barter trading. Additionally, Gensan and Bitung need to be enhanced with CIQS facilities, and Davao needs a new Ro-Ro terminal to serve the identified route. Similarly, the Tawau (Malaysia)–Tarakan (Indonesia)–Pantoloan (Indonesia) route, which is currently served by passenger ferries, has almost an equal prospect as the Davao/Gensan–Bitung route, if the required infrastructure is built or enhanced. Additionally, the

Table 11.1 Outcome of JICA's feasibility study.

Rating	Route	Connecting Countries	Divertible Existing Traffic	Available Infrastructure
1	Dumai–Melaka	Indonesia, Malaysia	Available at entire stretch	B (Dumai) C (Melaka)
2	Belawan–Penang	Indonesia, Malaysia	Available at entire stretch	B (Belawan) C (Penang)
3	Davao/Gensan–Bitung	Philippines, Indonesia	Available on part of the route	B (Gensan) B (Bitung) C (Davao)
4	Tawau–Tarakan–Pantoloan	Malaysia, Indonesia	Available on part of the route	C (Tawau) B (Tarakan) B (Pantoloan)
5	Muara–Zamboanga	Brunei, Philippines	Available on part of the route	A (Muara) C (Zamboanga)
None	Muara–Labuan–Brooke's Point	Brunei, Malaysia, Philippines	Available on part of the route	A (Muara) A (Labuan) D (Brooke's Point)
None	Belawan -Phuket	Indonesia, Thailand	No traffic observed	B (Belawan) B (Phuket)
None	Johor–Sintete	Malaysia, Indonesia	No traffic observed	A (Tg Belungkor) D (Sintete)

Source: Adapted from JICA (2013).

Muara (Brunei)–Zamboanga (Philippines) route was rated fifth with some prospects in term of available trade but will require the construction of Ro-Ro terminals at Zamboanga.

Although the last three routes were not rated and were considered not feasible, the sixth route involving Muara (Brunei)–Labuan (Malaysia) to Brooke's Point (Philippines) may still be revived, as there is some prospect due to the availability of significant barter trade activities by traditional boats. Since Brooke's Point is considered unsuitable for Ro-Ro operations due to shallow water, another suitable landing point in the Philippines' island of Palawan has been identified. It has been reported that construction of a Ro-Ro terminal and connecting roads are currently nearing completion at Buliluyan (Magdayao, 2018). This new Ro-Ro terminal is situated at the southern tip of Palawan Island, which makes it nearer to ports in Malaysia and Brunei by more than 100 km as compared to Brooke's Point.

4 Current situation of international SSS in ASEAN

The first intra-ASEAN Ro-Ro connection between Menumbok in Sabah and Muara in Brunei Darussalam (see Figure 11.4) was launched in late 2009 but has ceased operation after less than a year, citing a low load factor as the main reason behind the failure. The same vessel was then used to serve the Labuan–Muara route in 2010 and survives until today. On the other hand, the failed Menumbok–Labuan route was subsequently re-launched and enhanced with a Menumbok–Labuan–Muara connection since the end of 2015. In addition to the Ro-Ro connection with Brunei, the authorities of Malaysia and the Philippines are currently working on a connection between Kudat (Malaysia) and Baliluyan (Philippines) with the upgrading of the Ro-Ro terminal in Kudat, which was completed in June 2016 (Daily Express, 2016). The upgrading of the Baliluyan Ro-Ro port and road infrastructure connecting Baliluyan and the rest of Palawan Island is also

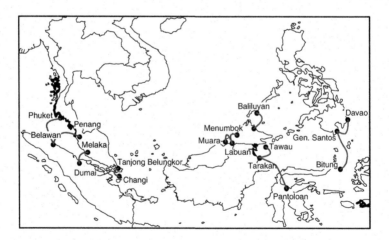

Figure 11.4 Short sea shipping in ASEAN.

nearing completion, allowing for the anticipated ASEAN Ro-Ro service between Kudat and Palawan to commence soon (Magdayao, 2018). Meanwhile, the Ro-Ro service connecting Davos–Gensan–Bitung that was launched on 30 April 2017 was temporarily halted, as it failed to secure enough cargo. The governments of both Indonesia and the Philippines are reportedly working towards the continuation of the service in 2019 (Colina IV, 2019).

Closer to mainland Southeast Asia, a Ro-Ro service between Tanjung Belungkor (Malaysia) and Changi (Singapore) that started in 2001 ceased operations in 2006 (JICA, 2013). Currently, the route is served by passenger ferries with two trips during weekdays and four trips during weekends. A feasibility study is currently being performed by a private operator to re-introduce it (Limbungan Maju, 2016). Similarly, the Belawan (Indonesia) and Penang (Malaysia) Ro-Ro service was terminated in 2006 after only a year of operation. The reasons cited for both terminations were low payload and the unwillingness to replace the ageing vessels employed (JICA, 2013; Limbungan Maju, 2016). The Belawan–Penang route was also previously served by a passenger ferry service. Currently, no regular Ro-Ro or passenger ferry service can be traced along the route. As for the Dumai (Indonesia)–Melaka (Malaysia) route, efforts are currently being undertaken to construct a Ro-Ro terminal at Tanjung Bruas Port in Melaka (Musa, 2018). Currently, the Dumai–Melaka route is served by a daily passenger ferry service.

The port of Phuket (Thailand) faces similar problems due to limited facilities, including no passenger terminal or Ro-Ro ramp. These challenges will have to be addressed to better realize the maritime connectivity with the island of Sumatra in Indonesia or Penang in Malaysia (IMT-GT, 2012, 2017). For the projected Ro-Ro route between Phuket and Belawan (Indonesia) to be realized, issues on the punctuality of cargo and passenger movement due to Ro-Ro networks, legislation and the required facilities need to be seriously addressed by both national authorities (Noh, 2018). In a recent survey involving 22 expert respondents from Indonesia, Malaysia and Thailand, it has been identified that the most critical factors before the Phuket–Belawan or Phuket–Penang–Belawan route could be successfully operationalized are regulatory, technical/infrastructure and safety issues, with the commercial and environmental factors listed below the top three.

5 A model for decision-making on Ro-Ro SSS

Due to the multiple failures of earlier interstate Ro-Ro SSS endeavours in the ASEAN countries, an analytic hierarchy process (AHP) study was conducted in 2015 to identify key determining factors to ensure future success with a focus on the ASEA sub-region. The AHP is one of the popular multi-criteria analysis instruments normally utilized for solving unstructured and complicated problems. The instrument that was introduced in 1980 by T. L. Saaty employs a procedure that utilizes a hierarchical model that contains goal, criteria and sub-criteria as well as alternatives (Saaty, 2008). This technique uses the concept of hierarchical structure and paired comparisons or network analysis in order to select the most suitable alternative between available feasible options (Saaty, 1997). The principal goal of AHP is to choose an alternative, which could satisfy a pre-determined set of factors or criteria from a set of possibilities or alternatives. It is also used to determine the weights of the factors involved in any suitable application by utilizing the experience and knowledge of the decision makers or panel of experts in a matrix of paired comparison of attributes (Saaty, 2008). For the purpose of decision-making using the AHP, Saaty (2008) emphasizes the necessity to:

1. Identify the issue or problem at hand;
2. Identify the purpose of the decision;
3. Identify the criteria and sub-criteria under examination;
4. Ascertain the groups and stakeholders that may be affected with the finding; and
5. Identify the choices or alternatives available for selection.

Through a process of content analysis from the available literature and Delphi surveys with expert respondents, ten key determining factors to enable interstate Ro-Ro SSS undertakings to be successful have been selected from an original list of 16 determining factors. As not all the factors gathered through the review of literature may be suitable as the key factors to facilitate the success of interstate Ro-Ro in the ASEA, a Delphi technique has been used to allow the selected panel of experts to choose the more important determinants among the 14 identified determining factors. The expert panel was also requested to nominate other important determinants that have not been addressed through the literature. Although nominated determinants were not addressed in the literature, they could be just as important for enabling the success of Ro-Ro short sea service in the ASEA due to the sub-region's uniqueness (Arof, Hanafiah and Ooi, 2016). The Delphi is a technique that necessitates knowledgeable and expert respondents reacting to the questions given individually and providing the feedback directly to the controller or researcher, who will process it by identifying the main tendencies and their justifications (Grisham, 2009). According to Rowe and Wright (1999), four key features that must be followed in the Delphi process are the anonymity of expert respondents, an iteration process allowing expert respondents to further refine their views, the provision of feedback to the respondents and statistical aggregation of the feedback received, which will allow for quantitative analysis and data interpretation. Because of the limited availability of maritime transport experts within the ASEA sub-region, the Delphi is arguably a more suitable instrument compared to some other common techniques, such as brainstorming and factor analysis, because no minimum number of experts is required for the Delphi as compared to the other techniques.

After the two-round Delphi survey, ten out of 16 identified determining factors to enable the realization of interstate Ro-Ro short sea service in ASEA sub-region were selected as the key factors, based on a rating of 6 and above on a 7-point Likert scale by the panel of experts from four countries within the ASEA sub-region (Arof and Nair, 2017). The key determining factors are:

1. government assistance at initial period;
2. adequate port facilities and equipment;
3. suitable ship's type in relation to payload, distance and speed;

4   good port access;
5   coordinated administrative and CIQS facilities;
6   security perception and safety of surrounding waters;
7   good intermodal link;
8   port efficiency;
9   regional agreements to relax shipping restriction; and
10 SSS service quality.

(Arof, 2018:37)

On the other hand, six other determining factors that have been judged not as critical as the ten determining factors identified earlier are

(1) harmonization of administrative procedures among ports; (2) balance payload or shipment volume; (3) large payload or shipment volume; (4) promotion of SSS; (5) weather and meteorological conditions; and (6) efficient and transparent government bureaucracy.

(Arof, 2018:37)

Subsequently, the ten key determining factors selected by the panel of experts were distributed between three clusters, namely 'Regulatory', 'Infrastructure' and 'Commercial'. Thereafter, 20 questionnaires were distributed to the AHP panel of experts to enable them to administer the paired comparisons. Out of the 20 questionnaires distributed, 19 were returned, but only 18 were found to be within the acceptable consistency ratio (CR). The aggregate result of the paired comparisons performed by the 18 experts shown in Table 11.2 contains the overall internal and global priority weights of the ten determining factors involved. Internal weight is the weight of a factor or variable as compared to other factors within the same cluster. Likewise, internal ranking is the standing of a factor or variable against other factors within the designated cluster.

On the opposite, global weight and global ranking represent the weight of the factor when judged against other factors across all clusters. Out of the three clusters involved, the 'Regulatory' cluster received a greater weight than the 'Infrastructure' and 'Commercial' clusters, which is comprehensible and typical in AHP when a cluster has more determining factors vis-à-vis other clusters with lesser determinants (Saaty, 1994). The 'Infrastructure' and 'Commercial' clusters, both with three determinants under them, obtained almost equal weight. The outcome was that the top four determining factors were justly represented from the three clusters: 'government assistance at the initial period', 'adequate port facilities and equipment', 'coordinated administrative and CIQS formalities' and 'suitable ship's type in relation to the payload, distance and speed'.

The outcome of the AHP pairwise comparisons has 80% similarity to the result of the Delphi technique performed earlier, in which 20 experts ascertained an aggregate score for the top five determining factors using a 7-point Likert scale with the following results:

a)   Government assistance at initial period (Mean 6.4).
b)   Adequate port facilities and equipment (Mean 6.4).

Table 11.2 Results of AHP paired comparisons.

Clusters	Weight	CR	Determining factors	Internal weight	Internal ranking	Global weight	Global ranking
Regulatory	0.428	0.0	Coordinated admin and CIQS	0.252	2	0.108	3
			Government assistance	0.351	1	0.150	1
			Agreements to relax shipping restrictions	0.201	3	0.086	7
			Security perception and safety	0.196	4	0.084	8
Physical and administrative infrastructure	0.284	0.0	Adequate port facilities	0.480	1	0.136	2
			Intermodal links	0.240	3	0.068	10
			Port access	0.270	2	0.077	9
Commercial	0.288	0.003	Port efficiency	0.332	2	0.096	5
			SSS service quality	0.312	3	0.090	6
			Suitable ship's type	0.356	1	0.103	4

Source: Adapted from Arof (2018).

c) Suitable ship's type in relation to the payload, distance and speed (Mean 6.25).
d) Good port access (Mean 6.15).
e) Coordinated administrative and Customs, Immigration, Quarantine and Security (CIQS) facilities (Mean 6.10).

(Arof, 2018:38)

The judgments made using the AHP paired comparisons judged the top two determining factors as similar to those determined by the earlier Delphi technique. Additionally, the 'coordinated administrative and CIQS facilities' was upgraded from fifth to third position, while 'suitable ship's type in relation to the payload, distance and speed' was moved down one step lower to fourth position. Nevertheless, the 'good port access' determinant was lowered from fourth place in the Delphi technique to ninth place in AHP aggregate paired comparisons. In fact, it is acceptable to see a minor re-arrangement of the determining factors in their AHP global rankings due to the reduced number of experts from 20 in the Delphi technique to only 18 in the AHP.

In reviewing the determining factors in Figure 11.5, the clusters were introduced due to the unsuitability in performing direct paired comparisons when more than seven variables are involved (Saaty and Ozdemir, 2003). It has also been argued in the literature that paired comparisons which involved five variables or more is prone to produce inconsistent results in individual judgments (Da Cruz et al., 2013; Kumar et al., 2009; Bodin and Gass, 2003). Therefore, based on the result of Round 1 of the Delphi survey, all the 16 determining factors identified

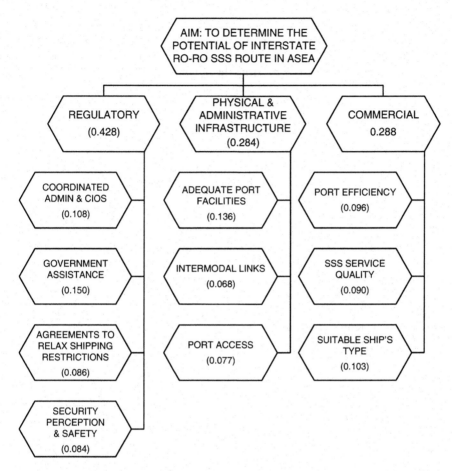

Figure 11.5 Decision-making model for interstate Ro-Ro SSS.
Source: Adapted from Arof (2018).

through literature review and proposed by the experts have been placed under four clusters. However, the 'weather and meteorological conditions' determinant that was placed under the 'Environmental' cluster was among the six determinants that were not selected through the Delphi process. Hence, the ten determining factors categorized as the key determinants are positioned under three clusters to attain a consistent outcome in the AHP paired comparisons.

6 Testing of AHP decision-making model

For the purpose of testing the AHP decision-making model illustrated in Figure 11.5, five experts who were known to have adequate knowledge on the three selected routes have been invited to provide their judgments. Based on the ten determinants that were used to develop the decision-making model, respondents were invited to evaluate the potential performance of the three interstate Ro-Ro SSS routes using a 5-point Likert scale ranging from 1 (poor) to 5 (excellent). The three routes were chosen because the expert respondents have witnessed Ro-Ro operations along the routes, including a test run between Kudat and Brooke's Point. Based on the availability of sufficient data involving the routes involved, expert judgments were expected to be accurate. The mean scores using the arithmetic mean method for all the judgments from the five nominated expert respondents are as per Table 11.3.

Subsequently, the values in Table 11.3 have been multiplied by the weight of each determinant. The results of the multiplication for each route were added to obtain the total ratings for all the routes under comparison as presented at Table 11.4.

Based on the outcome of the ratings given by the five expert respondents on the three selected routes and the multiplication of the ratings given by the weight of each variable in the SSS decision-making model, it can be witnessed from Table 11.4 that Route 2, which is the Muara–Labuan route, obtained the highest rating of 0.745 (3.727/5) from a maximum score of 1.0. This is a high score considering that it is very close to 75%. It is not surprising, as the Muara–Labuan interstate Ro-Ro SS operation has operated successfully since October 2010 with an increased number of passengers even after it was launched for only a year (Al-Haadi, 2011). Besides the success of Route 2 operation, further improvements can

Table 11.3 Mean score for selected routes.

Factor/Weight	R1	R2	R3	R4	P5	P6	P7	C8	C9	C10
Route	*0.108*	*0.15*	*0.086*	*0.084*	*0.136*	*0.068*	*0.077*	*0.096*	*0.09*	*0.103*
1 Muara to Menumbok	4	2.8	2.4	3.8	3.6	3.8	3.4	3.6	3.4	3.2
2 Muara to Labuan	4.6	3	2.6	3.8	4	4.2	4	4	3.6	3.8
3 Kudat to Brooke's Point	2.2	2.4	2.4	2.2	2	3.6	1.6	1.6	3	2.4

Legend
R1: Coordinated administrative and CIQS formalities
R2: Government assistance at initial period
R3: Regional agreements to relax shipping restriction
R4: Security perception and safety of surrounding waters
P5: Adequate port facilities and equipment
P6: Good intermodal links
P7: Good Port Access
C8: Port efficiency
C9: SSS service quality
C10: Suitable ship's type in relation to payload, distance and speed

Source: Author.

Table 11.4 Total ratings of selected routes.

Weight	R1	R2	R3	R4	P5	P6	P7	C8	C9	C10	TOTAL
Route	0.108	0.15	0.086	0.084	0.136	0.068	0.077	0.096	0.09	0.103	1.0
1 Muara to Menumbok	0.432 (.086)	0.42 (.084)	0.206 (.041)	0.319 (.064)	0.490 (.098)	0.258 (.052)	0.262 (.052)	0.346 (.069)	0.306 (.061)	0.33 (.066)	3.369/5 (.674)
2 Muara to Labuan	0.497 (.099)	0.45 (.09)	0.224 (.045)	0.319 (.064)	0.544 (.109)	0.286 (.057)	0.308 (.062)	0.384 (.077)	0.324 (.065)	0.391 (.078)	3.727/5 (.745)
3 Kudat to Brooke's Point	0.238 (.048)	0.36 (.072)	0.206 (.041)	0.185 (.037)	0.272 (.054)	0.245 (.049)	0.123 (.025)	0.154 (.031)	0.27 (.054)	0.247 (.049)	2.30/5 (.460)

Source: Author.

be undertaken on the shortcomings under determinants R2, R3 and C9 that scored less than the overall mean score of 75%.

In addressing element R2 (government assistance at initial period), government operational subsidy may no longer be relevant, as the company has successfully operated it for more than five years. However, certain incentives should be considered, as SSS is a more environmentally friendly mode of transportation compared to road transport. As a result, certain inducements that could be passed down to the SSS users would only encourage people to travel by sea more frequently.

As for R3, it could be argued that an agreement on cabotage relaxation could allow operators from neighbouring countries to include more than one port on their neighbour's territory as part of the route. This could result in better economies of scale, as more passengers and vehicles would utilize the SSS service. For instance, the Muara–Labuan operation that had initially failed has now successfully been extended to the Muara–Labuan–Menumbok service. As for C9, it would certainly attract more customers if the service quality that has been defined as a safe, regular and reliable service could be further improved.

As for Route 1 (Muara–Menumbok), which was once considered as one of ASEAN's flagship Ro-Ro programmes (Bandial, 2010), it achieved an overall score of 0.674, which can be considered as satisfactory. It is believed that with certain improvements on some critical determinants, the service that failed in 2010, after being in operation for less than a year, could be revived. Among the four top determinants that provide a combined weight of almost 0.5, or half the total weight, only R1 received a score of 79.6%. Other key determinants, for example R2, P5 and C10 that scored only 56%, 72% and 64% respectively, should be addressed. Among others, determinant R2 could be addressed by certain kinds of operational subsidies or tax incentives, as Route 2 competes directly with land transport. Additionally, P5 could be addressed by improving port facilities, such as the vehicle waiting area, and passenger terminal facilities, which are observed as lacking in Menumbok. In discussing determinant C10, it should be noted that when the service along Route 1 was initially started, it offered a daily schedule and suffered from a lack of passengers, particularly outside the school holiday period. In addressing this problem, a smaller vessel should be considered to cater to the limited demand. Otherwise, an additional port of call should be included, such as

Menumbok–Limbang–Muara, to increase the number of passengers. However, it has been reported that a new service from Menumbok–Labuan–Muara has been introduced after a contract was awarded to Labuan Mainlink Private Limited that will operate *MV Goodwill Star* with a maximum capacity of 500 passengers and 100 vehicles (Bernama, 2015).

As for Route 3 involving Kudat–Brooke's Point, which was delayed due to the incompletion of the Ro-Ro ramp in Kudat, the overall score achieved was only 0.460, far below the overall score for Route 2 and Route 1, which are 0.745 and 0.674 respectively. In fact, Route 3 scored the lowest for all determinants except for R3, where it shared second place with Route 1. Hence, before the SSS operation along this route commences, it is imperative for all the determinants, particularly the four key determinants R1, R2, P5 and C10, to be addressed. As maritime transport is an imperative means of transportation rather than a choice to connect the two rural ports, some kind of operational subsidies need to be introduced to sustain the service until it can secure sufficient payload to break even. Apart from the four key determinants, it has to be noted that Route 3 only obtained 44% for R4 as compared to 76.2% for both Route 1 and Route 2. Hence, Route 3 is still perceived by the experts as unsafe, unless law enforcement measures are further enhanced by the maritime authorities of both countries. Due to the unsuitability of Brooke's Point for Ro-Ro operations, the Philippines authority has identified Baliluyan as an alternative port for the Philippines–Malaysia connection (Colina IV, 2019).

7 Conclusion

In retrospect, the progress of interstate Ro-Ro SSS in the ASEAN has been very slow, although it has been highly encouraged by the ASEAN governments through the adoption of MPAC and MPAC 2025. Thus far, no incentives have been offered by the various governments to support the project, although it has been found through the AHP analysis that the regional experts considered 'government assistance at initial period' as the key determinant for the success of such operations. Without suitable government incentives, private investors will not commit their resources unless sufficient demand is available.

At present, the only successful routes are Labuan (Malaysia)–Muara (Brunei) and the Muara–Labuan–Menumbok (Malaysia), which prevail due to high demand. Other international routes that were operated earlier, especially Bitung (Indonesia)–Gensan (Philippines)–Davao (Philippines), Changi (Singapore)–Tanjung Belungkor (Malaysia) and Penang (Malaysia)–Belawan (Indonesia), will require a thorough study on the type of incentives suitable for enabling the operators to sustain the initial period of operations once services along those routes are re-introduced. As Ro-Ro shipping is considered a major component of the Motorways of the Sea, it is only sensible for it to be supply driven.

This study is unique and different from other previous research, as most recent research on SSS is centred in Europe and North America and is more focused on developing an economically and environmentally viable alternative mode of transportation that could remove some of the road freight transportation from congested roads and highways. Instead, the focus of this study is mostly on the ASEA sub-region of the ASEAN, where in many instances maritime connection is an imperative rather than an alternative. Instead of developing SSS as an alternative mode of transportation, this study is centred on the development of inter-island and interstate SSS connection in a less-developed sub-region, where SSS is imperative for further sub-regional development.

It is also hoped that this study will correct the perception that the failure of formal shipping services in the ASEAN is only attributed to a low load factor. In fact, 'large payload or shipment volume', which was listed as one of the 16 earlier determinants, was not even shortlisted as the ten key determinants to be included in the AHP decision-making model. This should be well understood particularly for the ASEA sub-region, because in certain situations maritime transport needs to operate in a supply-driven environment at the initial stage. This situation is similar to roads on land that need to exist before people can consider utilizing them for beneficial activities that include trade and tourism.

References

ADB (Asian Development Bank) (2010), Bridges across oceans: Initial impact assessment of the Philippines nautical highway system and lessons for Southeast Asia, ADB and Asia Foundation.
Al-haadi, Abu Bakar (2011), PKL eyes Menumbok RoRo service resumption, *Brunei Times*. 12 Jan. Available at http://newspaperhunt.com/papers/Brunei/Brunei-Times.php (accessed 13 January 2011).
Arof, A.M. (2018), Decision making model for Ro-Ro short sea shipping operations in Archipelagic Southeast Asia. *The Asian Journal of Shipping and Logistics*, 34 (1), pp. 33–42.
Arof, A.M., Hanafiah, R.M., & Ooi, I.U.J. (2016), A Delphi study on the potential benefits and obstacles of interstate short sea shipping in archipelagic Southeast Asia. *International Journal of e-Navigation and Maritime Economy*, 5, pp. 97–110.
Arof, A.M., & Nair, R. (2017), The identification of key success factors for interstate Ro-Ro short sea shipping in Brunei-Indonesia-Malaysia-Philippines: A Delphi approach. *International Journal of Shipping and Transport Logistics*, 9 (3), pp. 261–279.
ASEAN (2011), Master plan on ASEAN connectivity. Jakarta, ASEAN Secretariat.
ASEAN (2016), Master plan on ASEAN connectivity 2025. Jakarta, ASEAN Secretariat.
ASEANUP (2016), Available at https://aseanup.com/free-maps-asean-southeast-asia/ (accessed 1 June 2019).
Balduini, G. (1982), Short sea shipping in the economy of inland transport in Europe: Italy. European Council of Ministers of Transport, pp. 1–2.
Bandial, Quratul-ain (2010), Menumbuk ferry service a hit with Bruneian, The Brunei Time, 7 March. Available at www.bt.com.bn/news-national (accessed 8 March 2011).
Beh, Yuen Hui (2019), China remains ASEAN's top trading partner over a decade, *The Star Online* 3 March 2019 at http://www.thestar com.my/news/nation/2019/03/03 (accessed 24 Jan 2020).
Bernama (2015), Perkhidmatan feri baharu Labuan-Sabah-Brunei dilancar, 2 May. Available at http://mynewshub.cc/2015/05/02/dilancar/# (accessed 3 May 2018).

Bodin, L., & Gass, S.I. (2003), On teaching the analytic hierarchy process. *Computers & Operations Research*, 30 (10), pp. 1487–1497.

Colina IV, A.L. (2019), Davao-Gensan-Bitung route to resume this year. *Minda News*, 17 February. Available at www.mindanews.com (accessed 17 February 2019).

Da Cruz, M.R.P., Ferreira, J.J., & Azevedo, S.G. (2013), Key factors of seaport competitiveness based on the stakeholder perspective: An Analytic Hierarchy Process (AHP) model. *Maritime Economics & Logistics*, 15 (4), pp. 416–443.

Daily Express (2016), No hurry on Kudat Palawan ferry service, 2nd June. Available at www.dailyexpress.com.my/news.cfm?NewsID=110304 (accessed 3 June 2016).

Douet, M., & Cappuccilli, J.F. (2011), A review of short sea shipping policy in the European Union. *Journal of Transport Geography*, 19 (4), pp. 968–976.

Grisham, T. (2009), The Delphi technique: A method for testing complex and multifaceted topics. *International Journal of Managing Projects in Business*, 2 (1), pp. 112–130.

Indonesian-Malaysian-Thailand Growth Triangle (IMT-GT) (2012), Implementation Blueprint, 2012–2016. Available at http://imtgt.org/Documents/IMT-GT_Implementation_Blueprint_2012-2016.pdf.

Indonesian-Malaysian-Thailand Growth Triangle (IMT-GT) (2017), Implementation Blueprint, 2017–2021. Available at http://imtgt.org/Documents/IMT-GT_Implementation_Blueprint_2017-2021.pdf.

JICA (Japan International Cooperation Agency) (2013), The master plan & feasibility study on the establishment of an ASEAN RO-RO shipping network and short sea shipping, ASEAN/JICA.

Kumar, S., Parashar, N., & Haleem, A. (2009), Analytical hierarchy process applied to vendor selection problem: Small scale, medium scale and large scale industries. *Business Intelligence Journal*, 2 (2), pp. 355–362.

Limbungan Maju (2016), Tg Belungkor Feri Terminal Background. Available at www.tanjungbelungkor.com (accessed 5 October 2016).

Magdayao, A.G. (2018), Palawan needs few more months to start delayed PH – Malaysia Ro-Ro. *Philippines News Agency*, 29 May. Available at www.pna.gov.ph (accessed 30 May 2018).

Medda, F., & Trujillo, L. (2010), Short-sea shipping: An analysis of its determinants. *Maritime Policy & Management*, 37 (3), pp. 285–303.

Ministry of International Trade & Industry (2015), *MITI Weekly Bulletin*, Vol. 330, 17 March.

Musa, Z. (2018), Malaysia, Indonesia ports to start RoRo services. *The Star* Online, 2 February Available at www.thestar.com.my (accessed 2 February 2018).

Noh, F. N. (2018). Chairman of Joint Business Committee Indonesia-Malaysia-Thailand Growth Area, Personal Communication 18 December 2018.

Rowe, G., & Wright, G. (1999), The Delphi technique as a forecasting tool: Issues and analysis. *International Journal of Forecasting*, 15 (1999), pp. 353–375.

Saaty, T.L. (1994), How to make a decision: The analytic hierarchy process. *Interfaces*, 24 (6), pp. 19–43.

Saaty, T.L. (1997), Discussion: That is not the analytic hierarchy process: What the AHP is and what it is not. *Journal of Multi-Criteria Decision Analysis*, 6, pp. 324–335.

Saaty, T.L. (2008), Decision making with the analytic hierarchy process. *International Journal of Services Sciences*, 1 (1), pp. 83–98.

Saaty, T.L., & Ozdemir, M.S. (2003), Why the magic number seven plus or minus two. *Mathematical and Computer Modelling*, 38 (3–4), pp. 233–244.

12 Short sea shipping in Latin America
Analysis of the current logistics system

Delmo Moura and Rui Botter

1 Introduction

Short-sea shipping in Latin America is still governed by a system that provides market or flag reservation for national vessels in each country. Although there are some bilateral agreements between countries, such as Brazil and Argentina, Brazil and Chile, and Brazil and Uruguay, the reserve for maritime short sea shipping (SSS) still prevails for each country. The restriction for an SSS service is still extreme in Latin America, unlike the system implemented by the member countries of the European Union.

In Latin America, the term cabotage is used instead of SSS, and the service is different from that implemented in the European Union. In this region, cabotage is exclusive for national flag vessels of a particular country, maritime transport can only be carried out by a national crew and a country flagship cannot carry out a cabotage operation on the maritime coast of another country.

The only exception is when there is a bilateral agreement between countries. In this case, a flagship of a particular country may sail in the maritime waters of another country. However, it may not carry out cabotage service in the neighbouring country, only transport to the port of destination in the neighbouring country and return to its country of origin. This system is called big cabotage, in place through the bilateral agreements of Mercosul (Common Market of the South, South American Economic Bloc) between Brazil, Argentina and Uruguay.

There is a lack of coordination and interest among countries in integrating the maritime transport sector in Latin America. In addition, there are obstacles related to:

- The port authorities of the countries;
- Customs;
- Health; and
- Others affecting port productivity.

These factors automatically reflect on the logistics chain and port productivity. These problems require adequate public policies in each country related to maritime transport and its modal integration, with a focus on quality roads, rail and port infrastructure, to increase the logistics service and especially the proper integration between modes (Kuznetsov and Kirichenko, 2018).

The restrictions imposed by the Latin American countries in the maritime transport sector, especially in coastal shipping, make it challenging to develop the sector. The restrictions do not necessarily increase the country's shipbuilding sector, which is one of the arguments used by countries to restrict SSS transportation to flagship vessels that are not from their own countries. In fact, the shipbuilding sector in Latin America has no perceived sustainable development and, therefore, the countries of this region are not benefiting from the restriction imposed by each nation.

There should be an agreement between the countries to promote the growth of the region by using the lowest cost maritime transport and reducing the emission of polluting gases, aiming at an optimized modal integration between nations.

At 8,514,876 km2, Brazil's territory is vast, similar to a continent, and has more than 7367 km of coastline on the Atlantic Ocean. The majority of its population, about 80%, live at an average distance of 200 km from the east coast of the country. Currently, the Brazilian population is 209.3 million. Therefore, with these characteristics, its transport matrix should focus more on the use of maritime and waterway transport, since the country has several navigable rivers throughout its length.

The remainder of this chapter is organized as follows. Section 2 reviews the characteristics and legislation of SSS in Latin America and the Caribbean in the main coastal countries using the Atlantic and the Pacific oceans or the Caribbean Sea for transport. Section 3 reviews the current policies and legislation in the smaller economies of Latin America and the Caribbean. Section 4 reviews the existing bilateral agreements between some Latin American countries. Section 5 reviews the cargo flow of that region and the main products transported in SSS, as well as describes the main container handling operations in Latin America and the Caribbean in 2018. Section 6 reviews the characteristics of shipping in Brazil, focusing on current legislation and the role of the National Waterways Transportation Agency (ANTAQ). Section 7 reviews the flow of cargo transported by the maritime mode in Brazil. Section 8 reviews the development of multimodal transport in Brazil and its features. Section 9 reviews the need for actions to develop SSS in Brazil. Section 10 reviews the elements necessary to increase the use of SSS in Brazil to make it competitive and attractive to shipping companies and the market/users that depend on this type of transport for their goods. Section 11 is the conclusion, pointing out important elements that can leverage SSS in Brazil.

2 Characteristics of some Latin American and Caribbean countries in short sea shipping transport

2.1 Short sea shipping policies in major economies

2.1.1 Argentina

Until 1991, the Argentinean merchant navy benefited from a cargo reserve that ensured participation in national freight and foreign trade. Short sea shipping was an exclusive operation of Argentine flag vessels (Moura and Botter, 2019).

Since 1963, Argentina has had a Merchant Marine Fund, in the form of the Brazilian Merchant Marine Fund, which had as its objective the financing of shipbuilding in the country through long-term credits and which was set from a tax on maritime and river freight operations. In 1991, the process of deregulation of the Argentine maritime transport market began through Decree 1772/91 that allowed Argentinean shipowners to temporarily stop the registration of the vessel and thus to use the so-called flag of convenience. In 1992, the deregulation process continued with Decree 1493/92, which established the registration of foreign vessels. In its Article 6, the decree grants the right to be considered as national flag foreign vessels for navigation, communication and SSS. In the same period, the Merchant Marine Fund was extinguished.

Note that the motivations for the opening up of the Argentine maritime market were not only from the process of economic liberalization but also from a severe crisis that crossed the merchant navy with the national flag, making the country unable to provide transportation services of due to the aging of the fleet and its high operating costs.

However, during the period of deregulation, from 1991 to 2003, the Argentinean merchant marine fleet was reduced by 50% (from 149 vessels in 1991 to 66 vessels in 2003). Currently, there is an annual loss of foreign exchange of approximately 3.5 billion US dollars/year because of freight payments for foreign vessels.

In 2004, the Argentine government acknowledged that the decrees of the early 1990s did not have the expected results and prompted a new change in legislation by enacting Decree 1010/2004. The decree recapitulates the need for generating employment for crews and, in the maritime industry, the strengthening of national SSS and the national merchant navy.

This new policy brought no significant changes to the Argentine naval segment, nothing that could consolidate the naval industry and allow Argentina to stand out in the maritime market of South America or Latin America. The policy is a market protection practiced by the countries of Latin America to grow their shipbuilding industry, but without much success.

2.1.2 Brazil

Despite the recommendations on regulation and granting by the National Waterway Transport Agency (ANTAQ), which regulates the maritime and waterway transport sector in Brazil, Brazilian legislation regarding SSS is highly focused on the issue of cargo reserve to Brazilian companies and hardly focused at all on developing policy for a strong SSS sector. The objectives of SSS legislation are to protect domestic transport and shipbuilding.

In addition, several other government sectors, such as Anvisa (National Sanitary Surveillance Agency), the Federal Revenue Service and the Brazilian Navy, regulate aspects of SSS activity in specific laws, decrees and ordinances, making it difficult for companies interested in joining this activity to have a view of the restrictions imposed and rules to be followed. Legislation focusing on a single regulatory and oversight body would be much more convenient for the SSS sector.

Another point concerning legislation refers to the amount of documentation requested for SSS transport compared to the road mode of transportation. The market commonly refers to this factor as bureaucracy. Excessive paperwork is a drag on the industry, crippling the system and raising operating costs. For road transport, only four documents are required for cargo to cross the country, whereas SSS requires 12. In this respect, SSS in Brazil shares a common problem with its counterparts in the European Union, where similar complaints are recurrent.

2.1.3 Chile

The regulation of the Chilean merchant marine market is based on the Merchant Navy Act of 1979, amended in 1985 and 1988. The law provides that SSS is reserved for Chilean vessels and is based on three basic principles:

- Reciprocity: it allows the president of the republic to grant the right of vessels of other Latin American nations to carry SSS in Chile if the same nation grants this right to Chilean vessels;
- Special authorization: allows the president of the republic to grant the right of vessels of other nations to carry SSS in Chile in case of transportation deficiency; and
- Name of vessels: it allows Chilean shipowners to denominate as Chilean the vessel whose owner is Chilean or a resident of Chile, whose captain and officers are also Chilean and whose crew is composed of 75% Chileans.

The law also allows foreign vessels to operate in SSS when loading is less than 900 tonnes or when loading exceeds 900 tonnes and there are no Chilean flag vessels available. In the latter case, a public bidding process must be carried out.

Short sea shipping is, therefore, reserved in its entirety for Chilean shipping companies. A Chilean shipping company must meet the following requirements:

- Social object: the company must expressly establish in its status that it is dedicated to maritime transport;
- Means of transport: the company must own or rent a vessel with a Chilean flag or designate as Chilean vessels as determined by the Merchant Marine Law; and
- Nationality: The Chilean shipowner must have Chilean flag vessels, in which the owners must have more than 50% of the capital, are Chilean (natural or legal) and have a primary domicile or permanent headquarters in Chile and the president, directors or administrators are Chilean.

2.1.4 Other significant economies in Latin America

It is also useful to briefly review the situation in other significant economies of Latin America. In Uruguay, for example, coastal navigation is reserved for

Uruguayan flag vessels, commanded by a Uruguayan captain and with at least one-third of the crew Uruguayans. Uruguay states that its SSS law is not intended to protect a small domestic industry but to conform to the practices of other countries in the region.

The Colombian legislation establishes that the National Maritime Transport or SSS is the one practiced between Colombian ports. Therefore, the service may only be provided by incorporated companies that follow the legal provisions, are duly authorized and authorized to operate and operate national flag vessels. Colombia also believes that its SSS laws protect the domestic maritime industry. Colombian law requires that at least 80% of the crew on board should be Colombian citizens and that national flag vessels operating in domestic service should have a minimum of 60% Colombian officers on board.

As regards Mexico, 1994 legislation represents a substantial liberalization of SSS policy. Before the 1994 act, vessels operating in Mexican SSS were required to be 100% Mexican citizens and staffed by Mexican nationals. The 1994 act favours Mexican vessels in SSS operations, but in some instances, foreign shipowners or vessels may participate in Mexican SSS if the country in which the vessel is owned or registered has negotiated reciprocity or equivalence with Mexico.

Related to maritime transport of SSS, Venezuelan legislation established the Organic Waterway Law which refers to the navigation performed between points and ports located in those over which the country exercises sovereignty and jurisdiction. The legislation states that SSS shall be carried out on vessels registered in the Venezuelan Naval Register (RNV), without prejudice to the provisions of international conventions or treaties to the republic. The National Merchant Marine Protection and Development Act exists to protect Venezuelan citizens by requiring that vessels involved in SSS be at least 80% owned nationally and employ at least 80% of Venezuelan citizens.

3 Short sea shipping policies in smaller economies

3.1 Bahamas

Short sea shipping in the Bahamas is tied to generating employment for the citizens of that country. International tourism is an excellent source of income and moves the economy there, so the local government has defined that any vessel that makes more than one berth in the national ports must register this vessel in the country and, when possible, employ Bahamians in its crew.

3.2 Ecuador

Ecuadorian flag vessels must have more than 50% national ownership and, similar to Colombia, at least 80% of the crew engaged in domestic service must have Ecuadorian citizenship, including the captain and chief engineer. Ecuador indirectly subsidizes the domestic operation of its ships by providing low-cost fuel.

3.3 Honduras

Honduras participates in the Central American Economic Integration Program, which seeks to liberalize trade between Honduras, Nicaragua, El Salvador, Guatemala and Costa Rica. This movement towards open trade, however, did not violate the protection of national SSS. Short sea shipping laws in Honduras exist to favour vessels operating under the Honduran flag to increase government revenues with the registration of new vessels. National flag vessels operating in domestic service should be 100% Honduran and maintain a crew of at least 90% of Honduran citizens if possible.

3.4 Panama

The only activity restricted to national flag vessels in Panama is fishing.

3.5 Peru

Peru is in stark contrast to Panama. Peru, Brazil, Indonesia and the United States are the only countries in the world that meet registration, crew, property and shipbuilding requirements to participate in domestic shipping.

4 Bilateral agreements

Countries such as Chile, Venezuela and Colombia consider within their laws that they reserve SSS maritime transport to companies or ships of the national flag, except certain specific circumstances that allow carrying out this activity to a company or ship of a foreign flag. In any case, the bilateral maritime transport agreements between Brazil, Chile and Argentina and the flag reserve adopted in SSS create several inefficiencies in the region's transportation system, for example:

- A Chilean vessel on the Valparaíso (Chile)–Buenos Aires (Argentina)–Santos (Brazil) route cannot transport cargo from Buenos Aires to the port of Santos, as this would disregard the bilateral agreement between Brazil and Argentina. An Argentine vessel cannot move between Santos and Valparaiso for the same reason; and
- A Brazilian vessel on the Valparaíso–Punta Arenas (Chile)–Puerto Madryn (Argentina)–Buenos Aires–Santos–Fortaleza route cannot transport cargo from Valparaiso and Punta Arenas or between Puerto Madryn and Buenos Aires, as it would break the reservation rule of the flag. The same SSS restrictions apply to vessels from Argentina or Chile sailing in other countries.

5 Cargo flows in short sea shipping

A characteristic feature of the flow of goods in the region is the intensive use of the road mode of transportation, partly explained by the difficulties that countries encounter in the development of their SSS sector.

Table 12.1 Main trade flows.

Countries	Products
Argentina–Brazil	Automotive vehicles, parts for vehicles and tractors, machinery, plastics, iron ore, manufactured goods
Brazil–Chile	Mineral fuels and oils
Chile–Ecuador	Mineral fuels and oils
Ecuador–Peru	Mineral fuels and oils
Brazil–Venezuela	Meat and fuels
Brazil–Uruguay	Mineral fuels and oils
Brazil–Chile	Copper, manufactured products, beef

Source: Seabra *et al.* (2017).

Table 12.2 Exports of some Mercosul (Common Market of the South) member/associate countries.

Countries	%
Argentina	15
Brazil	17
Paraguay	14
Uruguay	12
Venezuela	5

Source: ECLAC (2017).

Table 12.1 shows the most substantial flows of products transported by member countries of Mercosul and associated countries or through bilateral agreements between countries.

Data from the ECLAC (Economic Commission for Latin America and the Caribbean) report of 2017 points out that between 2016 and 2017, exports from some Mercosul member/associate countries to Latin America were as shown in Table 12.2.

Figure 12.1 shows the port containerized cargo units (TEUs). About 10% of this turnover is related to SSS.

6 Characteristics of maritime transportation in Brazil

Brazil is by far the largest economy in Latin America, and the peculiarities of maritime transportation deserve a special attention. It is first important to mention that the maritime sector is subject to the rules and regulations of the Ports and Coasts Directorate of the Brazilian Navy, the National Waterways Transportation Agency (ANTAQ) and the National Petroleum Agency (ANP).

ANTAQ, the main regulatory body, was created under Law 10.233/2001, which provides for the restructuring of water and land transport and creates the National Council for Transport Policy Integration, the National Land Transport Agency, the National Transport and the National Department of Transport Infrastructure.

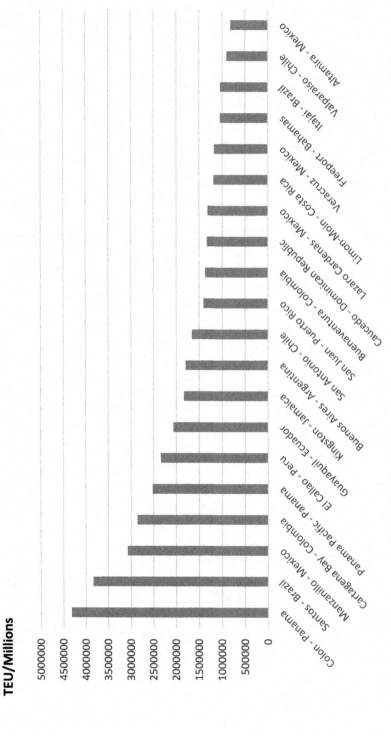

Figure 12.1 Port activities in 2018 – Latin America and the Caribbean.
Source: ECLAC (2018).

This law establishes that ANTAQ is responsible for regulating, supervising and inspecting the waterway sector (as part of its sphere of activity are navigations of port, river, lake, crossing, maritime, SSS and long-distance support), the transport of dangerous or unusual cargo waterways, organized ports and private port terminals and the exploitation of federal waterway infrastructure (Moura and Botter, 2017).

Brazil has 37 public ports and more than 147 terminals for private use (TUP) along its maritime coast. For this reason, SSS can promote a change in the transport matrix of Brazil, depending less on the road sector, since most of the Brazilian population is approximately 200 km from the Brazilian coast.

The National Logistics Plan in Brazil aims to increase the use of water-based modes of transportation, specifically SSS, over the next 10 years, and reduce the use of the road mode of transportation, which today is approximately 61.1% of the transport matrix, while the water-based modes represent 13.6%, the rail mode corresponds to approximately 20.7%, pipeline 4.2% and air transport 0.4%.

The private sector operates in SSS with 40 companies through authorization provided by ANTAQ. The estimated fleet is 153 vessels. The largest companies operating in the sector are Transpetro (Petrobras' transportation subsidiary), Aliança, Norsul, Elcano, Log-in and Mercosur (Fonseca, 2015).

The shipping company Norsul owns 24 ships and is a specialist in the transportation of bulk, general cargo and barge ships in SSS in Brazil. This company has dedicated lines for its clients in the transportation of wood, pulp and steel. Elcano operates bulk carriers, oil tankers and liquefied gases (Fonseca, 2015).

Regarding the transport of cargo with regular services, there is the Aliança (BR-Marítima), Log-in and Mercosul lines, which carry out door-to-door transport. These companies offer regular lines operating in SSS in Brazil and extend the service to Argentina and Uruguay. The Maestra shipping company operates in the container transportation sector and offers regular SSS services (Fonseca, 2015).

In 2018, the container movement in SSS in Brazil was 1,355,074 TEUs, a growth of 13% compared to 2017. Comparing 2010 to 2018, the growth in SSS was 146%, and 49% had its origin or destination in the São Paulo, the largest state in Brazil.

Petrobras, which owns Transpetro (a subsidiary of Petrobras' transportation area), operates in the transportation of oil and oil products, natural gas, ethanol and biofuels.

7 Cargo flows in short sea shipping in Brazil

A significant part of cargo flows in Brazil consists of mineral fuels and oils. The following values refer to 2016:

- Extracted in deep waters – 135.2 million tonnes or 66% of SSS operations.
- Transportation of bauxite – enables the aluminium production chain in the states of Maranhão and Pará.
- Transportation of forest products (wood and pulp) – moving more than 5.3 million tonnes. It supplies the paper industry.

- Coil transportation – 3.1 million tonnes. It supplies the metallurgical industry of the south of the country.
- Transportation of Manaus free zone products – transportation in containers of products of higher added value manufactured in the Manaus Free Trade Zone.
- Salt transport – movement of 868 thousand tonnes. It is used for consumption and as input for basic industry (chlorine, prepared foods, etc.).

Approximately 66% of everything transported by SSS refers to oil and its derivatives. There is fierce competition between the road mode and the maritime mode for the transportation of cargo in Brazil. Most of the cargo transported in Brazil is by road (approximately 61.1%).

The transport policy implemented today favours road transport to the detriment of maritime SSS. As a characteristic of this mode of transportation, one can cite the higher speed, depending on the route and distance covered, and higher offer and frequency. The remaining transport is carried out using the rail mode, which corresponds to approximately 20.7% of freight transport, the waterway mode with 13.6%, pipeline with 4.2% and air with 0.4% (Moura and Botter, 2017).

The maritime mode of SSS lost competitiveness in freight because of the development of the road, construction and maintenance of highways, the technological development of vehicles and fuel subsidies, given by the federal government in the 50s and 90s (Moura and Botter, 2019).

8 Measures for the development of multimodal transportation in Brazil

Multimodal transportation is a service performed by a multimodal transport operator (OTM). Law 9.611 of 19 February 1998 defines not only the operation of multimodal cargo transport but also the responsibilities of the agents involved; it presents the legal definitions for the OTM and the single transport contract, critical elements of the operation.

A single transport contract characterizes the multimodal transport operation, in which two or more modes of transport are used from the origin to the destination. This task is performed under the sole responsibility of an OTM. This operator is a company contracted to carry out the multimodal transport of the cargo from origin to destination, either by own means or through third parties (Moura and Botter, 2017). In addition to the transport itself, multimodal cargo transport includes the services of collection, consolidation, cargo handling and storage, deconsolidation and delivery, in short, all the essential steps to complete the task. It is essential that the services provided are frequent and reliable to operate in potential markets. It is also imperative to minimize intermodal costs and have a team vision, control operations, integrated systems, an intermodal structure (own or outsourced), intermodal terminals and integrated decision-making.

When it comes to shipping, an essential factor for the user market refers to aspects of multimodality or intermodality that Brazilian SSS needs to meet efficiently and effectively. If some deficiencies are inherent in the activity – slower speed, lack of versatility – they are barriers to entry for the sector that needs to integrate and coordinate with other modes (Castells *et al.*, 2012). Considering this, the following actions need to be taken to develop the sector (Bergqvist *et al.*, 2015):

- Plan in an integrated way between the various modes and as a door-to-door service;
- Regulate the process of cargo transhipment to reduce bureaucratic procedures and facilitate the emergence of feeder service for Brazil and Latin America;
- Invest in information technology to integrate modalities, facilitate the tracking and clearance of the cargo and allow the decision-making optimized by the cargo transporter;
- Invest in mechanisms to monitor the market, to allow the preparation of forecasts and the identification of potential for investments;
- Invest in the integration of communication systems between the Latin American ports aiming at the Latin American feeder service and a possible integrated market in the medium term;
- Intervene, as a regulatory agency, in the mechanism for releasing Merchant Marine Fund (FMM) resources and linked accounts, to protect the national fleet, guaranteeing the supply of vessels in the future and the technological advancement of the fleet for the transportation of containers;
- Carry out institutional campaigns on the advantages of SSS transport for the user and for transport operators interested in entering the sector;
- Invest in computerized systems to follow the SSS routes, companies involved and freights practiced, to identify the possible formation of cartels.

9 Measures for the development of short sea shipping in Brazil

The aspects to be eliminated, or the aspects deficient in the sector that are still threatened by the external environment, can be divided into two broad categories:

- Port restrictions;
- Legal charges on costs.

The low productivity of the national ports threatens the entire sector and can create an unfavourable situation for the SSS vessel in the port operation in private terminals. In the same sense, the costs of the shipping company are affected by aspects of legislation and regulation that create unfavourable competition when compared to the mode of transportation. There are, therefore, necessary actions for the development of the sector (Moura and Botter, 2017):

- Ensure, as a regulatory agency, that coastal shipping vessels are not impaired in port service, due to congestion or the least economic interest in their service (Douet and Cappuccilli, 2011);
- Act to reduce the number of port taxes applied in SSS, to reduce bureaucracy and rationalize the taxation of the sector;
- Ensure, as a regulatory agency, the isonomy in the value paid for fuels by the coastal vessels;

- Regulate the clearance of the SSS cargo to expedite the port operation;
- Accompany the supply and demand of the shipbuilding market: shipyards, orders under construction, orders in portfolios, age of the fleet, forecast of renewal, resources available in the Merchant Marine Fund, etc.
- Publicize the market situation and act to ensure the supply of yards for the renewal of the national fleet in the long term;
- Invest in information technology to monitor Brazilian port productivity.

It is also interesting to note the main proposed solutions, according to the National Transport Confederation, a major stakeholder in this sector. These are the following (CNT, 2018):

- Decrease bureaucracy and simplify processes and volumes of documents requested for transportation via SSS and obtaining funding;
- Increase the supply of port infrastructure, aiming to expand the terminals, berths and retro areas;
- Implement hub ports and feeder ports to promote long haul and SSS navigation;
- To increase the number of skilled labours in the market, both technical and official, which would require increasing the number of entities that form these professionals;
- Promote the development of the shipbuilding sector, through economic mechanisms, promote the renewal of the fleet, reduce bureaucratic access to credit lines and reduce the number of procedures for access to the FMM.

The FMM is an accounting fund from AFRMM (Additional Freight for Merchant Marine Renewal), which collects funding to provide resources for the development of merchant shipping and the maritime industry. The following banks operate it: BNDES, Banco do Brasil, Caixa Econômica Federal, Bando da Amazônia and Banco do Nordeste. The main advantages of FMM are that it lowers interest rates and grants exemption of some contributions. However, significant disadvantages of FMM still exist, such as the financing only occurring for vessels produced in the national shipyards and a long, bureaucratic and time-consuming process. The request for financing from FMM resources must be carried out by the companies concerned and takes 20 steps to complete; this can take an average of 25 months.

10 Measures for the development of the maritime transport sector in Brazil

The measures to boost the maritime transport sector in Brazil that should be adopted by the government are proposed as follows (Aperte and Baird, 2013):

a   Modernization of ports and improvement of port infrastructure for SSS cargos;

b   Reduction of bureaucracy around SSS cargos, including the possibility of providing exclusive terminals so that the SSS cargo does not compete with that of foreign vessels within the port terminals;
c   Reduction of the high percentage of taxes that affect the supply of ships on the Brazilian coast (PIS, COFINS, ICMS, CIDE, etc.). To enforce the legislation that establishes the isonomy in the price of fuel for national and international ships;
d   Promotion of the use multimodal transport, where more than one type of transport is used between origin and destination (characterized as a door-to-door service) under a single service contract. The use of multimodality has been seen as a viable alternative for reducing transport costs and, consequently, logistical costs;
e   Provision of efficient and effective intermodal terminals appropriate for transhipment operations of the products with a coordinated connection;
f   Development of a transport modernization programme (to have sources of financing to revitalize the transport sector), an infrastructure improvement plan (to ensure availability of roads, ports and terminals) and sector, adjusting legislation and improving inspection;
g   Definition of a simplified customs procedure for redesignation in feeder ships. Feeder services currently suffer from the existence of some procedures currently adopted by the Internal Revenue Service, such as the issuance of the DTA (Customs Transit Declaration), which imposes delays and adds costs to the service. The action consists of simplifying the customs procedures of the international transhipment cargos in a national port, for later distribution along the coast. This procedure could be replaced by the issuance of the CTAC (knowledge of waterway transportation of cargo) and MCC (SSS cargo manifesto), accompanied by a copy of the B/L – bill of lading – original for the international section. Also, technological advances now allow the B/L to be printed, signed and shipped in advance rather than necessarily at the port of origin, reducing the times involved in the process;
h   The standardization of the procedures adopted by the State Secretariats of the Farm (SEFAZ) in each port is an action that can bring higher speed in the liberation of maritime cargos, making SSS more competitive in Brazil;
i   Reformation of the current support system for the purchase of ships, which is composed of economic incentives granted by the Merchant Marine Fund, through the Additional Freight for Merchant Marine Renewal. These subsidies may only be used for the construction of ships on national shipyards. The main difficulty in enabling the acquisition of ships at competitive prices is that currently national shipyards lack enough productivity and scale of construction to allow the construction of ships at internationally competitive prices. One solution to alleviate the problem could be a plan to attract national and international investments aimed at the restructuring and recovery of the productive capacity of the shipbuilding sector in Brazil.

11 Conclusion

This chapter describes the main difficulties faced by SSS in Latin America and particularly in Brazil. It concludes that maritime integration between the Latin American countries must be thought of as a win-win relationship, since the market reserve that each imposes on the SSS sector does not add value or promote the development of this mode of transport in Latin America.

The chapter also concludes that bilateral agreements are incipient and restrictive and do not promote the region's growth. There is a need for better agreements between countries to develop an efficient and effective maritime transport system, with effective integration between the main ports in Latin America, with less bureaucracy and better customs and port agility. These barriers inhibit better trade between nations and do not promote maritime transport.

Investing more in SSS transport would be a smart and sustainable logistics solution, aimed at reducing operational costs and providing a better quality of service, integrating the other modalities (road, rail and waterway) and focusing on optimized and integrated operations (Liljestrand, 2016).

It is an enormous challenge for Brazil to increase the use of the waterway model in its transportation matrix and reduce roadway trips, which cross the country from north to south and from east to west, increasing the operational costs of logistics operations. Lack of infrastructure of national highways contributes to the precarious road network. It interferes, for instance, with the international competitiveness of Brazilian soybeans, when compared with American or Asian markets.

The transportation by SSS, with integration with the other modalities, is the most sensible and correct solution for Brazil to become logistically competitive. Also necessary are public and private investments in highways and access to the national ports, as well as investments in each country's own public and private ports. In addition, customs bureaucratization and port legislation to implement rapid terminals for short sea shipping should aim at reducing transportation time, documentation and processes.

References

Aperte, X.G., & Baird, A.J. (2013), Motorways of the sea policy in Europe. *Maritime Policy and Management*, 40 (1), pp. 10–26.

Bergqvist, R., Macharis, C., & Woxenius, J. (2015), Making hinterland transport more sustainable a multi criteria analysis. *Research in Transportation Business & Management*, 14, pp. 80–89.

Castells, M., Usabiaga, J.J., & Martínez, F. (2012), Road and maritime transport environmental performance: Short sea shipping vs road transport. *Journal of Maritime Research*, 9 (3), pp. 45–53.

CNT (2018), National Transport Confederation. CNT transport and logistics plan 2018. Available at https://cbic.org.br/infraestrutura/wp-content/uploads/sites/26/2018/08/Plano-CNT-Transporte-Pesquisa-Completa.pdf (accessed 2 March 2017).

Douet, M., & Cappuccilli, J.F. (2011), A review of short sea shipping policy in the European Union. *Journal of Transport Geography*, 19, pp. 968–976.

ECLAC – Economic Commission for Latin America and the Caribbean (2017), Report.
ECLAC – Economic Commission for Latin America and the Caribbean (2018), Port Activity in 2018.
Fonseca, R.O. (2015), The navigation of loading cabotage in Brazil. *Mercator, Fortaleza, Brazil*, 14 (1), January–April, pp. 21–46.
Kuznetsov, A.L., & Kirichenko, A.V. (2018), Methodological problems of modern transportation logistics. *The International Journal on Marine Navigation and Safety of Sea Transportation*, 12 (3), September, pp. 611–616.
Liljestrand, K. (2016), Improvement actions for reducing transport's impact on climate: A shipper's perspective. *Transportation Research Part D*, 48, pp. 393–407.
Moura, D.A., & Botter, R.C. (2017), Challenges for implementation of the green corridor in Brazil. In C. Guedes Soares and Ãngelo P. Teixeira (eds.) *International Maritime Association of the Mediterranean – IMAM – Maritime Transportation and Harvesting of Sea Resources*, vol. 1. Lisbon, Portugal: CRC Press, pp. 151–156.
Moura, D.A., & Botter, R.C. (2019), The potential for the growth of maritime transport in Brazil: Focus on cabotage/short sea shipping. In *XXVI Congreso Panamericano de Ingeniería Naval, Transporte Marítimo e Ingeniería Portuaria*, vol. 1. Cartagena, Colombia: COPINAVAL, pp. 15–28.
Seabra, F., Flores, G.P., & Balistieri, T. (2017), Perspectives of short sea shipping in Mercosur Countries. *Revista Espacios*, 38 (44).

Part IV
Information and communications technology in support of short sea shipping

13 Short sea shipping in the age of information and communications technology

Tiago A. Santos and C. Guedes Soares

1 Introduction

Literature on short sea shipping (SSS) lists an extensive number of areas in which information and communications technology (ICT) might assist in the promotion of SSS and, in general, multimodality. Such technologies benefit not only SSS but also deep sea shipping and have the potential to cover more aspects than merely the commercial promotion of specific market segments or modes of transportation. A useful systematization of ICT applications is provided by the European Parliament and Commission (2013a, 2013b), through Regulations 1315/2013 and 1316/2013, which established the trans-European transport network. This network comprises transport infrastructures but also information and communications technology, the so-called telematic applications. These regulations indicate that these applications are necessary for optimizing traffic, transport operations and traffic safety and improving related services. Such applications are defined as 'systems using information, communication, navigation or positioning/localisation technologies in order to manage infrastructure, mobility and traffic . . . for safe, secure, environmentally sound and capacity-efficient use of the network', emphasizing safety, security and sustainability. These telematic systems include the intelligent transport system (ITS), the Single European Sky ATM Research (SESAR), the Vessel Traffic Monitoring and Information Systems (VTMIS), the River Information Services (RIS), the e-Maritime Services (maritime single windows) and European Rail Traffic Management System (ERTMS). This chapter will consider how developments in VTMIS and e-Maritime Services may assist in the development of SSS and will cover developments in electronic data sharing platforms, which are more focused on the commercial promotion of, optimization of and assistance to freight transportation, including intermodal transport using SSS, when possible.

The potential areas of SSS improvement using information and communications technology, leading to increased utilization of SSS, have been listed in, for example, CENIT *et al.* (2015) and the Portuguese Port Association (2007):

1 Integration of the logistics chain stakeholders (shipowners, carriers, forwarders) in a one-stop shop (IT systems), allowing the monitoring of cargo flows and transparency.

2　Avoidance of discrimination of SSS in relation to deep sea shipping.
3　Year-round navigability (no restrictions due to ice, bad weather, drought).
4　Availability of water depth with no tidal restrictions.
5　Simplification of rules governing the operation of ports.
6　Reduced bureaucracy and complex documentation, namely in customs.
7　Improvement of the overall reliability of the terminal.
8　Establishment and monitoring of a set of service performance indicators.

These aspects, which require further improvement if SSS is to provide a more attractive solution for freight transportation, may in fact be addressed by ICT at different levels. Figure 13.1 shows the scope of the three main types of electronic facilities along the full span of the logistics chain.

Firstly, it is necessary to recognize that certain aspects (listed previously) requiring improvement in SSS relate mainly to safety, although also to the performance of transportation. These aspects include year-round navigability, availability of water depth and, to some degree, avoiding discrimination of SSS ships and reliability of the port terminal. Existing vessel traffic systems (VTMIS) address most of these aspects. It is also important to remember that SSS takes place mainly in European waters, often in congested maritime areas or crossing busy sea routes, where VTMIS is of the utmost importance. Furthermore, as will be discussed, some projects in the EU, Korea and Singapore are aiming at increasing the role of ICT in vessel traffic monitoring, taking it to the next level: sea traffic management. Management of sea traffic, rather than mere monitoring of traffic, although focused primarily on safety could also assist in avoiding conflicts between arriving SSS ships and larger deep sea ships and in re-arranging schedules, taking into account actual arrival times rather than estimated arrival times.

Secondly, such aspects as the simplification of rules governing port operations and reducing bureaucracy and complex documentation (mainly customs) are addressed through the national maritime single window (MSW) systems, port community systems and customs information systems. MSW systems have been deployed in many European ports in recent years and, in many cases, are already integrated with port service providers (part of port community) and customs.

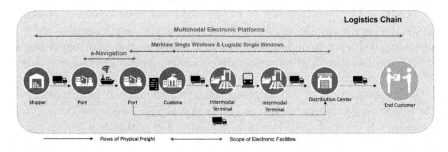

Figure 13.1 Scope of electronic facilities involved in the logistics chain.
Source: Adapted from Fergadioti (2016).

These electronic facilities cover generally one port and allow a set of formalities to be carried out and services to be requested at port level. In fewer cases, these facilities are also being developed to cover the stakeholders involved in at least part of the transport chain across the port's hinterland. MSW systems play a proportionally more important role for SSS ships, as these call in ports more often than deep sea ships do and are thus critical to the competitiveness of SSS. Furthermore, the performance of transport modes across the hinterland is, for SSS, proportionally more important than for deep sea shipping, as this land component of the transport chain represents a larger proportion of the overall transit time and cost.

Thirdly, some electronic data sharing platforms aim at integrating all stakeholders in the logistics chain, with the main purpose of optimizing the general performance of logistics chains from a commercial point of view, using considerations related to cost and transit time. These platforms may also have a role in monitoring cargo flows, that is providing tracking and tracing of cargos, therefore increasing the visibility along the logistics chain, which has also been one of the traditional major complaints of shippers when using intermodal transport solutions and SSS. Such platforms are also in good position to provide service performance indicators (KPIs) along the logistics chain, which is another concern of shippers regarding intermodal performance. Most importantly, data sharing in common platforms offers an enormous potential for identifying opportunities for cargo bundling, permitting liner services of shipping companies affiliated to these platforms to be operated with consistently high utilization rates, which are necessary to ensure that regular services are economically feasible, a factor that has proven in the past to be critical in maintaining these services.

In addition to the systems just described, all of which involve some form of collaboration between different stakeholders in the logistics chain, it should be recognized that digitalization will have impact also at the level of individual companies, organizations and agencies involved in transportation. At this stage, more or less every stakeholder – customs, port authorities, terminal operators, logistics companies, shipping companies – has its own electronic platforms for data collection, storage and treatment. In the specific case of shipping companies, many are now receiving from ships in their fleets huge volumes of data on a variety of aspects, including emissions of CO_2, NO_x and SO_x, average speed between ports versus cruise speed, total time at port per round trip, time per individual port and fuel consumption (per TEU.km). This data is then analyzed with more or less detail for various purposes, mainly computing KPIs and monitoring the efficiency of operations. Terminal operators also operate significant electronic facilities for monitoring and managing the operations in the quay, yard and gates. In any case, such individual electronic systems are left out of the scope of this chapter, as their contribution to the improvement of shipping efficiency is deemed less important than the three types of collaborative systems indicated earlier.

Several concerns surround the development of these collaborative electronic systems, namely the interoperability and standardization of data exchange and the preservation of data property and confidentiality. This is especially relevant when the information has a commercial nature, as its dissemination to competitors could entail significant economic consequences. In this respect, transport data sharing is the most difficult to achieve in practice.

The remainder of this chapter is organized to cover the developments in digitalization that may assist short sea shipping. Section 2 addresses developments in e-navigation, focusing primarily on vessel traffic systems and sea traffic management which may facilitate appropriate and accurate timing of arrival of ships engaged in SSS in order to prevent operational conflicts with larger deep sea ships and delays related to weather conditions, heavy traffic and tidal restrictions. Section 3 addresses developments in ICT systems, namely maritime single windows that facilitate the handling of the significant bureaucracies involved in SSS, which are frequently mentioned by shippers and shipping companies as a major drawback of SSS. Section 4 reviews the role of multimodal transport electronic platforms in stimulating, organizing and monitoring the demand for SSS, increasing also the overall transparency of multimodal transport. Section 5 draws general conclusions from this literature review.

2 Electronic navigation (e-navigation)

2.1 European vessel traffic management and information service

Vessel traffic monitoring and information services (VTMIS, henceforth designated as VTS), are an important component of so-called electronic navigation (e-navigation). This concept has been defined in IMO (2018) as 'the harmonized collection, integration, exchange, presentation and analysis of marine information on board and ashore by electronic means to enhance berth to berth navigation and related services for safety and security at sea and protection of the marine environment' (p. 1). This definition implies that both ships and centres located ashore will be involved in the described activities. Typically, in the EU, VTS take up such functions, which while applicable to all ships in EU waters, will certainly be especially relevant for ships engaged in SSS due to the nature and regional scope of their activities.

In what concerns VTS in EU waters, it is important to have in mind the definition in Directive 2002/59/EC: 'a service designed to improve the safety and efficiency of vessel traffic and to protect the environment, which has the capability to interact with the traffic and to respond to traffic situations developing in the VTS area' (p. 14). At the origin of the vessel traffic systems was the necessity of coastal states to be informed on the movements of ships carrying dangerous or polluting materials and on the precise nature of their cargo. This information is obviously critical for maintaining safety of navigation and, most important, preventing marine pollution. In line with these objectives, Council Directive 93/75/EEC (European Council 1993) set up minimum requirements for vessels bound for or leaving Community ports and carrying dangerous or polluting goods and introduced a system for competent authorities to receive information regarding ships bound for or leaving a Community port and carrying dangerous or polluting goods. The system should also include information on incidents at sea.

Directive 2002/59/EC (European Parliament and Council 2002a) carried the process one step further by demanding that member states establish a vessel traffic monitoring and information system with a view to enhancing the safety and the efficiency of maritime traffic. Such a system is also critical for improving authorities' responses to incidents, accidents or potentially dangerous situations at sea. Finally, it should assist in search and rescue operations and in the prevention and detection of pollution by ships. A system such as this builds upon the mandatory use of key technological progress in the area of on-board equipment. This includes the automatic identification of ships (AIS systems) and the voyage data recorder (VDR) systems. The first allows the tracking of ships while the second facilitates investigations following accidents.

The same directive also required member states to install appropriate equipment and shore-based installations for receiving and utilizing the AIS information, a process to be completed by the end of 2007, including the provision of duly qualified personnel. The system should also be able to exchange electronic information with national systems of other member states on ships carrying dangerous or polluting goods and leaving ports of the EU, this forming the basis of the SafeSeaNet (Community maritime information and exchange system). Finally, these systems should comply with IMO (1997a) guidelines for vessel traffic services and closely monitor ship compliance with any ship-routing systems in place in specific locations, as defined in IMO (1997b) and according to the guidelines in IMO (2003).

More recently, Directive 2009/17/EC introduced amendments to Directive 2002/59/EC (see European Parliament and Council, 2002, 2009b) to facilitate the implementation and operation of SafeSeaNet in a uniform way across Europe. It also established a European long range identification and tracking (LRIT) data centre and extended the directive to fishing vessels over 15 m long, as smaller vessels have been involved in a significant number of maritime accidents over the years.

2.2 Sea traffic management

Within the European Union, efforts have been underway to carry the process of monitoring maritime traffic one step further. In fact, operations in the maritime industry have been generally characterized by low interaction between an extensive number of actors. This is different from the practice in many other industries, where close partnerships have stimulated systems integration and standardization of information exchange. Several research projects in the EU have allowed progress in this field, including the development of the sea traffic management (STM) platform, shown in Figure 13.2. In addition, in Korea the SMART Navigation[1] project is underway and Singapore is providing a test bed for the SESAME Solution II.[2]

A move in this direction has been mainly fostered by the Swedish Maritime Administration, by setting up STM, a methodology developed within the framework of the MonaLisa and MonaLisa 2.0 projects, supported by the European Commission. These projects supported the definition of a set of systems and procedures to guide and monitor sea traffic in a manner close to air traffic management.

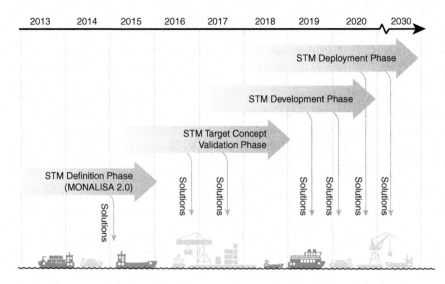

Figure 13.2 Sea traffic management implementation and deployment strategy.
Source: Adapted from STM (2019).

A maritime digital infrastructure is currently being developed, as leading system suppliers of on-board navigation systems (ECDIS), vessel traffic service systems, maritime service providers and authorities have agreed to adapt to the standard formats used in STM.

Currently, further research projects are continuing the development and validation of the concept (EfficientFlow, Real Time Ferries, STM Validation, among others). The goal is to fully deploy STM by 2030, as shown in Figure 13.2, and achieve a 50% reduction of accidents, 10% reduction in voyage costs, 30% reduction in waiting time for berthing, 7% lower fuel consumption and 7% lower greenhouse gas emissions (all in comparison with 2015). The validation of the system has been carried out for test cases primarily in the Baltic Sea, North Sea and western Mediterranean Sea, implying that the goals just mentioned will be felt mainly in SSS.

At this stage, STM provides the following services for ships and shore centres:

- Nordic Pilot Route Service;
- Baltic Navigational Warning Service;
- SSPA Route Optimization Service;
- SMHI route ETA forecasts;
- Winter navigation service;
- Ship-to-ship route exchange;
- STM search and rescue; and
- Enhanced monitoring service.

The Nordic Pilot Route Service is an onshore service that, for a submitted route, returns pilot routes based on the waypoint coordinates in the route. It assists in voyage planning when the captain is not familiar with the ports and can thus plan the voyage from pilot station to pilot station.

The Baltic Navigational Warning Service will display in the ECDIS system only the navigational warnings relevant to a specific route, considering both the current position of the ship currently and the anticipated times at which it will pass certain waypoints. Warnings will be deleted when they expire.

The SSPA Route Optimization Service, using a shore-based centre, provides an optimized version of a route manually planned consisting of a number of waypoints, the waypoint spatial distribution and waypoint estimated time of departure. Optimization considers as objective the bunker consumption (linked to total ship resistance) as affected by water depth, wind, current, waves and ice. Weather conditions are accounted for a period of 5 days ahead and 7 days prior to the current date.

SMHI route ETA forecasts are a service for providing multiple route optimizations during long voyages in order to provide a realistic estimated time of arrival (ETA) at port, considering the weather conditions, sea currents and ship characteristics. A probable time of arrival to each waypoint on the route as well as a calculated time window for the ETA are systematically provided to the ship. This allows adjusting engine settings for fuel efficiency, leading to cost savings and environmental benefits, and unlocks the possibility of ports handling more efficiently inbound ships.

The winter navigation service provides assistance to ships related to icebreaking capability in the northern Baltic. Routes and other operative information may be directly shared by ships, icebreakers and shore centres using machine-to-machine interfaces, enabling improved route planning and assistance during the voyage.

Ship-to-ship route exchange is a service consisting of the exchange between ships which are in the vicinity of their intended routes (a limited number of waypoints), creating an enhanced situational awareness among all ships (for example, to avoid ending up in a close-quarter situation). Such information is an aid to navigation and does not allow existing watch-keeping practices and compliance with the COLREGs to be observed.

STM search and rescue (SAR) service aims at enhancing the performance of search and rescue operations, particularly in coordinating the efforts of Maritime Rescue and Coordination Centres (MRCC) and the on-scene coordinators (OSC). MRCCs may then send distress positions, search areas and search routes or patterns to a SAR unit, a passing vessel or an airplane, with such information directly displayed on on-board navigation systems.

The enhanced monitoring service is provided through shore centres, covering much larger areas than a VTS. This service is characterized by a higher level of automation and receives advance information from ships on their route and schedule. This information allows shore centres to review the ships' intentions and act accordingly and proactively. This service has the potential to predict dense traffic situations in time and space, while also transmitting information regarding temporarily restricted areas (areas with military exercises or SAR operations).

In addition to these services already implemented in STM, system development has proceeded in the direction of integrating port operations with STM, as reported in Michaelides *et al.* (2019). This integration is designated as port collaborative decision-making (PortCDM) and relies on improved data sharing to increase situational awareness. Data sharing may be done on a port-to-port or ship-to-port basis. Such collaboration should be able to enable more efficient processes and enhanced decision-making during port calls, thus increasing the efficiency of port calls for all stakeholders.

The PortCDM electronic facility has been validated in four ports in the Mediterranean (Limassol, Sagunto, Valencia and Barcelona) and five ports in northern Europe (Gothenburg, Brofjorden, Vaasa, Umeå and Stavanger). Tests included the transmission to ports of better estimates of times of arrival and departure (ETA and ETD). The transmitted information allowed the evaluation of the predictability of ship arrival at each of four critical states (arrival traffic area, departure traffic area, arrival berth and departure berth), with and without PortCDM. Results confirmed its great potential for improving operational planning for all stakeholders (shipping companies, terminals, port authority, shipping agents, pilots, tugs, etc.), as this depends critically on reliable estimates of ship arrival time.

It has been claimed that more accurate estimates of ETA, combined with port data on berth availability, could enable slow steaming and the so-called virtual arrival of the ship, thus promoting the sustainability of shipping, as demonstrated in Jia *et al.* (2017) and Andersson and Ivehammar (2017). However, more recently, authors such as Poulsen and Sampson (2019) found that commercial policies of charterers and shipping companies often prevented the use of slow steaming, even though there are now charter contracts which include a virtual arrival clause that could enable such practices.

A further development of PortCDM might be, according to traffic situation in port approaches and the occupation of terminal berths, to send a recommended time of arrival (RTA) to a ship that has previously shared its planned time of arrival with the port. However, it is not clear whether ports are willing to send, in the short term, such an RTA because of the competitive nature of ports (first come, first served principle) and the uncertainty surrounding such RTA (congestion at berth, uncertainties in planning).

Some major port authorities (e.g. Rotterdam)[3] are also developing research on several aspects related to this field, namely ETA prediction, nautical traffic management, smart ships, intelligent barge port stays, blockchain applications in shipping and synchromodality. All these areas have in common the fact that electronic data exchange is required between collaborating electronic systems, enabling through data analysis the derivation of benefits in terms of optimization of transport parameters, improved assets capacity utilization, greater reliability and increased transparency.

Many of these developments are especially important for SSS, given that ships in this segment typically make a larger number of port calls per year than do deep sea ships, often with tight schedules. In this respect, collaboration and exchange of information with ports and terminals is especially interesting, as shipping companies engaged in this market segment often complain about discrimination against their comparatively smaller ships by terminal operators and port authorities. Collaborative decision-making could certainly avoid significant conflicts with larger deep sea ships for use of harbour approaches and channels, as well as berths in terminals.

3 Maritime single windows

3.1 National and European single windows

UNECE (2005) provides a simple and general definition of single window: a 'facility that allows parties involved in trade and transport to lodge standardized information and documents with a single entry point to fulfil all import, export and transit related regulatory requirements' (p. 3). In the EU, national maritime single windows are defined in European Parliament and Council (2019) as a

> nationally established and operated technical platform for receiving, exchanging and forwarding electronically information to fulfil reporting obligations, which includes commonly defined management of access rights, a harmonised reporting interface module and a graphical user interface for communication with declarants, as well as links with the relevant authorities' systems and databases at national and at Union level, which enables messages or acknowledgements covering the widest range of decisions taken by all of the participating relevant authorities to be communicated to declarants, and which could also allow, where applicable, for the connection with other reporting means.
>
> (p. 69)

A complete review of the development of maritime single windows may be found in Wawruch (2015).

The concept of maritime single windows first came up within the scope of the development of electronic facilities for handling the standardized facilitation forms for ships to fulfil certain reporting formalities when they arrive in or depart from a port. In this respect, information technologies certainly have also facilitated SSS in what concerns the reporting formalities when accessing EU ports. The reporting formalities consist mainly of a set of forms required as per the Convention on Facilitation of International Maritime Traffic, known as FAL forms, which include the following: general information, cargo, ship's stores, crew's effects, crew list, passenger list and dangerous goods. These forms were set up initially under the International Maritime Organisation's Convention on Facilitation of International Maritime Traffic, IMO (1965a). Directive 2002/6/EC (see European Parliament and Council, 2002) required member states of the EU to use and recognize a common standard version of the FAL forms, with the objective to facilitate maritime transport and to further strengthen the position of shipping in the transport system as an alternative and complement to other transport modes in a door-to-door logistics chain. Also mentioned is the possibility of member states accepting the provision of ship's reporting information (FAL forms) in electronic form, provided that data conformed to international standards.

In 2010, Directive 2010/65/EU was published (it is known as the Reporting Formalities Directive, RFD). This directive, as may be seen in European Parliament and Council (2010), recognized that several other European and international regulations required the transmission of diverse information (see European Parliament and Council, 2000, 2002b, 2004, 2009b; IMO, 1965a, 1965b). This additional information includes data on ship-generated waste and residues (see European Parliament and Council, 2000), data for traffic monitoring and information, security data (see European Parliament and Council, 2004), port state control data (see European Parliament and Council, 2009a) and dangerous goods data. Considering this increase in data reporting formalities, Directive 2010/65/EU aimed at simplifying and harmonizing, as far as possible, the administrative procedures applicable to maritime transport. In this respect, it required the electronic transmission of information to became standard and more rational, namely by member states accepting the fulfilment of reporting formalities in electronic format. This required the transmission of information via a single window (national single window) as soon as possible and in any case no later than 1 June 2015. This single window should link SafeSeaNet, e-Customs and other electronic systems, with all information reported once and made available to the various competent authorities and member states.

As regards SSS and for those ships operating between ports situated in the customs territory of the Union, Directive 2010/65/EU grants an exemption from the obligation to send the information referred to in the FAL forms. This applies when the ships do not come from, call at or head towards a port situated outside that territory or a free zone subject to type I controls and already constitutes a simplification of procedures.

In 2016, the Commission launched an evaluation of the RFD together with the VTMIS directive. The outcome of the support study (see PWC and Panteia, 2017), leads to the conclusion that the objectives of the reporting formalities directive were only partially attained. The main points of concern, summarized by the Commission, are the following:

- Paper reporting is still used in more than 50% of ports, often as duplication;
- Only a few EU countries allow fully digitalised and harmonized reporting;
- Only a few EU countries have in place single windows allowing submit only-once reporting available;
- The information is seldom shared and re-used, notably between EU countries;
- Not enough progress has been made on the EU level harmonization of national single windows.

These conclusions led to the latest regulatory development of maritime single windows, as contained in Regulation 2019/1239 (see European Parliament and Council, 2019). This regulation responds to demands of shipping companies for more interoperability and more comprehensive, user-friendly communication and information flows, in order also to improve the functioning of the internal market. Therefore, this regulation lays down harmonized rules for the information that is required for port calls, namely by ensuring that the same data sets are reported to each maritime national single window. It also aims at facilitating the transmission of information between declarants, relevant authorities, providers of port services (as defined in European Parliament and Council (2017)) and other member states. An important innovation is the introduction of a European maritime single window environment (EMSWe), which should be technologically neutral and interoperable and based on the national single windows. Also, the front-end interfaces of those maritime national single windows on the side of the declarants should be harmonized at Union level, obviously reducing administrative burdens.

Regulation 2019/1239 also takes in account that ports are actually not the final destination of goods and that the efficiency of the ship port calls has impact on logistics chains. This aspect is particularly important for SSS, as it is frequently in direct competition with other modes of transportation and needs an efficient integration between modes. Thus, the regulation specifies that national single windows should allow for the possibility of exchanging relevant information, such as arrival and departure times, with similar frameworks developed for other transport modes, enhancing the interoperability, multimodality and integration of maritime transport within the overall logistics chain.

Overall, these developments are directly in line with the policy recommendations outlined in ECSA (2016) for streamlining and rationalizing reporting requirements applicable to Union goods and to ships engaged in SSS. ECSA actually proposes a review of reporting requirements to alleviate the administrative burden and enhance the competitiveness of SSS in comparison with trucking. According to ECSA (2016), goods carried in trucks (within containers) between, for example, Rotterdam and Sweden, only have to possess a CMR letter (document implying the existence of a Contract for the International Carriage of Goods by Road, as per the CMR convention), whereas when carrying the container using SSS, at least 12 different reporting formalities have to be fulfilled (split between road haulage companies, ports, terminals and shipping companies). Port and logistic single windows, described in the next section, hopefully will contribute to alleviating this bureaucratic burden.

3.2 Port single window and logistic single window

One example of national single window is the Portuguese JUP (port single window). It is an electronic platform implementing a single contact point within the port, which puts all the stakeholders in connection. Stakeholders exchange information about ships and cargos using common standards like EDI and XML, thus increasing the collective efficiency of the port community.

The system is generally fed by shipping agents and allows different port call formalities at arrival and departure and requests for services to be made using only the electronic contact point. Upon ship arrival, documents – such as arrival notice, ISPS declaration, residue declaration, list of stores, list of crew, list of passengers, health declaration, entry manoeuvre request, IMO entry declaration, request for VAT exemption and bill of lading (cargos to be unloaded) – may be uploaded. Regarding ship services, at least the following may be requested: pilotage, tuggage, mooring, on-board entry, equipment rental, on-board works, divers, request for control, change of shipping agency and supplies/bunkering. Upon departure, documents such as exit notice, list of crew, list of passengers, IMO exit declaration, departure manoeuvre and bill of lading (cargos loaded) may be uploaded. All relevant entities and service providers may have access permissions to the system and can then grant the necessary authorizations or apply for providing the requested services.

Recently, development has started to extend the concept of the port single window (JUP) to the entire logistics chain, as shown in Figure 13.3, by involving the road haulage companies, rail companies, logistics operators and dry port operators. This upgraded system is called logistic single window (JUL). The objectives are now to achieve an integrated management of transportation modes, the simplification and uniformization of information on entry and exit of cargos from ports, the reduction in port time through paperless and simplified processes, the elimination of administrative errors and an increase in data reliability, the provision of tracking of containers, the increase in control of cargos in connection with customs and immigration services and an improved management of human and material resources.

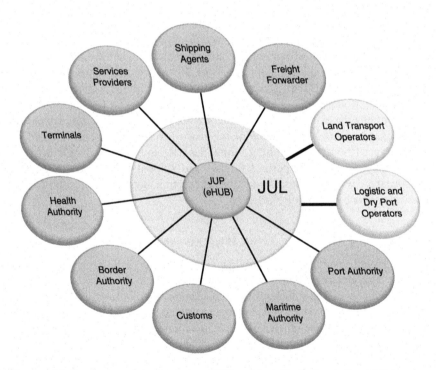

Figure 13.3 Scope of port single window (JUP) and logistic single window (JUL).
Source: Adapted from www.projeto-jul.pt/.

4 Multimodal transport electronic platforms

4.1 Data sharing platforms

The White Paper 'Roadmap to a Single European Transport Area' (European Community, 2011) identified significant remaining barriers to the completion of the transport internal market. It recognizes that more efficient electronic information exchange is key to optimizing freight transport efficiency. This could simplify administrative procedures, allowing cargo tracking and tracing and optimizing schedules and traffic flows. On the other hand, the same document also states that larger volumes of freight should be carried jointly to their destination by the most efficient (combination of) modes, thus recognizing the importance of multimodality.

Following the findings of the White Paper, one of the actions undertaken by the European Commission was setting up a Digital Transport and Logistics Forum (DTLF), which is a collaborative platform of member states, public entities and organizations to exchange knowledge, coordinate policy and provide technical recommendations for the European Commission, in the fields of transport (all modes) and logistics digitalization. In the first mandate of DTLF (2015–2018), recommendations and preparatory work for a regulation on electronic freight transport information (EFTI) was undertaken and the concept of digital corridor information systems ('federative platform') was developed. This aims at facilitating data sharing between all types of supply chain stakeholders through connecting existing IT platforms.

In what concerns the development of multimodality in the EU, it must be recognized that transportation remains largely focused on road haulage, with SSS, inland waterways and rail not obtaining volume increases and in some cases actually declining. This contributes to road congestion, air pollution and degradation of road infrastructure, among other undesirable external effects. The pressure on road transportation is such that a shortage of truck drivers has emerged in the EU. In parallel, rail infrastructure is underutilized and novel SSS services could be readily deployed to assist in alleviating the road infrastructure across many important transport corridors. However, increasing the attractiveness of these modes of transportation may only be obtained if significant cost reductions are offered, which may compensate for the inherent disadvantages of these modes, mainly the increased transportation time and the dependence on other modes of transportation for last-mile delivery. Cost reductions may be obtained by ensuring high utilization levels of trains, barges and ships, which are only possible, in many cases, through the bundling of cargo of different shippers.

However, the prevailing situation in logistics is currently one in which each actor is optimizing individually its own logistics, resulting only in limited volumes, insights and gains. Based on these limited insights, shippers thus limit themselves to taking ad hoc measures with impact only in each individual company. More significant gains are possible, however, through collaboration between companies, starting with shippers. This is increasingly being made through data sharing platforms, in which data ownership is retained by the origin organization and is anonymized and aggregated for developing collaborative transport solutions.

Figure 13.4 shows the types of services provided by such platforms to shippers. If only one mode of transportation is to be used, the platform allows optimized vehicle filling and optimized round trips to be generated, with cargos of multiple shippers being mixed within a single truck, provided that such cargos are bound for the same geographical area (same transport lane). In certain transport lanes, the aggregation of cargos of different shippers may present opportunities to minimize imbalances in cargo flows.

When intermodal transport solutions are possible, Figure 13.4 shows that cargo bundling may be used to ensure appropriate utilization levels of barges, trains or ships and, in some cases, even the increase of frequency of services offered by transport operators. The aggregation of data also allows going one step further, namely by identifying transport lanes (corridors) lacking offers of high-capacity transport solutions, thus enabling collaboration with transport operators in setting up new transport solutions across parts of or entire transport lanes.

One example of such data sharing platforms applied to multimodal transportation is CargoStream.[4] This is an independent pan-European platform aiming at aggregating shippers to create economies of scale in multimodal transportation. This platform promotes modal shift through the use of bundling of cargos of different shippers, thus assisting in realizing the EU Commission goals of shifting 30% of road freight over 300 km to other modes such as rail or waterborne transport by 2030, and more than 50% by 2050 (see European Commission, 2011). The developers of this multimodal platform claim that a 10% reduction in transportation costs, 20% reduction in CO_2 emissions and 10% increase in reliability may be achieved by using the platform.

CargoStream is an interconnected, neutral and open network on which shippers, intermodal terminals, rail and barge operators, logistics service providers, trustees and optimizers collaborate by synchronizing supply chain requirements with an appropriate mix of transport modes. The platform operates on the basis of the shipper's communications regarding their regular transportation needs. These are anonymized, and the needs of several shippers are aggregated along specific

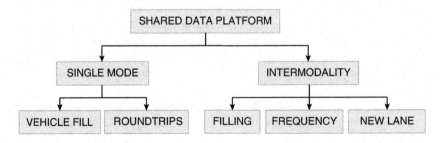

Figure 13.4 Services provided by transport data sharing platform.
Source: Adapted from www.clusters20.eu.

lanes. The data is made available to trustees and optimizers, who analyze, optimize and contact logistics service providers, thus generating suitable collaborative transport proposals. The platform also offers additional features to shippers, such as the analysis of their own transport lanes, existing intermodal lanes and the availability of free slots, potential collaboration to increase the frequency of intermodal lanes, or even the creation of new lanes.

An ongoing research project, Clusters 2.0,[5] is currently undertaking the deployment of CargoStream in well-established logistics clusters (PLAZA, Duisport, Interporto, etc.) to ensure improved coordination between the local actors in the cluster and improved connectivity and coordination between different logistics clusters. Also, the data sharing platform could minimize negative impacts such as congestion, noise, land use and local pollution. In the future, hopefully, CargoStream would become a pan-European community for freight sharing and collaboration.

Another data sharing platform has been developed within the SELIS[6] (Shared European Logistics Intelligence Space) project (see SELIS, 2018). This project also aims at developing an innovative collaboration-driven supply chain optimization tool (data sharing platform), supported by services that take into account network status, service level agreements (SLAs), cost, speed, time, utilization level and environmental KPIs. This project puts some emphasis on the need for a secure and trusted platform to share data and information, as this has been a common drawback of such data sharing platforms.

This platform offers to users KPIs on green logistics (freight consolidation, CO_2 reduction, route optimization), quality of service, reliability, resilience, agility, costs and assets utilization. Based upon the information provided by users of the platform, SELIS is also fitted with big data analytics capacities, including the analysis of the whole logistics community using knowledge graphs (KG), which capture the semantics of all entities and relationships associated with community. For a complete overview of big data analytics and its applications for logistics and supply chain management, see Govindan *et al.* (2018).

Finally, two aspects are worth noting concerning these data sharing platforms. Most of them are mainly focused on transport and logistics chains at regional levels within the EU, rather than global chains, and primarily on land modes of transportation, although inland waterways are also readily included in the platforms. Short sea shipping is often omitted, although it could be easily accommodated for those corridors where it is a real option.

4.2 Synchromodality

Data sharing platforms provide an excellent opportunity for bringing into reality the concept of synchromodality. This concept has been around for some time, but it is highly dependent upon the availability of information in real time on infrastructure conditions and the progress made along the logistics chain by individual cargos. Synchromodality consists of making optimal use of all modes of transportation and their available capacity, at all times, offering as an integrated transport solution. The goals would be to decrease transit time, decrease transportation costs and increase the efficiency and reliability of transportation. Planning of transportation would be done within the framework of a data sharing platform to optimize transportation not only at the beginning of the route but also, dynamically, along the route and in accordance with updates on actual progress being made by cargo. This would be possible by using:

- Dynamic planning and routing, with decision-making based on cost, transit time and network utilization;
- Switching modes of transport in real time; and
- Collaboration between shippers to combine transport flows.

A fundamental prerequisite for synchromodality to work is the availability and visibility of detailed information in real time regarding cargo flows through the transport system. To allow a real-time choice of transportation modes, it is essential for transport to be contracted with flexibility as to the mode of transportation (mode-free booking).

Giusti *et al.* (2019) provide a comprehensive review of synchromodal logistics and its open research questions, while, for example, Lucassen and Dogger (2012) present a case study on the utilization of synchromodality to convey cargo from Rotterdam to Tilburg, in the Netherlands, using several transport options as indicated in Figure 13.5. It is interesting to note that these authors conclude that this

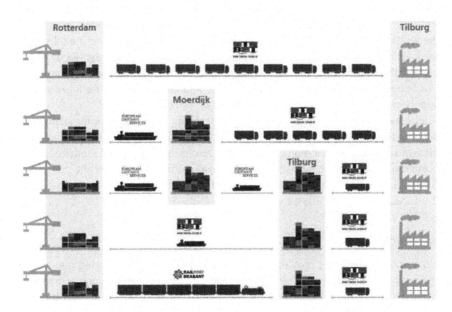

Figure 13.5 Synchromodal options between Rotterdam and Tilburg.
Source: Adapted from Lucassen and Dogger (2012).

concept is more appealing to transport operators than to shippers, as operators are able to cooperate between themselves, decreasing their needs for investment and increasing the utilization of their infrastructure and transport assets. However, from a shipper's perspective, it would certainly be necessary to provide access to an electronic platform supporting these transport solutions, as the shipper would be especially keen on monitoring closely the progress of its cargos along the network, if indeed he or she was to allow such mode-free booking to be used.

5 Conclusions

This chapter has addressed developments in three key areas where information and communications technology may assist the EU goals of promoting multimodality and short sea shipping and achieving a truly common transport internal market, namely e-navigation, maritime single windows and multimodal transport electronic platforms. The descriptions and analysis provided earlier allow some important conclusions to be drawn.

First, European authorities have strived for a steady and significant improvement in the EU of vessel traffic systems, within the broader context of e-navigation, and research and technological work is currently underway to develop a fully functional sea traffic management system. This system has the potential to increase the safety of maritime transportation, in general, and of SSS in particular. Furthermore, it will allow the cooperation between ports and between ships and ports in sharing routes and estimates of particulars of the ship's voyage (updated estimates of arrival time), thus allowing a much improved coordination of port activities, the avoidance of conflicts between deep and short sea ships, the avoidance of ice-, tide- and weather-motivated restrictions and a greater efficiency in the utilization of port and terminal resources. In addition, significant fuel savings could be obtained, contributing to the greening of the complete transport chain.

Significant achievements have also been obtained regarding maritime single windows, which are now in place in most European countries, greatly alleviating bureaucracy entailed by complex documentation (most notably customs) and with multiple requests of various port services. This is particularly important for ships engaged in SSS, as these ships make a proportionally larger number of calls in port per year than do deep sea ships. Initiatives are currently underway to extend the scope of these maritime single windows to the port hinterland, bringing into this common framework the stakeholders involved in logistics chains (transport operators, intermodal terminal operators), thus allowing an enlargement of services to cargo provided by these electronic platforms.

The European Commission is also very active in promoting a single transport internal market, supported by multimodal freight solutions, in which SSS plays a significant role, especially along geographical areas where Motorways of the Sea are located. Electronic transport data sharing platforms are currently emerging, mostly developed by private companies, which have the potential to promote the cooperation between shippers in the bundling of cargos, in the reduction of cargo imbalances or in the identification of corridors where further transport services are necessary. All of these developments could greatly assist SSS, because liner services typically need a consistently high degree of utilization to be profitable and ships have high cargo capacities which are sometimes difficult to fill. A high degree of utilization is also a requisite for SSS to be truly a green transport solution. Failure in this aspect has frequently led, in the past, to the closure of short sea services. In the near future, it is also possible that true synchromodality will be able to take advantage of these electronic facilities.

Finally, these three types of electronic systems, especially if a significant degree of collaboration exists between them, enclose the potential to allow shippers a much larger degree of transparency in the follow-up of cargos along the transport chain, thus addressing another significant drawback, from the perspective of shippers, of short sea shipping and, more generally, of multimodal transport and intermodal solutions.

Acknowledgements

The research presented in this chapter received support from the research project PTDC/ECI-TRA/28754/2017, financed by the Portuguese Foundation for Science and Technology (Fundação para a Ciência e Tecnologia – FCT).

Notes

1 http://smartnav.org/
2 http://sesamesolution2.org/
3 http://smart-port.nl
4 www.cargostream.net
5 www.clusters20.eu/
6 www.selisproject.eu/

References

Andersson, P., & Ivehammar, P. (2017), Green approaches at sea – The benefits of adjusting speed instead of anchoring. *Transportation Research Part D: Transport and Environment*, 51, March, pp. 240–249.

CENIT, VITO, COWI (2015), Analysis of recent trends in EU shipping and analysis and policy support to improve the competitiveness of short sea shipping in the EU, Final Report, European Commission, DG Mobility and Transport.

ECSA (2016), *Short Sea Shipping – The Full Potential Yet to Be Unleashed*. European Community Shipowners' Associations, Brussels, Belgium.

European Commission (2011), White Paper Roadmap to a single European transport area – towards a competitive and resource-efficient transport system. COM (2011) 144 final.

European Council (1993), Council Directive 93/75/EEC concerning minimum requirements for vessels bound for or leaving community ports and carrying dangerous or polluting goods.

European Parliament and Council (2000), Directive 2000/59/EC on port reception facilities for ship-generated waste and cargo residues.

European Parliament and Council (2002a), Directive 2002/59/EC on establishing a community vessel traffic monitoring and information system.

European Parliament and Council (2002b), Directive 2002/6/EC on reporting formalities for ships arriving in and/or departing from ports of the member states of the community.

European Parliament and Council (2004), Regulation (EC) No. 725/2004 on enhancing ship and port facility security.

European Parliament and Council (2009a), Directive 2009/16/EC of the European parliament and of the council of 23 April 2009 on port state control.

European Parliament and Council (2009b), Directive 2009/17/EC amending directive 2002/59/EC establishing a community vessel traffic monitoring and information system.

European Parliament and Council (2010), Directive 2010/65/EU on reporting formalities for ships arriving in and/or departing from ports of the member states and repealing directive 2002/6/EC.

European Parliament and Council (2013a), Regulation (EU) no 1315/2013 of 11 December 2013 on union guidelines for the development of the trans-European transport network and repealing decision no 661/2010/EU. Strasbourg.

European Parliament and Council (2013b), Regulation (EU) no 1316/2013 of 11 December 2013 establishing the connecting Europe facility, amending regulation (EU) no 913/2010 and repealing regulations (EC) no 680/2007 and (EC) no 67/2010. Strasbourg.

European Parliament and Council (2017), Regulation (EU) 2017/352 establishing a framework for the provision of port services and common rules on the financial transparency of ports.

European Parliament and Council (2019), Regulation (EU) 2019/1239 establishing a European maritime single window environment and repealing directive 2010/65/EU.

Fergadioti, I. (2016), SELIS: Towards a shared European logistics intelligent information space. 11th ITS European Congress – Delivering Future Cities Now, Glasgow, Scotland, 6–9 June.

Giusti, R., Manerba, D., Bruno, G., & Tadeia, R. (2019), Synchromodal logistics: An overview of critical success factors, enabling technologies, and open research issues. *Transportation Research Part E: Logistics and Transportation Review*, 129, September, pp. 92–110.

Govindan, K., Cheng, T.C.E., Mishrac, N., & Shukla, N. (2018), Big data analytics and application for logistics and supply chain management. *Transportation Research Part E: Logistics and Transportation Review*, 114, June, pp. 343–349.

IMO (1965a), International Maritime Dangerous Goods Code (with subsequent amendments).

IMO (1965b), International Maritime Organisation's Convention on Facilitation of International Maritime Traffic (FAL convention).

IMO (1997a), Resolution A.857(20) Guidelines for vessel traffic services.

IMO (1997b), Resolution A.851(20) General principles for ship reporting systems and ship reporting requirements, including guidelines for reporting incidents involving dangerous goods, harmful substances and/or marine pollutants.

IMO (2003), Circular MSC/Circ.1060 Guidance note on the preparation of proposals on ship routing systems and ship reporting systems for submission to the sub-committee on safety of navigation.

IMO (2018), IMO e-navigation Strategy Implementation Plan (SIP) – Update 1, MSC.1/Circ.1595.

Jia, H., Adland, R., Prakash, V., & Smith, T. (2017), Energy efficiency with the application of virtual arrival policy. *Transportation Research Part D: Transport and Environment*, 54, July, pp. 50–60.

Lucassen, I.M.P.J., & Dogger, T. (2012), Synchromodality pilot study – identification of bottlenecks and possibilities for a network between Rotterdam, Moerdijk and Tilburg. Report TNO 2012 P10128 v1.0.

Michaelides, M.P., Herodotou, H., Lind, M., & Watson, R.T. (2019), Port-2-Port communication enhancing short sea shipping performance: The case study of Cyprus and the eastern Mediterranean. *Sustainability*, 11, p. 1912. doi:10.3390/su11071912.

Portuguese Port Association (2007), Organization and configuration of pilot actions for the development of motorways of the sea in Portugal. Report D13 of PortMos, Lisbon, Portugal.

Poulsen, R.T., & Sampson, H. (2019), 'Swinging on the anchor': The difficulties in achieving greenhouse gas abatement in shipping via virtual arrival. *Transportation Research Part D: Transport and Environment*, 73, August, pp. 230–244.

PWC and Panteia (2017), Ex-post evaluation of Reporting Formalities Directive (RFD) and Directive on Vessel Traffic Monitoring and Information Systems (VTMIS). Final Report for Directorate-General for Mobility and Transport Directorate D – Waterborne Transport, Brussels, Belgium.

SELIS (2018), White paper – creating business value through intelligent supply chain collaboration.

STM (2019), Sea traffic management validation project – final report.

UNECE (2005), Recommendation and Guidelines on establishing a Single Window to enhance the efficient exchange of information between trade and government (Recommendation No. 33), United Nations, New York and Geneva.

Wawruch, R. (2015), The concept of a single window in e-navigation and according to the EU regulations. *TransNav, the International Journal on Marine Navigation and Safety of Sea Transportation*, 9 (4), December, pp. 551–556.

Index

accompanied transport 51, 52, 186–195, 207–218
Adriatic Sea 201
Africa 10, 154–160, 169
Agência Nacional de Transportes Aquaviários (ANTAQ) 260, 261, 265, 267
analytic hierarchy process (AHP) 249–256
Asia 11, 242, 243, 249
Association of Southeast Asian Nations (ASEAN) 242–256
automatic identification system (AIS) 13, 280–281

Ballast Water Management (BWM) Convention 15
Baltic Sea 10, 15, 22, 26, 28, 95, 282
Belt and Road Initiative (BRI) 3, 11
Black Sea 10, 22, 95
bottlenecks 5, 12, 141
bottom-up approach 13, 91
Brazil 259–272
Brexit 146
Bulgaria 10, 11
bureaucracy 10, 48, 56, 130, 251, 262, 269, 270–272, 278, 293

cabotage (maritime) 22, 259
cargo aggregation 290
China 3, 11, 26, 242
Clusters 2.0 project 291
cold ironing *see* shore power (cold ironing)
competitiveness 10, 56, 61, 63, 64, 89, 90, 93, 96, 108, 110, 112, 116, 145, 147, 148, 150, 154, 156, 184, 194, 199, 200, 201, 204, 205, 211, 220, 221, 226, 268, 272, 279, 287
congestion 3, 4, 6, 16, 22, 61, 66, 77, 91, 92, 98, 99, 100, 110, 116, 121, 141, 163, 178, 183, 199, 200, 210, 220, 224, 237, 238, 269, 284, 289, 291

Connect Europe Facility (CEF) 3, 5, 7
Container Security Initiative 12
core network corridors 5–7, 141
cross-border connections 5

decision matrix 142, 145, 146, 151
dedicated SSS terminal 12, 22–55
deep sea shipping 11, 18, 47, 48, 277, 278, 279
design of Ro-Ro SSS terminals 53–55
discrete event simulation
dockers *see* port labour
door-to-door transport 22, 94, 108, 109, 117, 142, 154, 184, 267
dwell time 51, 52, 53, 56, 61, 66, 67, 78, 97, 99, 154, 214, 215, 218

Eastern Africa 154–160
economic assessment 31, 62–64, 76, 85–86, 90–91, 117, 163–179, 183–195
EcoPorts network 13
emission control area (ECA) 15, 16, 66, 72, 76, 77, 84
emissions 3, 5, 13, 14, 15, 17, 18, 25, 26, 27, 63, 89–112, 164, 183, 186, 199, 279, 282, 290
emissions inventory 13
EU enlargement 4, 10
European Community Shipowners' Association (ECSA) 16, 287
European Sea Ports Organization (ESPO) 10
European Transport policy 3, 5, 6, 9, 63, 89, 141, 163–164, 183, 185, 199, 224, 243, 245, 260–264
European Union (EU) 3, 11, 15, 22, 61, 89, 91, 109, 116, 141, 142, 163, 164, 183, 259, 262, 281
Eurostat 200

Index

Euro-vignette 17
external cost 3, 16–17, 90–93, 99–103, 110–111, 199, 237

Far East 11
feasibility 55, 62, 63, 69, 79, 81, 83, 84, 86, 106, 117, 154, 227, 243, 245, 246, 247, 249
ferry 22, 23, 25, 26, 27, 49, 51, 52, 106, 107, 108, 109, 111, 112, 147, 163, 164, 175, 178, 244, 245, 249
fleet sizing 61–86
food and perishables 79, 146, 228
Food Port Project 146, 147, 150
France 14, 51, 64, 118, 119, 129, 130, 131, 134, 135, 137, 138, 147, 163, 168, 169, 170, 172, 178, 206, 207, 210
Freight Logistics Action Plan 11
Freight Transport Logistics Action Plan 5
frequency of service 49, 86, 117, 124, 138, 146, 148, 163, 178, 185, 192, 199–220, 268, 290–291

global sulphur cap 3, 16
Greece 10, 63, 90, 95, 103–112, 202, 224–239
green freight transport 5, 9, 13, 90, 164, 238, 293, 294
greenhouse gas (GHG) emissions 3, 5, 13, 15, 17, 18, 89, 93, 103, 237
green transportation logistics 5
green transport corridors for freight (Green Corridors) 5

Iceland 22, 170
IMO 3, 4, 5, 11, 13, 15, 17, 18, 93, 96, 102, 103, 157, 280, 281, 285, 286, 288
information and communication technology (ICT) 5, 269, 277–280, 285
Initial IMO strategy 3, 4, 17, 18
inland waterways 15, 61, 89, 90, 92, 95, 96, 116, 224, 237, 289, 291
innovation 17, 22, 23, 24, 55, 287
Intergovernmental Panel on Climate Change (IPCC) 17
intermodality 2, 4, 6, 9–18, 44–47, 56, 61–86, 80–112, 116–138, 141–160, 183–194, 199–221, 243, 251, 253, 268, 277–279, 290
intermodal units 44–47
internalization 4, 16–17, 91, 92, 111, 238–239

International Association of Ports and Harbors (IAPH) 13
International Ship and Port Security Code (ISPS) 11, 12, 48, 287
investment analysis *see* shipping finance
Irish Sea 28
Italy 50, 95, 184, 188, 189, 191, 193, 195, 199–221, 226

Latin America 63, 259–262, 265, 266, 269, 271, 272
liquefied natural gas (LNG) 14, 25, 26, 27, 92, 93, 163, 164, 165, 179
LNGHIVE2 Project 164
logistics 11, 15, 48, 61, 67, 98, 108, 117–119, 121, 124, 125–126, 130, 131, 137, 138, 141, 185–186, 194, 205, 220, 238, 245, 259, 267, 271–272, 277, 278, 279, 287–293

many-to-many transport problem 120, 143, 160
Marco Polo 4, 63, 91, 92, 105, 116, 224
maritime single window 285–288, 293
market access to port services 9–10
market share 195, 225, 233
Mediterranean Sea 22, 28, 64, 192, 282
Middle East 10
modal integration 5, 259, 260
modal shift 10, 16–18, 23, 141, 184–186, 200, 205, 220, 224–238, 290
Monte Carlo (simulation) 145, 146, 151–154
Motorways of the Sea (MoS) 4, 48, 63, 75–76, 116, 141–154, 163–178, 183–188, 199–221, 224, 256, 293
multi-criteria decision making 64, 142–146, 151–154, 160
multimodality 6, 238, 260, 268–269, 277, 280, 283, 287, 289–291, 293
multimodal transport platform 277, 279, 289–291, 293

North Africa 10, 169
North America 6, 15, 65, 256
Norway 14, 22
NUTS 2 65, 75, 78, 79, 81, 82, 86, 93, 94, 96, 100

operating costs 3, 226, 229, 231, 233, 261, 262

Pilot Actions for Combined Transport (PACT) 11
Poland 11, 27, 168
pollution 3, 15, 16, 61, 89, 90, 91, 92, 92, 93, 99, 100, 103, 116, 141, 199, 224, 237, 238, 243, 280, 281, 243, 280, 281, 289, 291
Port Environmental Review System (PERS) 13
port hinterland 55, 119, 155, 156, 187, 199, 279, 293
port labour 9–11, 50
port security 4, 11, 12
port services 9, 10, 154, 199, 287, 293
Portugal 61, 65, 67, 76, 78, 79, 85, 86, 95, 116, 118, 119, 130, 131, 134, 135, 137, 138, 168, 169, 171, 178
priority rules 11
protectionism 116, 261, 263–264, 269

questionnaires 188–194

rail 3, 4, 5, 6, 11, 17, 22, 23, 48, 50, 53, 54, 56, 89–112, 116, 141, 186, 199, 200, 224–225, 229, 239, 259, 267, 272, 288, 289, 290
rail freight corridor (RFC) 4, 6, 11, 56
reliability 48, 90, 116–138, 146, 160, 185, 202–203, 220, 278, 284, 288, 290–292
risk analysis 145–146, 234
road haulage 10, 61, 62, 67, 78, 94, 96–98, 103, 106, 116–117, 183–195, 202, 218, 218, 287–289
road tolls 17
roll-on/roll-off (Ro-Ro) 14, 16, 17, 22, 23, 95, 99, 101, 116, 117, 159, 163, 183, 184, 200, 226, 227, 229, 230, 231, 232, 234, 235, 236, 239, 243, 245, 250
Romania 10, 11
Ro-Pax ship 14, 23, 24, 26, 27, 28, 29, 32, 33, 35, 36, 39, 41, 44, 52, 55, 56, 63, 101, 155, 179, 190
RoRoSECA project 16
Ro-Ro ship 22, 23, 25, 28, 29, 30, 31, 35, 36, 41, 44, 46, 49, 51, 52, 55, 56, 61, 64, 73, 103, 117, 155, 225, 230, 243
Russia 11, 170

schedule 123, 124, 129, 130, 166, 202, 239, 245, 255, 278, 283, 284, 289
Scotland 146, 147, 148, 150, 151, 152, 160
sea traffic management 281–284
self-handling 50

SELIS project 291
sensitivity analysis 142, 145–146, 151, 234–236
SESAME Solution II project 281
shipowners 28, 48, 73, 75, 261, 262, 263, 277
shippers 16, 61, 118, 138, 184, 185, 193, 194, 245, 279, 280, 289, 290, 291, 292, 293, 294
shipping finance 224–236
shore power (cold ironing) 14
short sea shipping (SSS) 3, 6, 9–10, 15, 16, 22–23, 28, 44, 47, 53, 61, 63–64, 68, 79, 89, 90, 93, 101, 103, 105, 108, 112, 116, 119, 141, 146, 154, 155, 157, 160, 183–188, 193–195, 199, 224, 237, 238, 242–245, 248, 250–251, 253–257, 259, 260–263, 267, 269–270, 291, 293–294, 277–280, 286, 287
Singapore 243, 245, 249, 256, 278, 281
SMART Navigation project 281
South America 259, 261
Spain 61, 64, 116, 137, 149, 163, 166, 168, 169, 171, 177, 178, 184, 188, 189, 193, 195
stevedoring *see* port labour
Sulphur Emission Control Area (SECA) 16
SuperGreen project 11
supply chain 12, 16, 23, 112, 116, 119–120, 137, 184, 226, 238, 289–291
sustainability 5, 13, 61, 89–113, 116, 163, 164, 183, 186, 190, 194, 260, 277, 284
Sustainable Development Goals (SDGs) 13
Sweden 14, 27, 168, 287

telematics 6, 277
terminal operator 50, 51, 52, 67, 98, 138, 279, 285, 293
tourism 163, 166, 169, 170, 172, 173, 174, 175, 176, 177, 178, 257, 263
Trans-European Transport Network (TEN-T) 3, 141, 199
transport chain 12, 61, 90, 108, 112, 117, 118, 142, 186, 189–190, 194, 279, 293–294
transport demand 28, 61–86, 117–118, 138, 164, 166, 173.174, 178, 184, 190, 200, 204, 213, 216, 218, 224, 226–229, 245, 247, 256
transport network 4, 5, 6, 7, 11, 13, 61, 89–113, 116, 185–186, 199.221,

237–238, 243, 245, 248, 249, 272, 277, 292–293
truck drivers 23, 48, 51, 54, 55, 66, 97, 168, 210, 220, 289
Turkey 10, 51

unaccompanied transport 51, 52, 53, 119, 183–195, 208–219
uncertainty 6, 62, 68, 116, 284
unimodal 65–79, 119–138, 151, 190
unions *see* port labour

United Nations (UN) 13
United States 6, 264

vessel traffic system 277, 280–283, 293
VTMIS *see* vessel traffic system
VTS *see* vessel traffic system

World Ports Climate Initiative (WPCI) 13
World Ports Sustainability Program (WPSP) 13